RECORD VALUES—THEORY AND APPLICATIONS

Mohammad Ahsanullah

University Press of America,® Inc.
Dallas · Lanham · Boulder · New York · Oxford

Copyright © 2004 by
University Press of America,® Inc.
4501 Forbes Boulevard
Suite 200
Lanham, Maryland 20706
UPA Acquisitions Department (301) 459-3366

PO Box 317
Oxford
OX2 9RU, UK

All rights reserved
Printed in the United States of America
British Library Cataloging in Publication Information Available

Library of Congress Control Number: 2004101216
ISBN 0-7618-2794-3 (hardcover : alk. ppr.)

∞™ The paper used in this publication meets the minimum
requirements of American National Standard for Information
Sciences—Permanence of Paper for Printed Library Materials,
ANSI Z39.48—1984

To my wife, Masuda

CONTENTS

PREFACE   vii

ABBREVIATIONS   viii

CHAPTER 1 - RECORD STATISTICS

1.0	Introduction and Examples of Record Values	1
1.1	Definition of Record Values and Record Times	2
1.2	The Exact Distribution of Record Values	2
1.3	Moments of Record Values	8
1.4	Distribution of Inter-Record Times	25
1.5	Relation Between Occurrences of Records and Poisson Processes	37
1.6	Number of Records In A Sequence of Observations	39
1.7	Distribution of Inter-Record Times	42
1.8	The K-Records	43
1.9	Entropies of Record Values	60

CHAPTER 2 - EXPONENTIAL DISTRIBUTION

2.0	Introduction	63
2.1	Distribution of Record Values	64
2.2	Moments of Record Values	66
2.3	Estimation of Parameters	74
2.4	Characterizations	78
2.5	Prediction of Record values	96
2.6	Limiting Distributions of Record Values	98

Chapter 3 - GENERALIZED EXTREME VALUE DISTRIBUTION

3.0	Introduction	101
3.1	Distributional Properties	104
3.2	Recurrence Relations Between Moments	106
3.3	Estimation of Parameters	112
3.4	Prediction of Record Values	122

3.5	Characterizations	123
3.6	Applications	125
3.7	Limiting Distributions	129

Chapter 4 - GENERALIZED PARETO DISTRIBUTION

4.0	Introduction	131
4.1	Distributional Properties	132
4.2	Recurrence Relations of Moments	134
4.3	Estimation of Parameters	142
4.4	Prediction of Record Values	146
4.5	Classical Pareto Distribution	137
4.6	Lomax Distribution	150

Chapter 5 - Power Function Distribution

5.0	Introduction	155
5.1	Distributional Properties	156
5.2	Recurrence Relations Between Moments	158
5.3	Estimation of Parameters	165
5.4	Prediction of Record Values	169
5.5	One Parameter Uniform Distribution	171

Chapter 6 - Discrete Distribution

6.0	Introduction	177
6.1	Geometric Distribution	181
6.2	Records of Non-Identically Distributed Random Variables	192
6.3	Weak Records	195

Chapter 7 - Some Selected Distributions

7.0	Introduction	209
7.1	Logistic Distribution	209
7.2	Normal Distribution	215
7.3	Rayleigh Distribution	218
7.4	Two Parameter Uniform Distribution	224
7.5	Weibull Distribution	233

| 7.6 | Distributions Where Consecutive Record Values Have Linear Regression | 240 |

Chapter 8 - Additional Topics

8.0	Introduction	249
8.1	Limiting Distribution of Inter-Record times	249
8.2	Limiting Distribution of Record Values	252
8.3	Limiting Distribution of Record Times	254
8.4	Representation of Records	256
8.5	Limiting Distribution of Number of Records	258
8.6	Random Record Model	261
8.7	Records of Dependent Sequence	267
8.8	Concomitants	269

APPENDIX

A.1	Stirling Numbers of the First Kind	275
A.2	Bernoulli Numbers	276
A.3	Cauchy Type Functional Equation	277

COMPLEMENTS AND PROBLEMS ... 281

REFERENCES ... 293

INDEX   315

PREFACE

This book deals with the Theory of Record values in complete details. Since I wrote a book on Record Statistics (Nova Science Publishers Inc) 1995, there have been substantial advances in the field of record values. A large number of article have appeared in leading statistical journals dealing with record value theories and applications The aim of this book is to present the recent developments of record values and their applications in complete and easy understandable form.

The prerequisites for reading the book are probability theory and calculus.. Some familiarities with statistics and distribution theories will be of advantage. The book is intended for researchers, mathematicians, statisticians, advanced undergraduate and graduate students of mathematical and statistical sciences,. The applied statisticians will be able to find in this book various useful results.

Summer research grants and sabbatical leave from Rider University enabled me to complete this book. The author thanks Janet Miller and Barbara Damico for helping and resolving several difficulties in the process of my typing the manuscript.

I wish to thank the University Press of America for willing to publish this manuscript.

I could not have completed the book without the help and encouragement of my wife, Masuda. I dedicate this book to her.

M. Ahsanullah
Upper Holland, PA,USA
October 2003

ABBREVIATIONS

BLIE	best linear invariant estimator
BLUP	best linear unbiased predictor
cdf	cumulative distribution function
Cov(X,Y)	covariance of X and Y
E(X)	expectation of X
i.i.d.	Independent and identically distributed
MSE	Mean Square Error
MVLUE	minimum variance linear unbiased estimator
NBU	new better than used
NWU	new worse than used
P(A)	probability of an event A
ρ(X,Y)	correlation coefficient of X and Y
pdf	probability density function
pmf	probability mass function
rv	random variable
V(X)	variance of X

Chapter 1

RECORD STATISTICS

In this chapter the basic concepts and properties of the record values are presented. For simplicity the descriptions are confined here to the sequence of independent and identically distributed continuous random variables.

1.0. INTRODUCTION AND EXAMPLES OF RECORD VALUES

Suppose we consider the weighing of objects on a scale missing its spring. An object is placed on the scale and its weight is measured. The 'needle' indicated the correct weight but does not return to zero when the object is removed. If various objects are placed on the scale, only the weights greater than the previous ones can be recorded. These recorded weights are the upper record value sequence. If X_{ij} be the height water level of a river on the jth day of the ith location. If one is interested to study at each location the local maximum values of X_{ij}, then the local maxima are the upper record values.

Let us consider a sequence of products that may fail under stress. We are interested to determine the minimum failure stress of the products sequentially. We test the first product until it fails with stress less than X_1 then we record its failure stress, otherwise we consider the next product. In general we will record stress X_m of the mth product if $X_m < \min(X_1,..., X_{m-1})$, $m > 1$. The recorded failure stresses are the lower record values. One can go from lower records to upper records by replacing the original sequence of random variables $\{X_j\}$ by $\{-X_j, j \geq 1\}$ or if $P(X_j > 0) = 1$ by $\{1/x_j, i \geq 1\}$, $j=1,2,...$

Chandler (1952) introduced the record values, record times and inter record times. He proved the interesting result that for any given distribution of the random variables the expected value of the inter record time is infinite. Feller (1952) gave some examples of record values with respect to gambling problems.

1.1. DEFINITION OF RECORD VALUES AND RECORD TIMES

Suppose that $X_1, X_2, \ldots$ is a sequence of independent and identically distributed random variables with cumulative distribution function $F(x)$. Let $Y_n = \max (\min)\{X_1, X_2, \ldots, X_n\}$ for $n \geq 1$. We say X_j is an upper(lower) record value of $\{X_n, n \geq 1\}$, if $Y_j > (<) Y_{j-1}, j > 1$. By definition X_1 is an upper as well as a lower record value. One can transform the upper records to lower records by replacing the original sequence of $\{X_j\}$ by $\{-X_j, j \geq 1\}$ or (if $P(X_i > 0)=1$ for all i) by $\{1/X_i, i \geq 1\}$; the lower record values of this sequence will correspond to the upper record values of the original sequence.

The indices at which the upper record values occur are given by the record times $\{U(n)\}$, $n > 0$, where $U(n) = \min\{j|j>U(n-1), X_j > X_{U(n-1)}, n > 1\}$ and $U(1) = 1$. The record times of the sequence $\{X_n, n \geq 1\}$ are the same as those for the sequence $\{F(X_n), n \geq 1\}$. Since $F(X)$ has an uniform distribution, it follows that the distribution of $U(n)$, $n \geq 1$ does not depend on F. We will denote $L(n)$ as the indices where the lower record values occur. By our assumption $U(1) = L(1) = 1$. The distribution of $L(n)$ also does not depend on F.

1.2. THE EXACT DISTRIBUTION OF RECORD VALUES

Many properties of the record value sequence can be expressed in terms of $R(x)$, where $R(x) = -\ln \overline{F}(x)$, $0 < \overline{F}(x) < 1$ and $\overline{F}(x) = 1 - F(x)$. Here 'ln' is used for the natural logarithm. If we define $F_n(x)$ as the distribution function of $X_{U(n)}$ for $n \geq 1$, then we have

$$F_1(x) = P[X_{U(1)} \leq x] = F(x)$$

$$F_2(x) = P[X_{U(2)} \leq x]$$

(1.2.1)

$$= \int_{-\infty}^{x} \int_{-\infty}^{y} \sum_{i=1}^{\infty} (F(u))^{i-1} dF(u) dF(y)$$

$$= \int_{-\infty}^{x} \int_{-\infty}^{y} \frac{dF(u)}{1-F(u)} dF(y)$$

$$= \int_{-\infty}^{x} R(y) dF(y) \qquad (1.2.2)$$

If $F(x)$ has a density $f(x)$, then the probability density function (pdf) of $X_{U(2)}$ is

$$f_2(x) = R(x) f(x) \qquad (1.2.3)$$

The distribution function $F_3(x) = P(X_{U(3)} \leq x)$

$$= \int_{-\infty}^{x} \int_{-\infty}^{y} \sum_{i=0}^{\infty} (F(u))^{i} R(u) dF(u) dF(y)$$

$$= \int_{-\infty}^{x} \int_{-\infty}^{y} \frac{R(u)}{1-F(u)} dF(u) dF(y)$$

$$= \int_{-\infty}^{x} \frac{(R(u))^2}{\Gamma(3)} dF(u) . \qquad (1.2.4)$$

The pdf $f_3(x)$ of $X_{U(3)}$ is

$$f_3(x) = \frac{(R(x))^2}{\Gamma(3)} f(x), -\infty < x < \infty \qquad (1.2.5)$$

It can similarly be shown that the pdf $F_n(x)$ of $X_{U(n)}$ is

$$F_n(x) = P(X_{U(n)} \leq x)$$

$$= \int_{-\infty}^{x} f(u_n) du_n \int_{-\infty}^{u_n} \frac{f(u_{n-1})}{1-F(u_{n-1})} du_{n-1} \cdots \int_{-\infty}^{u_2} \frac{f(u_1)}{1-F(u_1)} du_1.$$

$$= \int_{-\infty}^{x} \frac{R^{n-1}(u)}{\Gamma(n)} dF(u), \quad -\infty < x < \infty. \quad (1.2.6)$$

This can be expressed as

$$F_n(x) = \int_{-\infty}^{R(x)} \frac{u^{n-1}}{\Gamma(n)} e^{-u} du, \quad -\infty < x < \infty$$

$$\overline{F}_n(x) = 1 - F_n(x) = \overline{F}(x) \sum_{j=0}^{n-1} \frac{(R(x))^j}{\Gamma(j+1)}$$

$$= e^{-R(x)} \sum_{j=0}^{n-1} \frac{(R(x))^j}{\Gamma(j+1)}$$

The pdf $f_n(x)$ of $X_{U(n)}$ is

$$f_n(x) = \frac{R^{n-1}(x)}{\Gamma(n)} f(x), \quad -\infty < x < \infty. \quad (1.2.7)$$

A random variable X is said to be symmetric around zero if X and -X has the same distribution function. If f(x) is their density function, then f(x) = f(-x) for all x. Two random variables X and Y with cdfs $F_1(x)$ and $F_1^*(y)$ are said to be mutually symmetric i.e. $F_1(-x) = 1 - F_1^*(x)$ or equivalently if the corresponding pdfs $f_1(x)$ and $f_1^*(y)$ exit, then $f_1(-x) = f_1^*(x)$. If the sequence of i.i.d. random variables are symmetric around zero, then they are also mutually symmetric around zero but not conversely. For symmetric or mutually (around zero) symmetric sequence $\{X_n, n \geq 1\}$ of random variables, it can easily be seen that in that case $X_{U(n)}$ is identically distributed as $-X_{L(n)}$.

The joint pdf $f(x_1, x_2, \ldots, x_n)$ of the n record values $X_{U(1)}, X_{U(2)}, \ldots, X_{U(n)})$ is given by

$$f(x_1, x_2, \ldots, x_n) = r(x_1) r(x_2) \ldots r(x_{n-1}) f(x_n)$$

for $-\infty < x_1 < x_2 < \ldots < x_{n-1} < x_n < \infty,$ \quad (1.2.8) where $r(x) = \dfrac{d}{dx}R(x) = \dfrac{f(x)}{1-F(x)}$, $0 < F(x) < 1$.

The function $r(x)$ is known as hazard rate.

The joint pdf of $X_{U(i)}$ and $X_{U(j)}$ is

$$f(x_i, x_j) = \frac{(R(x_i))^{i-1}}{\Gamma(i)} r(x_i) \frac{(R(x_j) - R(x_i))^{j-i-1}}{\Gamma(j-i)} f(x_j) \qquad (1.2.9)$$

for $-\infty < x_i < x_j < \infty$.

In particular for $i = 1$ and $j = n$ we have

$$f(x_1, x_n) = r(x_1) \frac{(R(x_n) - R(x_1))^{n-2}}{\Gamma(n-1)} f(x_n)$$

for $-\infty < x_1 < x_n < \infty$.

Suppose we use the transformation $Y_1 = R(X_{U(i)})$ and $Y_2 = R(X_{U(i)}) / R(X_{U(j)}), 1 \leq i < j$, then using (1.2.9), it can be shown that the pdf $f_2^*(y)$ of Y_2 is as follows:

$$f_2^*(y) = \frac{\Gamma(j)}{\Gamma(i)} \frac{1}{\Gamma(j-i)} \cdot y^{i-1}(1-y)^{j-i-1}, \quad 0 < y < \infty. \qquad (1.2.10)$$

Thus Y_2 is distributed as Beta distribution with parameters i and j (i.e. $B(i,j-i)$). The mean and variance of Y_2 are

$$E(Y_2) = \frac{i}{j} \quad \text{and} \quad \mathrm{Var}(Y_2) = \frac{ij}{(j+1)j^2}.$$

If we use the transformation $V_i = R(X_{U(i)})$, then the joint pdf of V_i, $i = 1,2,\ldots,n$, is

$$f(v_1, v_2, \ldots, v_n) = e^{-v_n}, \quad 0 < v_1 < v_2 < \cdots < v_n < \infty. \qquad (1.2.11)$$

The joint distribution of V_m and V_r, $r > m$, is

$$f(v_m, v_r) = \frac{1}{\Gamma(m)} \frac{(v_r - v_m)^{r-m-1}}{\Gamma(r-m)} \cdot e^{-v_r} \quad 0 < v_m < v_r < \infty$$

= 0, otherwise.

$$E(V_k^l) = \int_0^\infty t^l \frac{1}{\Gamma(k)} t^{k-1} e^{-t} dt = \frac{\Gamma(k+l)}{\Gamma(k)}.$$

Thus $E(V_k) = k$ and $Var(V_k) = k$. The conditional pdf of $X_{U(j)}|$ $X_{U(i)} = x_i$ if $(x_j | X_{U(i)} = x_i)$

$$= \frac{f_{ij}(x_i, x_j)}{f_i(x_i)}$$

$$= \frac{(R(x_j) - R(x_i))^{j-i-1}}{\Gamma(j-i)} \frac{f(x_j)}{1 - F(x_i)} \quad (1.2.12)$$

for $-\infty < x_i < x_j < \infty$.

For $j = i+1$

$$f(x_{i+1} | X_{U(i)} = x_i) = \frac{f(x_{i+1})}{1 - F(x_i)} \quad (1.2.13)$$

for $-\infty < x_i < x_{i+1} < \infty$.

For $i > 0$, $1 \leq k < m$, the joint conditional pdf of $X_{U(i+k)}$ and $X_{U(i+m)} | X_{U(i)}$ is

$f_{i+k, i+m}(x, y | X_{U(i)} = z)$

$$= \frac{1}{\Gamma(m-k)} \frac{1}{\Gamma(k)} [R(y) - R(x)]^{m-k-1} [R(X) - R(z)]^{k-1} \frac{f(y)r(x)}{\overline{F}(z)}$$

for $-\infty < z < x < y < \infty$.

The marginal pdf of the nth lower record value can be derived by using the same procedure as that of the nth upper record value. Let $H(u) = -\ln F(u)$, $0 < F(u) < 1$ and $h(u) = -\frac{d}{du} H(u)$, then

$$P(X_{L(n)} \leq x) = \int_{-\infty}^x \frac{\{H(u)\}^{n-1}}{\Gamma(n)} dF(u) \quad (1.2.14)$$

and the corresponding the pdf $f_{(n)}$ can be written as

$$f_{(n)}(x) = \frac{(H(x))^{n-1}}{\Gamma(n)} f(x). \quad (1.2.15)$$

The joint pdf of $X_{L(1)}, X_{L(2)}, \ldots, X_{L(m)}$ can be written as

$f_{(1),(2),\ldots,(m)}(x_1, x_2, \ldots, x_m) = h(x_1) h(x_2) \ldots h(x_{m-1}) f(x_m)$

$$-\infty < x_m < x_{m-1} < ... < x_1 < \infty$$
$$= 0, \text{ otherwise.} \qquad (1.2.16)$$

The joint pdf of $X_{L(r)}$ and $X_{L(s)}$ is

$$f_{(r),(s)}(x,y) = \frac{(H(x))^{r-1}[H(y)-H(x)]^{s-r-1}}{\Gamma(r)\,\Gamma(s-r)} h(x) f(y)$$

for $s > r$ and $-\infty < y < x < \infty$. $\qquad (1.2.17)$

Using the transformations $U = H(y)$ and $W = H(x)/H(y)$ in (1.2.17), it can be shown easily that W is distributed as $B(r, s-r)$.

Proceeding as in the case of upper record values, we can obtain the conditional pdfs of the lower record values.

Example 1.2.1. Let us consider the exponential distribution with pdf $f(x)$ as

$$f(x) = e^{-x}, 0 \le x < \infty$$

and the cumulative distribution function (cdf) $F(x)$ as

$$F(x) = 1 - e^{-x}, \ 0 \le x < \infty.$$

Then $R(x) = x$ and

$$f_n(x) = \frac{x^{n-1}}{\Gamma(n)} e^{-x}, \ x \ge 0$$
$$= 0, \quad \text{otherwise.}$$

The joint pdf of $X_{U(m)}$ and $X_{U(n)}$, $n > m$ is

$$f_{m,n}(x,y) = \frac{x^{m-1}}{\Gamma(m)\,\Gamma(n-m)}(y-x)^{n-m-1} e^{-y}$$
$$0 \le x < y < \infty$$
$$= 0, \quad \text{otherwise.}$$

The conditional pdf of $X_{U(n)} \mid X_{U(m)} = x$ is

$$f(y \mid X_{U(m)} = x) = \frac{(y-x)^{n-m-1}}{\Gamma(n-m)} e^{-(y-x)}$$
$$0 \le x < y < \infty$$
$$= 0, \quad \text{otherwise.}$$

Thus the conditional distribution of $X_{U(n)} - X_{U(m)}$ given $X_{U(m)}$ is the same as the unconditional distribution of $X_{U(n-m)}$ for $n > m$.

Example 1.2.2. Suppose that the random variable X has the Gumbel distribution with pdf $f(x) = e^{-x}e^{-e^{-x}}$, $-\infty < x < \infty$. Let $F_{(n)}$ and $f_{(n)}$ be the cdf and pdf of $X_{L(n)}$. It is easy to see that

$$F_{(n)}(x) = \int_{-\infty}^{x} \frac{e^{-nu}}{\Gamma(n)} e^{-e^{-u}} du$$

and $\quad f_{(n)}(x) = \dfrac{e^{-nx}}{\Gamma(n)} e^{-e^{-x}}, \qquad -\infty < x < \infty$.

Let $f_{(m,n)}(x,y)$ be the joint pdf of $X_{L(m)}$ and $X_{L(n)}$, $m < n$. Using (1.2.16), we get for the Gumbel distribution

$$f_{(m,n)}(x,y) = \frac{\left(e^{-y} - e^{-x}\right)^{n-m-1}}{\Gamma(n-m)} \frac{e^{-mx}}{\Gamma(m)} e^{-y} e^{-e^{-y}},$$

$-\infty < y < x < \infty$

Thus the conditional pdf $f_{(n|m)}(y|x)$ of $X_{L(n)} | X_{L(m)} = x$ is given by

$$f_{(n|m)}(y|x) = \frac{(e^{-y} - e^{-x})^{n-m-1}}{\Gamma(n-m)} e^{-y} e^{-(e^{-y} - e^{-x})},$$

$-\infty < y < x < \infty$

1.3. MOMENTS OF RECORD VALUES

Let μ_n^r and $\mu_{(n)}^r$ be the rth moment of $X_{U(n)}$ and $X_{L(n)}$ respectively, then

$$\mu_n^r = \int_{-\infty}^{\infty} x^r \frac{(R(x))^{n-1}}{\Gamma(n)} f(x) dx \text{ and}$$

$$\mu_{(n)}^r = \int_{-\infty}^{\infty} x^r \frac{(H(x))^{n-1}}{\Gamma(n)} f(x) dx$$

$\text{Var}(X_{U(n)}) = \mu_n^2 - (\mu_n^1)^2$ and $\text{Var}(X_{L(n)}) = \mu_{(n)}^2 - (\mu_{(n)}^1)^2$.

We will denote

$$\mu_{m,n}^{r,s} = E(X_{U(m)}^r X_{U(n)}^s)$$

and

$$\mu_{(m),(n)}^{r,s} = E(X_{L(m)}^r X_{L(n)}^s)$$

We have $\text{Cov}(X_{U(m)}, X_{U(n)}) = \mu_{m,n}^{1,1} - \mu_m^1 \mu_n^1$
and
$$\text{Cov}(X_{L(m)}, X_{L(n)}) = \mu_{(m),(n)}^{1,1} - \mu_{(m)}^1 \mu_{(n)}^1.$$

If we take $V_k = R(X_{U(k)})$, $k=1,2,..$, then

$$E(V_m V_r) = \int_0^\infty \int_0^y xy \frac{x^{m-1} (y-x)^{r-m-1}}{\Gamma(m) \Gamma(r-m)} e^{-y} dxdy$$

Using the transformation $t = yx$ and $w = y$, we get on simplification

$$E(V_m V_r) = \frac{\Gamma(m+1)}{\Gamma(m)} \frac{\Gamma(r-m)}{\Gamma(r+1)} \frac{\Gamma(r+2)}{\Gamma(r-m)} = m(r+1), \ m < r.$$

$\text{Cov}(V_m V_r) = m(r+1) - m\,r = m = \text{Var}(V_m)$, $m < r$..

If $\rho_{m,n}$ = the correlation coefficient between V_m and V_n, $m < n$, is

$$\rho_{m,n} = \sqrt{m/n}.$$

Example 1.3.1.

For the exponential distribution with $f(x) = e^{-x}$, $0 < x < \infty$.

$$\mu_n^r = \int_0^\infty x^r \frac{x^{n-1}}{(n-1)!} e^{-x} dx = \frac{(n+r-1)!}{(n-1)!}$$

$= n^{(r)}$, where $x^{(k)} = x(x+1)(x+2)...(x+k-1), k > 0$,

$= x^{(k)} = 1$ if $k = 0$

Thus $E(X_{U(n)}) = n$, $\text{Var}(X_{U(n)}) = n(n+1) - n^2 = n$.
For $m < n$,

$$\mu_{m,n}^{r,s} = \int_0^\infty \int_x^\infty x^r y^s \frac{x^{m-1}}{\Gamma(m)\Gamma(n-m)} (y-x)^{n-m-1} e^{-y} dxdy$$

$$= \sum_{k=0}^s \frac{\Gamma(m+r+s-k)}{\Gamma(m)} \frac{\Gamma(n-m+k)}{\Gamma(n-m)}$$

and $\text{Cov}(X_{U(m)}, X_{U(n)}) = \mu_{m,n}^{1,1} - \mu_m^1 \mu_n^1 = nm + m - nm = m = \text{Var}(X_{U(m)})$.

Let $\rho_{m,n}$ be the correlation between $X_{U(n)}$ and $X_{U(m)}$, then

$$\rho_{m,n} = \sqrt{m/n}.$$

It can easily be shown that $E[X_{U(n)}-X_{U(m)}]^r = (n-m)^{(r)}$.

Example 1.3.2.
For the Gumbel distribution with $f(x) = e^{-x}e^{-e^{-x}}, -\infty < x < \infty$,

$$E(X_{L(r)}) = \int_{-\infty}^{\infty} x \frac{e^{-rx}}{\Gamma(r)} e^{-e^{-x}} dx = -\frac{d}{dr}\ln\Gamma(r) = -\psi(r), \text{ where } \psi$$

(r) is the Psi (Digamma) function. Thus

$$E(X_{L(r)}) = \upsilon_r^*$$
$$\upsilon_1^* = \upsilon$$
$$\upsilon_j^* = \upsilon_{j-1}^* - (j-1)^{-1}, j \geq 2.$$

Here υ is the Euler's constant.
Let $f_{(m),(n)}(x,y)$ be the joint pdf of $X_{L(m)}$ and $X_{L(n)}$, $m < n$,. Using (1.2.17), we get for the Gumbel distribution

$$f_{(m),(n)}(x,y) = \frac{(e^{-y}-e^{-x})^{n-m-1}}{\Gamma(n-m)} \frac{e^{-x}}{\Gamma(m)} e^{-my} e^{-e^{-y}}.,$$

$-\infty < y < x < \infty$.
Thus the conditional pdf $f_{(n|m)}(y|x)$ of $X_{L(n)} | X_{L(m)} = x$ is given by

$f_{(n|m)}(y|x) =$

$$\frac{(e^{-y}-e^{-x})^{n-m-1}}{\Gamma(n-m)} e^{-y} e^{-(e^{-y}-e^{-x})}, -\infty < y < x < \infty.$$

$$E(X_{L(m)}X_{L(n)}) = \int_{-\infty}^{\infty}\int_{y}^{\infty} xy f_{(m),(n)}(x,y) dx dy$$

$$= \int_{-\infty}^{\infty}\int_{y}^{\infty} xy \frac{(e^{-y}-e^{-x})^{n-m-1}}{\Gamma(n-m)} \cdot \frac{e^{-mx}}{\Gamma(m)} e^{-y} e^{-e^{-y}} dx dy.$$

Substituting $y-x = t$, we get

$$\int_{-\infty}^{\infty} \int_{y}^{\infty} xy \frac{(e^{-y}-e^{-x})^{n-m-1} e^{-mx}}{\Gamma(n-m) \Gamma(m)} e^{-y} e^{-e^{-y}} dx dy$$

$$= \int_{-\infty}^{\infty} \int_{0}^{\infty} \Gamma(n) (\Gamma(m)\Gamma(n-m))^{-1} y(y+t)$$

$$\cdot (1-e^{-t})^{n-m-1} e^{-mt} f_{(n)}(y) dt\, dy$$

$$= E(X_{L(n)}^{2}) + E(T)E(X_{L(n)})$$

where $\quad E(T) = \int_{0}^{\infty} \Gamma(n) (\Gamma(m)\Gamma(n-m-1))^{-1} (1-e^{-t})^{n-m-1} e^{-mt}\, dt$

Similarly it can be shown that

$$E(X_{L(m)}) = E(X_{L(n)}) + E(T)$$

Thus $\quad \text{Cov}(X_{L(m)} X_{L(n)}) = \text{Var}(X_{L(n)})$. and

$$\text{Var}(X_{L(r)}) = \int_{-\infty}^{\infty} x^2 f_{(r)}(x) dx - \left(\int_{0}^{\infty} x f_{(r)}(x) dx \right)^2$$

$$= \frac{d}{dr} \psi(r) = \frac{\pi^2}{6} - \sum_{k=1}^{r-1} \frac{1}{k^2}, k > 1$$

$$= \frac{\pi^2}{6} \text{ for } k = 1.$$

Let $\text{Var}(X_{L(r)}) = V_{r,r}^{*}$, $r = 1, 2, \ldots$, then

$$V_{1,1}^{*} = \frac{\pi^2}{6}$$

$$V_{j,j}^{*} = V_{j-1,j-1}^{*} - (j-1)^{-2}, j \geq 2$$

Further

$$E(X_{L(m)}) = E(X_{L(n)}) + \sum_{p=m}^{n-1} \frac{1}{p}$$

$$\text{Var}(X_{L(n-1)}) - \text{Var}(X_{L(n)}) = (n-1)^{-2}$$

Let $\rho_{(m,n)}$ be the correlation coefficient between $X_{L(m)}$ and $X_{L(n)}$, then

$$\rho_{(m,n)} = \sqrt{\frac{\text{Var}(X_{(n)})}{\text{Var}(X_{(m)})}}.$$

Example 1.3.3.

A random variable is said to have generalized Pareto distribution if its probability density function is of the following form:

$$f_0(x,\mu,\sigma,\beta) = \frac{1}{\sigma}(1+\beta(\frac{x-\mu}{\sigma}))^{-(1+\beta^{-1})}$$

$x \geq \mu$, for $\beta > 0$,

$\mu < x \leq \mu - \sigma\beta^{-1}$, for $\beta < 0$

$$= \frac{1}{\sigma}e^{-(x-\mu)\sigma^{-1}}, x \geq \mu \text{ for } \beta = 0$$

$= 0$, otherwise.

It can be shown that for $\beta \neq 0$

$$X_{U(n)} \stackrel{d}{=} \mu - \frac{\sigma}{\beta} + \frac{\sigma}{\beta}\prod_{i=1}^{n} U_i$$

where $U_1, U_2, ..., U_n$ are independently and identically distributed with

$$P(U_i \leq x) = 1-(x)^{-\beta^{-1}}, \quad x \geq 1, \beta > 0,$$

$$= (x)^{-\beta^{-1}}, \quad \beta < 0, 0 < x < 1.$$

For $\beta = 0$, we have

$$X_{U(n)} \stackrel{d}{=} \mu + \sigma \sum_{i=1}^{n} Z_i$$

where $Z_1, Z_2, ..., Z_n$ are independently and identically distributed with

$P(Z_i \leq z) = 1 - e^{-z}$, $z > 0$, here $\stackrel{d}{=}$ denotes the equality in distribution.
For $\beta \neq 0$, we have

$$E(X_{U(n)}) = \mu + \frac{\sigma}{\beta}\{(1-\beta)^{-n} - 1\}, \beta < 1$$

$$\text{Var}(X_{U(n)}) = \sigma^2 \beta^{-2}\{(1-2\beta)^{-n} - (1-\beta)^{-2n}\}, \beta < \frac{1}{2}.$$

$$\text{Cov}(X_{U(m)}, X_{U(n)}) = \sigma^2 \beta^{-2}(1-\beta)^{m-n}\{(1-2\beta)^{-m} - (1-\beta)^{-2m}\}$$

Let $\rho_{m,n}$ be the correlation coefficient between $X_{U(m)}$ and $X_{U(n)}$, then

$$\rho_{m,n} = (1-\beta)^{m-n}\left[\frac{(1-2\beta)^{-m} - (1-\beta)^{-2m}}{(1-2\beta)^{-n} - (1-\beta)^{-2n}}\right]^{\frac{1}{2}}, \beta < 1/2.$$

$$= \{(t^m - 1)/(t^n - 1)\}^{1/2}, \text{ where } t = \frac{(1-\beta)^2}{1-2\beta} \text{ and } \beta < 1/2.$$

As $\beta \to 0$, $\rho_{m,n} \to \sqrt{(m/n)}$ which is the correlation coefficient between $X_{U(m)}$ and $X_{U(n)}$ when $\beta = 0$ i.e. for the exponential distribution.

Example 1.3.4.

A random variable is said to have Type II extreme value distribution if its cumulative distribution function is of the following form:

$$F(x) = e^{-(\frac{x-\mu}{\sigma})^{-\delta}}, x > \mu, \sigma > 0, \delta > 0.$$

Suppose $X_{L(1)}, X_{L(2)}$ .... be the sequence of lower record values and $f_{(n)}(x)$ is the pdf of $X_{L(n)}$, $n = 1, 2, ...$
We can write

$$f_{(n)}(x) = \frac{(H(x))^{n-1}}{\Gamma(n)} f(x)$$

$$= \frac{\delta^n (\frac{x-\mu}{\sigma})^{-(n\delta+1)}}{\sigma \Gamma(n)} e^{-(\frac{x-\mu}{\sigma})^{-\delta}}$$

We can write $\dfrac{X_{L(n)}-\mu}{\sigma} \stackrel{d}{=} (W_1+W_2+\ldots+W_n)^{-\frac{1}{\delta}}$, where $W_1, W_2, \ldots, W_n$ are independent and identically distributed as exponential with unit mean.

Let $Y_{L(n)} = \dfrac{X_{L(n)}-\mu}{\sigma}$, and $U_n = W_1+W_2+\cdots+W_n$, then

$E(Y_{L(n)}) = E((U_n)^{-1/\delta})$

$= \displaystyle\int_0^\infty \dfrac{u^{-\frac{1}{\delta}} u^{n-1} e^{-u}}{\Gamma(n)} du = \dfrac{\Gamma(n-\frac{1}{\delta})}{\Gamma(n)}$

$E(Y_{L(n)})^2 = E((U_n)^{-2/\delta})$

$= \displaystyle\int_0^\infty \dfrac{u^{-\frac{2}{\delta}} u^{n-1} e^{-x}}{\Gamma(n)} du = \dfrac{\Gamma(n-\frac{2}{\delta})}{\Gamma(n)}$

Thus

$E(X_{L(n)}) = \mu + \sigma \dfrac{\Gamma(n-\frac{1}{\delta})}{\Gamma(n)}$,

$\text{Var}(X_{L(n)}) = \sigma^2 \left[\dfrac{\Gamma(n-\frac{2}{\delta})}{\Gamma(n)} - \left(\dfrac{\Gamma(n-\frac{1}{\delta})}{\Gamma(n)}\right)^2 \right]$

For $m < n$,

$E(Y_{L(m)} \cdot Y_{L(n)})$

$= \displaystyle\int_0^\infty \int_0^\infty \dfrac{u^{-\frac{1}{\delta}} (u+v)^{-\frac{1}{\delta}}}{\Gamma(m)\Gamma(n-m)} e^{-u} u^{m-1} e^{-v} v^{n-m-1} du\, dv$

Substituting

$y_1 = u$ and $y_2 = \dfrac{u}{u+v}$, we get on simplification,

$$E(Y_{L(m)} \cdot Y_{L(n)})$$

$$= \int_0^\infty \int_0^1 \frac{(y_1)^{n-1-\frac{2}{\delta}} e^{-y_1} (1-y_2)^{n-m-1}}{\Gamma(m)\Gamma(n-m)} (y_2)^{m-1-\frac{1}{\delta}} dy_1 dy_2$$

$$= \frac{\Gamma(n-\frac{2}{\delta})\Gamma(m-\frac{1}{\delta})}{\Gamma(m)\Gamma(n-\frac{1}{\delta})}$$

Thus $\text{Cov}(X_{L(m)} X_{L(n)})$

$$= \sigma^2 \left\{ \frac{\Gamma(m-\frac{1}{\delta})}{\Gamma(m)} \left[\frac{\Gamma(n-\frac{2}{\delta})}{\Gamma(n-\frac{1}{\delta})} - \frac{\Gamma(n-\frac{1}{\delta})}{\Gamma(n)} \right] \right\}.$$

We rewrite the covariance expression as
$\text{Cov}(X_{L(m)} X_{L(n)}) = \sigma^2 \, a_m b_n$, where

$$a_m = \frac{\Gamma(m-\frac{1}{\delta})}{\Gamma(m)} \quad \text{and} \quad b_n = \frac{\Gamma(n-\frac{2}{\delta})}{\Gamma(n-\frac{1}{\delta})} - \frac{\Gamma(n-\frac{1}{\delta})}{\Gamma(n)}, \; 1 \le m \le n.$$

$$\text{Corr}(X_{L(m)} X_{L(n)}) = \sqrt{\frac{a_m b_n}{a_n b_m}}.$$

The following theorem gives the condition for the existence of the moments of the nth record value.

Theorem 1.3.1.

If $\int_{-\infty}^{\infty} |x|^{r+\delta} dF(x) < \infty$, for some $\delta > 0$, then $E(X_{U(n)})^r$ is finite for all $n \geq 1$.

Proof.

We define the inverse function $R^{-1}(y) = \inf\{x : R(x) \geq y\}$

$$E(|X_{U(n)}|^r)$$

$$= \int_{-\infty}^{\infty} \frac{1}{\Gamma(n)} |x|^{r+\delta} (R(x))^{n-1} dF(x) < \infty, \text{ for } \delta > 0,$$

$$= \frac{1}{\Gamma(n)} \int_0^{\infty} |R^{-1}(y)|^r y^{n-1} e^{-y} dy$$

$$= \frac{1}{\Gamma(n)} (\int_0^{\infty} |R^{-1}(y)|^{rp} e^{-y} dy)^{1/p} (\int_0^{\infty} y^{nq} e^{-y} dy)^{1/q}$$

by Holder's inequality, where $\frac{1}{p} + \frac{1}{q} = 1$, $p > 1$, $q > 1$,

$$= \frac{1}{\Gamma(n)} (\int_0^{\infty} |R^{-1}(y)|^{r+\delta} e^{-y} dy)^{1/p} (\int_0^{\infty} y^{nq} e^{-y} dy)^{1/q},$$

where $p = \frac{r+\delta}{r}$;

$$= \frac{1}{\Gamma(n)} (E(|x|)^{r+\delta})^{1/p} (\int_0^{\infty} y^{nq} e^{-y} dy)^{1/q} < \infty.$$

Theorem 1.3.2.

If $E(X) = 0$ and $Var(X) = 1$, then $|E(X_{U(n+1)})| \leq \sqrt{\binom{2n}{n} - 1}$.

Proof:

Let

$$F^{-1}(u) = \text{Sup}\{x : F(x) \leq u\}, 0 < u < 1,$$

$$F^{-1}(1) = \text{Sup}\{F^{-1}(u), u < 1\}$$

$$0 = E(X) = \int_0^{\infty} x f(x) dx = \int_0^{\infty} \overline{F}^{-1}(t) dt.$$

$$1 = E(X^2) = \int_0^{\infty} x^2 f(x) dx = \int_0^{\infty} \{\overline{F}^{-1}(t)\}^2 dt.$$

$$E(X_{U(n+1)}) = \int_{-\infty}^{\infty} x \frac{\{-\ln \overline{F}(x)\}^n}{\Gamma(n+1)} f(x) dx$$

$$= \int_0^1 \overline{F}^{-1}(t) \frac{\{-\ln(1-t)\}^n}{\Gamma(n+1)} dt$$

$$= \int_0^1 \overline{F}^{-1}(t)[\frac{\{-\ln(1-t)\}^n}{\Gamma(n+1)} - \lambda] dt.$$

Using Cauchy and Schwarz inequality, we get

$$|E(X_{U(n+1)})| \le \{\int_0^1 [\overline{F}^{-1}(t)]^2 dt\}^{\frac{1}{2}} \{\int_0^1 (\frac{(-\ln(1-t))^n}{\Gamma(n+1)} - \lambda)^2 dt\}^{\frac{1}{2}}.$$

Now

$$\int_0^1 \{\overline{F}^{-1}(t)\}^2 dt = 1,$$

and

$$\int_0^1 (\frac{(-\ln(1-t))^n}{\Gamma(n+1)} - \lambda)^2 dt = \binom{2n}{n} + \lambda^2 - 2\lambda$$

Since the minimum value of $\lambda^2 - 2\lambda$ is -1, we get

$$E(X_{U(n)})| \le \sqrt{\binom{2n}{n} - 1} \qquad (1.3.1)$$

$$\approx \frac{2^{2n}}{\sqrt{n\pi}}, \text{ for large n.}$$

For symmetric distribution the upper bound of $|E(X_{U(n)})|$ is smaller. The bound of the symmetric distribution is given in the following theorem.

Theorem 1.3.3.

Suppose the random variable X is symmetric about zero and has variance 1,

then $E(X_{U(n+1)}) \le \frac{1}{\sqrt{2}} \{\binom{2n}{n} \frac{1}{[\Gamma(n+1)]^2} \int_0^\infty [\ln(1-u)\ln u]^n du\}^{\frac{1}{2}}$.

Proof:

$$E(X_{U(n+1)}) = \int_{-\infty}^{\infty} x \frac{\{-\ln \bar{F}(x)\}^n}{\Gamma(n+1)} f(x) dx$$

$$= \int_{0}^{\infty} x \frac{\{-\ln \bar{F}(x)\}^n}{\Gamma(n+1)} f(x) dx$$

$$- \int_{0}^{\infty} x \frac{\{-\ln F(x)\}^n}{\Gamma(n+1)} f(x) dx$$

$$= \frac{1}{2\Gamma(n+1)} \int_{0}^{1} F^{-1}(u) [\{-\ln(1-u)\}^n - \{-\ln u\}^n] du.$$

Now

$$\int_{0}^{1} \{F^{-1}(u)\}^2 du = 1$$

and

$$\int_{0}^{1} [\{-\ln(1-u)\}^n - \{-\ln u\}^n]^2 du$$

$$= 2\Gamma(2n+1) - 2 \int_{0}^{1} [\ln(1-u)\ln u]^n du$$

Hence using the Cauchy and Schwarz inequality, we get

$$E|X_{U(n+1)}| \leq \frac{1}{\sqrt{2}} \left\{ \binom{2n}{n} - \frac{1}{[\Gamma(n+1)]^2} \int_{0}^{\infty} [\ln(1-u)\ln u]^n du \right\}^{\frac{1}{2}}.$$

(1.3.2)

The following table gives the upper bounds of the inequalities given by (1.3.1) and (1.3.2). For large n, the ratio of the bounds as given by (1.3.2) and (1.3.1) is approximately $\sqrt{2}$.

Let $h(n) = \frac{1}{\sqrt{2}} \left\{ \binom{2n}{n} - \frac{1}{[\Gamma(n+1)]^2} \int_{0}^{\infty} [\ln(1-u)\ln u]^n du \right\}^{\frac{1}{2}}$,

$g(n) = \sqrt{\binom{2n}{n} - 1}$ and $b(n) = \frac{g(n)}{h(n)}$.

Thus g(n) is the upper bound of $|E(X_{U(n)})|$ and h(n) is the upper bound of $E(X_{U(n)})$, when the distribution of X_i, i=1,2,... is symmetric.

Table 1.3.1 Values of h(n), g(n) and b(n)

N	h(n)	g(n)	b(n)
1	0.906896	1	1.102662
2	1.726929	2.236068	1.294824
3	3.162147	4.358899	1.378462
4	5.916078	8.306624	1.404076
5	11.224972	15.84298	1.411405
6	21.494185	30.380915	1.413448
7	41.424630	58.574739	1.414008
8	80.218452	113.441615	1.414159
9	155.916644	220.497166	1.414199
10	303.937494	429.831362	1.414210

Nevzorov (1992) gave an interesting upper bounds of the correlation coefficient between any two upper record values. The result is given in the following theorem.

Theorem 1.3.4.

Let { X_i, i=1,2,...} be a sequence of independent and identically distributed random variables and suppose that for $1 \leq m < n$, $E(X_1^2(\ln(1-F(X_1)))^{n-1} < \infty$. Then

$$\rho(X_{U(m)}, X_{U(n)}) \leq \sqrt{m/n},$$

where $\rho(X, Y)$ is the correlation between X and Y. The equality holds if and only if X_1 is distributed as exponential.

Proof:

We will give here the original proof of Nevzorov(1992). The Theorem is proved using the Laguerre polynomials
($L_n^\alpha(s), n = 1,2,...., \alpha > -1$), some of its properties and a relation

between the m th ($m \geq 1$) upper record of a continuous distribution with the m th upper record of the exponential distribution.

$$L_n^\alpha(x) = \frac{1}{n!} e^x x^{-\alpha} \frac{d^n}{dx^n}(e^{-x} x^{n+\alpha})$$

$$= \sum_{m=0}^{n} (-1)^n \binom{n+\alpha}{n-m} \frac{x^m}{m!}$$

We need the following properties of Laguerre polynomials:

$L_0^\alpha(x) = 1$, $L_1^\alpha = \alpha + 1 - x$;

$$\int_0^1 (1-x)^{\mu-1} x^\alpha L_n^\alpha(ax) dx \frac{\Gamma(\alpha+n+1)\Gamma(\mu)}{\Gamma(\alpha+\mu+n+1)} L_n^{\alpha+\mu}(a)$$

$$\int_0^\infty e^{-x} x^\alpha L_n^\alpha(x) L_m^\alpha(x) dx$$

$= 0, \quad m \neq n, \alpha > -1$

$$= \frac{\Gamma(\alpha+n+1)}{\Gamma(n+1)}, m = n.$$

Let $X_{U(n)}$ be the nth upper record value from a continuous distribution function $F(x)$ and $Z_{U(n)}$ be the nth upper record value from the exponential distribution, $E(0,1)$, then

$$X_{U(n)} \stackrel{d}{=} G(Z_{U(n)}), n = 1, 2, \ldots,$$

where $G(x) = F^{-1}(1 - e^{-x})$, F^{-1} is the inverse of F.
It can be shown that

$$Z_{U(n)} \stackrel{d}{=} \xi_1 + \xi_2 + \ldots + \xi_n,$$

where $\xi_1, \xi_2, \ldots, \xi_n$ are independent exponential random variables.

$$E(X_{U(n)}) = E[X\{-\ln(1-F(x))\}^{n-1}],$$

similarly

$$E\{(X_{U(n)})^2\} = E[X^2\{-\ln(1-F(x))\}^{n-1}]$$

Thus the condition $E(X_1^2(\ln(1-F(X_1)))^n < \infty$ implies $X_{U(n)}$ and $X_{U(m)}$ have finite variances. We will maximize $\rho(h_1(Z_{U(m)}), h_2(Z_{U(n)}))$, over all functions h_1 and h_2 subject to the conditions

$E[h_1\{Z_{U(m)}\}]^2 < \infty$ and $E[h_2\{Z_{U(n)}\}]^2 < \infty$.
Let
$$h_1(x) = \sum_{r=0}^{\infty} a_r L_r^{m-1}(x), \quad h_2(x) = \sum_{r=0}^{\infty} b_r L_r^{n-1}(x).$$
Then
$$E(h_1(Z_{U(m)})) = \frac{1}{\Gamma(m)} \int_0^{\infty} h_1(x) x^{m-1} e^{-x} dx$$
$$= \frac{1}{\Gamma(m)} \sum_0^{\infty} a_r \int_0^{\infty} L_r^{m-1}(x) x^{m-1} e^{-x} dx$$
$$= a_0.$$
Now
$$E(h_1(Z_{U(m)}))^2 = \frac{1}{\Gamma(m)} \int_0^{\infty} (h_1(x))^2 x^{m-1} e^{-x} dx$$
$$= \frac{1}{\Gamma(m)} \sum_0^{\infty} a_r^2 \int_0^{\infty} \{L_r^{m-1}(x)\}^2 x^{m-1} e^{-x} dx$$
$$= \sum_{r=0}^{\infty} a_r^2 \frac{\Gamma(r+m)}{\Gamma(m)\Gamma(r+1)}$$
and
$$\text{Var}(h_1(Z_{U(m)})) = \sum_{r=1}^{\infty} a_r^2 \frac{\Gamma(r+m)}{\Gamma(m)\Gamma(r+1)}$$
Similarly
$$\text{Var}(h_2(Z_{U(n)})) = \sum_{r=1}^{\infty} b_r^2 \frac{\Gamma(r+n)}{\Gamma(n)\Gamma(r+1)}$$
and

$E[h_1(Z_{U(m)}) \cdot h_2(Z_{U(n)})]$

$$= \int_0^{\infty} \int_0^{\infty} h_1(x) h_2(x+y) \frac{1}{\Gamma(m)} x^{m-1} e^{-x} \frac{1}{\Gamma(n-m)} y^{n-m-1} e^{-y} dx dy$$

$$= \frac{1}{\Gamma(m)\Gamma(n-m)} \int_0^\infty h_2(v) v^{n-1} e^{-v} \{ \int_0^1 h_1(uv) u^{m-1} (1-u)^{n-m-1} du \} dv$$

$$= \frac{1}{\Gamma(m)\Gamma(n-m)} \sum_{r=0}^\infty a_r \sum_{s=0}^\infty b_s \int_0^\infty L_s^{n-1}(v) v^{n-1} e^{-v}$$

$$\cdot \{ \int_0^1 L_r^{m-1}(uv) u^{m-1}(1-u)^{n-m-1} du \} dv$$

$$= \sum_{r=0}^\infty a_r b_r \frac{\Gamma(m+r)}{\Gamma(m)\Gamma(r+1)}.$$

Hence

$$\text{Cov}[h_1(Z_{U(m)}), h_2(Z_{U(n)})]$$
$$= \text{Cov}[h_1(Z_{U(m)}) \cdot h_2(Z_{U(n)})] - E[h_1(Z_{U(m)})] E[h_2(Z_{U(n)})]$$
$$= \sum_{r=1}^\infty a_r b_r \frac{\Gamma(m+r)}{\Gamma(m)\Gamma(n-m)}.$$

Thus

$$\rho(Z_{U(m)}, Z_{U(n)})$$

$$= \sum_{r=1}^\infty a_r b_r \frac{\Gamma(m+r)}{\Gamma(m)\Gamma(r+1)} \left(\sum_{r=1}^\infty a_r^2 \frac{\Gamma(r+m)}{\Gamma(r+1)\Gamma(m)} \sum_{r=0}^\infty b_r^2 \frac{\Gamma(r+n)}{\Gamma(r+n)\Gamma(n)} \right)^{-\frac{1}{2}}$$

Since $\dfrac{\Gamma(m+r)}{\Gamma(n+r)} < \dfrac{\Gamma(m+1)}{\Gamma(n+1)}, r=2,3,\ldots$, and

$$\Gamma(m+r) < \left(\frac{\Gamma(n+r)\Gamma(m+r)\Gamma(m+1)}{\Gamma(n+1)} \right)^{\frac{1}{2}},$$

we have

$$|\rho(Z_{U(m)}, Z_{U(n)})| \leq \sum_{r=1}^\infty |a_r| \left(\frac{\Gamma(m+r)}{\Gamma(r+1)} \right)^{\frac{1}{2}} |b_r| \left(\frac{\Gamma(n+r)}{\Gamma(r+1)} \right)^{\frac{1}{2}} \left(\frac{\Gamma(m+1)}{\Gamma(n+1)} \right)^{\frac{1}{2}}$$

$$\cdot \left(\sum_{r=1}^\infty a_r^2 \frac{\Gamma(m+r)}{\Gamma(r+1)} \sum_{r=1}^\infty b_r^2 \frac{\Gamma(n+r)}{\Gamma(r+1)} \right)^{-\frac{1}{2}} \left(\frac{\Gamma(m)}{\Gamma(n)} \right)^{-\frac{1}{2}},$$

with the equality being satisfied if and only if $a_r b_r = 0$ for $r = 2,3,...$
Thus we get

$$|\rho(Z_{U(m)}, Z_{U(n)})| \leq \left(\frac{m}{n}\right)^{\frac{1}{2}},$$

only if $a_r = b_r = 0$ for $r = 2,3,...$ and $a_1 b_1 > 0$. Hence
$$h_1(x) = a_0 + a_1 L_1^{m-1}(x) = a_0 + a_1(m-x)$$
and
$$h_2(x) = b_0 + b_1 L_1^{n-1}(x) = b_0 + b_1(m-x).$$
Thus

$\rho(X_{U(m)}, X_{U(n)})$ takes its upper limit $\left(\frac{m}{n}\right)^{\frac{1}{2}}$ only when

$h_1(x) = c_1 + c_2 x$ and
$h_2(x) = d_1 + d_2 x$ with $c_2 d_2 > 0$.

So when $\rho(X_{U(m)}, X_{U(n)}) = \left(\frac{m}{n}\right)^{\frac{1}{2}}$, we have

$G(x) = F^{-1}(1 - e^{-x}) = c_1 + c_2 x$ for $x \geq 0$.
Thus
$F(x) = 1 - e^{-(x-c_1)/c_2}$, for $x \geq c_1$.

Rohtagi and Szekely (1992) gave an alternative proof of this Theorem by using the linear property of $E(X|Y)$ and $E(Y|X)$ when X and Y have finite variances

We will call F is "new better than used" (NBU) if for $x, y \geq 0$, $\overline{F}(x+y) \leq \overline{F}(x)\overline{F}(y)$, and F is "new worse than used" (NWU) if for $x, y \geq 0$, $\overline{F}(x+y) \geq \overline{F}(x)\overline{F}(y)$. We will say F belongs to the class C_1 if either F is NBU or NWU. The following Theorem is based on NBU(NWU) properties.

Theorem 1.3.5.

Let $\{X_n, n \geq 1\}$ be a sequence of independent and identically distributed random variables with distribution function F(x) and the corresponding density function f(x). If $E(X_n)$, $n \geq 1$ is finite and F belongs to the class C_1, then $E\{X_{U(m+1)} - X_{U(m)}\} \leq (\geq) E(X_n)$, for any fixed m and n according as F is NBU(NWU).

Proof.
From (1.2.9), we can write the $E\{X_{U(m+1)} - X_{U(m)}\}$ as

$$E\{X_{U(m+1)} - X_{U(m)}\} = \int_0^\infty \int_0^\infty \frac{1}{\Gamma(n)}(R(u))^{n-1} f(u) \frac{\overline{F}(u+z)}{\overline{F}(u)} du\,dz$$

$$\leq (\geq) \int_0^\infty \int_0^\infty \frac{1}{\Gamma(n)}(R(u))^{n-1} f(u)\overline{F}(z) du\,dz,$$

according as $\overline{F}(x+y) \leq (\geq) \overline{F}(x)\overline{F}(y)$. Hence $E\{X_{U(m+1)} - X_{U(m)}\} \leq (\geq) E(X_n)$ according as F is NBU(NWU).

If F(x) has the density f(x), the ratio $r(x) = \frac{f(x)}{\overline{F}(x)}$, for $\overline{F}(x) > 0$ is called the failure (hazard) rate hazard rate, we will say F belongs to the class C_2 if the failure rate, r(x), is either monotone increasing (IFR) or monotone decreasing (DFR).

Theorem 1.3.6.

Let $\{X_i, i=1,2,\ldots\}$ be ac sequence of i.i.d. continuous non-negative rv's with common cdf F(x) and pdf f(x). Suppose that $X_{U(1)}, X_{U(2)}, \ldots$ are the upper record values of this sequence and $Z_{n+1,n} = X_{U(n+1)} - X_{U(n)}$, $n = 1,2,\ldots$ with $X_{U(0)}=0$. If $E(D_{n+1})$ exists and F belongs to class C_2, then $E(Z_{n+1}) > (<) E(Z_n)$ according as F is IFR or DFR.
Proof.

For $n = 1,2,\ldots$, the joint pdf of $X_{U(n)}$ and $X_{U(n+1)}$ is given by

$$f_{n,n+1}(x,y) = \frac{(R(x))^{n-1}}{(n-1)!} r(x) f(y)$$

for $-\infty < x < y < \infty$.

The joint pdf of $X_{U(n)}$ and $Z_{n+1,n}$ is

$$f_{n,Z}(x,z) = \frac{(R(x))^{n-1}}{(n-1)!} r(x) f(z+x)$$

Now for $0 < x, z < \infty$.

$$E(Z_{n+1,n}) = \int_0^\infty \int_0^\infty z \frac{(R(x))^{n-1}}{(n-1)!} r(x) f(z+x) dx dz.$$

Since $\int_0^\infty z f(z+x) dz = \int_0^\infty \vec{F}(z+x) dz$, we obtain

$$E(Z_{n+1,n}) = \int_0^\infty \int_0^\infty \frac{(R(x))^{n-1}}{(n-1)!} r(x) \vec{F}(z+x) dx dz.$$

On integrating by parts and using the relation $R'(x) = r(x)$, we get

$$E(Z_{n+1,n}) = \int_0^\infty \int_0^\infty \frac{(R(x))^n}{n!} f(z+x) dx dz$$

$$= \int_0^\infty \int_0^\infty \frac{(R(x))^n}{n!} r(z+x) \overline{F}(z+x) dx dz$$

$$\geq (\leq) \int_0^\infty \int_0^\infty \frac{(R(x))^n}{n!} r(z) \overline{F}(z+x) dx dz$$

according as $r(x)$ is IFR or DFR

$$= E(Z_{n+2,n+1})..$$

1.4 DISTRIBUTION OF INTER-RECORD TIMES

Let $\Delta_r = U(r+1) - U(r)$ and $\Delta_{(r)} = L(r+1) - L(r)$, $r = 1, 2, ...$ We will call Δ_r and $\Delta_{(r)}$ as the upper and lower inter record times respectively. Since $U(1) = 1 = L(1)$, we have $U(r+1) = 1 + \Delta_1 + \Delta_2 + ... + \Delta_r$. Similarly $L(r+1) = 1 + \Delta_{(1)} + \Delta_{(2)} + ... + \Delta_{(r)}$.

Lemma 1.4.1

For any $n \geq 1$, $P(\Delta_n < \infty) = 1 = P(\Delta_{(n)} < \infty)$.

Proof:

$$P(\Delta_1 = \infty) = P(\bigcap_{i=2}^\infty X_i \leq X_1) \qquad (1.4.1)$$

$$= \lim_{m \to \infty} P(\bigcap_{i=2}^{\infty} X_i \leq X_1)$$

$$= \lim_{m \to \infty} P(\max(X_2, X_2, ..., X_m) \leq X_1)$$

$$= \lim_{m \to \infty} \frac{1}{m} = 0.$$

It is obvious that $P(\Delta_{(1)} = \infty) = 0$.

Similarly it can be shown that for $n \geq 2$.

$$P(\Delta_n = \infty) = 0 = P(\Delta_{(n)} = \infty).$$

Theorem 1.4.1.

$$P(\Delta_n = k) = \sum_{i=0}^{k-1} \binom{k-1}{i} (-1)^i \frac{1}{(2+i)^n}.$$

Proof.

$$P(\Delta_1 = k | X_1 = x_1) = P[U(2) = k+1 | X_1 = x_1]$$
$$= (F(x_1))^{k-1} \overline{F}(x_1)$$

Thus

$$P(\Delta_1 = k) = \int_{-\infty}^{\infty} (F(x_1))^{k-1} (1-F(x_1)) f(x_1) dx_1 \qquad (1.4.2)$$

$$= \frac{1}{k} - \frac{1}{k+1} = \frac{1}{k(k+1)}$$

Similarly it can be shown that

$$P(\Delta_n = k | X_{U(n)} = x_n) = (F(x_n))^{k-1}(1-F(x_n))$$

$$P(\Delta_n = k) = \int_{-\infty}^{\infty} (F(x))^{k-1} (1-F(x)) \frac{(-\ln(1-F(x))^{n-1}}{\Gamma(n)} f(x) dx$$

$$= \sum_{i=0}^{k-1} \binom{k-1}{i} (-1)^i \frac{1}{(2+i)^n}. \qquad (1.4.3)$$

$$P(\Delta_n > k) = \int_0^\infty \sum_{j=k}^\infty (F(x))^{j-1}(1-F(x)) \frac{\{-\ln(1-F(x))\}^{n-1}}{\Gamma(n)} f(x) dx$$

$$= \sum_{i=0}^{k-1} \binom{k-1}{i} (-1)^i \frac{1}{(1+i)^n} \quad (1.4.4)$$

Proceeding similarly, the following theorem can be proved.

Theorem 1.4.2.

$$P(\Delta_{(n)} = k) = \sum_{I=0}^{k-1} \binom{k-1}{i} (-1)^i \frac{1}{(2+i)^n}$$

For all $n \geq 1$, Δ_n and $\Delta_{(n)}$ are identically distributed. Their pdfs are independent of the parent distribution $F(x)$.

Joint Distribution of Record Values with Record Times and Inter Record Times

For any $-\infty < x_1 < x_2 < .. x_{n+1} < \infty$ and $1 = u(1) < u(2) < ... < u(n+1)$, we have $P(X_{U(1)} \leq x_1, X_{U(2)} \leq x_2, ... X_{U(n+1)} \leq x_n, U(1) = 1, U(2) = u(2),..., U(n+1) = u(n+1)) = P(X_1 \leq x_1, \max\{X_2,..., X_{u(2)-1}\} \leq X_1 < X_{u(2)} \leq x_2,..., \max\{X_{u(n)},...X_{u(n+1)-1}\} < X_{u(n)} < X_{u(n+1)} \leq x_{n+1}\} =$

$$\int_{-\infty}^{x_1} ... \int_{-\infty}^{x_{n+1}} \{\prod_{r=1}^{n} F^{u(r+1)-u(r)-1}(w_r)\} f(w_1) f(w_2)....f(w_{n+1})$$

$$dw_1 dw_2 ...dw_{n+1} \quad (1.4.5)$$

Let $f_{1,2,...,n+1,(1),(2),..(n)}(x_1, x_2,...x_{n+1}, u(1), u(2),..u(n+1))$ be the density function of the continuous random variables $X_{U(1)}, X_{U(2)},..., X_{U(n+1)}$ and the discrete record times $U(1), U(2),..., U(n+1)$ is obtained by differentiating (1.4.5) with respect to $x_1, x_2,..x_n$. Thus

$f_{1,2,...,n+1,(1),(2),..(n+1)}(x_1, x_2,...x_{n+1}, u(1), u(2),..u(n+1))$

$$= \{\prod_{r=1}^{n} F^{u(r+1)-u(r)-1}(x_r)\} f(x_1) f(x_2)....f(x_{n+1})$$

for $-\infty < x_1 < x_2 < .. x_{n+1} < \infty$ and $1 = u(1) < u(2) < ... < u(n+1)$,

= 0, otherwise. (1.4.6)

Let $\Delta_r = U(r+1) - U(r)$ and $d_r = u(r+1) - u(r)$, $r = 1, 2, ..., n$, then the density function $^*f_{1,2,...,n,1,2,...,n+1}(x_1,x_2,...x_{n+1},d_1,d_2,...d_n)$ of the continuous random variables $X_{U(1)}, X_{U(2)},..., X_{U(n+1)}$ and the discrete inter record times $\Delta_1, \Delta_2,..., \Delta_n$ is

$^*f_{1,2,...,n+1,1,2,...,n}(x_1,x_2,...x_{n+1},d_1,d_2,...d_n)$

$$= \{\prod_{r=1}^{n} F^{d_r-1}(x_r)\} f(x_1) f(x_2)....f(x_{n+1})$$

for $-\infty < x_1 < x_2 <.. x_{n+1} < \infty$ and $d_r > .0, r = 1,2,...,n$,
= 0, otherwise.

The joint density function of $X_{L(1)}, ..., X_{L(n+1)}$ and $\Delta_{(r)}$, $r = 1,...,n$ is similar.
The conditional probability of $\Delta_1, ..., \Delta_n$, given $X_{U(1)}, X_{U(2)},..., X_{U(n+1)}$ is
$P(\Delta_1 = d_1, ..., \Delta_n = d_{n-1}| X_{U(1)} = x_1, ..., X_{U(n+1)} = x_{n+1})$

$$= \frac{\{\prod_{r=1}^{n} F^{d_r-1}(x_r)\} f(x_1) f(x_2)....f(x_{n+1})}{r(x_1)...r(x_n) f(x_{n+1})}$$

$$= \prod_{r=1}^{n} F^{d_r-1}(x_r)(1 - F(x_r))$$

Thus the inter record times $\Delta_1, ..., \Delta_n$, given $X_{U(1)}, X_{U(2)},..., X_{U(n+1)}$ are independent. Hence

$P(\Delta_n = m| X_{U(n)} = x_n) = (F(x_n))^{m-1}(1-F(x_n))$

and

$E(\Delta_n | X_{U(n)} = x_n) = (1 - F(x_n))^{-1}$

$Var(\Delta_n | X_{U(n)} = x_n) = F(x_n)(1 - F(x_n))^{-2}$

Similarly, we will have

$E(\Delta_{(n)} | X_{L(n)} = x_{(n)}) = (F(x_n))^{-1}$

$Var(\Delta_{(n)} | X_{L(n)} = x_{(n)}) = (1 - F(x_{(n)}))(F(x_{(n)}))^{-2}$.

Theorem 1.4.3.

$$E(\Delta_n^{-1}) = n(S_{n+1} - 1), \text{ where}$$

$$S_n = \sum_{j=1}^{\infty} (j)^{-n}$$

Proof.

$E(\Delta_n^{-1})$

$$= \frac{1}{\Gamma(n)} \int_{-\infty}^{\infty} \sum_{k=1}^{\infty} k^{-1}(F(x))^{k-1}(1-F(x))(-\ln(1-F(x)))^{n-1} f(x) dx$$

$$= \frac{1}{\Gamma(n)} \int_{-\infty}^{\infty} (F(x))^{-1}(1-F(x))(-\ln(1-F(x)))^n f(x) dx$$

$$= \frac{1}{\Gamma(n)} \int_0^{\infty} y^n e^{-2y}(1-e^{-y})^{-1} dy$$

$$= n \sum_{k=1}^{\infty} (k+1)^{-(n+1)}.$$

The following table gives the value of $E(\Delta_n^{-1})$ for some selected values of n.

Table 1.4.1. Values of $E(\Delta_n^{-1})$

n	$E(\Delta_n^{-1})$
1	0.644934
2	0.404114
3	0.246970
4	0.147711
5	0.086715
6	0.050096
7	0.028541
8	0.016067
9	0.008951
10	0.004942
15	0.000229

Using the relation between S_{2n} and the Bernoulli numbers (see Appendix A) we can express $E(\Delta_n^{-1})$ for odd n in terms of the Bernoulli numbers.

Theorem 1.4.4.
$$P(\Delta_n \geq s) = \frac{1}{s} \sum_{j=1}^{s} P(\Delta_{n-1} \geq j)$$

Proof.

$P[\Delta_n \geq s]$

$$= \frac{1}{\Gamma(n)} \int_{-\infty}^{\infty} (1-F(x))\{-\ln(1-F(x))\}^{n-1} \sum_{k=s}^{\infty} (F(x))^{k-1} f(x) dx$$

$$= \frac{1}{\Gamma(n)} \int_{-\infty}^{\infty} (F(x))^{s-1} \{-\ln(1-F(x))\}^{n-1} f(x) dx$$

$$= \frac{1}{\Gamma(n)} \int_0^1 t^{s-1} \{-\ln(1-t)\}^{n-1} dt$$

$$= \frac{1}{s\Gamma(n-1)} \int_0^1 \frac{1-t^s}{1-t} \{-\ln(1-t)\}^{n-2} dt, \; n \geq 2,$$

$$= \frac{1}{s} \sum_{j=1}^{s} P(\Delta_{n-1} \geq j), \, n \geq 2. \qquad (1.4.9)$$

In particular
$$P(\Delta_1 > s) = \frac{1}{s+1},$$
and
$$P(\Delta_2 > s) = \frac{1}{s+1} \sum_{j=1}^{s} (1+j)^{-1}.$$

Let $P_g(\Delta_n(s))$ be the probability generating function of Δ_n ($|s| < 1$), then
$$P_g(\Delta_1(s)) = \sum_{x=1}^{\infty} P(\Delta_1 = x) s^x = \sum_{x=1}^{\infty} \frac{1}{x(x+1)} s^x = 1 + \frac{1-s}{s} \ln(1-s),$$

Record Statistics

$$E[s^{\Delta_n} \mid X_{U(n)} = x_n] = \sum_{k=1}^{\infty} s^k (F(x_n))^{k-1} (1-F(x_n)) = s \frac{1-F(x_n)}{1-sF(x_n)}$$

and

$$P_g(\Delta_n(s)) = \int_{-\infty}^{\infty} s \frac{1-F(x)}{1-tF(x)} \cdot \frac{(-\ln(1-F(x)))^{n-1}}{\Gamma(n)} f(x)dx$$

$$= \int_0^1 \frac{s(1-u)}{1-su} \cdot \frac{(-\ln(1-u))^{n-1}}{\Gamma(n)} du$$

$$= 1 - \sum_{j=0}^{\infty} (-1)^j \frac{s^j}{(1-s)^j} \cdot \frac{1}{(1+j)^n}, \mid s \mid < 1. \quad (1.4.10)$$

The following table gives the values of $P(\Delta_n < k)$ for some selected values of n. From (1.4.4), we have

$$P(\Delta_n < m) = 1 - \sum_{j=0}^{m-1} \binom{m-1}{j} (-1)^j \frac{1}{(1+j)^n}$$

Table 1.4.2. Values of $P(\Delta_n < m)$

M \ n	1	2	3	4	5	6
2	0.5000	0.2500	0.1250	0.0625	0.0313	0.0156
5	0.8000	0.5433	0.3323	0.1890	0.1039	0.0552
10	0.9000	0.7071	0.4936	0.3143	0.1870	0.1058
15	0.9333	0.7788	0.5803	0.3926	0.2459	0.1451
20	0.9500	0.8201	0.6365	0.4484	0.2912	0.1773
30	0.9667	0.8668	0.7071	0.5251	0.3586	0.2283
50	0.9800	0.9100	0.7813	0.6153	0.4460	0.3002
100	0.9900	0.9481	0.8573	0.7209	0.5615	0.4062
200	0.9950	0.9706	0.9095	0.8047	0.6657	0.5137
500	0.9980	0.9864	0.9522	0.8836	0.7780	0.6453
1000	0.9950	0.9925	0.9712	0.9235	0.8425	0.5985
5000	0.9998	0.9982	0.9916	0.9734	0.9353	0.7798

Theorem 1.4.5.

$E(\Delta_n^{\alpha}) = \infty$ and $E(\Delta_n^{-\alpha}) < \infty$ for $\alpha \geq 1$ and $n \geq 1$.

Proof

$$E(\Delta_n) = \sum_{s=0}^{\infty} P[\Delta_n > s]$$

$$= \int_0^{\infty} \frac{y^{n-1} e^{-y}}{\Gamma(n)} \sum_{s=0}^{\infty} (1-e^{-y})^s \, dy, \quad (1.4.11)$$

$$= \int_0^{\infty} \frac{y^{n-1}}{\Gamma(n)} dy = \infty,$$

and $E(\Delta_n^{\alpha}) > E(\Delta) = \infty$, $\alpha > 1$.

For $0 < \alpha < 1$,

$$E(\Delta_n^{\alpha}) = \frac{1}{\Gamma(n)} \int_{-\infty}^{\infty} \sum_{k=1}^{\infty} k^{\alpha} (F(x))^{k-1} \overline{F}(x) \{-\ln \overline{F}(x)\}^{n-1} f(x) dx$$

$$= \frac{1}{\Gamma(n)} \int_0^{\infty} e^{-2t} t^{n-1} \sum_{k=1}^{\infty} k^{\alpha} (1-e^{-t})^{k-1} dt.$$

Now

$$\sum_{k=1}^{\infty} k^{\alpha} (1-e^{-t})^{k-1} \leq \int_0^{\infty} (s+1)^{\alpha} e^{-s\ln(1-e^{-t})^{-1}} ds$$

$$= \int_1^{\infty} u^{\alpha} e^{-(u-1)\ln(1-e^{-t})^{-1}} du$$

$$\leq (1-e^{-t})^{-1} \int_0^{\infty} u^{\alpha} e^{-u\ln(1-e^{-t})^{-1}} du$$

$$= (1-e^{-t})^{-1} \frac{\Gamma(1+a)}{\{-\ln(1-e^{-t})\}^{a+1}} \leq (1-e^{-t})^{-1} \Gamma(1+a) e^{(1+a)t}.$$

Thus

$$E(\Delta_n^{\alpha}) \leq \frac{\Gamma(1+\alpha)}{\Gamma(n)} \int_0^{\infty} (1-e^{-t})^{-1} e^{-(1-\alpha)t} t^{n-1} \, dt.$$

Since $x \leq x(1-e^{-x})^{-1} \leq x+1$, we have

$$E(\Delta_n{}^\alpha) \leq \frac{\Gamma(1+\alpha)}{\Gamma(n)} \int_0^\infty e^{-(1-\alpha)x}(x+1)x^{n-2} dx$$

$$= \frac{\Gamma(1+\alpha)}{(1-\alpha)^n}\{1+\frac{1-\alpha}{n}\}.$$

The probability of the event $(\Delta_1 = k_1 \cap \Delta_2 = k_2)$ is

$$P(\bigcap_{i=1}^{2} \Delta_i = k_i)$$

$$\iint_{-\infty<x_0<x_1<\infty}(F(x_0))^{k_1-1}(F(x_1))^{k_2-1}\overline{F}(x_0)\overline{F}(x_1)r(x_0)f(x_1)\,dx_0\,dx_1$$

$$= \int_{-\infty}^{\infty}(F(x_0))^{k_1-1}\overline{F}(x_0)r(x_0)[\frac{1}{k_2}(1-(F(x_0))^{k_2})$$

$$-\frac{1}{k_2+1}(1-(F(x_0))^{k_2+1})]dx_0$$

$$= \frac{1}{k_1 k_2} - \frac{1}{k_2(k_1+k_2)} - \frac{1}{(k_2+1)k_1} + \frac{1}{k_2+1}\cdot\frac{1}{k_1+k_2+1}$$

$$= \frac{1}{k_1(k_1+k_2)(k_1+k_2+1)}.$$

Using the probability of inter-record times, we can easily obtain various probabilities of the record times.

$$P[U(2) = n_1] = P[\Delta_1 = n_1 - 1] = \frac{1}{n_1-1}\cdot\frac{1}{n_1}.$$

$$P[U(3) = n_2, U(2) = n_1] = P[\Delta_2 = n_2 - n_1, \Delta_1 = n_1 - 1]$$

$$= \frac{1}{n_1-1}\cdot\frac{1}{n_2-1}\cdot\frac{1}{n_2}.$$

$$P(U(3)=n_2) = = \frac{1}{n_2-1}\cdot\frac{1}{n_2}\sum_{j=2}^{n_2-1}\frac{1}{j-1}.$$

In general

$$P[U(m+1)=n_m, U(2)=n_1, U(3)=n_2,...,U(m)=n_{m-1}]$$
$$= \frac{1}{n_1-1} \cdot \frac{1}{n_2-1} \cdots \frac{1}{n_m-1} \cdot \frac{1}{n_m}.$$

$$P[U(m+1)=n_m \mid U(2)=n_1, U(3)=n_2,...,U(m)=n_{m-1}]$$
$$= \frac{n_{m-1}}{n_m(n_m-1)},$$

$$= P[U(m+1)=n_m \mid U(m)=n_{m-1}]$$

Thus the sequence $\{U(n+1), n \geq 0\}$ forms a homogeneous Markov chain with the transition probability p_{ij}, where

$$p_{ij} = \frac{i}{j(j-1)}, \quad j > i$$
$$= 0, \quad \text{for } j \leq i.$$

Now

$$E(U(2)) = \sum_{n=2}^{\infty} \frac{n}{n(n-1)} = \infty.$$

Since $U(2) < U(3) < ....$, we have $E\{U(m+1)\} = \infty$, for $m \geq 1$. This result can also be established by noting that $U(m+1) = 1 + \sum_{i=1}^{m} \Delta_i$ and $E(\Delta_1) = \infty$.

We can write $P(U(2)=m) = |S(1,m-2)|/m!$, where $S(r,m)$ = coefficient of x^r in the expression $P(x,m)$, where
$P(x,m) = x(x-1)(x-2)...(x-m+1)$. $S(r,m)$ is known as Stirling numbers of the first kind.

$$P(U(2)=k, U(3)=m) = \frac{1}{(k-1)m(m-1)}, \quad k=2,..,m-1....$$

Thus

$$P(U(3)=m) = (1+...+\frac{1}{m-2})\frac{1}{m(m-1)}, \quad m=3,...$$

Using the Stirling's number we have
$P(U(3)=m) = |S(2,m-1)|/m!$.
In general
$P(U(n) = m) = |S(n-1, m-1)|/m!$, $m = n, \ldots$
Let $P_{gU(n)}(t)$ be the probability generating function of $U(n)$. We have

$$P_{gU(n)}(t) = E(t^{U(n)}) = \sum_{m=n}^{\infty} t^m |S(n-1, m-1)|/m!$$

Using the relation

$$\sum_{m=n}^{\infty} t^m |S(k,m)|/m! = (-\ln(1-t))^k/k!,$$

we get

$$P_{gU(n)}(t) = \int_0^t \frac{(-\ln(1-u))^{n-1}}{(n-1)!} du = \int_0^{-\ln(1-t)} \frac{v^{n-1}}{(n-1)!} e^{-v} dv \qquad (1.4.12)$$

$$= 1 - (1-t) \sum_{j=0}^{n-1} \frac{(-\ln(1-t))^j}{j!}.$$

The following Theorem is due to Nevzorov.

Theorem 1.4.6.

If $h(n) = 1 + 1/2 + \ldots + 1/n$, then $Eh(U(n)) = n$

Proof:

$$E(h(U(n))|U(n-1)=i) = E \sum_{j=i+1}^{\infty} h(j) | U(n-1) = i \sum_{j=i+1}^{\infty} h(j)/(j(j-1))$$

$$= i \sum_{j=i+1}^{\infty} h(j)/(j(j-1))$$

$$= i \sum_{j=i+1}^{\infty} h(j)/(j-1) - i \sum_{j=i+1}^{\infty} h(j)/j$$

$$= i \sum_{j=i+1}^{\infty} h(j)/(j-1) - i \sum_{j=i+1}^{\infty} (h(j+1) - 1/(j+1))/j$$

$$= i\sum_{j=i+1}^{\infty} h(j)/(j-1) - i\sum_{j=i+2}^{\infty}(h(j)/(j-1) - i\sum_{j=i+1}^{\infty} 1/(j+1)j)$$
$$= h(i+1)+i/(i+1) = 1+h(i)$$

Thus

$Eh(U(n)| U(n-1)) = E(h(U(n-1))) +1$

Hence we have

$E(h(U(n)| U(n-1)) = E(h(U(n-1))) +1 = \ldots = E(h(U(1)))+n-1 = n$

Williams (1973) showed that the following representation for $U(r)$, $r = 1,2,\ldots$ where $U(1) = 1$, $U(n+1) = [U(n) \exp(W_n)] + 1$, $n=1,2,\ldots$ where $W_1, W_2, \ldots$ are i.i.d random variables from exponential distribution with unit mean and $[x]$ denotes the integer part of x.

The proof can be established by noting the fact

$P(\exp(-W_n) < x = P(W_n > -\ln x) = x$, $0<x<1$ and

$P(U(n+1) = j| U(n) = m) = P([L(n)/V_n + 1| L(n) = m)$,

where V_n is uniformly distributed random variable on $[0,1]$ and is independent of $L(n)$, variable on $[0,1]$. Thus

$P(U(n+1) =j| U(n) =m) = P([m/V_n]+1 =j| U(n) =m)$

$$= P([m/V_n +1 =j)$$

$$= p[i/m < V_n < i/(m-1)] = \frac{i}{m(m-1)}$$

Galambos and Seneta (1975) proved that if

$$T(n) -1 < U(n)/U(n-1) \leq T(n), n=2,3,\ldots, \text{ then}$$

$T(r)$, $r =2,3,\ldots$ are independent and identically distributed with

T(r), r =2,3,... are independent and identically distributed with
$$P(T(r) = j) = P(U(2) = j) = \frac{1}{j(j-1)}, j = 2,3,...$$

1.5. RELATION BETWEEN OCCURRENCE OF RECORDS AND POISSON PROCESS

In this section we restrict the discussion to upper record values. The corresponding results for lower record values are similar.

Let $\{X_n, n \geq 1\}$ be a sequence of i.i.d. random variable with continuous cdf F such that $F(0) = 0$. We define the process $N_{(0,t]}$ for $0 < t < \infty$ as
$$N_{(0,t]} = \#\{m: X_{U(m)} \leq t\}.$$
It is easy to see that
$$F_m(t) = P[X_{U(m)} \leq t] = P(N_{(0,t]} \geq m).$$

Hence
$$P(N_{(0,t]} \geq m) = \int_0^t \frac{\{R(u)\}^{m-1}}{\Gamma(m)} f(u) du$$

Thus assuming $E(N_{(0,t]}) < \infty$, we get
$$E(N_{[0,t]}) = \sum_{m=1}^\infty P(N_{[0,t]} \geq m)$$
$$= \sum_{m=1}^\infty \int_0^t \frac{\{R(u)\}^{m-1}}{\Gamma(m)} f(u) du$$

Now interchanging the summation and the integral and simplifying, we obtain
$$E(N_{(0,t]}) = \int_0^t \frac{f(u)}{\overline{F}(u)} du = -\ln \overline{F}(t)$$

Since
$$P(N_{(0,t]} \geq m) = \int_0^t \frac{\{R(u)\}^{m-1}}{\Gamma(m)} f(u) du,$$

$$P(N_{[0,t]} = k) = P(N_{(0,t]} \geq k) - P(N_{(0,t]} \geq k+1)$$

$$= \int_0^t \frac{(R(u))^{k-1}}{\Gamma(k-1)} f(u)du - \int_0^t \frac{(R(u))^k}{\Gamma(k)} f(u)du$$

$$= \overline{F}_k(t) - \overline{F}_{k-1}(t).$$

Using the relation

$$\overline{F}_n(x) = 1 - F_n(x) = \overline{F}(x) \sum_{j=0}^{n-1} \frac{(R(x))^j}{j!}$$

$$= e^{-R(x)} \sum_{j=0}^{n-1} \frac{(R(x))^j}{j!}$$

we have

$$P(N_{[0,t]} = k) = e^{-R(t)} \frac{(R(t))^{k-1}}{(k-1)!}, \; k = 1, 2, \ldots$$

Thus the point process $N_{(0,t]}$ is a Poisson Process with mean $= R(t) = -\ln \overline{F}(t)$.

Example 1.5.1

Suppose $\{X_n, n \geq 1\}$ is a sequence of i.i.d. random variables with $F(x) = 1 - e^{-\lambda x}$, $x > 0$ and $\lambda > 0$. Then $F_n(x) = \int_0^x \frac{u^{n-1}}{(n-1)!} e^{-u} du$ and $N_{(0,t]}$ is a homogeneous Poisson Process with $E(N_{(0,t]}) = \lambda t$ and intensity function δ_t ($\delta_t = -\frac{\overline{F}'(t)}{\overline{F}(t)}$) $= \lambda$.

1.6. NUMBER OF RECORDS IN A SEQUENCE OF OBSERVATIONS

We will consider here the number of upper records among the sequence of observations $X_1, X_2, \ldots, X_n$, the result for the lower records are identical.

Let M_n be the number of upper records among the sequence $X_1, ..., X_n$.

$P[M_n < 2] = P[U(2) > n] = P[\Delta_1 > n-1] = \dfrac{1}{n}$.

$P[M_n < 3] = P[U(3) > 3]$

$$= \sum_{m=1}^{n-1} p[\Delta_1 = n-m, \Delta_2 > m-1]$$

$$= \dfrac{1}{n} \sum_{m=1}^{n-1} \dfrac{1}{n-m}$$

In general

$P[M_n < k+1] = P[U(k+1) > n]$

$$= \dfrac{1}{n} \cdot \sum_{1 < m_1 < ... < m_k < n} \dfrac{1}{n-m_k} \cdot \dfrac{1}{n-m_{k-1}} ... \dfrac{1}{m_1}.$$

Theorem 1.6.1.

$$E(M_n) = \sum_{i=1}^{n} \dfrac{1}{i}$$

and $\quad Var(M_n) = \sum_{i=1}^{n} \dfrac{i-1}{i^2}, n \geq 1.$

Proof.

Let $Z_i = 1$, if $X_i = \max(X_1, ..., X_n)$
$\quad\quad\quad = 0$, otherwise.

Then

$E(Z_i) = P(Z_i = 1) = P(X_i = \max(X_1, ..., X_n)) = \dfrac{1}{i}$.

$Var(Z_i) = E(Z_i^2) - (E(Z_i))^2 = \dfrac{1}{i} - \dfrac{1}{i^2} = \dfrac{i-1}{i^2}$.

For $j > i$

$E(Z_i Z_j) = P(Z_i = 1 \text{ and } Z_j = 1)$

$$= P(X_i = \max(X_1, ..., X_i) < \max(X_{i+1}, ..., X_j) = X_j)$$
$$= P(X_i = \max(X_1, ..., X_i)) \cdot P(\max(X_1, ..., X_i) = X_i)$$
$$< \max(X_{i+1}, ..., X_j) \cdot P(X_j = \max(X_{i+1}, ..., X_j))$$
$$= \frac{1}{i} \cdot \frac{j-i}{j} \cdot \frac{1}{j-i} = \frac{1}{i} \cdot \frac{1}{j}$$

Thus
$$E(Z_i Z_j) = \frac{1}{i} \cdot \frac{1}{j} = E(Z_i) E(Z_j), \text{ i.e. } Z_i \text{ and } Z_j \text{ are not}$$
correlated. We can express M_n in terms of Z_i,
$$M_n = \sum_{i=1}^{n} Z_i.$$

The probability generating function, $P_M(s)$ ($=E(s^{M_n})$), of M_n is the product of the n probability generating functions of the Bernoulli rvs $Z_1, ..., Z_n$.
Thus
$$P_M(s) = \frac{1}{n!} \prod_{i=1}^{n} (x+i+1) = \frac{\Gamma(n+s)}{\Gamma(n+1)\Gamma(s)} \qquad (1.6.1)$$

$$P(M_n = r) = \text{coefficient of } x^r \text{ in } \frac{1}{n!} \prod_{i=1}^{n} (x+i+1)$$
$$= \frac{S(r,n)}{n!},$$
where $S(r,n)$ is the Stirling number of the first kind.
Using the recurrence relation
$$\frac{n}{n+1} \frac{|S(r,n)|}{n!} = \frac{1}{n+1} \frac{|S(r-1,n)|}{n!} + \frac{|S(r-1,n)|}{n!}, \text{ it follows that}$$
$$E(M_n) = \frac{d}{ds} P_M(s)|_{s=1}$$
$$= \frac{d}{ds} \frac{\Gamma(n+s)}{\Gamma(n+1)\Gamma(s)}|_{s=1}$$
$$= (\psi(n+1) - \Psi(1).),$$

where $\psi()m) = \dfrac{\Gamma'(m)}{\Gamma(m)}$ is the digamma function.

Hence

$$E(M_n) = \sum_{i=1}^{n} \frac{1}{i} \cong \ln n + \gamma.$$

$$E(M_n(M_n-1)) = \frac{d^2}{ds} P_M(s)|_{s=1} = \frac{d^2}{ds^2} \frac{\Gamma(n+s)}{\Gamma(n+1)\Gamma(s)}|_{s=1}$$

$$= (\psi(n+1) - \Psi(1))^2 + \psi'(n+1) - \psi'(1).,$$

and

$$\text{Var}(M_n) = E(M_n(M_n-1)) - (E(M_n))^2 + E(M_n)$$

$$= \sum_{i=1}^{n} \frac{1}{i} - \sum_{i=1}^{n} \frac{1}{i^2} = \sum_{i=1}^{n} \frac{i-1}{i^2} \cong \ln n + \gamma - \frac{\pi^2}{6}.$$

For $n \to \infty$, $E(M_n) - \text{Var}(M_n) \to \pi^2/6$.

$$E(2^{M_n}) = P_M(2) = \frac{\Gamma(n+2)}{\Gamma(n+1)\Gamma(2)} = n+1$$

and

$$\text{Var}((2^{M_n}) = E((2^{M_n})^2 - (E(2^{M_n}))^2$$
$$= P_M(4) - (P_M(2))^2$$
$$= \frac{\Gamma(n+4)}{\Gamma(n+1)\Gamma(4)} - \left(\frac{\Gamma(n+2)}{\Gamma(n+1)\Gamma(2)}\right)^2$$

Thus $2^{M_n} - 1$ is an unbiased estimate of n.

The following table gives the exact and asymptotic values of $E(M_n)$ and $\text{Var}(M_n)$..

Table 1.6.1 Exact and Asymptotic Values of $E(M_n)$ and $Var(M_n)$.

N	$E(M_n)$	$Var(M_n)$	$E(M_n)$	$Var(M_n)$
10	2.929	1.379	2.880	1.235
100	5.187	3.552	5.182	3.537
500	6.793	5.150	6.792	5.147
1000	7.485	5.842	7.485	5.840

(The last two columns are asymptotic values)

1.7. DISTRIBUTION OF INTER-RECORD TIMES AMONG n OBSERVATIONS

If the rth record value occurs at the k_r th observation then the rth inter-record time $\delta_{r,n}$ among the n observation is $k_{r+1} - k_r$. Let $P(\delta_{1,n} = i)$ = Probability that the second value occurs at the i + 1 th observation. Thus

$$P(\delta_{1,n} = i) = \frac{(i-1)!}{(i+1)!} = \frac{1}{i(i+1)}, \quad 0 < i < n. \tag{1.7.1}$$

Let $\delta_{r,n} = 0$ be the event that $\delta_{r,n}$ does not exit i.e. there are less than r+1 records among the n observations.

Using (1.6.1), we can express $P(\delta_{1,n} = 0)$ in terms of Stirling numbers (see Appendix A)

$$P(\delta_{1,n} = 0) = \frac{|s(1,n)|}{n!}. \tag{1.7.2}$$

The following table gives the values of $P(\delta_{1,n} = 0)$ for $1 \leq r \leq n \leq 8$.

Table 1.7.1: Values of $P(\delta_{r,n} = 0)$

n/r	1	2	3	4	5	6	7	8
2	$\frac{1}{2}$	1						
3	$\frac{2}{6}$	$\frac{5}{6}$	1					
4	$\frac{6}{24}$	$\frac{17}{24}$	$\frac{23}{24}$	1				
5	$\frac{24}{120}$	$\frac{74}{120}$	$\frac{109}{120}$	$\frac{119}{120}$	1			
6	$\frac{120}{720}$	$\frac{394}{720}$	$\frac{619}{720}$	$\frac{619}{720}$	$\frac{719}{720}$	1		
7	$\frac{720}{5040}$	$\frac{2484}{5040}$	$\frac{4108}{5040}$	$\frac{4843}{5040}$	$\frac{5018}{5040}$	$\frac{5039}{5040}$	1	
8	$\frac{5040}{40320}$	$\frac{18108}{40320}$	$\frac{31240}{40320}$	$\frac{38009}{40320}$	$\frac{39969}{40320}$	$\frac{40291}{40320}$	$\frac{40319}{40320}$	1

1.8. The k- Records

Suppose that X_1, X_2, ... is a sequence of independent and identically distributed random variables with cdf F(x) and pdf f(x). We define

$U(1,k) = k$

$U(n,k) = \min \{ j: j > U(n-1, k), X_j > X_{U(n-1,k)-k+1,\ U(n-1,k)} \}$

and

$L(1,k) = k$

$L(n,k) = = \min \{ j: j > L(n-1, k), X_j < X_{k,\ L(n-1,k)} \}$,

where $X_{j,m}$ is the jth order statistic in a random sample of size m .Then U(m,k) and L(m,k) are the mth upper and m^{th} lower - record indices The corresponding upper and lower k-record values are $X_{U(m,k)} = X_{U(m,k)-k+1,\ U(m,k)}$ and $X_{L(m,k))} = X_{k,\ L(m,k)}$ for m =1,2,. . If k =1, then this k- records will coincide with the records. The pdf of $X_{Un,k}$ ($X_{L(n,k)}$) is the same as the pdf of $X_{U(n)}$ ($X_{L(n)}$) from a random variable X with cdf as $1-(1-F(x))^k$. The lower record values of a sequence $\{X_n, n \geq 1\}$ are defined as the upper record values of the sequence $\{X_n, n \geq 1\}$. Thus the lower k-record values of a sequence $\{X_n, n \geq 1\}$ are defined as the same as the upper k-record values of the sequence $\{X_n, n \geq 1\}$..

Let $f_{n,k}(x)$ be the pdf of $X_{U(n,k)}$, then

$$f_{n,k}(x) = \frac{k^n}{\Gamma(n)}\{-\ln(\overline{F}(x))\}^{n-1}(\overline{F}(x))^{k-1} f(x), \; n = 1, 2, \ldots \quad (1.8.1)$$

$$F_{n,k}(x) = P[XU(n,k) < x] = \int_{-\infty}^{x} \frac{k^n}{\Gamma(n)}\{-\ln(\overline{F}(u))\}^{n-1}(\overline{F}(u))^{k-1} f(u)du$$

$$= \int_{0}^{-k\ln \overline{F}(x)} \frac{w^{n-1}e^{-w}}{\Gamma(n)} dw \quad (1.8.2)$$

For m<n, the joint pdf $f_{m,n,k}(x,y)$ of $X_{U(m,k)}$ and $X_{U(n,k)}$ is defined as

$$f_{m,n,k}(x,y) = \frac{k^n}{\Gamma(m)\Gamma(n-m)}\{-\ln \overline{F}(x)\}^{m-1}[-\ln \overline{F}(x) - \ln \overline{F}(y)]^{n-m-1}$$

$$\cdot \frac{f(x)}{\overline{F}(x)}\{\overline{F}(y)\}^{k-1} f(y), \; x < y \quad (1.8.3)$$

The joint pdf $f_{1,2,\ldots,n}(x_1, x_2, \ldots, x_n)$ of $X_{U(1,k)}, X_{U(1,k)}, \ldots X_{U(n,k)}$ is defined as

$f_{1,2,\ldots,n}(x_1, x_2, \ldots, x_n) =$

$$k^n [\overline{F}(x_n)]^{k-1} f(x_n) \prod_{i=1}^{n-1} \frac{f(x_i)}{\overline{F}(x_i)}, \; -\infty < x_1 < x_2 < \ldots < x_n < \infty,$$

$= 0$, otherwise. $\quad (1.8.4)$

The joint pdf $f_{n|1,2,\ldots n-1,k}$ of $X_{U(n,k)}$ given $X_{U(1,k)}, \ldots X_{U(n-1,k)}$ is

$$f_{n|1,2,\ldots n-1,k}(x_n| x_1, x_2, \ldots, x_{n-1}) = \frac{k(\overline{F}(x_n))^{k-1} f(x_n)}{(\overline{F}(x_{n-1}))^k}$$

$= f_{n|n-1,k}(x_n | x_{n-1})$, the pdf of $X_{U(n,k)} | X_{U(n-1,k)} = x_{n-1}$.

Thus the sequence $X_{U(1,k)}$, $X_{U(2,k)}$,....is a Markov chain for any $k \geq 1$.
The joint pdf $f_{(1,2,...,m)}(x_1, x_2, ..., x_m)$ of $X_{L(1,k)}, X_{L(2,k)},....X_{L(m,k)}$ is defined as

$f_{(1,2,...,n)}(x_1, x_2, ..., x_n) =$

$$k^n [F(x_n)]^{k-1} f(x_n) \prod_{i=1}^{n-1} \frac{f(x_i)}{F(x_i)}, \quad -\infty < x_n < x_{n-1} < ... < x_1 < \infty,$$

$= 0$, otherwise. (1.8.5)

$$f_{(n,k)}(x) = \frac{k^n}{\Gamma(n)} \{-\ln(F(x))\}^{n-1} (F(x))^{k-1} f(x), \quad -\infty < x < \infty. \quad (1.8.6)$$

Example 1.8.1. Let us consider the exponential distribution with pdf f(x) as

$f(x) = e^{-x}, 0 \leq x < \infty$ and the cumulative distribution function (cdf) F(x) as

$F(x) = 1 - e^{-x}, 0 \leq x < \infty$.
We have $\ln(1-F(x)) = x$ and the pdf $f_{n,k}(x)$ of $X_{U(n,k)}$ is

$$f_{n,k}(x) = \frac{k^n}{\Gamma(n)} x^{n-1} e^{-kx}, x \geq 0, n = 1, 2, ...$$

$= 0$, otherwise.

Thus $X_{U(n,k)} \stackrel{d}{=} (W_1 + W_2 + ... + W_k)/k$

The joint pdf of $X_{U(m,k)}$ and $X_{U(n,k)}$, n > m is

$$f_{m,n,k}(x,y) = \frac{k^n x^{m-1}}{\Gamma(m)\Gamma(n-m)}(y-x)^{n-m-1} e^{-ky}$$

$0 \leq x < y < \infty$

$= 0$, otherwise.

The conditional pdf of $X_{U(n,k)} | X_{U(m,k)} = x$ is

$$f(y|X_{U(m,k)} = x) = \frac{k^{n-m}(y-x)^{n-m-1}}{\Gamma(n-m)} e^{-k(y-x)}$$

$0 \leq x < y < \infty$

$= 0$, otherwise.

Thus the conditional distribution of $X_{U(n,k)} - X_{U(m,k)}$ given $X_{U(m,k)}$ is the same as the unconditional distribution of $X_{U(n-m,k)}$ for n > m.

We will define $\Delta_n(k) = U(n+1,k) - U(n,k)$, $n = 1,2,\ldots$, $U(1,k) = k$, $\Delta_{(n)}(k) = L(n+1,k) - L(n,k)$, $n = 1,2,\ldots$ and $L(1,k) = k$, If $k = 1$, then $\Delta_n(k)$ and $\Delta_{(n)}(k)$ coincide with Δ_n and $\Delta_{(n)}$ respectively. We know that $E(U(n)) = \infty$ for $n \geq 2$ but we will prove that $EU(n,k) < \infty$ for $n \geq 2$ and $k > 1$. $P(\Delta_1(k) = r) = P(U(2,k) = k + r) =$

$$\int_{-\infty}^{\infty} (F(x))^{r-1} k(\overline{F}(x))^k f(x) dx$$

$$= \int_0^1 u^{r-1} k(1-u))^k du$$

$$= k \frac{k!(r-1)!}{(k+r)!}$$

$E(U(2,k)) = \sum_{r=1}^{\infty} k \frac{k!(r-1)!}{(k+r-1)!} = \frac{k^2}{k-1}.$

$P(\Delta_2(k) = r) = \int_{-\infty}^{\infty} (F(x))^{r-1} k\{-k \ln(\overline{F}(x))\} (\overline{F}(x))^k f(x) dx$

$$= -k^2 \int_0^1 u^k (1-u)^{r-1} \ln u \, du$$

$$= \sum_{j=0}^{r-1} \binom{r-1}{j}(-1)^j \frac{k^2}{(k+j+1)^2}$$

$E(\Delta_2(k)) = -k^2 \int_0^1 \sum_{r=1}^{\infty} r u^k (1-u)^{r-1} \ln u \, du$

$$= -k^2 \int_0^1 u^{k-2} \ln u \, du = \frac{k^2}{(k-1)^2}, k \geq 2.$$

Thus

$E(U(3,k)) = E(\Delta_2(k)) + E(U(2,k)) = \frac{k^2}{(k-1)^2} + \frac{k^2}{k-1} = \frac{k^3}{(k-1)^2}$

$P(\Delta_n(k) = r) =$

$$= \int_{-\infty}^{\infty} (F(x))^{r-1} \frac{k\{-k\ln(\overline{F}(x))\}^{n-1}}{\Gamma(n)} (\overline{F}(x))^k f(x) dx$$

$$= \frac{k^n \int_0^1 u^k (1-u)^{r-1} (-\ln u)^{n-1} du}{\Gamma(n)}$$

$$= \sum_{j=0}^{r-1} \binom{r-1}{j}(-1)^j \frac{k^n}{(k+j+1)^n} \qquad (1.8.7)$$

For k=1, $P(\Delta_n(k) = r)$ coincides with $P(\Delta_n = r)$ given in (1.4.3).

$$E((\Delta_n(k)) = \sum_{r=1}^{\infty} \int_{-\infty}^{\infty} r(F(x))^{r-1} \frac{k\{-k\ln(\overline{F}(x))\}^{n-1}}{\Gamma(n)} (\overline{F}(x))^k f(x) dx$$

$$= \frac{k^n}{\Gamma(n)} \sum_{r=1}^{\infty} \int_0^1 r u^k (1-u)^{r-1} (-\ln u)^{n-1} du$$

$$= k^n \int_0^1 \frac{u^{k-2}(-\ln u)^n}{\Gamma(n)} du$$

$$= \frac{k^n}{(k-1)^n}, \quad k>1, n \geq 1. \qquad (1.8.8)$$

Hence

$E(U(n+1,k)) = E((\Delta_n(k)) + E(\Delta_{n-1}(k)) + ... + E(\Delta_1(k)) + k$

$$= \frac{k^{n+1}}{(k-1)^n}, \quad k>1, n \geq 0. \qquad (1.8.9)$$

The probability of the event $\Delta_1(k) = k_1 \cap \Delta_2(k) = k_2$ is

$P(\Delta_1(k) = k_1 \cap \Delta_2(k) = k_2))$
$$= \iint_{-\infty < x_0 < x_1 < \infty} (F(x_0))^{k_1-1} (F(x_1))^{k_2-1} \overline{F}(x_0)\overline{F}(x_1) r(x_0) f(x_1) dx_0\, dx_1$$

$$= \int_{-\infty}^{\infty} k^2 (F(x_0))^{k_1-1} \overline{F}(x_0) r(x_0) u_0(x) dx_0,$$

where

$$u_0(x) = \sum_{j=0}^{k} \binom{k}{j}(-1)^j \frac{1}{k_2+1}(1-F(x_0))^{k_2+j}$$

$$= \int_{-\infty}^{\infty} k^2 [\sum_{j=0}^{k} \binom{k}{j}(-1)^j u_1(x) f(x) dx$$

and $u_1(x) = \frac{1}{k_2+j}((F(x))^{k_1-1} - (F(x))^{k_1+k_1+j-1})$

$$= k^2 [\sum_{j=0}^{k} \binom{k}{j}(-1)^j \frac{1}{k_1(k_1+k_2+j)}] \qquad (1.8.10)$$

The conditional probability distribution of $\Delta(n,k) \mid X_{U(n,k)}$ is geometric with

$$P(\Delta_n(k)=m \mid X_{U(n,k)} = x_m) = p(1-p)^{m-1}, \ m=1,2,...., \qquad (1.8.11)$$

where

$$p = 1 - F(x_m).$$

Using the probability of inter-record times, we can easily obtain various probabilities of the record times.

$$\frac{k^2}{(k-1)^2} + \frac{k^2}{k-1} \ P[U(2,k)=n_1] = P[\Delta_1(k) = n_1 - k]$$

$$= k \ \frac{k!(n_1-k-1)!}{n_1!}.$$

$P[U(3)=n_2, U(2)=n_1] = P[\Delta_2 = n_2 - n_1, \Delta_1 = n_1 - 1]$

$$= k^2 [\sum_{j=0}^{k} \binom{k}{j}(-1)^j \frac{1}{(n_1-k)(n_2-k+j)}] = \frac{k^2 k!(n_2-k)!}{(n_1-k)(n_2-k)n_2!}$$

$P[U(3,k)=n_2 \mid U(2,k)=n_1] = P[\Delta_2(k) = n_2 - n_1 \mid \Delta_1(k) = n_1 - 1]$

$= k \dfrac{(n_1 - k + 1)(n_1 - k + 2)....(n_2 - k + 1)}{(n_1 + 1)(n_1 + 2)....n_2}$, $n_2 > n_1 > k > 1$.

$= k \dfrac{(n_2 - k - 1)! n_1!}{n_2!(n_1 - k)!}$

In general

$P[\; P[U(m+1,k)=n_m, U(2,k)=n_1, U(3,k)=n_2,...,U(m,k)=n_{m-1}\;]$

$= \dfrac{k^{m-1}(n_m - 1)!}{n_m!} \cdot \dfrac{k!}{(n_1 - 1)(n_2 - k)(n_3 - k).....(n_m - k)}$

$P(U(m+1,k)=n_m \mid U(2,k)=n_1, U(3,k)=n_2,...,U(m)=n_{m-1})$

$= \dfrac{k(n_{m-1} + 1 - k)(n_{m-1} + 2 - k)...(n_m - k - 1)}{(n_{m-1} + 1)(n_{m-1} + 2).....(n_m - 1)n_m}$

$= \dfrac{k\, n_{m-1}!(n_m - k - 1)!}{(n_{m-1} - k)! n_m!}$

$= P(U(m+1,k)=n_m \mid U(m,k)=n_{m-1})$.

Thus the sequence $\{U(n,k), k>1, n \geq 1\}$ forms a Markov chain.

$E(U(2,k)) = \sum\limits_{r=1}^{\infty} k(k+r) \dfrac{k!(r-1)!}{(k+r)!} = \dfrac{k^2}{k-1}$.

$E(U(m+1,k) \mid U(m,k)= m+k) = \sum\limits_{r=1}^{\infty} \dfrac{k(m+k)!(m+r-1)!}{m!(m+k+r-1)!}$

$= \dfrac{k(m+k)}{k-1}$, $k > 1$.

Thus

$E(U(3,k)) = \dfrac{k}{k-1} E(U(2,k)) = \dfrac{k^3}{(k-1)^2}$, $k>1$.

Hence by induction, we have

$E(U(n,k)) = \dfrac{k^n}{(k-1)^{n-1}}$, $k>1$, $n \geq 1$.

$$P(\Delta_1(k) = r) = P(U(2,k) = k + r) = \int_{-\infty}^{\infty} (F(x))^{r-1} k(\overline{F}(x))^k f(x)\, dx$$

$$= \int_0^1 u^{r-1} k(1-u)^k\, du$$

$$= k\, \frac{k!(r-1)!}{(k+r)!}$$

$$E\left(\frac{1}{U(2,k)+1}\right) = k \sum_{r=1}^{\infty} \frac{k!(r-1)!}{(k+r+1)!} = \frac{k}{(k+1)^2}$$

$$E\left(\frac{1}{(U(2,k)+1)(U(2,k)+2)}\right) = \sum_{r=1}^{\infty} \frac{k\, k!(r-1)!}{(k+r+2)!} = \frac{k}{(k+1)(k+2)^2}$$

$$E\left(\frac{1}{(U(2,k)+1)(U(2,k)+2)(U(2,k)+3)\ldots(U(2,k)+m)}\right) = \sum_{r=1}^{\infty} \frac{k\, k!(r-1)!}{(k+r+m)!}$$

$$= \frac{1}{(k+1)(k+2)\ldots(k+m-1)} \cdot \frac{k^2}{(k+m)^2} \quad . \quad (1.8.12)$$

$$E(U(2,k)(U(2,k)-1)) = \sum_{r=1}^{\infty} k(k+r)(k+r-1)\frac{k!(r-1)!}{(k+r)!} = \frac{k^2(k-1)}{k-2}, k>2.$$

For k>m, we have

$$E(U(2,k)(U(2,k)-1)\ldots(U(2,k)-m+1)) =$$

$$\sum_{r=1}^{\infty} k(k+r)(k+r-1)(k+r-m+1)\frac{k!(r-1)!}{(k+r)!}$$

$$= \sum_{r=1}^{\infty} k^2 \frac{k!(r-1)!}{(k+r-m)!} = \frac{k^2(k-m+1)(k-m+2)\ldots(k-1)}{k-m}, k>m.$$

$$= \frac{k^2(k-1)!}{(k-m)(k-m)!} \quad .. \quad (1.8.13).$$

For m = k-1, k>1, we have

$$E(U(2,k)(U(2,k)-1)\ldots(U(2,k)-k+2)) = k^2(k-1)$$

For k>m,

$$\left(\frac{k-m}{k}\right) E(U(2,k))(U(2,k)-1)\ldots(U(2,k)-m+1) = \frac{\Gamma(k+1)}{\Gamma(k-m+1)}$$

We have

$E(U(3,k)(U(3,k)-1)\ldots(U(3,k)-m+1)|\ U(2,k) = r+s)$

$$= \frac{k\Gamma(k+r+1)}{\Gamma(k+r-m+2)}[1 + \frac{r+1}{k+r-m+2} + \frac{(r+1)(r+2)}{(k+r-m+2)(k+r-m+3)} + \ldots]$$

$$= \frac{k\Gamma(k+r+1)}{\Gamma(k+r-m+2)} \cdot \frac{k+r-m+1}{k-m}$$

$$= \frac{k}{k-m} \cdot \frac{\Gamma(k+r+1)}{\Gamma(k+r-m+1)}.$$

Thus
$E(U(3,k)(U(3,k)-1)\ldots(U(3,k)-m+1))$

$$= \frac{k}{k-m} \cdot \sum_{r=1}^{\infty} \frac{\Gamma(k+r+1)}{\Gamma(k+r-m+1)} \cdot \frac{k\, k!(r-1)!}{(k+r)!}$$

$$= \frac{k^2\,\Gamma(k+1)}{k-m} \cdot \sum_{r=1}^{\infty} \frac{(r-1)!}{\Gamma(k+r-m+1)}$$

$$= \frac{k^2\,\Gamma(k+1)}{(k-m)^2\,\Gamma(k-m+1)}.$$

Hence

$$\left(\frac{k-m}{k}\right)^2 E(U(3,k)(U(3,k)-1)\ldots(U(3,k)-m+1)) = \frac{\Gamma(k+1)}{\Gamma(k-m+1)}.$$

It can be proved by induction that

$$\left(\frac{k-m}{k}\right)^{n-1} E(U(n,k)(U(n,k)-1)\ldots(U(n,k)-m+1)) = \frac{\Gamma(k+1)}{\Gamma(k-m+1)}, 1 \leq m < k$$

(1.8.14)

Using (1.8.14) we can obtain the higher moments of $U(n,k)$. We have

$$\text{Var}(U(n,k)) = \frac{k^n(k-1)}{(k-2)^{n-1}} + \frac{k^n}{(k-1)^{n-1}} - \frac{k^{2n}}{(k-1)^{2n-2}}, \; n \geq 1.$$

Now

$$E(\Delta_1(k))^2) = \sum_{r=1}^{\infty} kr^2 \frac{k!(r-1)!}{(k+r)!} = \sum_{r=1}^{\infty} kr(r+1)\frac{k!(r-1)!}{(k+r)!} - E(\Delta(1,k))$$

$$\frac{k^2(k-1)}{k-2} + \frac{k^2}{k-1} - \frac{k^4}{(k-1)^2} = \frac{k^2(k-1)}{k-2} - \frac{k^3}{k-1}$$

$$\text{Var}((\Delta_1(k))) = \frac{k^2(k-1)}{k-2} - \frac{k^3}{k-1} - \frac{k^2}{(k-1)^2}$$

$$= \frac{k^2(k-1)}{k-2} + \frac{k^2}{k-1} - \frac{k^4}{(k-1)^2} = \text{Var}(U(2,k)).$$

$$E(\Delta_n(k)) = \sum_{r=1}^{\infty} \int_{-\infty}^{\infty} r\, (F(x))^{r-1} \frac{k\{-k\ln(\overline{F}(x))\}^{n-1}}{\Gamma(n)}(\overline{F}(x))^k f(x)\,dx$$

$$= \int_{-\infty}^{\infty} \frac{k\{-k\ln(\overline{F}(x))\}^{n-1}}{\Gamma(n)}(\overline{F}(x))^{k-2} f(x)\,dx$$

$$= k^n \int_0^1 \frac{u^{k-2}(-\ln u)^{n-1}}{\Gamma(n)}\,du$$

$$= \frac{k^n}{(k-1)^n}, \; k>2, n\geq 1$$

$E((\Delta_n(k)(\Delta_n(k)+1))$

$$= \sum_{r=1}^{\infty} \int_{-\infty}^{\infty} r(r+1)(F(x))^{r-1}$$

$$\cdot \frac{k\{-k\ln(\overline{F}(x))\}^{n-1}}{\Gamma(n)}(\overline{F}(x))^k f(x)\,dx$$

$$= \int_{-\infty}^{\infty} \frac{2k\{-k\ln(\overline{F}(x))\}^{n-1}}{\Gamma(n)}(\overline{F}(x))^{k-3} f(x)\,dx$$

$$= \int_0^1 \frac{2k^n}{\Gamma(n)} t^{k-3} (-\ln t)^{n-1} \, dt = 2\left(\frac{k}{k-2}\right)^n, \ k > 2.$$

Thus

$$E((\Delta_n(k))^2) = \frac{2k^n}{(k-2)^n} - \frac{k^n}{(k-1)^n}, \ k>2, \ n \geq 1$$

and

$$\text{Var}(\Delta_n(k)) = \frac{2k^n}{(k-2)^n} - \frac{k^n}{(k-1)^n} - \frac{k^{2n}}{(k-1)^{2n}} \qquad (1.8.15)$$

Let $P_g(\Delta_n(s,k))$ be the probability generating function of $\Delta_n(k)$, then
$P_g(,\Delta_n(s,k))$

$$= \sum_{r=1}^{\infty} \int_{-\infty}^{\infty} s^r (F(x))^{r-1} \frac{k\{-k\ln(\overline{F}(x))\}^{n-1}}{\Gamma(n)} (\overline{F}(x))^k f(x) \, dx$$

$$= \int_{-\infty}^{\infty} \frac{s}{1-sF(x)} \frac{k\{-k\ln(\overline{F}(x))\}^{n-1}}{\Gamma(n)} (\overline{F}(x))^k f(x) \, dx$$

$$= \int_0^1 \frac{s}{1-s+su} \frac{k^n (-\ln u)^{n-1}}{\Gamma(n)} u^k \, du$$

$$= 1 - \sum_{j=0}^{\infty} \frac{(-1)^j s^j}{(1-s)^j} \cdot \left(\frac{k}{k+j}\right)^n. \qquad (1.8.16)$$

For k=1, (1.8.8) coincides with 1.4.8.

Let $P_{gU(n,k)}(s)$ be the probability generating function of U(n,k). We have

$$P_{gU(2,k)}(s) = \sum_{r=1}^{\infty} s^{k+r} \frac{k\,k!(r-1)!}{(k+r)!}$$

$$= k s^{k+1} \int_0^1 \frac{(1-t)^k}{1-st} \, dt$$

$$= k^2 \int_0^{-\ln(1-s)} x e^{-kx} (1-(1-s)e^x)^{k-1} \, dx \qquad (1.8.17)$$

$$P_{gU(3,k)}(s) = EE(s^{U(3,k)}| U(2,k) = k+r)$$

$$= E\frac{ks^{k+r+1}}{k+r+1}[1+\frac{r+1}{k+r+2}s+\frac{(r+1)(r+2)}{(k+r+2)(k+r+3)}s^2$$
$$+...+]|U(2,k) = k+r)$$

$$= E\frac{ks^{k+r+1}}{k+r+1}\frac{\Gamma(k+r+2)}{\Gamma(r+1)\Gamma(k+1)}\int_0^1 t^r(1-t)^k\frac{1}{1-st}dt|U(2,k)=k+r$$

$$= \sum_{r=1}^{\infty}\frac{ks^{k+r+1}\Gamma(k+r+1)}{\Gamma(r+1)\Gamma(k+1)}(\int_0^1 t^r(1-t)^k\frac{1}{1-st}dt)\frac{k\,k!(r-1)!}{(k+r)!}$$

$$= \sum_{r=1}^{\infty}\frac{k^2 s^{k+r+1}}{r}(\int_0^1 t^r(1-t)^k\frac{1}{1-st}dt)$$

$$= k^2 s^{k+1}\int_0^1 (1-t)^k\frac{\ln(1-st)}{1-st}dt$$

$$= \frac{k^3}{\Gamma(3)}\int_0^{-\ln(1-s)} x^2 e^{-kx}(1-(1-s)e^x)^{k-1}dx$$

By induction it can be proved that

$$P_{gU(n,k)}(s) = k^n \int_0^{-\ln(1-s)} \frac{x^{n-1}}{\Gamma(n)} e^{-kx}(1-(1-s)e^x)^{k-1}dx \quad (1.8.18)$$

If we put k=1, then (1.8.18) coincides with (1.4.12)

Theorem 1.8.1.

If $h(n) = 1 + 1/2 + ... + 1/n$. then $E(h(U(n,k))) = h(k) + (n-1)/k$.

Proof:

$$P(U(n,k) = r| U(n-1,k) = j) = \frac{k(j-k+1)(j-k+2)....j}{(r-k)(r-k+1)...r}$$

Now

$$E(h(U(n,k))| U(n-1,k)=j) = \sum_{r=j+1}^{\infty} h(r) \frac{k(j-k+1)(j-k+2)\ldots j}{(r-k)(r-k+1)\ldots r}$$

$$= h(j+1) \frac{k(j-k+1)(j-k+2)\ldots j}{(j+1-k)(j+2-k)\ldots(j+1)}$$

$$+ h(j+2) \frac{k(j-k+1)(j-k+2)\ldots j}{(j+2-k)(j+3-k)\ldots(j+2)}$$

$$+ h(j+3) \frac{k(j-k+1)(j-k+2)\ldots j}{(j+3-k)(j+2-k)\ldots(j+3)}$$

$$+\ldots\ldots\ldots\ldots\ldots$$

$$= (h(j) + \frac{1}{j+1}) \frac{k(j-k+1)(j-k+2)\ldots j}{(j+1-k)(j+2-k)\ldots(j+1)}$$

$$+ (h(j) + \frac{1}{j+1} + \frac{1}{j+2}) \frac{k(j-k+1)(j-k+2)\ldots j}{(j+2-k)(j+3-k)\ldots(j+2)}$$

$$+ (h(j) + \frac{1}{j+1} + \frac{1}{j+2} + \frac{1}{j+3}) \frac{k(j-k+1)(j-k+2)\ldots j}{(j+3-k)(j+2-k)\ldots(j+3)}$$

$$+\ldots\ldots\ldots\ldots\ldots$$

$$= \sum_{r=j}^{\infty} h(j) \frac{k(j-k+1)(j-k+2)\ldots j}{(r+1-k)(r-k+1)\ldots(r-1)}$$

$$+ (\frac{1}{j+1}) \frac{k(j-k+1)(j-k+2)\ldots j}{(j+1-k)(j+2-k)\ldots(j+1)}$$

$$+ (\frac{1}{j+1} + \frac{1}{j+2}) \frac{k(j-k+1)(j-k+2)\ldots j}{(j+2-k)(j+3-k)\ldots(j+2)}$$

$$+ (\frac{1}{j+1} + \frac{1}{j+2} + \frac{1}{j+3}) \frac{k(j-k+1)(j-k+2)\ldots j}{(j+3-k)(j+2-k)\ldots(j+3)}$$

$$+\ldots\ldots$$

$$= h(j) + \sum_{r=j+1}^{\infty} \frac{(j-k+1)(j-k+2)\ldots j}{(r-k)(r-k+1)\ldots r}$$

$$= h(j) + 1/k$$

Since $U(1,k) = k$, we have $E(h(U(n,k))) = h(k) + (n-1)/k$.

If $k=1$, then we get the result given in Theorem 1.4.1.

The following theorem gives a bound on the expected value on $n+1^{th}$ k-record.

Theorem 1.8.2.

If $E(X) = 0$ and $Var(X) = 1$, then

$$|E(X_{U(n+1,k)})| \leq [\frac{k^{2n+2}}{(2k-1)^{2n+1}}\binom{2n}{n} - 1]^{1/2}..$$

Proof:
Let

$$F^{-1}(u) = \text{Sup}\{x: F(x) \leq u\}, 0 < u < 1,$$

$$F^{-1}(1) = \text{Sup}\{F^{-1}(u), u < 1\}$$

$$0 = E(X) = \int_0^\infty x f(x) dx = \int_0^\infty \overline{F}^{-1}(t) dt.$$

$$1 = E(X^2) = \int_0^\infty x^2 f(x) dx = \int_0^\infty \{\overline{F}^{-1}(t)\}^2 dt.$$

$$E(X_{U(n+1,k)}) = \int_{-\infty}^\infty x \frac{k^{n+1}\{-\ln \overline{F}(x)\}^n (\overline{F}(x))^{k-1}}{\Gamma(n+1)} f(x) dx$$

$$= \int_0^1 k^{n+1} \overline{F}^{-1}(t) [t^{k-1} \frac{\{-\ln t\}^n}{\Gamma(n+1)}] dt$$

$$= \int_0^1 k^{n+1} \overline{F}^{-1}(t) [t^{k-1} \frac{(-\ln t)^n}{\Gamma(n+1)} - \lambda] dt$$

We have

$$1 = E(X^2) = \int_0^\infty \{\overline{F}^{-1}(t)\}^2 dt \text{ and}$$

$$\int_0^1 [t^{k-1} \frac{(-\ln t)^n}{\Gamma(n+1)} - \lambda]^2 dt = \frac{\Gamma(2n+1)}{(\Gamma(n+1))^2} \cdot \frac{1}{(2k-1)^{n+1}} - 2\lambda \frac{1}{k^{n+1}} + \lambda^2.$$

The minimum value of $-2\lambda \frac{1}{k^{n+1}} + \lambda^2$ is $-\frac{1}{k^{2n+2}}$.

Thus using Cauchy and Schwarz inequality, we get

$$|E(X_{U(n+1,k)})| \le [\frac{k^{2n+2}}{(2k-1)^{2n+1}}\binom{2n}{n}-1]^{1/2}. \qquad (1.8.18)$$

We will denote $B_{k,n}(1) = [\frac{k^{2n+2}}{(2k-1)^{2n+1}}\binom{2n}{n}-1]^{1/2}$.

For k=1, this inequality will coincide with the one given in Theorem 1.3.2.

In that case the bound is attainable if
$$\overline{F}(x) = \exp[-\{\Gamma(n+1)((\binom{2n}{n}-1)^{1/2}x+1)\}^{1/n}],$$

for $-\frac{1}{(\binom{2n}{n}-1)^{1/2}} < x < \infty$

For k >1, the bound is not attainable.

Using the principal of greatest convex minorants Raqab (1997) improved the bound of $E(X_{U(n+1,k)})|$ as given below:

$$E(X_{U(n+1,k)})| \le [\frac{k^{2n+2}}{(2k-1)^{2n+1}}\binom{2n}{n}I_{u(1)}(2n+1)$$
$$+ \frac{k^{2n+2}}{(n!)^2}(-\ln(1-u_1))^{2n}(1-u_1)^{2k-1}$$
$$-2\{I_{u(2)}(n+1) + \frac{k^{n+1}}{n!}(-\ln(1-u_1))^n(1-u_1)^k\} + 1]^{1/2}$$
$$= B_{k,n}(2), \text{ say,}$$

where

u(1) = -(2k-1) ln(1-u_1), u(2) = -k ln(1-u_1), $I_p(r) = \frac{1}{\Gamma(r)}\int_0^p e^{-x}x^{r-1}dx$

and u_1 is the solution of following equation:

$$\frac{k^{n+1}}{\Gamma(n+1)}(-\ln(1-u_1))^n(1-u_1)^k = 1 - I_{-k\ln(1-u_1)}(n+1).$$

Theorem 1.8.3.

For symmetric random variable X, with E(X) =0 and $E(X^2)$ =1,

$|E(X_{U(n+1,k)})| \le$

$$[\frac{k^{2n+2}}{\sqrt{2}}\{\frac{1}{(2k-1)^{2n+1}}\binom{2n}{n}-1]^{1/2}.-A_{n(k)}\}^{1/2},$$

where $A_{n(k)} = \dfrac{1}{(\Gamma(n+1))^2} \int_0^1 [\ln u \ln(1-u)]^n [u(1-u)]^{n-1} du$

Proof:

We have

$$E(X_{U(n+1,k)}) = \int_{-\infty}^{\infty} x \frac{k^{n+1}\{-\ln \bar{F}(x)\}^n (\bar{F}(x))^{k-1}}{\Gamma(n+1)} f(x) dx$$

$$= \frac{k^{n+1}}{\Gamma(n+1)} \int_{\frac{1}{2}}^{1} F^{-1}(u)[h(u) - h(1-u)] du \;.,$$

$$= \frac{k^{n+1}}{2\Gamma(n+1)} \int_0^1 F^{-1}(u)[h(u) - h(1-u)] du$$

where $h(u) = [-\ln(1-u)]^n (1-u)^{k-1}$.

Using the facts

$$\int_0^1 \{F^{-1}(u)\}^2 du = 1,$$

$$\int_0^1 [\{h(u)\}^n - \{h(1-u)\}^n]^2 du$$

$$= \frac{2k \; \Gamma(2n+1)}{(2k-1)^{2n+1}} - 2 \int_0^1 [\ln(1-u)\ln u]^n u^{k-1} (1-u)^{k-1} du$$

and the Cauchy and Schwarz inequality, we get
$|E(X_{U(n+1),k})| \le.$

$$\frac{k^{n+1}}{\sqrt{2}}\{\frac{1}{(2k-1)^{2n+1}}\binom{2n}{n}$$

$$-[-\frac{1}{(\Gamma(n+1))^2}\int_0^1 \{\ln u \ln(1-u)\}^n \{u(1-u)\}^{k-1} du]\}^{\frac{1}{2}}$$

Record Statistics

$= B_{k,n}(3)$ say.

Using the convex minorate, Raqab (1997) gave the following improved bound for $|E(X_{U(n+1),k})|$.

$$|E(X_{U(n+1),k})| \le B_{k,n}(4) = \frac{H(1)}{\sqrt{2}} [\int_{1/2}^{1} \{h^*(u)\}^2 du]^{1/2}$$

$$H(x) = \int_{1/2}^{x} h(u) du, \quad h(u) = |h_1(u) - h_2(u)|$$

$$h_1(u) = \frac{k^n}{\Gamma(n) H(1)} [\{-\ln(1-u)\}^{n-1} (1-u)^{k-1}]$$

$$h_2(u) = \frac{k^n}{\Gamma(n) H(1)} [\{-\ln u\}^{n-1} u^{k-1}]$$

$h^*(u) = h(u), \; \frac{1}{2} \le u < u_2$
$\quad\quad = h(u_2), \; u_2 \le u \le 1$
and u_2 satisfies the equation
$1 - H(u_2) = h(u_2)(1 - u_2)$.

The following table gives the values of $B_{k,n}(j)$, j=1,2,3, 4 for some selected values of k and n.

Table 1.8.1 Bounds for the expected values of k-record values

k	n	$B_{k,n}(1)$	$B_{k,n}(2)$	$B_{k,n}(3)$	$B_{k,n}(4)$
2	2	0.43033	0.34507	0.21236	0.20702
2	5	1.62534	1.61707	1.34753	1.34256
3	3	0.63220	0.48066	0.34841	0.32403
3	8	1.95985	1.92171	1.55577	1.53182
3	10	2.80858	2.77564	2.10809	2.08619
4	4	0.76913	0.56198	0.45829	0.40895
4	10	1.92083	1.84058	1.53129	1.48118
4	15	3.65570	3.58306	2.67994	2.62867
5	8	1.24237	1.08310	1.1873	1.03270
5	12	1.53498	1.81150	1.54015	1.46311
5	18	1.54489	1.42668	2.60444	2.52411
6	10	1.38078	1.18611	1.20352	1.09479
6	12	1.65317	1.47770	1.36615	1.26162

1.9. ENTROPIES OF RECORD VALUES

Let X be a continuous random variable with the pdf f(x), then the entropy H(x) of X is defined as

$$H(x) = - \int_{-\infty}^{\infty} f(x) \ln f(x) dx$$

where f(x) ln f(x) is integrable.

In the case of continuous random variable the Y=a+bX will change the entropy of Y as

$$H(Y) = - \int_{-\infty}^{\infty} \frac{1}{b} f(\frac{x-a}{b}) \ln f(\frac{x-a}{b}) dx$$

$$= - \int_{-\infty}^{\infty} f(x) \ln \left(\frac{1}{b} f(x) \right) dx$$

$$= \ln b + H(x)$$

The concept of entropy has recently been used in statistical inference. Shannon was the first to compute the entropies of the normal, exponential and uniform distribution. We will discuss here the entropies of upper record values. The entropies of lower record values are similar.

Let $H_n(x)$ be the entropy of $X_{U(n)}$ for a continuous random variable, then

$$-H_n(x) = \int_{-\infty}^{\infty} f_n(x) \ln f_n(x) dx$$

$$= -\ln \Gamma(n) + (n-1) \int_{-\infty}^{\infty} \ln R(x) \frac{(R(x))^{n-1}}{\Gamma(n)} f(x) dx$$

$$+ \int_{-\infty}^{\infty} \ln f(x) \frac{(R(x))^{n-1}}{\Gamma(n)} f(x) dx$$

$$= -\ln \Gamma(n) + (n-1) \int_{0}^{\infty} \frac{t^{n-1}}{\Gamma(n)} e^{-t} \ln t \, dt + I,$$

where
$$= -\ln\Gamma(n)+(n-1)\psi(n)+I$$

$$I = \int_{-\infty}^{\infty} \ln f(x)\frac{(R(x))^{n-1}}{\Gamma(n)}f(x)dx = \int_{-\infty}^{\infty} f_n(x)\ln f(x)dx,$$

and $\psi(n)$ is the digamma function i.e. $\psi(n) = \dfrac{d}{dn}=\ln\Gamma(n)=\dfrac{\Gamma'(n)}{\Gamma(n)}$.

Example 1.9.1.

Suppose that the sequence of i.i.d. random variables X_n has the Weibull pdf, f(x) where

$$f(x) = \frac{c}{a}x^{c-1}e^{-x^c/a}, \; 0 < x, a, c < \infty.$$

In this case, we have

$$I = \int_0^{\infty} f_n(x)\ln f_n(x)dx$$

$$= \ln\frac{c}{a}+(c-1)\int_0^{\infty}\ln x\, f_n(x)dx - \int_0^{\infty}\frac{x^c}{a}f_n(x)dx$$

$$= \ln\frac{c}{a}+(c-1)(\ln a + \psi(n))-n$$

$$= \ln c - \frac{1}{c}\ln a + \frac{c-1}{c}\psi(n)-n.$$

Hence

$$H_n(x) = \ln\Gamma(n)-(n-\frac{1}{c})\,\psi(n)-\ln c + \frac{1}{c}\ln a + n.$$

If we take c=1, the we get the entropy of the nh upper record value of the exponential distribution as

$$H_n(x) = \ln\Gamma(n)-(n-1)\Psi(n)+n.$$

Example 1.9.2.

Suppose the sequence of independent and identically distributed random variables X_n, $n \geq 1$, has the Gumbel distribution with pdf f(x)

where

$$f(x) = e^{-x}e^{-e^{-x}}, -\infty < x < \infty,$$
$$= 0, \text{ otherwise.}$$

Let $H_{(n)}(x)$ be the entropy of the nth lower record value of the X_i's.

We have

$$-H_{(n)}(x) = \int_{-\infty}^{\infty} \ln f_{(n)}(x) f_{(n)}(x)\, dx$$

$$= \int_{-\infty}^{\infty} [-\ln\Gamma(n) - nx - e^{-x}] \frac{1}{\Gamma(n)} e^{-nx} e^{-e^{-x}}\, dx$$

$$-\ln\Gamma(n) + n\psi(n) - n$$

Hence

$$H_{(n)}(x) = \ln\Gamma(n) - n\psi(n) + n.$$

CHAPTER 2

EXPONENTIAL DISTRIBUTION

2.0. INTRODUCTION.

In this chapter we study the record values of the exponential distribution. Exponential distribution is widely is real life data. The distribution of record values from the exponential distribution is relatively easy to work with.
A continuous random variable X is said to be exponentially distributed with parameters μ and σ, $\sigma>0$, if its pdf is of the following form

$$f(x) = \sigma^{-1}\exp(-\sigma^{-1}(x-\mu)), \quad x \geq \mu$$
$$= 0, \quad \text{otherwise}. \quad (2.0.1)$$

The corresponding distribution function F(x) and the hazard rate r(x) of the rv X are respectively

$$F(x) = 1-\exp(-\sigma^{-1}(x-\mu)), \quad x \geq \mu$$

and

$$r(x) = f(x)/(1-F(x)) = \sigma^{-1}. \quad (2.0.2)$$

We will denote the exponential distribution with the pdf as given in (2.0.1) as $E(\mu,\sigma)$. The exponential distribution possesses the memory less property i.e. an item whose lifetime is exponentially distributed, the residual life does not depend on the past life. In terms of probability, we can write

$$P[X> s+t \mid X> t] = P[X>s] \quad (2.0.3)$$

In terms of the distribution function we can write (2.0.3) as

$$1-F(s+t) = [\,1-F(s)]\,[\,1-F(t)]\,. \quad (2.0.4)$$

This property is utilized in many characterization problems of the exponential distribution.

The exponential distribution possesses the memory less property i.e. an item whose lifetime is exponentially distributed, the residual life does not depend on the past life. In terms of probability, we can write

$$P[X> s+t \mid X> t] = P[X>s] \quad (2.0.3)$$

In terms of the distribution function we can write (2.0.3) as

$$1-F(s+t) = [\ 1-F(s)][\ 1-F(t)]. \quad (2.0.4)$$

This property is utilized in many characterization problems of the exponential distribution.

2.1. DISTRIBUTION OF RECORD VALUES

Using the relation (1.2.7) and noting $R(x)=\sigma^{-1}(x-\mu)$, we have

$$f_n(x) = \frac{\sigma^{-n}}{\Gamma(n)}(x-\mu)^{n-1}\exp(-\sigma^{-1}(x-\mu)), x \geq \mu$$
$$= 0, \text{otherwise}. \quad (2.1.1)$$

The corresponding cdf F is

$$F_n(x) = 1 - \sum_{k=0}^{n-1} \frac{1}{k!}\left(\frac{x-\mu}{\sigma}\right)^k e^{-\frac{x-\mu}{\sigma}}.$$

The joint pdf of $X_{U(m)}$ and $X_{U(n)}, n > m$ (by using 1.2.9) is

$$f_{m,n}(x,y) = \frac{\sigma^{-n}}{\Gamma(m)} \cdot \frac{(x-\mu)^{m-1}}{\Gamma(n-m)}(y-x)^{n-m-1}\exp(-\sigma^{-1}(x-\mu))$$
$$\mu \leq x < y < \infty,$$
$$= 0, \text{otherwise}. \quad (2.1.2)$$

It is easy to see that $X_{U(n)} - X_{U(n-1)}$ and $X_{U(m)} - X_{U(m-1)}$ are identically distributed for $1<m<n<\infty$. It can be shown that $X_{U(m)} \stackrel{d}{=} X_{U(m-1)} + U, (m>1)$ where U is independent of $X_{U(m)}$ and $X_{U(m-1)}$ and is identically distributed as X_i's iff $F(x) = 1 - e^{-x}$, $x>0$. The conditional pdf of $X_{U(n)} \mid X_{U(m)} = x$ is

$$f(y \mid X_{U(m)} = x) = \frac{\sigma^{m-n}}{\Gamma(n-m)}(y-x)^{n-m-1}\exp(-\sigma^{-1}(y-x))$$

Exponential Distribution

$$\mu \leq x < y < \infty,$$
$$= 0, \quad \text{otherwise}. \quad (2.1.3)$$

Thus $P[X_{U(n)} - X_{U(m)} = y \mid X_{U(m)} = x]$ does not depend on x. It can be shown that if $\mu = 0$, then $X_{U(n)} - X_{U(m)}$ is identically distributed as $X_{U(n-m)}$, $n > m$.

If we take $\mu = 0$ and $\sigma = 1$ and $W_n = X_{U(1)} + X_{U(2)} + \cdots + X_{U(n)}$, the characteristic function of W_n can be written as

$$\phi_n(t) = \frac{1}{1-it} \cdot \frac{1}{1-2it} \cdots \frac{1}{1-nit}. \quad (2.1.4)$$

Inverting (2.1.4), we obtain the pdf $f_W(w)$ of W_n as

$$f_W(w) = \sum_{j=1}^{n} \frac{1}{\Gamma(j)} \cdot \frac{(-1)^{n-j}}{\Gamma(n-j+1)} \cdot e^{-w/j} j^{n-2}. \quad (2.1.5)$$

Theorem 2.1.1.

Let X_j, $i = 1, 2, \ldots$ be independently and exponentially distributed with $\mu = 0$ and $\sigma = 1$. Suppose $\xi_i = \dfrac{X_{U(i)}}{X_{U(i+1)}}$ $i = 1, 2, m-1$ then ξ_i's are independent..

Proof.

The joint pdf of $X_{U(1)}, X_{U(2)}, \ldots, X_{U(m)}$ is

$f(x_1, x_2, \ldots, x_m) = (x_1 x_2 \ldots x_m)^{\gamma-1} e^{-x_m}$, $0 < x_1 < x_2 < \ldots < x_m < \infty$.

Let us use the transformation

$$\xi_o = X_{U(1)}, \text{ and } \xi_i = \frac{X_{U(i)}}{X_{U(i+1)}}, i = 2, \ldots, m-1.$$

The Jacobian of the transformation

$$J = \left| \frac{\partial(X_{U(1)}, X_{U(2)}, \ldots, X_{U(m)})}{\partial(\xi_o, \xi_1, \ldots, \xi_{m-1})} \right| = \frac{\xi_o^{m-1}}{\xi_1^m \xi_2^{m-1} \ldots \xi_{m-1}^2}$$

We can write the pdf of ξ_i, $i = 0, 1, \ldots, m-1$, as

$$f(e_o, e_1, \ldots, e_{m-1}) = \frac{\alpha^m e_o^{m-1}}{e_1^m e_2^{m-1} \ldots e_{m-1}^2} e^{-\left(\frac{e_o}{e_1 \ldots e_{m-1}}\right)}.$$

Now integrating the above expression with respect to e_0, we obtain the joint
pdf of ξ_i, $i = 1, \ldots, m-1$, as

$$f(e_1, \ldots, e_{m-1}) = \Gamma(m) \, e_2 \ldots e_{m-1}^{m-2}.$$

Thus ξ_i, $i = 1, 2, \ldots, m-1$ are independent and
$P(\xi_k \leq x) = x^k$, $1 \leq k \leq m$.
Since $R(x) = x$ for the exponential distribution with unit mean, the pdf of $\xi_i = X_{U(i)} / X_{U(i+1)}$, $i=1,2, \ldots, n-1$ can also be obtained using (1.2.10).

Corollary 2.2.1.
Let $W_k = (\xi_k)^k$, $k = 1, 2, \ldots, m-1$, then $W_1, W_2, \ldots, W_{m-1}$ are independent and identically distributed as uniform (over the interval (0,1)) random variable.

2.2. MOMENTS OF RECORD VALUES

Without any loss of generality we will consider in this section the standard exponential population, $E(0, 1)$, with pdf $f(x) = \exp(-x)$, $0 \leq x < \infty$, in which case we have $f(x) = 1 - F(x)$. From (2.1.1) it is obvious that $X_{U(n)}$ can be written as the sum of n i.e. random variables $V_1, V_2, \ldots, V_n$ each of which is distributed as $E(0, 1)$. We have already seen that

$$E(X_{U(n)}) = n$$
$$Var(X_{U(n)}) = n, \quad \text{and}$$
$$Cov(X_{U(n)}, X_{U(m)}) = m, \quad m < n. \tag{2.2.1}$$

Exponential Distribution

For $1 \leq m < n$,

$$E(X_{U(n)}^p X_{U(m)}^q)$$

$$= \int_0^\infty \int_0^u \frac{1}{\Gamma(m)} \cdot \frac{1}{\Gamma(n-m)} u^q e^{-x} v^{m+p-1}(u-v)^{n-m-1} dv du$$

Substituting $tu = v$ and simplifying we get

$$E(X_{U(n)}^p X_{U(m)}^q)$$

$$= \int_0^\infty \int_0^1 \frac{1}{\Gamma(m)\Gamma(n-m)} u^{n+p+q-1} e^{-x} t^{m+p-1}(1-t)^{n-m-1} dt du$$

$$= \frac{\Gamma(m+p)\Gamma(n+p+q)}{\Gamma(m)\Gamma(n+p)}$$

From (2.1.5), it can be shown that if $S_n = X_{U(1)} + X_{U(2)} + \ldots + X_{U(n)}$, then

$$E(S_n) = \frac{n(n+1)}{2} \text{ and } Var(S_n) = \frac{n(n+1)(2n+1)}{6}.$$

Some simple recurrence relations satisfied by single and product moments of record values are given by the following theorems.

Theorem 2.2.1

For $n \geq 1$ and $r = 0, 1, 2, \ldots$

$$E\left(X_{U(n)}^{r+1}\right) = E\left(X_{U(n-1)}^{r+1}\right) + (r+1)E\left(X_{U(n)}^r\right) \quad (2.2.2)$$

and consequently, for $0 \leq m \leq n-1$ we can write

$$E\left(X_{U(n)}^{r+1}\right) = E\left(X_{U(m)}^{r+1}\right) + (r+1)\sum_{p=m+1}^{n} E\left(X_{U(p)}^r\right) \quad (2.2.3)$$

with $E\left(X_{U(0)}^{r+1}\right) = 0$ and $E\left(X_{U(n)}^0\right) = 1$.

Proof.

For $n \geq 1$ and $r = 0, 1, \ldots$, we have from (1.2.7)

$$E(X^r_{U(n)}) = \frac{1}{\Gamma(n)} \int_0^\infty x^r \{R(x)\}^{n-1} f(x) dx$$

$$= \frac{1}{\Gamma(n)} \int_0^\infty x^r \{R(x)\}^{n-1} \{1-F(x)\} dx,$$

since $f(x) = 1 - F(x)$.

Upon integrating by parts treating x^r for integration and the rest of the integrand for differentiation, we obtain

$$E\left(x_{U(n)}^r\right) = \frac{1}{(\Gamma(n)(r+1))} [\int_0^\infty x^{r+1} \{R(x)\}^{n-1} f(x) dx$$

$$- (n-1) \int_0^\infty x^{r+1} \{R(x)\}^{n-2} f(x) dx]$$

$$= \frac{1}{r+1} [\int_0^\infty x^{r+1} \frac{1}{\Gamma(n)} \{R(x)\}^{n-1} f(x) dx$$

$$- \int_0^\infty x^{r+1} \frac{1}{\Gamma(n-1)} \{R(x)\}^{n-2} f(x) dx]$$

$$= \frac{1}{r+1} \{E(X_{U(n)}^{r+1}) - E(X_{U(n-1)}^{r+1})\},$$

which, when rewritten, gives the recurrence relation in (2.2.2). Then, by repeatedly applying the recurrence relation (2.2.2), we simply derive the recurrence relation in (2.2.3).

Remark 2.2.1. The recurrence relation in (2.2.2) can be used in a simple way to compute all the simple moments of all record values. Once again, using the property that $f(y) = 1-F(y)$, we can derive some simple recurrence relations for the product moments of record values.

Theorem 2.2.2.

For $m \geq 1$ and $r, s = 0, 1, 2, \ldots$

$$E(X_{U(m)}^r X_{U(m+1)}^{s+1}) = E(X_{U(m)}^{r+s+1}) + (s+1) E(X_{U(m)}^r X_{U(m+1)}^s), \quad (2.2.4)$$

Exponential Distribution

and for $1 \leq m \leq n-2$, $r,s = 0, 1, 2, \ldots$

$$E\left(X_{U(m)}^{r} X_{U(n)}^{s+1}\right)$$
$$= E\left(X_{U(m)}^{r} X_{U(n-1)}^{s+1}\right) + (s+1)E\left(X_{U(m)}^{r} X_{U(n)}^{s}\right)$$

(2.2.5)

Proof.

Let us consider $1 \leq m < n$ and $r,s = 0, 1, 2, \ldots$

$$E\left(X_{U(m)}^{r} X_{U(n)}^{s}\right) = \frac{1}{\Gamma(m)\Gamma(n-m)} \int_{0}^{\infty} x^{r} \{R(x)\}^{m-1}$$
$$\cdot \frac{f(x)}{1-F(x)} I(x) dx,$$

(2.2.6)

where

$$I(x) = \int_{x}^{\infty} y^{s} \{R(y) - R(x)\}^{n-m-1} f(y) dy$$

$$= \int_{x}^{\infty} y^{s} \{R(y) - R(x)\}^{n-m-1} \{1 - F(y)\} dy$$

$$= \int_{x}^{\infty} y^{s} \{R(y) - R(x)\}^{n-m-1} \{1 - F(y)\} dy$$

since $f(y) = 1 - F(y)$.

Upon integrating by parts treating y^{s} for integration and the rest of the integrand for differentiation, we obtain when $n = m+1$ that

$$I(x) = \frac{1}{s+1} \left[\int_{x}^{\infty} y^{s+1} f(y) dy - x^{s+1} \{1 - F(x)\} \right],$$

and when $n \geq m+2$, that

$$I(x) = \frac{1}{s+1}[\int_x^\infty y^{s+1}\{R(y)-R(x)\}^{n-m-1}f(y)dy.]$$
$$- (n-m-1)\int_x^\infty y^{s+1}\{R(y)-R(x)\}^{n-m-2}f(y)dy] \quad (2.2.7)$$

Upon substituting the above expressions of $I(x)$ in equation (2.2.6) and simplifying, we obtain when $n = m+1$ that

$$E(X_{U(m)}^r X_{U(m+1)}^s) = \frac{1}{s+1}\{E(X_{U(m)}^r X_{U(m+1)}^{s+1}) - E(X_{U(m)}^{r+s+1})\}$$

and when $n \geq m+2$, that

$$E(X_{U(m)}^r X_{U(n)}^s)$$
$$= \frac{1}{s+1}\{E(X_{U(m)}^r X_{U(n)}^{s+1}) - E(X_{U(m)}^r X_{U(n-1)}^{s+1})\}.$$

The recurrence relations in (2.2.4) and (2.2.5) follow readily when the above two equations are rewritten.

Remark 2.2.2. By repeated application of the recurrence relation in (2.2.5), with the help of the relation in (2.2.4), we obtain for $n \geq m+1$ that

$$E(X_{U(m)}^r X_{U(n)}^{s+1})$$
$$= E(X_{U(m)}^{r+s+1}) + (s+1)\sum_{p=m+1}^n E(X_{U(m)}^r X_{U(p)}^s)$$
$$(2.2.8)$$

Corollary 2.2.1. For $n \geq m+1$,

$$Cov(X_{U(m)}, X_{U(n)}) = Var(X_{U(m)}).$$

Proof:

By setting r =1 and s = 0 in (2.2.8), we obtain
$$E(X_{U(m)} X_{U(n)}) = E(X^2_{U(m)}) + (n-m)E(X_{U(m)}) \quad (2.2.9)$$

Similarly, by setting r = 0 in (2.2.3), we obtain
$$E(X_{U(n)}) = E(X_{U(m)}) + (n-m), \quad m > m. \quad (2.2.10)$$

With the help of (2.2.9) and (2.2.10), we get for $n \geq m+1$

$$Cov(X_{U(m)}, X_{U(n)})$$
$$= E(X_{U(m)} X_{U(n)}) - E(X_{U(m)}) E(X_{U(m)})$$
$$= E(X^2_{U(m)}) + (n-m)E(X_{U(m)})$$
$$- \{E(X_{U(m)})\}^2 - (n-m)E(X_{U(m)})$$
$$= Var(X_{U(m)})$$

Corollary 2.2.2. By repeated application of the recurrence relations in (2.2.4) and (2.2.5), we also obtained for $m \geq 1$

$$E(X_{U(m)}^r \, X_{U(m+1)}^{s+1}) = \sum_{p=0}^{s+1} (s+1)^{(p)} E(X_{U(m)}^{r+s+1-p})$$

and for $1 \leq m \leq n-2$

$$E(X_{U(m)}^r \, X_{U(n)}^{s+1}) = \sum_{p=0}^{s+1} (s+1)^{(p)} E(X_{U(m)}^r \, X_{U(n-1)}^{s+1-p}),$$

where
$$(s+1)^{(0)} = 1 \quad and \quad (s+1)^{(i)} = (s+1) \, s \ldots (s+1-i+1), \quad for \quad i \geq 1.$$

Remark 2.2.3. The recurrence relations in equations (2.2.4) and (2.2.5) can be used in a simple way to compute all the product moments of all records values.

Theorem 2.2.3

For $m \geq 2$ and r,s = 0,1,2...,

$$E(X_{U(m-1)}^{r+1} X_{U(m)}^{s}) = E(X_{U(m)}^{r+s+1}) - (r+1)E(X_{U(m)}^{r} X_{U(m+1)}^{s})$$

(2.2.11)

and for $2 \leq m \leq n-2$ and $r,s = 0,1,2..$,

$$E(X_{U(m-1)}^{r+1} X_{U(n-1)}^{s}) = E(X_{U(m)}^{r+1} X_{U(n-1)}^{s}) - (r+1)E(X_{U(m)}^{r} X_{U(m+1)}^{s})$$

(2.2.12)

Proof.

From (2.2.7), let us consider for $2 \leq m \leq n$ and $r,s = 0,1,2..$

$$E(X_{U(m)}^{r} X_{U(n)}^{s}) = \int_0^\infty \int_0^\infty x^r y^s f_{m,n}(x,y) dx dy$$

$$= \frac{1}{(m-1)!(n-m-1)!} \int_0^\infty y^s f(y) J(y) dy,$$

(2.2.13)

where

$$J(y) = \int_0^y x^r \{-\ln(1-F(x))\}^{m-1} \{-\ln(1-F(x))\}^{n-m-1} \frac{f(x)}{1-F(x)} dx$$

$$= \int_0^y x^r \{-\ln(1-F(x))\}^{m-1} \{-\ln(1-F(x)) + \ln(1-F(y))\}^{n-m-1} dx,$$

since $f(x) = 1-F(x)$. Upon integrating by parts treating x^r for integration and the rest of the integrand for differentiation, we obtain for $n = m+1$ that

$$J(y) = \frac{1}{r+1} \left[y^{r+1} \{-\ln(1-F(x))\}^{m-1} \right]$$

$$-(m-1) \int_0^y x^{r+1} \{-\ln(1-F(x))\}^{m-2} \frac{f(x)}{1-F(x)} dx$$

and when $n \geq m+2$ that

$$J(y) = \frac{1}{r+1}\left[(n-m-1)\int_0^y x^{r+1}\{-\ln(1-F(x))\}^{m-1}\frac{f(x)}{1-F(x)}\right.$$
$$\{-\ln(1-F(y))+\ln(1-F(x))\}^{n-m-2}\,dx$$
$$-(m-1)\int_0^y x^{r+1}\{-\ln(1-F(x))\}^{m-2}\frac{f(x)}{1-F(x)}dx$$
$$\left.\{-\ln(1-F(y))+\ln(1-F(x))\}^{n-m-1}\,dx\right]$$

Upon substituting the above expressions of J(y) in Equation (2.2.13) and simplifying, we obtain for n = m+1 that

$$E\left(X_{U(m)}^r X_{U(n)}^s\right) = \frac{1}{r+1}\{E(X_{U(m)}^{r+s+1}) - E(X_{U(m-1)}^{r+1} X_{U(m)}^s)\},$$

and when $n \geq m+2$ that

$$E\{X_{U(m)}^r X_{U(n)}^s\} = \frac{1}{r+1}\{E(X_{U(m)}^{r+1} X_{U9n}^s) - E[X_{U(m-1)}^{r+1} X_{U(n-1)}^s]\}$$

The recurrence relations of Equations (2.2.11) and (2.2.12) follow readily when the above two equations are rewritten.

Corollary 2.2.3. By repeated application of the recurrence relation in (2.2.12), with the help of the relation in (2.2.1), we obtain for $2 \leq m \leq n-1$ and r,s = 0,1,2..

$$E\{X_{U(m-1)}^{r+1} X_{U(n-1)}^s\} = E\{X_{U(n-1)}^{r+s+1}\} - (r+1)\sum_{p=m}^{n-1} E\{X_{U(p)}^r X_{U(n)}^s\}$$

Corollary 2.2.4. By repeated application of the recurrence relations in (2.2.11) and (2.2.12), we also obtain for $m \geq 2$

$$E\{X_{U(m-1)}^{r+1} X_{U(m)}^s\} = \sum_{p=0}^{r+1} (-1)^p (r+1)^{(p)} E\{X_{U(m+p)}^{r+s+1-p}\}$$

and for $2 \leq m \leq n-2$

$$E\{X_{U(m-1)}^{r+1} X_{U(n-1)}^s\} = \sum_{p=0}^{r+1} (-1)^p (r+1)^{(p)} E\{X_{U(m-p)}^{r+1-p} X_{U(n+1-p)}^s\}.$$

It is also important to mention here that this approach can easily be adopted to derive recurrence relations for product moments involving more than two record values.

2.3 ESTIMATION OF PARAMETERS

We shall consider here the linear estimation of μ and σ.

(a) Minimum Variance Linear Unbiased Estimates (MVLUE)

Suppose $X_{U(1)}, X_{U(2)}, ..., X_{U(m)}$ are the m record values from an i.i.d. sequence $E(\mu, \sigma)$. Let $Y_i = \sigma^{-1}(X_{U(i)} - \mu)$, $i = 1, 2, ..., m$, then

$$E(Y_i) = i = Var(Y_i), \quad i = 1, 2, ..., m,$$

and $Cov(Y_i, Y_j) = \min(i, j)$.

Let $X = (X_{U(1)}, X_{U(2)}, ..., X_{U(m)})'$, then

$$E(X) = \mu L + \sigma \delta$$
$$Var(X) = \sigma^2 V,$$

where

$$L = (1, 1, ..., 1)', \delta = (1, 2, ...m)'$$
$$V = (V_{ij}), V_{ij} = \min(i, j), \quad i, j = 1, 2, ..., m.$$

The inverse $V^{-1}(= V^{ij})$ can be expressed as

$$V^{ij} = \begin{array}{ll} 2 & \text{if } i = j = 1, 2, ..., m-1 \\ 1 & \text{if } i = j = m \\ -1 & \text{if } |i - j| = 1, \ i, j = 1, 2, ..., m \\ 0 & \text{otherwise.} \end{array}$$

The minimum variance linear unbiased estimates (MVLUE) $\hat{\mu}, \hat{\sigma}$ of μ and σ respectively are

$$\hat{\mu} = -\delta'V^{-1}(L\delta'-\delta L')V^{-1}X/\Delta$$
$$\hat{\sigma} = L'V^{-1}(L\delta'-\delta L')V^{-1}X/\Delta,$$

where

$$\Delta = (L'V^{-1}L)(\delta'V^{-1}\delta) - (L'V^{-1}\delta)^2$$

and

$$Var(\hat{\mu}) = \sigma^2 L'V^{-1}\delta/\Delta$$
$$Var(\hat{\sigma}) = \sigma^2 L'V^{-1}L/\Delta$$
$$Cov(\hat{\mu},\hat{\sigma}) = -\sigma^2 L'V^{-1}\delta/\Delta .$$

It can be shown that
$$L'V^{-1} = (1,0,0,...,0), \quad \delta'V^{-1} = (0,0,0,...,1),$$
$$\delta'V^{-1}\delta = m \quad \text{and} \quad \Delta = m-1.$$

On simplification we get
$$\hat{\mu} = (mX_{U(1)} - X_{U(m)})/(m-1)$$
$$\hat{\sigma} = (X_{U(m)} - X_{U(1)})/(m-1) \tag{2.3.1}$$

with
$$Var(\hat{\mu}) = m\sigma^2/(m-1), Var(\hat{\sigma}) = \sigma^2/(m-1) \quad \text{and}$$
$$Cov(\hat{\mu},\hat{\sigma}) = -\sigma^2/(m-1). \tag{2.3.2}$$

(b) Best Linear Invariant Estimators

The best linear invariant (in the sense of minimum mean squared error and invariance with respect to the location parameter μ) estimators (BLIE) $\tilde{\mu}$ $\tilde{\sigma}$ of μ and σ are

$$\tilde{\mu} = \hat{\mu} - \hat{\sigma}\left(\frac{E_{12}}{1+E_{22}}\right)$$

and

$$\tilde{\sigma} = \hat{\sigma}/(1+E_{22}) \quad ,$$

where
$\hat{\mu}$ and $\hat{\sigma}$ are MVLUE of μ and σ and

$$\begin{pmatrix} Var(\hat{\mu}) & Cov(\hat{\mu},\hat{\sigma}) \\ Cov(\hat{\mu},\hat{\sigma}) & Var(\hat{\sigma}) \end{pmatrix} = \sigma^2 \begin{pmatrix} E_{11} & E_{12} \\ E_{12} & E_{22} \end{pmatrix}$$

The mean squared errors of these estimators are

$$MSE(\tilde{\mu}) = \sigma^2 \left(E_{11} - E_{12}^2 (1 + E_{22})^{-1} \right) \text{ and}$$

$$MSE(\tilde{\sigma}) = \sigma^2 E_{22} (1 + E_{22})^{-1}$$

We have

$$E(\tilde{\mu} - \mu)(\tilde{\sigma} - \sigma) = \sigma^2 E_{12} (1 + E_{22})^{-1}.$$

Using the values of E_{11}, E_{12} and E_{22} from (2.3.2), we obtain

$$\tilde{\mu} = \{(m+1)X_{U(1)} - X_{U(m)}\}/m \quad ,$$

$$\hat{\sigma} = (X_{U(m)} - X_{U(1)})/m$$

$$Var(\tilde{\mu}) = \frac{m+1}{m}\sigma^2 \text{ and } Var(\hat{\sigma}) = \frac{m-1}{m^2}\sigma^2$$

2.4 CHARACTERIZATIONS

We will give several characterization theorems of the exponential distribution under various assumptions.

(a) Under the Assumption of Independence.

We have already seen that $X_{U(n)} - X_{U(m)}$ and $X_{U(m)}$, $n > m \geq 1$, are independent. This is a characteristic property of the exponential distribution. For n = 2 Tata (1969) proved the following characterization theorem.

Theorem 2.4.1

Let $\{X_n, n \geq 1\}$ be an i.i.d. sequence of non-negative random variables with cdf F(x) and pdf f(x). Then for X_n to belong to $E(\mu,\sigma)$, it is necessary and sufficient that $X_{U(2)} - X_{U(1)}$ and $X_{U(1)}$ are independent.

Exponential Distribution

Proof:

The property of the independence of $X_{U(2)} - X_{U(1)}$ and $X_{U(1)}$ will lead to the functional equation

$$\overline{F}(0)\overline{F}(x+y) = \overline{F}(x)\overline{F}(y), \quad 0 < x, y < \infty. \quad (2.4.1)$$

The continuous solution of this functional equation is $\overline{F}(x) = e^{-(x-\mu)\sigma^{-1}}$.

The following theorem is a generalization of theorem 2.4.1.

Theorem 2.4.2

Let $\{X_n, n \geq 1\}$ be a sequence of i.i.d. random variables with common distribution function F which is absolutely continuous with pdf f. Assume $F(0) = 0$. Then for $X_n \in E(0, \sigma)$ it is necessary and sufficient that $X_{U(n)}$ and $X_{U(n+1)} - X_{U(n)}$, $n \geq 1$, are independent.

Proof.

Let $Z_{n+1,n} = X_{U(n+1)} - X_{U(n)}$. It is easy to establish that $Z_{n+1,n}$ and $X_{U(n)}$ are independent. We will prove the sufficient condition. Suppose that $X_{U(n)}$ and $Z_{n+1,n}$ are independent. Now the joint pdf $f(z,u)$ of $Z_{n+1,n}$ and $X_{U(n)}$ can be written as

$$f(z,u) = \frac{(R(u))^{n-1}}{\Gamma(n)} r(u) f(u+z), \quad 0 < u, z < \infty. \quad (2.4.2)$$

$= 0,$ otherwise.

But the pdf $f_n(u)$ of $X_{U(n)}$ can be written as

$$f(u) = \frac{(R(u))^{n-1}}{\Gamma(n)} f(u), 0 < u < \infty,$$

$= 0,$ otherwise. $\quad (2.4.3)$

Since $Z_{n+1,n}$ and $X_{U(n)}$ are independent, we get from (2.4.2) and (2.4.3)

$$\frac{f(u+z)}{\overline{F}(u)} = g(z), \quad (2.4.4)$$

where g(z) is the pdf of $Z_{n+1,n}$. Integrating (2.4. 4) with respect z from 0 to z_1, we get

$$\overline{F}(u) - \overline{F}(u+z_1) = \overline{F}(u)G(z_1) \qquad (2.4.5)$$

Since $G(z_1) = \int_0^{z_1} g(z)dz$. Now $u \to 0^+$ and using the boundary condition, we see that $G(z_1) = F(z_1)$. Hence we get from (2.4.5)

$$\overline{F}(u+z_1) = \overline{F}(u)\,\overline{F}(z_1). \qquad (2.4.6)$$

The only continuous solution of (2.4.6) with the boundary condition $F(0) = 0$ (see Appendix A) is

$$\overline{F}(x) = e^{-\sigma^{-1} x} \qquad , x \geq 0 \qquad (2.4.7)$$

where σ is an arbitrary positive real number.

The following theorem is a generalization of the theorem (2.4.2)

Theorem 2.4.3.

Let $\{X_n, n \geq 1\}$ be independent and identically distributed with common distribution function F which is absolutely continuous and $F(0) = 0$ and $F(x) < 1$ for all $x > 0$. Then for $X_n \in E(0,\sigma)$, it is necessary and sufficient that $Z_{n,m}$ and $X_{U(m)}$ ($n > m > 0$) are independent. Here $Z_{n,m} = X_{U(n)} - X_{U(m)}$.

Proof.

The necessary condition is easy to establish. To proof the sufficient condition, we need the following lemma.

Lemma 2.4.1.

Let F(x) be an absolutely continuous function and $\overline{F}(x) > 0$, for all x > 0. Suppose that $\overline{F}(u+v)(\overline{F}(v))^{-1} = \exp\{-q(u,v)\}$ and $h(u,v) = \{q(u,v)\}^r \exp\{-q(u,v)\} \dfrac{\partial}{\partial u} q(u,v)$, for $r \geq 0$ Futher if $h(u,v) \neq 0$, and

Exponential Distribution

$\frac{\partial}{\partial u} q(u,v) \neq 0$ for any positive u and v. If h(u,v) is independent of v, then q(u,v) is a function of u only. Here $\overline{F}(x) = 1 - F(x)$.

Proof:

Let
$$g(u) = h(u,v)$$
$$= (q(u,v))^r \exp(-q(u,v)) \frac{\partial}{\partial v} q(u,v)$$
$$= \sum_{j=0}^{\infty} \frac{(-1)^j}{\Gamma(j+1)} \{q(u,v)\}^{r+j} \frac{\partial}{\partial u} q(u,v)$$
$$= \sum_{j=0}^{\infty} \frac{(-1)^j}{\Gamma(j+1)} \frac{1}{(r+j+1)} \frac{\partial}{\partial u} q(u,v).$$

Hence
$$\sum_{j=0}^{\infty} \frac{(-1)^j}{\Gamma(j+1)} (q(u,v))^{r+j+1} \frac{1}{(r+j+1)}$$
$$= c + \int g(u) du ,$$
$$= g_1(u) , \text{ say}. \qquad (2.4.8)$$

Here $g_1(u)$ is a function of u only and c is independent of u but may depend on v.

Now letting $u \to 0^+$, we see that $q(u,v) \to 0$ and hence from (2.4.8), we have c as independent of v.

Therefore
$$0 = \frac{\partial}{\partial v} g_1(v) = \sum_{j=0}^{\infty} \frac{(-1)^j}{\Gamma(j+1)} \{q(u,v)\}^{r+j} \frac{\partial}{\partial v} q(u,v)$$
$$= g(u) \frac{\partial}{\partial v} q(u,v) (\frac{\partial}{\partial u} q(u,v))^{-1}.$$

Now we know $g(u) = h(u,v) \neq 0$ and $\dfrac{\partial}{\partial u} q(u,v) \neq 0$, so we must have $\dfrac{\partial}{\partial v} q(u,v) = 0$.

Now we proof the sufficiency condition of the theorem 2.4.3.
The joint pdf of $Z_{n,m}$ ($= X_{U(n)} - X_{U(m)}$) and $X_{U(m)}$ is

$$f(z,u) = \frac{R^{m-1}(x)\, r(x)}{\Gamma(m)\,\Gamma(n-m)} \{R(z+x) - R(x)\}^{n-m-1} f(z+x)$$

for $0 < z < \infty$, $0 < x < \infty$.
The conditional pdf of $Z_{n,m}$ given $X_{U(m)} = x$ is

$$F(z|X_{u(m)} = x) = \frac{1}{\Gamma(n-m)} \{R(z+x) - R(x)\}^{n-m-1} \frac{f(z+x)}{\overline{F}(x)} \quad (2.4.9)$$

for $0 < z < \infty$, $0 < x < \infty$.
Since $Z_{n,m}$ and $X_{U(m)}$ are independent, we will have for all $z > 0$,

$$(R(z+x) - R(x))^{n-m-1} \frac{f(z+x)}{\overline{F}(x)} \quad (2.4.10)$$

as independent of x.

Now let $R(z+x) - R(x) = -\ln \dfrac{\overline{F}(z+x)}{\overline{F}(x)} = q(z,x)$, say.

Writing (2.4.10) in terms of q(z,x), we get

$$q(z,x)\}^{n-m-1} \exp\{-q(z,x)\} \frac{\partial}{\partial z} q(z,x) \quad (2.4.11)$$

as independent of x. Hence by the lemma 2.4.1, we have

$$-\ln\{\overline{F}(z+x)(\overline{F}(x))^{-1}\} = q(z+x) = c(z), \quad (2.4.12)$$

where c(z) is a function of z only. Thus

$$\overline{F}(z+x)\,(\overline{F}(x))^{-1} = c_1(z) \quad (2.4.13)$$

where $c_1(z)$ is a function of z only.

The relation (2.4.13) is true for all $z \geq 0$ and any arbitrary fixed positive number x. The continuous solution of (2.4.13) with the boundary condition $\overline{F}(0) = 1$ and $\overline{F}(\infty) = 0$ is

$$\overline{F}(x) = \exp(-x\,\sigma^{-1}) \quad (2.4.14)$$

for $x \geq 0$ and any arbitrary positive real number σ.

Exponential Distribution

The assumption of absolute continuity of F(x) in the theorem 2.4.3 can be replaced by the continuity of F(x).

(b) Under the Assumptions of Identical Distribution.

We have seen that if the sequence { X_n, n ≥ 1} of i.i.d. rvs are from $E(0,\sigma)$, then $X_{U(n)} \stackrel{d}{=} Z_1 + Z_2 + ... + Z_n$, where $Z_1, Z_2, ..., Z_n$ are i.i.d. $E(0,\sigma)$.

The following theorem gives a characterization of the exponential distribution using the above property.

If F is the distribution function of a non- negative random variable, we will call F is "new better than used " (NBU) if for x, y ≥ 0, $\overline{F}(x+y) \leq \overline{F}(x)\overline{F}(y)$, and F is " new worse than used" (NWU) if for x, y ≥ 0, $\overline{F}(x+y) \geq \overline{F}(x)\overline{F}(y)$. We will say F belongs to the class C_1 if either F is NBU or NWU.

Theorem 2.4.4.

Let X_n, n≥ 1 be a sequence of i.i.d. random variables which has absolutely continuous distribution function F with pdf f and F(0) = 0, Assume that F(x) < 1 for all x>0. If X_n belongs to the class C_1 and $Z_{n+1,n}$ ($= X_{U(n+1)} - X_{U(n)}$) has an identical distribution with X_k, k ≥ 1, then $X_k \in E(0,\sigma)$, k ≥ 1.

Proof.

The pdf g_n of $Z_{n+1,n}$ can be written as

$$g_n(x) = \int_0^\infty \frac{(R(u))^{n-1}}{\Gamma(n)} r(u) f(u+z) du, z \geq 0$$

= 0, otherwise. (2.4.15)

By the assumption of the identical distribution of $Z_{n+1,n}$ and X_k, we must have

$$\int_0^\infty \{R(u)\}^{n-1} \frac{r(u)}{\Gamma(n)} f(u+z) du = f(z), \text{ for all } z > 0. \quad (2.4.16)$$

Substituting

$$\int_0^\infty \{R(u)\}^{n-1} f(u)du = \Gamma(n), \qquad (2.4.17)$$

we have

$$\int_0^\infty \{R(u)\}^{n-1} r(u) f(u+z) du = f(z) \int_0^\infty \{R(u)\}^{n-1} f(u) du \qquad (2.4.18)$$

for all $z > 0$.

Thus

$$\int_0^\infty \{R(u)\}^{n-1} f(u) [f(u+z)(\overline{F}(u))^{-1} - f(z)] du = 0 \qquad (2.4.19)$$

for all $z > 0$.

Integrating the above expression with respect to z from z_1 to ∞, we get from (2.4.19),

$$\int_0^\infty \{R(u)\}^{n-1} f(u) [\overline{F}(u+z_1)(\overline{F}(u))^{-1} - \overline{F}(z_1)] du = 0 \qquad (2.4.20)$$

for all $z_1 > 0$.

If $F(x)$ is NBU, then (2.4.20) is true if

$$\overline{F}(u+z_1)(\overline{F}(u))^{-1} = \overline{F}(z_1), \qquad (2.4.21)$$

for all $z_1 > 0$.

The only continuous solution of (2.4.21) with the boundary conditions $\overline{F}(0) = 1$ and $\overline{F}(\infty) = 0$ is $\overline{F}(x) = \exp(0, \sigma^{-1})$, where σ is an arbitrary real positive number.

Similarly, if F is NWU then (2.4.20) is true if (2.4.21) is satisfied and hence

$X_k \in E(0,\sigma)$, $k \geq 1$.

The following theorem is proved under the assumption of monotone hazard rate. We will say F belongs to the class C_2 if $r(x)$ is either monotone increasing or decreasing.

Theorem 2.4.5.

Exponential Distribution

If X_k, $k \geq 1$ has an absolutely continuous distribution function F with pdf f and $F(0) = 0$. If $Z_{n+1,n}$ and $Z_{n,n-1}$, $n \geq 1$, are identically distributed and F belongs to C_2, then $X_k \in E(0,\sigma)$, $k \geq 1$.

Proof:

$$P(Z_{n+1,n} > z) = \int_0^\infty \{R(u)\}^{n-1} \frac{r(u)}{\Gamma(n)} \overline{F}(u+z)du, \text{ for all } z > 0,$$

$= 0$, otherwise.

Since $Z_{n+1,n}$ and $Z_{n,n-1}$ are identically distributed, we get using the above equation,

$$\int_0^\infty \{R(u)\}^n r(u)\overline{F}(u+z)du = n \int_0^\infty \{R(u)\}^{n-1} r(u)\overline{F}(u+z)du \quad (2.4.22)$$

for all $z > 0$.

Substituting the identity

$$n \int_0^\infty \{R(u)\}^{n-1} r(u)\overline{F}(u+z)du = \int_0^\infty \{R(u)\}^n f(u+z)du$$

in (2.4.22), we get on simplification

$$\int_0^\infty \{R(u)\}^{n-1} r(u)\overline{F}(u+z)\left[1 - \frac{r(u+z)}{r(u)}\right]du = 0, \quad (2.4.23)$$

for all $z > 0$.

Thus if $F \in C_2$, then (2.4.23) is true if for almost all u and any fixed $z > 0$,

$$r(u+z) = r(u). \quad (2.4.24)$$

The constant hazard rate i.e. the relation (2.4.24) is a well known characterization property of the exponential distribution. Hence, we have $X_k \in E(0,\sigma)$ for all $k \geq 1$.

Theorem 2.4.6.

Let X_n, $n \geq 1$ be a sequence of independent and identically distributed non-negative random variables with absolutely continuous distribution function $F(x)$ with $f(x)$ as the corresponding density function. If $F \in C_2$ and for some fixed n,m, $1 \leq m < n < \infty$, $Z_{n,m} \stackrel{d}{=} X_{U(n-m)}$, then $X_k \in E(0,\sigma)$, $k \geq 1$.

Proof.

The pdfs $f_1(x)$ of $X_{U(n-m)}$ and $f_2(x)$ of $Z_{n,m}$ ($= X_{U(n)} - X_{U(m)}$) can be written as

$$f_1(x) = \frac{1}{\Gamma(n-m)} (R(x))^{n-m-1} f(x), \quad \text{for } 0 < x < \infty, \quad (2.4.25)$$

and

$$f_2(x) = \int_0^\infty \frac{(R(u))^{m-1}}{\Gamma(m)} \frac{\{R(x+u) - R(x)\}^{n-m-1}}{\Gamma(n-m)} r(u) f(u+x) du, \quad (2.4.26)$$

for $0 < x < \infty$.

Integrating (2.4.25) and (2.4.26) with respect to x from 0 to x_0, we get
$F_1(x_0) = 1 - g_1(x_0)$ (2.4.27)
where

$$g_1(x_0) = \sum_{j=1}^{n-m} \frac{(R(x_0))^{j-1}}{\Gamma(j)} e^{-R(x_o)},$$

and
$F_2(x_0) = 1 - g_2(x_0, u)$ (2.4.28)

where
$g_2(x_o, u)$

$$= \sum_{j=1}^{n-m} \frac{\{R(u+x_o) - R(u)\}^{j-1}}{\Gamma(j)} \exp\{-(R(u+x_o) - R(u))\}.$$

Now equating (2.4.27) and (2.4.28), we get

$$\int_0^\infty \frac{\{R(u)\}^{m-1}}{\Gamma(m)} f(u) [g_2(u, x_o) - g_1(x_o)] du = 0, \quad (2.4.29)$$

for all $x_0 \geq 0$.
Now $g_2(x_0, 0) = g_1(0)$ and

$$= \frac{\{R(u) - R(u)\}^{n-m-1}}{\Gamma(n-m)} \exp\{-(R(u+x_o) - R(u))\}[r(x_o) - r(u+x_o)] .$$

Thus if $F \in C_2$, then (2.4.29) is true if
$r(u+x_0) = r(u)$ (2.4.30)

Exponential Distribution

for almost all u and any fixed $x_0 \geq 0$.
Hence $X_k \in E(0,\sigma)$ for all $k \geq 1$, here σ is an arbitrary positive real number.
Substituting $m = n-1$, we get $Z_{n,n-1} \stackrel{d}{=} X_1$ as a characteristic property of the exponential distribution.

Theorem 2.4.7.

Let $\{X_n, n \geq 1\}$ be a sequence of independent and identically distributed non-negative random variables with absolutely continuous distribution function $F(x)$ and the corresponding density function $f(x)$. If F belongs to C_2 and for some m, $m > 1$, $X_{U(m)} = X_{U(m-1)} + U$, where U is independent of $X_{U(m)}$ and $X_{U(m-1)}$ and is distributed as X_n's, then $X_n \in E(0, \sigma)$, for some $\sigma > 0$.

Proof:

The pdf $f_m(x)$ of $X_{U(m)}$, $m \geq 1$, can be written as

$$f_m(y) = \frac{(R(y))^{m-1}}{\Gamma(m)} f(y), 0 < y < \infty,$$

$$= \frac{d}{dy}\{-\overline{F}(y)\int_0^y \frac{(R(x))^{m-2}}{\Gamma(m-1)} r(x)dx + \int_0^y \frac{(R(x))^{m-1}}{\Gamma(m-1)} f(x)dx)$$

(2.4.31)

The pdf $f_2(y)$ of $X_{U(m+1)} + U$ can be written as

$$f_2(y) = \int_0^y \frac{(R(x))^{m-2}}{\Gamma(m-1)} f(y-x) f(x) dy$$

$$= \frac{d}{dy}(-\frac{(R(x))^{m-2}}{\Gamma(m-1)} \overline{F}(y-x) f(x) dx + \int_0^y \frac{(R(x))^{m-2}}{\Gamma(m-1)} f(x) dx)$$

(2.4.32)

Equating (2.4.31) and (2.4.32), we get on simplification

$$\int_0^y \frac{(R(x))^{m-1}}{\Gamma(m-1)} f(x) H_1(x,y) dx = 0,$$

where $H_1(x,y) = \overline{F}(y-x) - \overline{F}(y)(\overline{F}(x))^{-1}, 0<x<y<\infty$

(2.4.33)

Since $F \in C_1$, therefore for (2.4.33) to be true, we must have

$$H_1(x,y) = 0 \tag{2.4.34}$$

for almost all x, $0 < x < y < \infty$.

Now $H_1(x,y) = 0$ for almost all x, $0 < x < y < \infty$, implies

$$\overline{F}(y-x)\overline{F}(x) = \overline{F}(y) \tag{2.4.35}$$

for almost all x, $0 < x < y < \infty$.

The only continuous solution of (2.4.35) with the boundary conditions $\overline{F}(0) = 1$ and $\overline{F}(\infty) = 0$, is

$$\overline{F}(x) = e^{-x\sigma^{-1}} \tag{2.4.36}$$

where σ is an arbitrary positive number.

Remark 2.4.1. The theorem 2.4.7 can be used to obtain the following known results of a two parameter exponential distribution ($\overline{F}(x) = \exp\{-\sigma^{-1}(x-\mu)\}$).

$E(X_{U(m)}) = \mu + m\sigma$

$Var(X_{U(m)}) = m\sigma^2$

$Cov(X_{U(m)}, X_{U(n)}) = m\sigma^2$, $m < n$.

Theorem 2.4.8.

Let $X_1,...,X_m,...$ be independent and identically distributed random variables with probability density function $f(x)$, $x \geq 0$ and m is an integer valued random variable independent of X's and $P(m = k) = p(1-p)^{k-1}$, $k = 1, 2, ...$ and $0 < p < 1$. Then the following two properties are equivalent:

(a) X's are distributed as $E(0,\sigma)$, where σ is a positive real number,

Exponential Distribution

(b) $p \sum_{j=1}^{m} X_j \stackrel{d}{=} X_{U(n)} - X_{U(n-1)}$, for some fixed n, $n \geq 2$, $X_j \in c_2$
and $X_j \in c_2$ and $E(X_j) < \infty$.

Proof.

It is easy to verify (a) $\Rightarrow$ (b). We will prove here that (b) $\Rightarrow$ (a).
Let $\phi_1(t)$ be the characteristic function of $X_{U(n)} - X_{U(n-1)}$, then

$$\phi_1(t) = \int_0^\infty \int_0^\infty \frac{1}{\Gamma(n)} e^{itx} (R(u))^{n-1} r(u) f(u+x) du dx$$

$$= 1 + it \int_0^\infty \int_0^\infty \frac{1}{\Gamma(n)} e^{itx} (R(u))^{n-1} r(u) \overline{F}(u+x) du dx$$

n be written as

$$\Phi_2(t) = E(e^{itp \sum_{j=1}^{m} X_j})$$

$$= \sum_{k=1}^{\infty} (\Phi(tp))^k p(1-p)^{k-1},$$

where $\Phi(t)$ is the characteristic function of X's.

$$= p(\Phi(tp))(1 - q\Phi(pt))^{-1}, q = 1-p.$$

(2.4.38)

Equating (2.4.37) and (2.4.48), we get on simplification

$$\frac{\Phi(pt)-1}{1-q\Phi(pt)} \frac{1}{it} = \int_0^\infty \int_0^\infty \frac{1}{\Gamma(n)} e^{itx} (R(u))^{n-1} r(u) \overline{F}(u+x) du dx$$

(2.4.39)

Now taking limit of both sides of (2.4.50) as t goes to zero, we have

$$\frac{\Phi'(0)}{i} = \int_0^\infty \int_0^\infty \frac{1}{\Gamma(n)} (R(u))^{n-1} r(u) \overline{F}(u+x) du dx .$$

(2.4.40)

Writing

$$\frac{\Phi'(0)}{i} = \int_0^\infty \overline{F}(x)dx, \text{ we get from}(2.4.40)$$

$$\int_0^\infty \int_0^\infty (R(u))^{n-1} r(u) \{\overline{F}(u+x) - \overline{F}(u)\overline{F}(x)\} du dx = 0 \quad (2.4.41)$$

Since X's belongs to C_1, we must have

$$\overline{F}(u+x) = \overline{F}(x)\overline{F}(u) \quad (2.4.42)$$

for almost all x, u, $0 < u, x < \infty$.

The only continuous solution of (2.4.42) with the boundary condition $\overline{F}(0) = 1$ and $\overline{F}(\infty) = 0$, is

$$\overline{F}(x) = \exp(-x\,\sigma^{-1}), x \geq 0 \quad (2.4.43)$$

where σ is an arbitrary positive real number.

(c) Under the Assumption of Finite Moments.

We will proof the following characterization theorem under the assumption of the finite first moment.

Theorem 2.4.9.

Let X_n, $n \geq 1$ be a sequence of independent and identically distributed non-negative random variables with absolutely continuous distribution function F(x) and the corresponding density function f(x). Let a = inf$\{x|F(x) > 0\}$ = 0, F(x) < 1 for all x > 0. If F belongs to the class C_1 and $E(X_k)$, $k \geq 1$ is finite., then $X_k \in E(0,\sigma)$, if and only if for some fixed n, n > 1, $E(Z_n) = E(X_k)$.

Proof.

If $X_k \in E(o,\sigma)$, then it can easily be seen that $E(Z_n) = E(X_k)$. Suppose that for some foxed n, n > 1, $E(Z_n) = E(X_k)$, then we must have

Exponential Distribution

$$\int_0^\infty \int_0^\infty \frac{(R(u))^{n-1}}{\Gamma(n)} f(u)(\overline{F}(u))^{-1} du\, dx = \int_0^\infty \overline{F}(u) du \qquad (2.4.44)$$

But we know

$$\Gamma(n) = \int_0^\infty (R(u))^{n-1} f(u) du \qquad (2.4.45)$$

Substituting (2.4.45) in (2.4.44) and simplifying, we have

$$\overline{F}(u+z) = \overline{F}(u)\overline{F}(z) \qquad (2.4.46)$$

for all u,z, $0 < u,z < \infty$.

Now the continuous solution of (2.4.46) with the boundary conditions $\overline{F}(0) = 1$ and $F(\infty) = 0$, is $\overline{F}(x) = \exp\{-x\sigma^{-1}\}$, where σ is an arbitrary real number.

The following theorem uses the property of homocedasticity but does not use NBU or NWU property.

Theorem 2.4.10.

Let x_n, $n \geq 1$ be a sequence of independent and identically distributed random variables with common distribution function F which is absolutely continuous and $\inf\{ x| F(x) > 0\} = 0$ and $E(X_n^2) < \infty$. Then X_k, $k \geq 1$ has the exponential distribution if and only if $\text{var}(Z_n| X_{U(n)} = x) = b$ for all x, where b is a positive constant independent of x and $Z_n = X_{U(n+1)} - X_{U(n)}$.

Proof.

The 'if' condition is easy to establish.
We will prove here the ' only if ' condition.

$b = E(Z_n^2| X_{U(n)}) = x) - [E(Z_n | X_{U(n)} = x)]^2. \qquad (2.4.47)$

$E(Z_n^2| X_{U(n)} = x)$

$= \int_0^\infty z^2 (\overline{F}(x))^{-1} d\overline{F}(z+x) = 2 \int_0^\infty z(\overline{F}(x))^{-1} \overline{F}(z+x) dz$

$\qquad (2.4.48)$

and

$E(Z_n | X_{U(n)} = x)$
$$= \int_0^\infty z(\overline{F}(x))^{-1} d\overline{F}(z+x) = \int_0^\infty (\overline{F}(x))^{-1} \overline{F}(z+x) dz \qquad (2.4.49)$$

Substituting $G(x) = \int_0^\infty z\overline{F}(z+x)dz$ and denoting $G^{(r)}(x)$ as the r th derivative of $G(x)$, we have on simplification

$$G^{(1)}(x) = \int_0^\infty \overline{F}(z+x)dz, G^{(2)}(x) = \overline{F}(x) \text{ and } G^{(3)}(x) = -f(x).$$

Writing (2.4.48) and (2.4.49) in terms of $G(x)$ and $G^{(r)}(x)$, we get from (2.4.46),

$$2G(x)\{G^{(r)}(x)\}^{-1} - \{G^{(1)}(x)(G^{(2)}(x))^{-1}\}^2 = b \qquad (2.4.50)$$
for all $x > 0$.

Differentiating (2.4.50) with respect to x and simplifying, we obtain

$$2G^{(3)}(x)\{G^{(2)}(x)\}^{-3} - [(G^{(1)}(x))^2 - G(x)G^{(2)}(x)] = 0 \qquad (2.4.51)$$

Since $G^{(3)}(x) \neq 0$ for all $x > 0$, we must have

$$\{G^{(1)}(x)\}^2 - G(x)G^{(2)}(x) = 0, \qquad (2.4.52)$$

i.e.

$$\frac{d}{dx}\{G(x)(G^{(1)}(x))^{-1}\} = 0, \text{ for all } x > 0. \qquad (2.4.53)$$

The solution of (2.4.53) is

$$G(x) = a e^{-cx}, x > 0 \qquad (2.4.54)$$

where a and c are arbitrary constants.
Hence

$$\overline{F}(x) = G^{(2)}(x) = ac^2 e^{-cx}, x > 0.$$

Since $F(x)$ is a distribution function with $F(0) = 0$, it follows that

$$\overline{F}(x) = e^{-x\sigma^{-1}},$$ where σ is an arbitrary real positive number.

The following Theorem gives a characterization of the exponential distribution using the hazard rate.

Theorem 2.4.11.

Let $\{X_n, n \geq 1\}$ be a sequence of independent and identically distributed non negative random variables with continuous distribution

Exponential Distribution

function F(x) and the corresponding density function f(x). Let a = inf{x|F(x) = 0} = 0, F(x) < 1 for all x > 0 and F belongs to class C_2. Then $X_k \in E(0,\sigma)$, if and only if for some fixed n, $n \geq 1$, the hazard rate r_1 of $Z_{n+1,n}$ = the hazard rate r of X_k, where $Z_{n+1,n} = X_{U(n+1)} - X_{U(n)}$.

Proof.

If $X_k \in E(0,\sigma)$, then it can easily be shown that $r_1 = r$. Suppose $r_1 = r$. Using (2.1.2), we can write the joint pdf of $X_{U(n+1)}$ and $X_{U(n)}$ as

$$f_{n+1,n}(x,y) = \frac{1}{\Gamma(n)} \{R(x)\}^{n-1} r(x) f(y), \quad 0 < x < y < \infty,$$
$$= 0, \text{ otherwise.}$$

Substituting $Z_{n+1,n} = X_{U(n+1)} - X_{U(n)}$ and $V_n = X_{U(n)}$, we get the pdf of $Z_{n+1,n}$ and V_n as

$$f_1^*(z,u) = \frac{1}{\Gamma(n)} \{R(u)\}^{n-1} r(u) f(u+z) \quad (2.4.55)$$
$$\text{for } 0 < u,z < \infty,$$
$$= 0, \text{ otherwise.}$$

Thus by (2.4.55), we can write

$$r_1(z) = \frac{\int_0^\infty (R(u))^{n-1} r(u) f(u+z) du}{\int_0^\infty (R(u))^{n-1} r(u) \overline{F}(u+z) du} \quad (2.4.56)$$

for all $z \geq 0$. Since $r_1(z) = r(z)$ for all z, we must have

$$\frac{\int_0^\infty (R(u))^{n-1} r(u) f(u+z) du}{\int_0^\infty (R(u))^{n-1} r(u) \overline{F}(u+z) du} = \frac{f(z)}{\overline{F}(z)} \quad (2.4.57)$$

for all $z \geq 0$. Now simplifying (2,4.57), we have

$$\int_0^\infty (R(u))^{n-1} r(u) \overline{F}(z) \overline{F}(u+z) \{r(u+z) - r(z)\} du = 0 \quad (2.4.58)$$

for all $z \geq 0$. Since F belongs to class C_2, for (2.4.58) to be true, we must have
$$r(u+z) = r(u) \qquad (2.4.59)$$
for all $z \geq 0$ and almost al u, $u \geq 0$. Hence $X_k \in E(0,\sigma)$.

The exponential distribution can also be characterized using lower record values. The following result is due to Ahsanullah and Kirmani (1991).

Suppose $\{X_n, n \geq 1\}$ be a sequence of i.i.d. random variables with cdf F and $F(0) = 0$. Let N is the rv defined as $N = \min\{i > 1: X_i < X_1\}$. It can easily be shown that $P(N = n) = \dfrac{1}{n(n-1)}$, $n = 2, 3, \ldots$

Theorem 2.4.12.

The rvs NX_N and X_1 are identically distributed iff $F(x) = \exp(-\lambda x)$, $x > 0$, for some $\lambda > 0$.

In proving the theorem, we need the following Lemma.

Lemma 2.2.1.

$$P(NX_N > x) = \sum_{n=2}^{\infty} \dfrac{1}{n(n-1)} (\overline{F}(\dfrac{x}{n}))^n, \text{ for all } x \geq 0.$$

Proof.

$$P(NX_N > x) = \sum_{n=2}^{\infty} P(NX_N > x, N > n)$$

$$= \sum_{n=2}^{\infty} \int_{-\infty}^{\infty} P(nX_n > x, X_n < y, X_i > y \text{ for all } i = 2, 3, \ldots, n-1 | X_1 = y) \, dF(y)$$

$$= \sum_{n=2}^{\infty} \int_{x}^{\infty} P(\dfrac{x}{n} < x_n < y)(P(x_i > y))^{n-2} dF(y)$$

$$= \sum_{n=2}^{\infty} \int_{\frac{x}{n}}^{\infty} \{\overline{F}(\tfrac{x}{n}) - \overline{F}(y)\} \{\overline{F}(y)\}^{n-2} dF(y)$$

$$= \sum_{n=2}^{\infty} [\{\overline{F}(\tfrac{x}{n})\} \frac{(\overline{F}(\tfrac{x}{n}))^{n-1}}{n-1} - \frac{(\overline{F}(\tfrac{x}{n}))^{n}}{n}]$$

$$= \sum_{n=2}^{\infty} \frac{1}{n(n-1)} [\overline{F}(\tfrac{x}{n})]^{n}.$$

Proof of the Theorem 2.4.12.

Define $u(x) = -\dfrac{\ln \overline{F}(x)}{x}$, $x > 0$; $u(0) = u(0+)$ and suppose that $NX_N \stackrel{d}{=} X_1$.
Then

$$\sum_{n=2}^{\infty} \frac{1}{n(n-1)} e^{-xu(x/n)} = e^{-xu(x)}, \quad x > 0. \tag{2.4.60}$$

We shall show that the above holds iff $u(x)$ is a constant, i.e. given any $T > 0$

$$\min_{x \in [0,T]} u(x) = \max_{x \in [0,T]} U(x). \tag{2.4.61}$$

Let

$a_0 = \min_{x \in [0,T]} U(x), x_0 = \inf\{x \in [0,T] | u(x) = a_0\}$,

$a_1 = \max_{x \in [0,T]} U(x), x_1 = \inf\{x \in [0,T] | u(x) = a_1\}$.

It is obvious that (2.4.61) will be proved if we show that $x_0 = 0 = x_1$. By continuity of u, $x_0 \in [0,T]$ and $u(x_0) = a_0$. Hence

$$u(x_0) \leq u(x_0/n) \text{ for all } n \geq 1. \tag{2.4.62}$$

If equality holds for all $n \geq 2$, then $u(x_0) = u(0)$ which by definition of $x_0 = 0$. Suppose now that $x_0 > 0$ (so that $x_0/n \neq x_0$ for all n. Then, the strict inequality must hold for (2.4.62) for at least one value of $n > 1 \geq 2$. Now

$$e^{-x_0 u(x_0)} - \sum_{n=2}^{\infty} \frac{1}{n(n-1)} e^{-x_0 u(x_0/n)}$$

$$= \sum_{n=2}^{\infty} \frac{1}{n(n-1)} \{e^{-x_0 u(x_0)} - e^{-x_0 u(x_o/n)}\} > 0,$$

which contradicts(2.4.62). Therefore $x_0 = 0$. Similarly $x_1 = 0$. Thus $NX_N \underline{d} X_1 \Rightarrow u(x) \equiv$ constant. The converse can easily be verified.

Basak(1996) give a similar characterization based on k-records.

The result is given in the following theorem.

Theorem 2.4.13.

Suppose $\{X_n, n \geq 1\}$ be a sequence of i.i.d. random variables with cdf F with $F(0) = 0$.and $\lim_{x \to 0^+} \frac{F(x)}{x} = \lambda$, $\lambda > 0$. . If $(L(n,k) - k+1) X_{L(n,k)}$ and $X_{1,n}$, $k \geq 1$, are identically distributed, then X has the exponential distribution with $F(x) = \exp(-\lambda x)$..

Proof.

For any $-\infty < x_n < x_{n-1} < .. x_1 < \infty$ and $d(0) = 0$, $k = d(1) < d(2) < ... < d(n)$, we have
$P(X_{L(1,k)} \leq x_1, X_{L(2,k)} \leq x_2, ... X_{U(n,k)} \leq x_n$, $L(1,k) = k,$, $L(2,k) = d(2),...,$ $L(n,k) = d(n))$

$$= \int_{-\infty}^{x_1} ... \int_{-\infty}^{x_n} \{\prod_{r=1}^{n} (\overline{G}(w_r))^{d(r)-d(r-1)-1} g(w_1) g(w_2)....g(w_n)$$

$dw_1 dw_2 ... dw_n$, (2.4.63)

where $\overline{G}(x) = (\overline{F}(x))^k$ and $g(x) = -\frac{d}{dx}\overline{G}(x)$. The joint density function, $f_{(1,2,..,n),(1),(2),..(n)}(x_1,x_2,...x_n,d(1),d(2),..d(n))$, of the continuous random variables $X_{L(1,k)}, X_{L(2,k)},..., X_{L(n,k)}$ and the discrete record times

Exponential Distribution

L(1,k), L(2,k),..., L(n,k) is obtained by differentiating the above equation with respect to $x_1, x_2, ..x_n$. Thus

$f_{(1,2,..,n),(1),(2),..(n)}(x_1, x_2, ...x_n, d(1), d(2), ..d(n))$

$$= \prod_{r=1}^{n} (\overline{G}(w_r))^{d(r)-d(r-1)-1} g(w_1) g(w_2)....g(w_n)$$

for $-\infty < x_n < x_{n-1} < .. x_1 < \infty$ and $d(0) = 0$, $k = d(1) < d(2) < ... < d(n)$,

= 0, otherwise.

(2.4.64)

On integrating out and simplification, we obtain from (2.4.64) the joint density function of $X_{L(n,k))}$ and L(n,k) as

$$f(x, m_n) = \frac{|S(m_n - 1, n - 1)|}{\Gamma(m_n - k + 2)} (\overline{G}(x))^{m_n - k} g(x), \quad m_n \geq n-k+1$$

(2.4.65)

Let $U = (L(n,k) - k+1) X_{L(n,k)}$ and $M = L(n,k) - k+1$, then the probability density of U

$$f_U(x) = \sum_{m=n}^{\infty} \frac{|S(m-1, n-1)|}{\Gamma(m+1)} (\overline{G}(x/m))^{m-1} g(x/m), \quad m \geq n$$

(2.4.66)

On integrating (2.4.66) from x to ∞, we obtain

$$1 - F_U(x) = \sum_{m=n}^{\infty} \frac{|S(m-1, n-1)|}{\Gamma(m+1)} (\overline{G}(x/m))^{m}, \quad x \geq 0, m \geq n..$$

(2.4.67).

Since $U = (L(n,k) - k+1) X_{L(n,k)}$ and $X_{1,k}$, $k \geq 1$, are identically distributed, we must have

$$\sum_{m=n}^{\infty} \frac{|S(m-1, n-1)|}{\Gamma(m+1)} (\overline{G}(x/m))^{m} = \overline{G}(x) \quad (2.4.68)$$

for all $x \geq 0$.

The unique solution of the equation (2.4.64) with the conditions $F(0) = 0$. and $\lim_{x \to 0^+} \frac{F(x)}{x} = \lambda$ is

$$\overline{G}(x) = e^{-\lambda x/k}, \lambda > 0, k \geq 1 \text{ and } x \geq 0.$$

The following Theorem replaces the equality of distribution in Theorem (2.4.13) by the equality of expectation.

Theorem 2.4.14.

Suppose $\{X_n, n \geq 1\}$ be a sequence of i.i.d. random variables with cdf F with $F(0) = 0$. and $\lim_{x \to 0^+} \frac{F(x)}{x} = \lambda$, $\lambda > 0$. Further assume that $E(X_n) < \infty$. If $E((L(n,k) - k+1) X_{L(n,k)}) = E(X_{1,n})$ $k \geq 1$, then X_1 has the exponential distribution with $F(x) = \exp(-\lambda x)$..

Proof.

$E(L(n,k) - k+1) X_{L(n,)} =$

$$E(U) = \int_0^\infty \sum_{m=n}^\infty \frac{|S(m-1, n-1)|}{\Gamma(m+1)} (\vec{G}(x/m))^m \, dx,$$

by (2.4.67),

$$= \sum_{m=n}^\infty \frac{|S(m-1, n-1)|}{\Gamma(m+1)} \int_0^\infty (\vec{G}(x/m))^m \, dx$$

(2.4.68)

Now

$$E(X_{1,k}) = \int_0^\infty (\overline{G}(x)) \, dx$$

$$= = \sum_{m=n}^\infty \frac{|S(m-1, n-1)|}{\Gamma(m+1)} \int_0^\infty (\vec{G}(x))$$

(2.4.69).

Exponential Distribution

Equating (2.4.86) and (2.4.68) and following the proof of Theorem 2.4.13, the result can easily be established.

2.5. PREDICTION OF RECORD VALUES

We will predict the sth upper record value based on the first m record values for $s > m$.

Let $W' = (W_1, W_2, ..., W_m)$, where
$\sigma^2 W_i = Cov(X_{U(i)}, X_{U(s)}), i = 1, ..., m$ and $\alpha^* = \sigma^{-1} E(X_{U(s)} - \mu)$.

The best linear unbiased predictor of $X_{U(s)}$ is $\hat{X}_{U(s)}$, where

$$\hat{X}_{U(s)} = \hat{\mu} + \hat{\sigma}\alpha^* + W'V^{-1}(X - \hat{\mu}L - \hat{\sigma}\delta), \hat{X}_{U(s)}$$

$\hat{\mu}, \hat{\sigma}$ are the MVLUE of μ, σ respectively. It can be shown that $W'V^{-1}(X - \hat{\mu}L - \hat{\sigma}\delta) = 0$.

$$\hat{X}_{U(s)} = ((s-1)X_{U(m)} + (m-s)X_{U(1)})/(m-1) \quad (2.5.1)$$

$$E(\hat{X}_{U(s)}) = \mu + s\sigma$$

$$Var(\hat{X}_{U(s)}) = \sigma^2(m + s^2 - 2s)/(m-1).$$

$$MSE(\hat{X}_{U(s)}) = E(\hat{X}_{U(s)} - X_{U(s)})^2$$
$$= \sigma^2(s-m)(s-1)/(m-1).$$

Let $\tilde{X}_{U(s)}$ be the best linear invariant predictor of $X_{U(s)}$. Then it can be shown that

$$\tilde{X}_{U(s)} = \hat{X}_{U(s)} - C_{12}(1 + E_{22})^{-1}\hat{\sigma}, \quad (2.5.2)$$

where
$C_{12}\sigma^2 = Cov(\hat{\sigma}, (L - W'V^{-1}L)\hat{\mu} + (\alpha^* - W'V^{-1}\delta)\hat{\sigma})$
and $\sigma^2 E_{22} = Var(\hat{\sigma})$.

On simplification we get

$$\tilde{X}_{U(s)} = \frac{m-s}{m} X_{U(1)} + \frac{s}{m} X_{U(m)}$$

$$E(\widetilde{X}_{U(s)}) = \mu + \left(\frac{ms + m - s}{m}\right)\sigma$$

$$Var(\widetilde{X}_{U(s)}) = \sigma^2(m^2 + ms^2 - s^2)/m^2$$

$$MSE(\widetilde{X}_{U(s)}) = MSE(\hat{X}_{U(s)}) - \frac{(s-m)^2}{m(m-1)}\sigma^2$$

$$= \frac{s(s-m)}{m}.$$

It is well known that the best (unrestricted) least squares predictor $\widetilde{\widetilde{X}}$ of $X_{U(s)}$ is

$$\hat{\widetilde{X}}_{U(s)} = E\left(X_{U(s)} \mid X_{U(1)}, \ldots, X_{U(m)}\right) \qquad (2.5.3)$$
$$= X_{U(m)} + (s-m)\sigma..$$

But $\hat{\widetilde{X}}_{U(s)}$ depends on the unknown parameter σ. If we substitute the minimum variance linear unbiased estimate $\hat{\sigma}$ for σ, then $\hat{\widetilde{X}}_{U(s)}$ becomes equal to $\hat{X}_{U(s)}$. Now

$$E(\hat{\widetilde{X}}_{U(s)}) = \mu + s\sigma = E(X_{U(s)})$$
$$Var(\hat{\widetilde{X}}_{U(s)}) = m\sigma^2 \text{ and}$$
$$MSE(\hat{\widetilde{X}}) = E\left(\hat{\widetilde{X}}_{U(s)} - X_{U(s)}\right)^2 = (s-m)\sigma^2$$

By considering the mean square errors of $\hat{X}_{U(s)}, \widetilde{X}_{U(s)}$ and $\hat{\widetilde{X}}_{U(s)}$, it can be shown that

$$MSE(\hat{\widetilde{X}}) = E\left(\hat{\widetilde{X}}_{U(s)} - X_{U(s)}\right)^2 = (s-m)\sigma^2$$

2.6. LIMITING DISTRIBUTION OF RECORD VALUES

We have seen that for $\mu = 0$ and $\sigma = 1$, $E(X_{U(n)}) = n$ and $Var(X_{U(n)}) = n$. Hence

Exponential Distribution

$$P\left(\frac{X_{U(n)}-n}{\sqrt{n}} \le x\right) = P(X_{U(n)} \le n + x\sqrt{n})$$

$$= \int_{n+x\sqrt{n}}^{\infty} \frac{x^{n-1} e^{-x}}{\Gamma(n)} dx, \text{ by} \qquad (2.1.1).$$

$$= P_n(x), \text{ say.}$$

Let

$$\Phi(x) = \frac{1}{\sqrt{2\pi}} \int_{-\infty}^{x} e^{-\frac{t^2}{2}} dt.$$

The following table gives the values of $P_n(x)$ for various values of n, x and $\Phi(x)$

Table 2.6.1 Values of $P_n(x)$

N \ x	-2	-1	0	1	2
5	0.0002	0.1468	0.5575	0.8475	0.9590
10	0.0046	0.1534	0.5421	0.8486	0.9601
15	0.0098	0.1554	0.5343	0.8436	0.9653
25	0.0122	0.1568	0.5243	0.8427	0.9684
45	0.0142	0.1575	0.5198	0.8423	0.9698
$\Phi(x)$	0.0226	0.1587	0.5000	0.8413	0.9774

Thus for large n , $\Phi(x)$ is a good approximation of $P_n(x)$.
Suppose $X_{n,n} = \text{Max}(X_1, X_2, \ldots, X_n)$, then we know (see Ahsanullah and Nevzorov (2001)) that

$$P(X_{n,n} - \ln n \le x) \to \exp(-e^{-x}) \text{ as } n \to \infty, \text{ for all } -\infty < x < \infty.$$

Hence

$$P(X_{U(n)} - \ln L(n) \le x) \to \exp(-e^{-x}), \text{ as } n \to \infty,.$$

for all $-\infty < x < \infty$

Thus the asymptotic distributions of $X_{U(n)}$ from exponential distribution with random and nonrandom normalization are not same.

CHAPTER 3

GENERALIZED EXTREME VALUE DISTRIBUTIONS

3.0. INTRODUCTION

A random variable X is said to have the generalized extreme value distribution if its cumulative distribution function is of the following form:

$$F(x) = \exp[-\{1-\gamma\sigma^{-1}(x-\mu)\}^{1/\gamma}] \qquad (3.0.1)$$

where $\sigma > 0$, $\gamma \neq 0$ and

$$x < \mu + \sigma\gamma^{-1}, \text{ for } \gamma > 0$$
$$x > \mu + \sigma\gamma^{-1}, \text{ for } \gamma < 0. \qquad (3.0.2)$$

If $\gamma = 0$ then

$$F(x) = \exp[-\exp\{-(x-\mu)/\sigma\}], \sigma > 0, -\infty < x < \infty. \qquad (3.0.3)$$

We will write $X \in \text{GEV}(\mu,\sigma,\gamma)$ if X has the cdf as given in (3.0.1). Since

$$\lim_{\gamma \to 0}\{1-\gamma\sigma^{-1}(x-\mu)\}^{1/\gamma} = \exp\{-\sigma^{-1}(x-\mu)\}, \text{ we can take}$$

$$\lim_{\gamma \to 0} GEV(\mu,\sigma,\gamma) = GEV(\mu,\sigma,0).$$

The density function of GEV(μ,σ,γ) is

$$f(x) = \sigma^{-1}\{1-\gamma\sigma^{-1}(x-\mu)\}^{\frac{1-\gamma}{\gamma}} \exp[-\{1-\gamma\sigma^{-1}(x-\mu)\}^{1/\gamma}], \gamma \neq 0$$

$$x < 1/\gamma, \text{ for } \gamma > 0,$$

$$x > 1/\gamma, \text{ for } \gamma < 0,$$

and
$$f(x) = e^{-x}\exp(-e^{-x}), \text{ for } \gamma = 0, \text{ for all } x.$$

Figures 3.0.1 and 3.0.2 give the pdfs of GEV(0,1,1/2) and GEV(0,1,0).

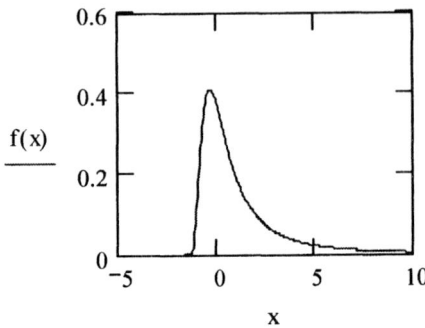

Figure 3.0.1. Pdf of GEV(0,1,1/2)

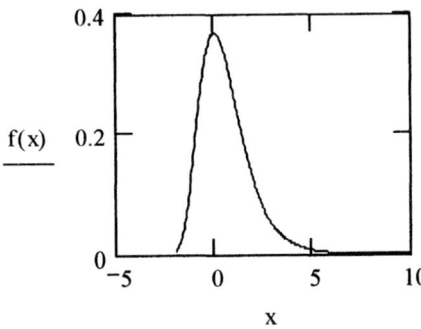

Figure 3.0.2. Pdf of GEV(0,1,0)

The extreme value distribution for $\gamma = 0$, is also known Gumbel distribution.

The largest order statistic $X_{n,n}$ when properly standardized tends to one of the following three types of limiting distributions as $n \to \infty$.

(1) Type 1: (Gumbel) $F(x) = \exp(-e^{-x})$, for all x,
(2) Type 2: (Frechet) $F(x) = \exp(-x^{-\delta})$, $x > 0$, $\delta > 0$
(3) Type 3: (Weibull) $F(x) = \exp(-(-x)^{\delta})$, $x<0$, $\delta >0$.

Since the smallest order statistic $X_{1,n} = Y_{n,n}$, where $Y = -X$, $X_{1,n}$ when properly standardized will also converge to one of the above three limiting distributions. Gumbel (1958) has given various applications of these distributions. The Type 1 (Gumbel distribution) is the limiting distribution of $X_{n,n}$ when F(x) is normal, log normal, logistic, gamma etc. The generalized extreme value distribution (3.0.1) has been discussed by Jenkinson (1955). It includes as special case the above three well known extreme value distributions.

The type 2 and type 3 distributions can be transformed to Type 1 distribution by the transformations $V_2 = \ln X$ and $V_3 = -\ln X$ respectively.

These distributions were originally introduced by Fisher and Tippet (1928). Extreme value distributions have been used in the analysis of data concerning floods, extreme sea levels and air pollution problems ; for details see Gumbel (1958), Horwitz (1980), Jenkinson (1955) and Roberts (1979).

For a given set of n observations, let $X_{1,n} < .... < X_{n,n}$ be the associated order statistics. Suppose that P{ a_n ($X_{n,n} - b_n$) < x } → G(x) as n → ∞ for some suitable constants a_n and b_n. Then it is known (see Leadbetter et al, 1983, p.33) that

$$P\{a_n(X_{n-m,n} - b_n) \leq x\} \xrightarrow{d} G(x) \sum_{s=0}^{m} \frac{[-\ln G(x)]^s}{\Gamma(s+1)}.$$

We have already seen that the right hand side of the above expression is the cdf of the m th lower record value from the distribution function G(x).

Thus the limiting distribution of the (n- m + 1)th order statistic (m finite) as n → ∞ from the generalized extreme value distribution is the same as the m th lower record value from the generalized extreme value distribution. In this chapter we will study the lower record values of GEV (μ,σ,γ).

3.1 Distributional Properties.

If $X \in GEV(\mu,\sigma,\gamma)$, then using (1.2.7) we can write for $\gamma \neq 0$, the pdf f(m) of the m th lower record value as

$$f_{(m)}(x) = \{1-\gamma\sigma^{-1}(x-\mu)\}^{(m-1)/\gamma} f_m^*(x) \qquad (3.1.1)$$

where

$$f_m^*(x) = \frac{\{1-\gamma\sigma^{-1}(x-\mu)\}^{(1-\gamma)/\gamma}}{\sigma(m-1)!} \exp\{-(1-\gamma\sigma^{-1}(x-\mu))\}^{1/\gamma}$$

and for $\gamma = 0$,

$$f_{(m)}(x) = \frac{e^{-m\sigma^{-1}(x-\mu)}}{\sigma(m-1)!} \exp\{-e^{-\sigma^{-1}(x-\mu)}\}, \; m = 1,2,. \qquad (3.1.2)$$

From (3.1.1) and (3.1.2) it can be shown that

$$X_{L(m)} \stackrel{d}{=} \mu + \sigma\gamma^{-1}\{1 - (W_1 + \cdots + W_m)^\gamma\}, \text{ for } \gamma \neq 0,$$

$$(3.1.3)$$

$$X_{L(m)} \stackrel{d}{=} X - \sigma(W_1 + \frac{W_2}{2} + \cdots + \frac{W_{m-1}}{m-1}), \text{ for } \gamma = 0,$$

$$(3.1.4)$$

where $W_1, W_2,\ldots,W_m$ are independently distributed as exponential random variables with unit mean and $\stackrel{d}{=}$ .denotes the equality in distribution. It can easily be shown that

$$E(X_{L(m)}) = \mu + \sigma\gamma^{-1} \cdot \{1 - \Gamma(m+\gamma)/\Gamma(m)\}.$$

$$\text{Var}(X_{L(m)})$$
$$= \sigma^2\gamma^{-2}[E(W_1 + \cdots + W_m)^{2\gamma} - \{E(W_1 + \cdots + W_m)^\gamma\}^2]$$
$$= \sigma^2\gamma^{-2}[\frac{\Gamma(m+2\gamma)}{\Gamma(m)} - \{\frac{\Gamma(m+\gamma)}{\Gamma(m)}\}^2].$$

For r < m

$$\gamma^2 \sigma^{-2} \text{Cov}(X_{L(r)}, X_{L(m)}) =$$

$$E\{(\sum_{j=1}^{r} W_j)^\gamma (\sum_{j=1}^{m} W_j)^\gamma - E(\sum_{j=1}^{r} W_j)^\gamma E(\sum_{j=1}^{m} W_j)^\gamma$$

$$= \int_0^\infty \int_0^\infty u^\gamma (u+v)^\gamma \frac{e^{-u} u^{r-1}}{\Gamma(r)} \frac{e^{-v} v^{m-r-1}}{\Gamma(m-r)} du\, dv$$

$$= \frac{\Gamma(r+\gamma)\Gamma(r+2\gamma)}{\Gamma(r)\Gamma(r+\gamma)} - \frac{\Gamma(r+\gamma)\Gamma(m+\gamma)}{\Gamma(r)\Gamma(m)},$$

since u and v are independent. We can write for r <m

$$\text{Cov}\{X_{L(r)}, X_{L(m)}\} = \sigma_o^2\, a_r\, b_m,$$

where

$$a_r = \frac{\Gamma(r+\gamma)}{\Gamma(r)}, \quad b_m = \frac{\Gamma(m+2\gamma)}{\Gamma(m+\gamma)} - \frac{\Gamma(m+\gamma)}{\Gamma(m)} \text{ and } \sigma_o^2 = \frac{\sigma^2}{\gamma^2}.$$

Using (3.1.4), we obtain for γ = 0,

$$E(X_{L(r)}) = \mu + \upsilon_r^* \sigma$$

$$\text{Var}(X_{L(m)}) = \sigma^2 V_{r,r}^*, r = 1, 2, \ldots$$

$$\text{Cov}(X_{L(r)}, X_{L(m)}) = \text{Var}(X_{L(m)}), r < m,$$

with

$$\upsilon_1^* = \upsilon$$

$$\upsilon_j^* = \upsilon_{j-1}^* - (j-1)^{-1}, j \geq 2,$$

$$V_{1,1}^* = \pi^2/6,$$

$$\ldots\ldots\ldots\ldots\ldots\ldots\ldots$$

$$V_{j,j}^* = V_{j-1,j-1}^* - (j-1)^{-2}, j \geq 2$$

Here υ (=0.57722..) is the Euler's constant.

For $X \in$ GEV $(\mu,\sigma,0)$, the joint pdf of $Y = H(X_{L(m+1)}) / H(X_{L(m)})$ is

$$f_Y^*(y) = m\, y^{m-1}, \quad 0 < y < \infty. \tag{3.1.5}$$

Thus $(Y)^m$ is distributed as uniform over the interval $(0,1)$. Consequently $m[-\ln H(X_{L(m)}) + \ln H(X_{L(m+1)})]$ is distributed as exponential distribution with mean unity. Since $-\ln H(x) = \dfrac{x - \mu}{\sigma}$, we have $m[X_{L(m)} - X_{L(m+1)}]$ is $E(0,\sigma)$.

Tables 3.1.1 and 3.1.2 give the values of $E(X_{L(n)})$ and $Var(X_{L(n)})$ for some selected values of n and γ.

Table 3.1.1. Expected Values of $X_{L(n)}$

n\γ	0	0.5	1.0	1.5
5	-1.5061	-2.3619	-4.0000	-7.3301
10	-2.2518	-4.2460	-9.0000	-21.1944
15	-2.6743	5.6817	-14.0000	-39.0221
20	-2.9705	-6.8886	-19.0000	-60.0718
25	-3.1987	-7.9501	-24.0000	-83.9094
30	-3.3844	-8.9089	-29.0000	-110.2405

Table 3.1.2. Variances of $X_{L(n)}$

N\γ	γ = 0	γ = 0.5	γ = 1.0	γ = 1.5
5	0.2213	0.9738	5.0000	29.3843
10	0.1052	0.9872	10.0000	108.7898
15	0.0689	0.9915	15.0000	238.1350
20	0.0513	0.9937	20.0000	417.5101
25	0.4080	0.9950	25.0000	646.8852
30	0.0339	0.9958	30.0000	926.2602

3.2. RECURRENCE RELATION BETWEEN MOMENTS

We will derive the recurrence relation for the moments of standardized extreme value distribution, GEV(0,1, γ). The distribution function of the standard generalized extreme value distribution can be written as

$$F(x) = e^{-\{1-\gamma x\}^{1/\gamma}}, x < 1/\gamma, \text{ when } \gamma > 0$$
$$x > 1/\gamma, \text{ when } \gamma < 0$$

and

$$F(x) = e^{-e^{-x}}, -\infty < x < \infty, \text{ when } \gamma = 0$$

The corresponding pdfs are

$$f(x) = e^{-\{1-\gamma x\}^{1/\gamma}} \cdot \{1-\gamma x\}^{\frac{1}{\gamma}-1}, \text{ when } x < 1/\gamma, \text{ when } \gamma > 0$$
$$x > 1/\gamma \text{ when } \gamma < 0$$

$$= e^{-e^{-x}} e^{-x}, -\infty < x < \infty, \gamma = 0$$

Note that for $\gamma \neq 0$

$$f(x) = F(x) \cdot \{1-\gamma x\}^{\frac{1}{\gamma}-1}$$

$$\Rightarrow \{1-\gamma x\} f(x) = F(x)\{1-\gamma x\}^{1/\gamma} = -F(x) \ln F(x) \quad (3.2.1)$$

(a) Let us consider the case. $\gamma \neq 0$

Let $X_{L(1)}, X_{L(2)}, \ldots$ be the sequence of lower record values from the above generalized extreme value distribution when $\gamma \neq 0$. Then, the pdf $f_n(x)$ of $X_{L(n)}$ (n>1) is given by

$$f_n(x) = \frac{1}{\Gamma(n)} \{-\ln F(x)\}^{n-1} f(x), x < 1/\gamma, \text{ when } \gamma > 0$$

$$, x > 1/\gamma, \text{ when } \gamma < 0$$

$$(3.2.2)$$

Theorem 3.2.1.

For n=1,2,.....and r = 0,1,2,.....,

$$E(X_{L(n+1)}^{r+1}) = \left\{1 + \frac{\gamma(r+1)}{n}\right\} E(X_{L(n)}^{r+1}) - \frac{r+1}{n} E(X_{L(n)}^{r})$$

(3.2.3)

Proof.

From (3.2.2), let us consider for n>1 and r=0,1,

$$E(X_{L(n)}^{r}) - \gamma E(X_{L(n)}^{r+1}) = \frac{1}{\Gamma(n)} \int_{-\infty}^{\infty} (x^r - \gamma x^{r+1})\{-\ln F(x)\}^{n-1} f(x) dx$$

$$= \frac{1}{\Gamma(n)} \int_{-\infty}^{\infty} x^r \{-\ln F(x)\}^n F(x) dx$$

Upon using (3.2.1). Upon integrating by parts, we obtain

$$E(X_{L(n)}^{r}) - \gamma E(X_{L(n)}^{r+1}) = \frac{1}{\Gamma(n)(r+1)} \int_{-\infty}^{\infty} nx^{r+1}\{-\ln F(x)\}^{n-1} f(x) dx$$

$$- \int_{-\infty}^{\infty} x^{r+1}\{-\ln F(x)\}^n f(x) dx$$

$$= \frac{n}{(r+1)} \left\{E(X_{L(n)}^{r+1}) - E(X_{L(n+1)}^{r+1})\right\}.$$

The relation in (3.2.3) is derived upon rewriting the above equation.

Remark 3.2.1. By starting with the first k raw moments of the generalized extreme value distribution, Theorem 1 will enable one to determine the first k raw moments of all the lower record values.

Corollary 3.2.1.

For n > 1,

$$E(X_{L(n+1)}) = \left(1 + \frac{\gamma}{n}\right) E(X_{L(n)}) - \frac{1}{n}$$

(3.2.4)

consequently, for n > 1

$$E(X_{L(n+1)}) = E(X_{L(1)}) \prod_{i=1}^{n}\left(1+\frac{\gamma}{i}\right) - \sum_{i=1}^{n-1}\prod_{j=i+1}^{n}\left(1+\frac{\gamma}{i}\right)\frac{1}{n}$$

(3.2.5)

Proof.

Relation in (3.2.4) follows from (3.2.3) by setting r = 0. Repeated application of (3.2.4) gives (3.2.5). The joint density function of $X_{L(m)}$ and $X_{L(n)}$, $1 < m < n$, is given by

$$f_{(m),(n)}(x,y)$$
$$= \frac{1}{\Gamma(m)\Gamma(n-m)}\{-\ln F(x)\}^{m-1}\frac{f(x)}{F(x)}\{-\ln F(y)+\ln F(x)\}^{n-m-1}f(y)$$

for x > y   (3.2.6)

Proceeding along the lines of Theorem 3.3.1, we can then prove the following relations for the product moments of record values.

Theorem 3.2.2

For m = 1,2,..... and r,s = 0,1,2,.....,

$$E(X_{L(m)}^{r+1} X_{L(m+1)}^{s}) = \frac{1}{m+\gamma(r+1)}\{(r+1)E(X_{L(m)}^{r} X_{L(m+1)}^{s}) + mE(X_{L(m+1)}^{r+s+1})\}$$

(3.2.7)

and for 1 < m < n-2 and r, s = 0,1,2,.....,

$$E(X_{L(m)}^{r+1} X_{L(n)}^{s}) = \frac{1}{m+\gamma(r+1)}\{(r+1)E(X_{L(m)}^{r} X_{L(n)}^{s}) + mE(X_{L(m+1)}^{r+1} X_{L(n)}^{s})\}$$

(3.2.8)

Corollary 3.2.2.

For m = 1,2,.....

$$E(X_{L(m)} X_{L(m+1)}) = \frac{1}{m+\gamma}\{E(X_{L(m+1)}) + mE(X_{L(m+1)}^2)\}$$ (3.2.9)

and for 1 < m < n-2

$$E(X_{L(m)} X_{L(m+1)}) = \frac{1}{m+\gamma} \{ E(X_{L(n)}) + m E(X_{L(m+1)} X_{L(n)}) \}$$

(3.2.10)

Proof.

Relations in (3.2.9) and (3.2.10) follow from Theorem 3.2.2 simply by setting r = 0 and s = 1.

Remark 3.2.2. The recurrence relations in (3.2.9) and (3.2.10) will enable one to determine the product moments (and hence the covariance) of all lower record values in a simple recursive manner.

Corollary 3.2.3.

Let $V_{m,n} = \text{Cov}(X_{L(m)}, X_{L(n)})$ and $V_{m,m} = \text{Var}(X_{L(m)})$, then for m = 1,2,...,

$$V_{m,m+1} = \frac{m}{m+\gamma} V_{m+1,m+1}$$

and for $1 < m < n-2$

$$V_{m,n} = \frac{(n-1)^{(n-m)}}{(n-1+\gamma)^{(n-m)}} V_{n,n}.$$

Here

$$r^{(-i)} = r(r-1)\ldots(r-i+1) \quad \text{for } i=1,2,\ldots$$
$$= 0 \quad \text{for } i = 0.$$

Proof.

The above relations follow simply from (3.2.9) and (3.2.10) upon using (3.2.3). It is also important to mention here that the method used in proving Theorems 3.2.2 and 3.2.3 can be extended to derive recurrence relations for product moments involving more than two record values.

(b) case γ = 0.
When γ = 0, the generalized extreme value distribution is also known as the Gumbel distribution or type I extreme value distribution. Let us consider the standard type I extreme value distribution with pdf

Generalized Extreme Value Distribution

$$f(x) = e^{-e^{-x}} e^{-x}, -\infty < x < \infty, \quad (3.2.11)$$

and cdf

$$F(x) = e^{-e^{-x}}, -\infty < x < \infty. \quad (3.2.12)$$

It is easy to see from (3.2.11) and (3.2.12) that for the standard type I extreme value distribution

$$f(x) = F(x) \{ -\ln F(x) \}, -\infty < x < \infty. \quad (3.2.13)$$

We can make use of this property of the type I extreme distribution to derive some recurrence relations for the single and product moments of lower record values.

Theorem 3.2.3.

For $n \geq 1$ and $r = 0, 1, 2, \ldots$,

$$E(X_{L(n+1)}^{r+1}) = E(X_{L(n)}^{r+1}) - \frac{r+1}{n} E(X_{L(n)}^r) \quad (3.2.14)$$

and, consequently, for $n \geq 1$ and $r = 0, 1, 2, \ldots$,

$$E(X_{L(n+1)}^{r+1}) = E(X_{L(1)}^{r+1}) - (r+1) \sum_{p=1}^{n} E(X_{L(r)}^r)/p \quad (3.2.15)$$

Proof.

The pdf $f_{(n)}(x)$ of $X_{L(n)}$, $n \geq 1$, is given by

$$f_{(n)}(x) = \frac{1}{\Gamma(n)} \{-\ln F(x)\}^{n-1} f(x), -\infty < x < \infty.$$

From (3.2.2), let us consider $n \geq 1$ and $r = 0, 1, 2, \ldots$,

$$E(X_{L(n)}^r) = \frac{1}{\Gamma(n)} \int_{-\infty}^{\infty} x^r \{-\ln F(x)\}^{n-1} f(x) dx$$

$$= \frac{1}{\Gamma(n)} \int_{-\infty}^{\infty} x^r \{-\ln F(x)\}^n F(x) dx \quad (\text{by } 3.2.13)$$

Upon integrating by parts treating x^r for integration and the rest of the integrand for differentiation. We simply obtain

$$E(X_{L(n)}^r) = \frac{1}{(r+1)\Gamma(n)} [n \int_{-\infty}^{\infty} x^{r+1} \{-\ln F(x)\}^{n-1} f(x) dx$$

$$-\int_{-\infty}^{\infty} x^{r+1}\{-\ln F(x)\}^n f(x)dx$$

$$= \frac{n}{r+1}\left[\int_{-\infty}^{\infty} \frac{x^{r+1}}{\Gamma(n)}\{-\ln F(x)\}^{n-1} f(x)dx\right.$$

$$\left. -\int_{-\infty}^{\infty} \frac{x^{r+1}}{\Gamma(n+1)}\{-\ln F(x)\}^{n-1} f(x)dx\right.$$

$$= \frac{n}{r+1}\left\{ E(X_{L(n)}^{r+1}) - E(X_{L(n+1)}^{r+1}) \right\}$$

Upon rewriting the above equation, we derive the recurrence relation in (3.2.14). By repeatedly applying (3.2.14), we obtain (3.2.15). Substituting r = 0 in Theorem (3.2.3), we obtain
$E(X_{L(n+1)}) = E(X_{L(n)}) - 1/n$ and

$$E(X_{L(n+1)}) = E(X_{L(m)}) - \sum_{p=m}^{n} p^{-1}.$$

Using the relation (3.2.13), we can easily proof the following Theorem.

Theorem 3.2.4.

For $m \geq 1$ and $r,s = 0,1,2,\ldots$,

$$E(X_{L(m)}^{r+1} X_{L(n)}^{s}) = E(X_{L(m+1)}^{r+s+1}) + \frac{r+1}{m} E(X_{L(m)}^{r} X_{L(m+1)}^{s}); \quad (3.2.16)$$

for $1 \leq m \leq n-2$ and $r,s = 0,1,2,\ldots$,

$$E(X_{L(m)}^{r+1} X_{L(n)}^{s}) = E(X_{L(m+1)}^{r+1} X_{L(n)}^{s}) + \frac{r+1}{m} E(X_{L(m)}^{r} X_{L(n)}^{s})$$
$$(3.2.17)$$

Using Theorem 3.2.3 and Theorem 3.2.4, it can be shown that

$$\text{Cov}(X_{L(n)}, X_{L(m)}) = E(X_{L(n)}, X_{L(m)}) - E(X_{L(n)}) E(X_{L(m)})$$
$$=$$
$$E(X_{L(n)}^2) + E(X_{L(n)})\sum_{pm}^{n-1} \frac{1}{p} - E(X_{L(n)})\{E(X_{L(n)}) + \sum_{p=m}^{n-1} \frac{1}{p}\}$$

$$= \text{Var}(X_{L(m)})$$

3.3. ESTIMATION OF PARAMETERS

(a) Estimation of μ and σ for known γ

3.3.1. MINIMUM VARIANCE LINEAR UNBIASED ESTIMATES (MVLUE)

The following theorem gives the minimum variance linear unbiased estimators of μ and σ when γ is known.

Theorem 3.3.1.1.

Suppose $\gamma \neq 0$. Then the MVLUE $\hat{\mu}$ and $\hat{\sigma}_o$ of μ and σ_o respectively, based on the observed m record values $r_1, r_2, \ldots, r_m$ are:

$$\hat{\mu} = D^{-1}\{r_m(1'V^{-1}\alpha) - \alpha_m 1'V^{-1}r\}$$

where

$$\hat{\sigma}_o = -D^{-1}\{r_m(1'V^{-1}1) - 1'V^{-1}r\}$$

$$D = \Gamma(m+k)\{\frac{1'V^{-1}1}{\Gamma(m)} - \frac{1}{b_m}\}, V = \{V^{ij}\},$$

$$V^{11} = \frac{(1+\gamma)^2}{\gamma^2}\frac{1}{\Gamma(1+2\gamma)}, V^{mm} = \frac{b_{m-1}}{b_m}\frac{m-1+\gamma}{\gamma^2}\cdot\frac{\Gamma(m)}{\Gamma(m-1+\gamma)}$$

$$V^{ii} = \frac{\Gamma(i)}{\Gamma(i+2\gamma)}\cdot\frac{1}{\gamma^2}\{(i+\gamma)^2+(i-1)(i-1+2\gamma)\}, i=2,\ldots,m-1,$$

$$V^{ij} = V^{ji} = -\frac{i+\gamma}{\gamma^2}\frac{\Gamma(i+1)}{\Gamma(i+2\gamma)}, j=i+1, i=1,\ldots,m-1$$

and

$V^{ij} = 0$, if $|i - j| > 1$, here

$1' = (1,\ldots,1), r' = (r_1,\ldots,r_m), \alpha' = (\alpha_1,\ldots,\alpha_m),$

$\alpha_i = 1 - \frac{\Gamma(i+\gamma)}{\Gamma(i)}, i = 1, 2, \ldots, m,$

$$Var(\hat{\mu}) = \sigma_o^2 \{b_m(1'V^{-1}1) - 2 + \frac{\Gamma(m+\gamma)}{\Gamma(m)}\}/D$$

$$Var(\hat{\sigma}_o) = \sigma_o^2 b_m \{1'V^{-1}1\}/D$$

and

$$Cov(\hat{\mu}, \hat{\sigma}_o) = -\sigma_o^2 \{b_m(1'V^{-1}1) - 1\}/D.$$

Proof:
Let $R = (X_{L(1)}, ..., X_{L(m)})$. Then we can write
$$E(R) = \mu \underline{1} + \sigma_0 \alpha$$
$$Var(R) = \sigma_o^2 V,$$
where

$$\alpha' = (\alpha_1, ..., \alpha_m), \quad \alpha_i = 1 - \frac{\Gamma(i+\gamma)}{\Gamma(i)},$$

$\underline{1}' = (1, ..., 1)$, $V = \{V_{ij}\}$, $V_{ij} = a_i b_j$, $1 \le i, j \le m$

, $a_i = \frac{\Gamma(i+\gamma)}{\Gamma(i)}, b_i = \frac{\Gamma(i+2\gamma)}{\Gamma(i+\gamma)} - \frac{\Gamma(i+\gamma)}{\Gamma(i)}$ and $\sigma_0^2 = \frac{\sigma^2}{\gamma^2}$.

Let $V^{-1} = \{V^{ij}\}$. Then

$$V^{11} = \frac{a_2}{a_1(a_2 b_1 - a_1 b_2)} = \frac{1}{\gamma^2} \frac{(1+\gamma)^2}{\Gamma(1+2\gamma)}$$

$$V^{ii} = \frac{a_{i+1} b_{i-1} - a_{i-1} b_{i+1}}{(a_i b_{i-1} - a_{i-1} b_i)(a_{i+1} b_i - a_i b_{i+1})}$$

$$= \frac{\Gamma(i)}{\gamma^2 \Gamma(i+2\gamma)} \{(i+\gamma)^2 + (i-1)(i-1+2\gamma)\}, i = 2, ..., m-1$$

$$V^{mm} = \frac{b_{m-1}}{b_m} \frac{1}{a_m b_{m-1} - a_{m-1} b_m} = \frac{b_{m-1}}{b_m} \frac{m+1-\gamma}{\gamma^2} \frac{\Gamma(m)}{\Gamma(m-1+\gamma)},$$

$$V^{ij} = V^{ji} = -\frac{1}{a_{i+1} b_i - a_i b_{i+1}} = -\frac{i+\gamma}{\gamma^2} \frac{\Gamma(i+1)}{\Gamma(i+2\gamma)}$$

$j = i+1, i = 1, 2, ..., m-1$,

and

Generalized Extreme Value Distribution

$V_{ij} = 0$, if $|i-j| > 1$.

It follows from the method of Lloyd (1952) that the MVLUE of μ and σ_0 based on the observed value r of R are, respectively,

$$\hat{\mu} = -\alpha' V^{-1} \{1\alpha' - \alpha 1'\} V^{-1} r / \Delta$$

$$\hat{\sigma}_0 = 1' V^{-1} \{1\alpha' - \alpha 1'\} V^{-1} r / \Delta$$

where

and

$$\Delta = \{1' V^{-1} 1\} \{\alpha' V^{-1} \alpha\} - \{1' V^{-1} \alpha\}^2$$

$$Var(\hat{\mu}) = \sigma_o^2 (\alpha' V^{-1} \alpha)/\Delta$$

$$Var(\hat{\sigma}_o) = \sigma_o^2 (1' V^{-1} 1)/\Delta$$

$$Cov(\hat{\mu}, \hat{\sigma}_o) = \sigma_o^2 (1' V^{-1} \alpha)/\Delta.$$

It can be shown that, upon simplification,

$$1' V^{-1} \alpha = 1' V^{-1} 1 - 1/b_m$$

$$\alpha' V^{-1} \alpha = 1' V^{-1} 1 - 1/b_m + a_m/b_m$$

$$\alpha' V^{-1} r = 1' V^{-1} r - r_m/b_m,$$

and

$$\Delta = \Gamma(m + \gamma) \left\{ \frac{1' V^{-1} 1}{b_m \Gamma(m)} \right\} - \frac{1}{b_m^2}.$$

The Theorem follows by using these relations.

Theorem 3.3.1.2

Suppose $\gamma = 0$. Then the MVLUE $\hat{\mu}, \hat{\sigma}$ of μ and σ respectively based on the observed record values $r_1, r_2, ..., r_m$ are

Suppose $\gamma = 0$. Then the MVLUE $\hat{\mu}, \hat{\sigma}$ of μ and σ respectively based on the observed record values $r_1, r_2, \ldots, r_m$ are:

$$\hat{\mu} = r_m - v_m^* \hat{\sigma}$$

$$\hat{\sigma} = (m-1)^{-1} \sum_{i=1}^{m-1} r_i - r_m$$

Their corresponding variances and covariance are

$$Var(\hat{\mu}) = \sigma^2 \{(v_m^*)^2 (m-1)^{-1} + V_{mm}^*\}$$

$$Var(\hat{\sigma}) = \sigma^2 / (m-1), \text{ and}$$

$$Cov(\hat{\mu}, \hat{\sigma}) = -\sigma^2 v_m^* / (m-1),$$

where

$$v_m^* = E(X_{L(m)}) \text{ and } v_{mm}^* = Var(X_{L(m)}).$$

Proof.

For $\gamma = 0$, we know (see section 3.1)

$$E(X_{L(r)}) = \mu + v_r^* \sigma$$

$$Var(X_{L(m)}) = \sigma^2 V_{r,r}^*, r = 1, 2, \ldots$$

$$Cov(X_{L(r)}, X_{L(m)}) = Var(X_{L(m)}), r < m,$$

with

$$v_1^* = v$$

$$v_j^* = v_{j-1}^* - (j-1)^{-1}, j \geq 2,$$

$$V_{1,1}^* = \frac{\pi^2}{6},$$

$$\ldots\ldots\ldots\ldots\ldots\ldots$$

$$V_{j,j}^* = V_{j-1,j-1}^* - (j-1)^{-2}, j \geq 2,$$

Generalized Extreme Value Distribution 117

where υ is the Euler's constant.

Let $\Omega = V^{-1} = (V^{ij})$, then

$$V^{ii} = i^2 + (i-1)^2, \ i = 1,2,..., m-1$$

$$V^{ij} = -\min(i^2, j^2), \ i \neq j, \ |i-j| = 1$$

$$= 0, \ \text{if} \ |i-j| > 1$$

$$V^{mm} = (m-1)^2 + 1/V^*_{mm}.$$

$$1' V^{-1} = (0,0,...,1/V^*_{mm})0$$

$$\alpha' V^{-1} = (1,1,...,\alpha_m / V^*_{mm} - (m-1)$$

$$\alpha' V^{-1} 1 = \alpha_m / V^*_{mm},$$

$$\alpha' V^{-1} \alpha = (\alpha_m)^2 / V^*_{mm} + m - 1$$

and

$$\Delta = (m-1) / V^*_{mm}.$$

Substituting these values in the expression of $\hat{\mu}$ and $\hat{\sigma}$, where

$$\hat{\mu} = -\alpha'^{/} V^{-1} \{1\alpha'^{/} - \alpha 1'^{/}\} V^{-1} r / \Delta$$

$$\hat{\sigma} = 1'^{/} V^{-1} \{1\alpha'^{/} - \alpha 1'^{/}\} V^{-1} r / \Delta$$

the results follow.

For example for m = 6, the MVLUE of μ and σ for the type I extreme value distribution is given by

$$\hat{\sigma} = .2 \ (r_1 + r_2 + r_3 + r_4 + r_5 \ ) - r_6$$

and

$$\hat{\mu} = 0.3412(r_1 + r_2 + r_3 + r_4 + r_5) - 0.7061 r_6$$

$Var(\hat{\mu})=0.7635\sigma^2$,
$Var(\hat{\sigma})=0.2000\sigma^2$, and
$Cov(\hat{\mu},\hat{\sigma})=-0.3412\sigma^2$.

3.3.2 BEST INVARIANT ESTIMATES (BLIE)

Theorem 3.3.2.1

Suppose $\gamma \neq 0$. Then the best linear invariant (best in the sense of minimum mean squared error and invariant with respect to the location parameter μ) estimators $\tilde{\mu}$ and $\tilde{\sigma}_o$ of μ and σ_0 are respectively

$$\tilde{\mu}=\hat{\mu}-c_1\hat{\sigma}_o,$$
$$\tilde{\sigma}=c_2\hat{\sigma}_o$$

where

$$c_1 = \frac{b_m\{1'V^{-1})b_m-1\}}{\{\Gamma(m+2\gamma)/\Gamma(m+\gamma)\}\{b_m(1'V^{-1}1)-1\}}$$

and

$$c_2 = \frac{D}{D+b_m(1'V^{-1}1)}.$$

Proof.

The BLIE $\tilde{\mu}$ and $\tilde{\sigma}_o$ of μ and σ_0 are :

$$\tilde{\mu}=\hat{\mu}-\hat{\sigma}_o\{E_{12}(1+E_{22})^{-1}\},$$

and

$$\tilde{\sigma}_o=\hat{\sigma}_o(1+E_{22})^{-1},$$

where

$$\sigma_o^2 \begin{pmatrix} E_{11} & E_{12} \\ E_{12} & E_{22} \end{pmatrix}$$

defines the covariance matrix of the MVLUEs of $\tilde{\mu}$ and $\tilde{\sigma}_o$. The mean squares errors (MSE) of $\tilde{\mu}$ and $\tilde{\sigma}_o$ are :

Generalized Extreme Value Distribution 119

$$MSE(\tilde{\mu}) = \sigma_o^2 \{E_{11} - E_{12}^2 (1+E_{22})^{-1}\},$$

$$MSE(\tilde{\sigma}_o) = \sigma_o^2 E_{22}(1+E_{22})^{-1},$$

$$E(\tilde{\mu}-\mu)(\tilde{\sigma}_o-\sigma) = \sigma_o^2 E_{12}(1+E_{22})^{-1}$$

Substituting the values of E_{11}, E_{12} and E_{22}, the results follow on simplification.

Theorem 3.3.2.2

Suppose $\gamma = 0$. Then the BLIE $\tilde{\mu}$ and $\tilde{\sigma}$ of μ and σ are:

$$\tilde{\mu} = \hat{\mu} - v_m^* \hat{\sigma}/m$$

$$\tilde{\sigma} = \hat{\sigma}(m-1)/m$$

and
$$MSE(\tilde{\mu}) = \sigma^2 [V_{mm}^* + (v_m^*)^2/m]$$

$$MSE(\tilde{\sigma}) = \sigma^2/m,$$

where $\hat{\mu}$ and $\hat{\sigma}$ are the MVLUE of μ and σ when $\gamma = 0$.

Proof.

We know

$$Var(\hat{\mu}) = \sigma^2 \{(v_m^*)^2 (m-1)^{-1} + V_{mm}^*\}$$

$$Var(\hat{\sigma}) = \sigma^2/(m-1), \text{ and}$$

$$Cov(\hat{\mu},\hat{\sigma}) = \sigma^2 v_m^*/(m-1),$$

Since $1 + E_{22} = \dfrac{m}{m-1}$, on simplification, we get the results. For m = 6,

$$\hat{\sigma} = \frac{1}{6}(r_1 + r_2 + r_3 + r_4 + r_5) - \frac{5}{6}r_6,$$

$$\hat{\mu} = 0.3981(r_1 + r_2 + r_3 + r_4 + r_5) - 0.9904 r_6$$

$$MSE(\tilde{\mu}) = 0.6665 \sigma^2$$

and

$$MSE(\tilde{\sigma}) = 0.1667 \sigma^2 .$$

3.3.3 Maximum Likelihood Estimates (MLE)

Suppose $\gamma \neq 0$. Then we can write the log likelihood function L based on the observed record values $r_1, r_2, \ldots, r_m$ are :

$$\ln L = \sum_{i=1}^{m-1} \ln\{\frac{f(r_i)}{F(r_i)}\} + \ln f(r_m) . \qquad (3.3.3.1)$$

Differentiating (3.4.3.1) with respect to μ and equating to zero, we get

$$(-1+\gamma^{-1}) \sum_{i=1}^{m} (\gamma \sigma^{-1})\{1 + \gamma \sigma^{-1}(r_i - \mu)\}^{-1}$$

$$- \sigma^{-1}\{1 + \gamma \sigma^{-1}(r_m - \mu)\}^{-1+\gamma^{-1}} = 0$$

$$(3.3.3.2)$$

Differentiating (3.3.3.1) with respect to σ and equating to zero, we get

$$- m\sigma^{-1} - (1+\gamma^{-1}) \sum_{i=1}^{m} \gamma (r_i - \mu) \sigma^{-2} \{1 + \gamma \sigma^{-1}(r_i - \mu)\}$$

$$- \gamma \sigma^{-2}(r_m - \mu)\{1 + \gamma \sigma^{-1}(r_m - \mu)\}^{-1+\gamma^{-1}} = 0.$$

$$(3.3.3.3)$$

From (3.3.3.2) and (3.3.3.3), we obtain the maximum likelihood estimators $\widehat{\mu}_\ell$ and $\widehat{\sigma}_\ell$ of μ and σ assuming γ as known are the solutions of the following equations.

$$\hat{\mu}_\ell = r_m - \frac{\sigma}{\gamma}(1-m^\gamma)$$

$$\sum_{i=1}^{m-1} \frac{1}{m^\gamma - \gamma(r_i - r_m)/\sigma} = \frac{m^{1-\gamma}}{1-\gamma} - m^{-\gamma} \qquad (3.3.3.4)$$

A closed form solution can be found if m = 2:

$$\hat{\sigma}_\ell = \frac{(1+\gamma)(r_1 - r_2)}{2^{\gamma+1}}$$

$$\hat{\mu}_\ell = r_2 - \frac{\hat{\sigma}_\ell}{\gamma}(1-2^\gamma) \qquad (3.3.3.5)$$

A closed form solution can also be found if $\gamma = 0$. In this case

$$\ln L = -m \ln\sigma - \sum_{i=1}^{m} \frac{r_i - \mu}{\sigma} - \exp\{-\sigma^{-1}(r_m - \mu)\}$$

$$\frac{\partial \ln L}{\partial \mu} = 0 \Rightarrow \frac{m}{\sigma} - \frac{1}{\sigma}\exp\{-\sigma^{-1}(r_m - \mu)\} \qquad (3.3.3.6)$$

$$\frac{\partial \ln L}{\partial \sigma} = 0 \Rightarrow -\frac{m}{\sigma} + \frac{1}{\sigma^2}\sum_{i=1}^{m}(r_i - \mu) - \frac{r_m - \mu}{\sigma^2}\exp\{-\sigma^{-1}(r_m - \mu)\} = 0$$

The solutions of the equations as given in (3.3.3.6) will give the MLE of μ and σ as

$$\hat{\sigma}_\ell^\circ = \bar{r} - r_m$$

$$\hat{\mu}_\ell^\circ = r_m + \hat{\sigma}_\ell^\circ \ln m \qquad (3.3.3.7)$$

where

$$\bar{r} = (r_1 + \ldots + r_m)/m.$$

It can easily be shown that

$$E(\hat{\sigma}_\ell^\circ) = \frac{m}{m-1}\sigma.$$

The bias in $\hat{\sigma}_\ell^\circ$ is $-\frac{\sigma^2}{m-1}$. The variance of $\hat{\sigma}_\ell^\circ$ is

$$Var(\hat{\sigma}_\ell^\circ) = \left(\frac{m}{m-1}\right)^2 \frac{\sigma^2}{m}.$$

$$E(\hat{\mu}_\ell^\circ) = \mu + \sigma(v_m^* + \frac{m-1}{m}(\ln m)).$$

Since $v_m^* = \upsilon - 1 - \frac{1}{2}\frac{1}{3} \cdots \frac{1}{m-1}$, the bias in $E(\hat{\mu}_\ell^\circ)$ is slight. We obtain on simplification, $Var(\hat{\mu}_\ell^\circ) = \sigma^2 [v_{r,r} + (\frac{m-1}{m})^2 \frac{(\ln m)^2}{m}].$

(b) Estimation of γ for known μ and σ.

We will assume without any loss of generality that $\mu = 0$ and $\sigma = 1$. A maximum likelihood estimator of γ can be obtained as the numerical value that maximizes by solving the equation (3.3.3.1) for known μ and σ For unknown μ and σ the , numerical selection of (γ,μ, σ) that maximizes (3.3.3.1) subject to the constraints (3.1.1) can be obtained.

Using the following two identities :

$$E\left(\sum_{i=1}^{m-1} Y_i\right) = m - 1 - \gamma E\left(\sum_{i=1}^{m-1} X_i\right)$$

where

$$Y_i = i(X_{L(i)} - X_{L(i+1)})$$

and

$(i+\gamma) E(X_{L(i)}) = 1 + i E(X_{L(i+1)}), i = 1, 2, \ldots, m-1,$

we can obtainr the moment estimators of γ as :

$$\gamma_1^\circ = \frac{1 - \bar{y}}{\bar{r}},$$

3.4. PREDICTION OF RECORD VALUES

Suppose $\gamma \neq 0$. Assume $s > m$ and let $U' = (U_1, \cdots, U_m)$, where $\sigma_o^2 U_i = Cov(X_{L(i)}, X_{L(s)})$, $i = 1, \ldots, m$.

The best linear unbiased predictor (BLUP) of $X_{L(s)}$ is
$$\hat{X}_{L(s)} = \hat{E}(X_{L(s)}) + U'V^{-1}(R - \hat{\mu}1 - \hat{\sigma}_o),$$
where
$$\hat{E}(X_{L(s)}) = \hat{\mu} + \alpha_s \hat{\sigma}_o, \alpha_s'' = \sigma_o^{-1} E(X_{L(s)} - \mu)$$
and $\hat{\mu}$ and $\hat{\sigma}_o$ are the MVLUE of μ and σ as given in Theorem 3.3.1.1.

Since $U' = bs(1' - \alpha')$,

$$\hat{T}_s = \hat{\mu} + \alpha_s \hat{\sigma}_o + b_s (1' - \alpha')V^{-1}(R - \hat{\mu}1 - \hat{\sigma}_o \alpha)$$
(3.4.1)
$$= \hat{\mu} + \alpha_s \hat{\sigma}_o + b_s b_m^{-1}(X_{L(m)} - \hat{\mu} - \alpha_m \hat{\sigma}_o)$$

Using

we have
$$Var(X_{L(s)}) = \sigma_o^2 a_s b_s, \text{ and } U'V^{-1}U = a_m b_m^{-1} b_s^2,$$

$$E(\hat{X}_{L(s)}) = \mu + \alpha_s \sigma_o, \text{ and}$$
$$MSE(\hat{X}_{L(S)}) = Var(X_{L(s)}) + \sigma_0^2 (c_{11}^* - U'V^{-1}U),$$
where

$$\sigma_o^2 c_{11}^* = Var\{(1 - U'V^{-1}1)\hat{\mu} + (\alpha_s - U'V^{-1}\alpha)\hat{\sigma}_o$$

$$= \sigma_o^2 \{(1 - b_s b_m^{-1})^2 E_{11} + (1 - b_s b_m^{-1})(\alpha_s b_m^{-1} \alpha_m)E_{11}$$
$$+ (\alpha_s - b_m^{-1} b_s \alpha_m)^2 E_{22}\}$$

For $\gamma = 0$, since $U'V^{-1}(r-\hat{\mu}1-\hat{\sigma}_o\alpha)=0$,

$$\hat{X}_{L(s)}=\hat{\mu}+\alpha_s\hat{\sigma}$$

and

$$Var(\hat{X}_{L(s)})=\sigma^2\{V_{mm}+(\alpha_s-\alpha_m)^2(m-1)^{-1}\}.$$

The best invariant predictor (best in the sense of minimum mean squares error and invariant with respect to location parameter μ) $\tilde{X}_{L(s)}$ of $X_{L(s)}$ is for $\gamma \neq 0$,

$$\tilde{X}_{L(s)}=\hat{X}_{L(s)} -c_{12}^*(1+E_{22})^{-1}\hat{\sigma}_o$$

where

$$\sigma_0^2 c_{12}^* = Cov\{\hat{\sigma}_o,(1-U'V^{-1}1)\hat{\mu}+(\alpha_s-U'V^{-1}\alpha)\hat{\sigma}_0\}$$

$$=\sigma_o^2\{(1-b_s b_m^{-1})E_{12}+(\alpha_s-b_s b_m^{-1}\alpha_m)E_{22}\}$$

Also,

$$MSE(\tilde{X}_{L(s)})=MSE(\hat{X}_{L(s)})-\sigma_o^2 E_{12}^2(1+E_{22}),$$

and hence

$$MSE(\tilde{X}_{L(s)})\leq MSE(\hat{X}_{L(s)})$$

For $\gamma = 0$, $\tilde{X}_{L(s)}$ reduces to

$$\tilde{X}_{L(s)}=X_{L(m)}+(m-1)m^{-1}(\upsilon_s^\bullet-\upsilon_m^\bullet)\hat{\sigma}_o.$$

3.5 CHARACTERIZATION

We have $S_{(m)} = m(X_{L(m)} - X_{L(m+1)})$, $m=1,2,\ldots$ as identically distributed exponential. random variables. Arnold and Villasenor (1997) raised the question whether the identical distribution of $S_{(1)}$ and $2 S_{(2)}$ as exponential with unit mean can characterize the Gumbel distribution. As an answer to this question, Al-Zaid and Ahsanullah (2003) proved the following theorem.

Theorem 3.5.1.

Let $\{X_j, j =1,....\}$ be a sequence of independent and identically distributed random variables with absolutely continuous (with respect to Lebesgue measure) distribution function $F(x)$. Then the following two statements are identical.

(a) $F(x) = e^{-e^{-x}}, \quad -\infty < x < \infty,$

(b) for a fixed m >1, the condition $X_{L(m)} \underset{=}{d} X_{L(m+1)} + \frac{W}{m}$, where
W is independent of $X_{L(n)}$ and $X_{L(n+1)}$ and $X_{L(n+1)}$ and is distributed as exponential with unit mean and $F(0) = e^{-1.}$.

Proof.

It is easy to show that (a) $\Rightarrow$ (b),
We will prove here that (b) $\Rightarrow$ (a).

Suppose that for a fixed m > 1, $X_{L(m)} \underset{=}{d} X_{L(m+1)} + \frac{W}{m}$, then

$$F_{(m)}(x) = \int_{-\infty}^{x} P(W \le m(x-y)) f_{(m+1)}(y) dy$$

$$= \int_{-\infty}^{x} [1 - e^{-m(x-y)}] f_{(m+1)}(y) dy$$

$$= F_{(m+1)}(x) - \int_{-\infty}^{x} e^{-m(x-y)} f_{(m+1)}(y) dy . \quad (3.5.1)$$

Thus

$$e^{mx}[F_{(m+1)}(x) - F_{(m)}(x)] = \int_{-\infty}^{x} e^{my} f_{(m+1)}(y) dy \quad (3.5.2)$$

Using the relation (1.1.7), we obtain

$$e^{mx} \frac{F(x) H^m(x)}{\Gamma(m+1)} = \int_{-\infty}^{x} e^{my} f_{(m+1)}(y) dy \quad (3.5.3)$$

Taking the derivatives of both sides of (3.5.3), we obtain

$$\frac{d}{dx}\left[e^{mx} \frac{H^m(x)}{\Gamma(m+1)} F(x) \right] = e^{mx} f_{(n+1)}(x) \quad (3.5.4)$$

This implies that

$$\frac{d}{dx}\left[e^{mx}\frac{H^m(x)}{\Gamma(m+1)}\right]F(x) = 0 \ . \tag{3.5.5}$$

Thus

$$\frac{d}{dx}\left[e^{mx}\frac{H^m(x)}{\Gamma(m+1)}\right] = 0 \ . \tag{3.5.6}$$

Hence

$$H(x) = c\ e^{-x},\ -\infty < x < \infty \tag{3.5.7}$$

Thus

$$F(x) = e^{-ce^{-x}}\ -\infty < x < \infty\ . \tag{3.5.8}$$

Since $F(x)$ is a distribution, assuming $F(0) = e^{-1}$, we obtain

$$F(x) = e^{-e^{-x}},\ -\infty < x < \infty. \tag{3.5.9}$$

Corollary 3.5.1. If for some fixed $m > 1$, $X_{U(m+1)} \stackrel{d}{=} X_{U(m)} + \frac{W}{m}$, then we get a characterization of the Gumbel distribution with $F(x) = 1 - e^{-e^x}$, $-\infty < x < \infty$.

Corollary 3.5.2. If $m = 1$, then relation $X_{U(2)} \stackrel{d}{=} X_{U(1)} + W$, will give a characterization of the exponential distribution.

Remark 3.5.1. The condition that any one of the statistics $m(X_{L(m)} - X_{L(m+1)})$, $m(X_{U(m+1)} - X_{U(m)})$, $(X_{L(m)} - X_{L(m+1)})$ or $(X_{U(m+1)} - X_{U(m)})$ is distributed as negative exponential do not characterize any distribution.

3.6. APPLICATIONS

Example 3.6.1

The following table (Table 3.6.1) shows the one hour mean concentration of SO_2 from Long Beach, California (taken from Roberts (1979)) from 1979 to 1974. Roberts(1979) fitted the Gumbel distribution $F(x) = \exp(-e^{-a(x-b)})$ to the annual maxima of the hourly concentration of

Generalized Extreme Value Distribution

SO$_2$. SO$_2$. He obtained by using complete data with a variant of the least squared method, the estimates $\hat{a}, \hat{b}$ of a and b as $\hat{a} = 0.081$ and $\hat{b} = 31.5$. In terms of our notation σ 1/a and μ=b. From the annual of the hourly concentration of SO$_2$, we obtain 47,41,32,27,20 and 18 as lower records values.

Table 3.6.1. Sulfur dioxide, 1-hour average concentration (pphm). Monthly and annual maxima.

YEAR	JAN	FEB	MAR	APR	MAY	JUN	JULY	AUG	SEP	OCT	NOV	DEC	MAX
1956	47	31	44	12	13	3	14	21	33	33	40	32	47
1957	22	19	20	32	20	23	18	16	13	14	41	25	41
1958	15	13	30	12	24	13	37	20	32	27	27	68	68
1959	20	32	20	15	3	6	8	15	17	15	29	20	32
1960	22	18	23	20	8	13	14	9	13	16	27	20	27
1981	25	20	20	16	10	10	8	10	12	16	14	43	43
1962	20	13	15	18	10	1	10	10	11	11	14	7	20
1963	12	16	27	21	2	7	4	4	15	19	18	18	27
1964	16	10	3	3	19	9	16	25	4	14	18	21	25
1965	16	18	9	14	8	10	18	18	14	12	12	14	18
1966	27	33	25	10	17	30	13	18	22	15	25	23	32
1967	30	40	32	10	8	7	8	26	10	40	18	17	40
1968	51	30	18	22	10	19	22	25	26	29	50	40	51
1969	37	13	55	14	9	10	13	17	33	13	15	44	55
1970	23	18	19	11	15	12	25	40	25	20	12	8	40
1971	22	26	20	28	10	15	20	55	38	41	26	25	55
1972	30	32	18	27	37	13	23	19	21	31	25	13	37
1973	10	8	8	12	11	16	25	16	11	28	10	23	28

For the estimations of the location and scale parameters, we will use the first six lower records i.e. m = 6. The minimum variance linear unbiased estimators of μ and σ are

$\hat{\sigma}$ = 0.2 (47 +41 + 32 + 27 + 20) - 18 = 15.4

$\hat{\mu}$ = 0.3412(47 + 41 + 32 + 27 +20) - 0.7061(18) = 44.3

The best linear invariance estimators of μ and σ are

$\tilde{\mu} = \hat{\mu} - v_m^* \hat{\sigma}/m = 48.7$

$\tilde{\sigma} = \hat{\sigma}(m-1)/m = 12.8$

The maximum likelihood estimators of μ and σ are

$\hat{\sigma}_\ell^\circ = \bar{r} - r_m = 12.8$

$\hat{\mu}_\ell^\circ = r_m + \hat{\sigma}_\ell^\circ \ln m = 51.7$

Example 3.6.2

We consider the progression of Olympic records since 1912 for the 100 meter women's free style swim (see Mellon (1988)). Table 3.5.2 gives the record values for each Olympics where a new record was set.

Table 3.6.2 Olympic Records: Women's 100 Meter Free style

Year	Records(times in seconds)
1912	79.80
1920	73.60
1924	72.20
1928	71.00
1932	66.80
1936	65.90
1952	65.50
1956	62.00
1960	61.20
1964	59.50
1972	58.89
1976	55.65
1980	54.79

Generalized Extreme Value Distribution

The generalized extreme value distribution was fitted to the record values shown in Table 3.6.1. Parameters μ and σ were estimated using both minimum variance linear unbiased and minimum variance linear invariance methods. Best linear invariant predictors of the next 5 lower records were calculated. The results are shown in Table 3.6.2. The BLIE appear to be somewhat superior to the MVLUE's in terms of the estimated mean square error and log liklihood. The best linear invariant predictor of the next record is 54.36 seconds, or 0.12 seconds below the record set by Jenny Thompson of United States in 1992 Olympic at Barcelonan, Spain.

$\gamma = 0.60$,
$\hat{\mu}=78.74, \hat{\sigma}=3.97$, log likelihood for MVLUE's = 78.33
$\hat{Var}(\hat{\mu})=0.78\sigma^2, \hat{Var}(\hat{\sigma})= 0.13\sigma^2$
$\tilde{\mu}=78.33, \tilde{\sigma}=3.51, \tilde{MSE}(\tilde{\mu})= 0.77\sigma^2$ and $\tilde{MSE}(\tilde{\sigma})=0.12\sigma^2$.
The Log likelihood for BLIE's = -21.70.

Table 3.6.3 Best Linear Invariant prediction of next records.

S	Predictor	MSE
1	54.36	0.10
2	53.91	0.20
3	53.46	0.29
4	53.01	0.38
5	52.56	0.47

3.7. Limiting Distribution

In this section we will consider the limiting distribution of $X_{L(n)}$ for the standard Type I distribution i.e. GEV(0,1,0).

Let $M_n = E(X_{L(n)})$ and $Var(X_{L(n)}) = V_{nn}$. We have seen the values of M_n and V_{nn} in Tables 3.2.1 and 3.2.2.

$$P_{(n)}(x) = P(\frac{X_{L(n)} - M_n}{\sqrt{V_{nn}}} \leq x) = \int_{-\infty}^{M_n + x\sqrt{V_{nn}}} \frac{e^{-nt} e^{-e^{-t}}}{\Gamma(n)} dt$$

Table 3.7.1 gives the values of $P(\frac{X_{L(n)}-M_n}{\sqrt{V_{nn}}} \leq x)$ for selected values of n and x. It is found that these values are closer to the values of the cumulative normal distribution function, $\Phi(x)$, where

$$\Phi(x) = \frac{1}{\sqrt{2\pi}} \int_{-\infty}^{x} e^{-\frac{t^2}{2}} dt .$$

Table 3.7.1 values of $P_n(x)$ and $\Phi(x)$

n \ $P_n(x)$	x = -2	x = -1	x = 0	x = 1	x = 2
5	0.010356	0.154023	0.530360	0.845021	0.966426
10	0.013946	0.156442	0.521256	0.843232	0.969291
15	0.015575	0.157208	0.517290	0.842617	0.970651
20	0.016549	0.157581	0.514951	0.842306	0.971486
30	0.017703	0.157949	0.512185	0.841990	0.972497
$\Phi(x)$	0.022750	0.158655	0.500000	0.841345	0.977250

CHAPTER 4

GENERALIZED PARETO DISTRIBUTION

4.0 INTRODUCTION

A random variable (rv) X is said to have the generalized Pareto distribution if its probability density function (pdf) is of the following form:

$$f(x) = \frac{1}{\sigma}(1+\beta(\frac{x-\mu}{\sigma}))^{-(1+\beta^{-1})}$$

$$x \geq \mu, \text{ for } \beta > 0,$$

$$\mu < x < \mu - \sigma/\beta, \text{ for } \beta < 0,$$

$$= \frac{1}{\sigma}e^{-(x-\mu)\sigma^{-1}}, x \geq \mu \text{ for } \beta = 0,$$

$$= 0, \text{ otherwise,}$$

for $\sigma > 0$. (4.0.1)

We will say that $X \in GP(\mu,\sigma,\beta)$ if X has the pdf as given in (4.0.1). For $\beta > 0$, $GP(\mu,\sigma,\beta)$ is known as Pareto type II or Lomax distribution. For $\beta = -1$, $GP(\mu,\sigma,\beta)$ coincide with the uniform distribution on $(\mu, \mu + \sigma)$. Figure 4.0.1 gives the pdf of $GP(0,1,1)$

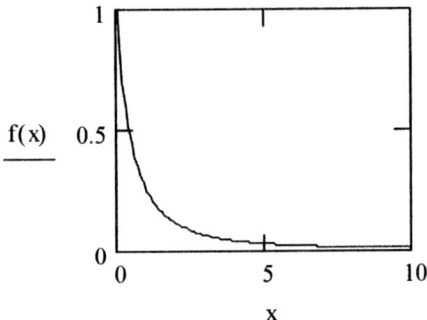

Figure 4.0.1, Pdf of GP(0,1,1)

The generalized Pareto distribution was introduced by Pickands(1975). Some of its applications include its uses in the analysis of the extreme events, in the modeling of large insurance claims and to describe the annual maximum flood at river gauging station. GP(μ,σ,β) has finite variance if $\beta < 1/2$. GP(μ,σ,β) for $\beta = 0$ is the exponential distribution which is discussed in chapter 2. In this chapter we will take $\beta \neq 0$.

If $X \in$ GP(μ,σ,β), then
$$r(x) = \frac{1}{\sigma}[1+\beta(x-\mu)\sigma^{-1}]^{-1}$$
and
$$R(x) = \frac{1}{\beta}\ln[1+\beta(x-\mu)\sigma^{-1}].$$

The hazard rate $r(x)$ is monotonically increasing (decreasing) in x if $\beta > (<) 0$ and $r(x)$ is constant for $\beta = 0$.

4.1. DISTRIBUTIONAL PROPERTIES OF RECORD VALUES

We will consider the upper record values from GP(μ,σ,β). The marginal pdf of $X_{U(n)}$ is

$$f_n(x) = \frac{1}{\Gamma(n)} \{\frac{1}{\beta}\ln[1+\frac{\beta(x-\mu)}{\sigma}]\}^{n-1} \frac{1}{\sigma}[1+\frac{\beta(x-\mu)}{\sigma}]^{-(1+\beta^{-1})}$$
(4.1.1)
$$\mu < x < \infty, \beta > 0.$$

Substituting $\frac{1}{\beta}\ln[1+\frac{\beta(x-\mu)}{\sigma}] = t$, we have

$$E(X_{L(n)}) = \frac{1}{\Gamma(n)} \int_0^\infty t^{n-1}[\mu+\frac{\sigma}{\beta}(e^{\beta t}-1)]e^{-t}\, dt$$

$$= \mu + \frac{\sigma}{\beta}\{(1-\beta)^{-n} - 1\}, \text{ if } \beta < 1.$$

Similarly

$$E(X_{L(n)})^2 = \frac{1}{\Gamma(n)} \int_0^\infty t^{n-1}[\mu+\frac{\sigma}{\beta}(e^{\beta t}-1)]^2 e^{-t}\, dt$$

$$= (\mu - \frac{\sigma}{\beta})^2 + 2(\mu - \frac{\sigma}{\beta})\frac{\sigma}{\beta}(1-\beta)^{-n} + \frac{\sigma^2}{\beta^2}(1-2\beta)^{-n}, \text{ if } \beta < 1/2.$$

$$\text{Var}(X_{L(n)}) = \sigma^2 \beta^{-2} \{(1-2\beta)^{-n} - (1-\beta)^{-2n}\}, \qquad \beta < 1/2$$

Using (4.1.1), we can write

$$X_{U(n)} \stackrel{d}{=} \mu - \frac{\sigma}{\beta} + \frac{\sigma}{\beta} \prod_{i=1}^n U_i, \qquad (4.1.2)$$

where U_1, U_2, U_n are independent and identically distributed as
$$P[U_i \leq x] = 1 - (x)^{-1/\beta}, x \geq 1, \beta > 0,$$
$$= (x)^{-1/\beta}, 0 < x < 1, \beta < 0. \qquad (4.1.3)$$

From (4.1.2) and (4.1.3), we have

$$\text{Cov}(X_{U(m)}, X_{U(m)}) = a_m b_n \sigma^2 \beta^{-2}, \quad m < n,$$
(4.1.4)

where

$$a_m = (1-\beta)^m \{(1-2\beta)^{-m} - (1-\beta)^{-2m}\}, \beta < 1/2$$
$$b_n = (1-\beta)^{-n}, \beta \neq 1$$

Example 4.1.1.

If $\beta = -1$, i.e. when X is distributed uniformly in the interval $(\mu, \mu + \sigma)$, then

$$E(X_{U(n)}) = \mu + (1 - 2^{-n}) \sigma$$
$$Var(X_{U(n)}) = (3^{-n} - 4^{-n}) \sigma^2$$
$$Cov(X_{U(m)}, X_{U(n)}) = 2^{m-n} Var(X_{U(m)}), \, m < n.$$

Example 4.1.2.

For the classical Pareto distribution with the cumulative distribution function F(x), where

$$F(x) = 1 - (\frac{\theta}{x})^\nu, 0 < \theta \leq x < \infty, \nu > 0,$$

$$E(X_{U(n)}) = \theta \left(\frac{\nu}{\nu-1}\right)^n, \text{ if } \nu > 1$$

$$Var(X_{U(n)}) = \theta^2 \left[(\frac{\nu}{\nu-2})^n - (\frac{\nu}{\nu-1})^{2n}\right], \text{ if } \nu > 2$$

$$Cov(X_{U(m)}, X_{U(n)}) = \theta^2 \left(\frac{\nu}{\nu-1}\right)^{n-m} Var(X_{U(m)}), \, m < n.$$

4.2. RECURRENCE RELATIONS FOR MOMENTS

We will consider in this section without any loss of generality $\mu = 0$ and $\sigma = 1$ i.e.

$$f(x) = (1 + \beta x)^{-(1+\beta^{-1})}, x \geq 0, \text{for } \beta > 0, \quad (4.2.1)$$

$$0 < x < -\beta^{-1} \text{ for } \beta < 0$$

$$= e^{-x}, \quad x \geq 0 \text{ for } \beta = 0,$$

$$= 0, \text{ otherwise.}$$

In this section some recurrence relations satisfied by the single and product moments of upper record values from the generalized Pareto distribution in (4.2.1). These recurrence relations will enable one to obtain all the single and product moments of all record values in a simple recursive manner. It is shown here that the results for the exponential distribution proved in chapter 2 can be deduced from the results established in this section by letting the shape parameter β tend to 0.

We will derive some recurrence relations between moments and product moments of the record values. These results are given by Balakrishnan and Ahsanullah(1994).

(a) Relations for single moments
First of all, we may note that for the generalized Pareto distribution in (4.2.1)

$$f(x)(1+\beta x)=1-F(x). \qquad (4.2.2)$$

The relation in (4.2.2) will be exploited in this section to derive recurrence relations for the moments of record values from the generalized Pareto distribution.

Let $X_{U(1)}<X_{U(2)}<\ldots$ be the sequence of upper record values from (4.2.1). For convenience, we shall also take $X_{U(0)} = 0$. Then the pdf of $X_{U(n)}$, $n=1,2,\ldots$, is given by

$$f_n(x)=\frac{1}{(n-1)!}\{-\ln(1-F(x))\}^{n-1}f(x) \qquad (4.2.3)$$

For the existance of the (r+1)th moment (r+1) β must be less than 1.

Theorem 4.2.1.

For $n \geq 1$ and $r = 0,1,2,\ldots$,

$$E(X_{U(n)}^{r+1})=\frac{1}{1-(r+1)\beta}\left\{(r+1)E\left(X_{U(n)}^{r}\right)+E(X_{U(n)}^{r+1})\right\} \qquad (4.2.4)$$

for $\beta<(r+1)^{-1}$.

Proof.

For $n \geq 1$ and $r = 0,1,2,\ldots$, we have from (4.2.3)

$$E(X_{U(n)}^{r})+\beta E(X_{U(n)}^{r+1})=\int(x^r+\beta x^{r+1})f_n(x)dx$$

$$=\int_x x^r \frac{1}{(n-1)!}\{-\ln(1-F(x))\}^{n-1}(1+\beta x)f(x)dx$$

$$=\frac{1}{(n-1)!}\int_x x^r\{-\ln(1-F(x))\}^{n-1}(1-F(x))dx$$

upon using the relation in (4.2.2). Integrating now by parts treating x^r for integration and the rest of the integrand for differentiation, we get

$$E(X^r_{U(n)}) + \beta E(X^{r+1}_{U(n)}) =$$

$$= \frac{1}{(r+1)(n-1)!}[-(n-1)\int_x^\infty x^{r+1}\{-\ln(1-F(x))\}^{n-2}f(x)dx$$

$$+ \int_x^\infty x^{r+1}\{-\ln(1-F(x))\}^{n-2}f(x)dx]$$

$$\frac{1}{r+1}\left[E(X^{r+1}_{U(n)}) - E(X^{r+1}_{U(n-1)})\right]$$

The relation in (4.2.4) is derived simply by rewriting the above equation.

Remark 4.1.1. The recurrence relation in Theorem 4.2.1 can be used in a simple recursive manner to compute all the single moments of all record values. By setting r=0 in (3.1.3), for example, we get the relation

$$E(X_{U(n)}) = \frac{1}{1-\beta}\{1 + E(X_{U(n-1)})\}, n \geq 2, \beta < 1. \quad (4.2.5)$$

Repeated application of (4.2.5) will readily yield

$$E(X_{U(n)}) = \frac{1}{1-\beta} + \frac{1}{(1-\beta)^2} + \cdots + \frac{1}{(1-\beta)^{n-1}} = \frac{1}{\beta}\left[\frac{1}{(1-\beta)^n} - 1\right]$$

an expression given by Ahsanullah (1992).

(b) Relations for product moments

Next, we have the joint density function of $X_{U(m)}$ and $X_{U(n)}$, $1 \leq m < n$, as

Generalized Pareto Distribution

$$f_{m,n}(x,y) = \frac{1}{\Gamma(m)\Gamma(n-m)}\{-\ln(1-F(x))\}^{m-1}$$

$$\cdot\{-\ln(1-F(y))+\ln(1-F(x))\}^{n-m-1}\cdot\frac{f(x)}{1-F(x)}f(y), x<y$$

(4.2.6)

Once again, upon using the relation in (4.2.2), we derive some simple recurrence relations for the product moments of record values.

Theorem 4.2.2.

For $m \geq 1, r, s = 0, 1, 2, \ldots$,

$$E(X_{U(m)}^{r} X_{U(m+1)}^{s+1}) = \frac{1}{1-(s+1)\beta}\left[(s+1)E(X_{U(m)}^{r} X_{U(m+1)}^{s}) + E(X_{U(m)}^{r+s+1})\right]$$

(4.2.7)

for $\beta < \frac{1}{s+1}$; for $1 \leq m \leq n-2$ and $r, s = 0, 1, 2, \ldots$,

$$E(X_{U(m)}^{r} X_{U(n)}^{s+1}) = \frac{1}{1-(s+1)\beta}\left[(s+1)E(X_{U(m)}^{r} X_{U(n)}^{s}) + E(X_{U(m)}^{r} X_{U(n-1)}^{s+1})\right]$$

(4.2.8)

for $\beta < \frac{1}{s+1}$.

Proof:

From (4.2.6), let us consider for $1 \leq m \leq n-1$ and $r, s = 0, 1, 2, \ldots$

$$E(X_{U(m)}^{r} X_{U(n)}^{s}) + \beta E(X_{U(m)}^{r} X_{U(n)}^{s+1}) = \iint_{x<y}(x^r y^s + \beta x^r y^{s+1})f_{m,n}(x,y)dydx$$

$$= \frac{1}{(m-1)!(n-m-1)!}\int_{x} x^r \{-\ln(1-F(x))\}^{m-1} \frac{f(x)}{1-F(x)} I(x)dx, \quad (4.2.9)$$

where

$$I(x) = \int_{y>x} y^s (1+\beta y)\{-\ln(1-F(y))+\ln(1-F(x))\}^{n-m-1} f(y)dy$$

$$= \int_{y>x} y^s \{-\ln(1-F(y)) + \ln(1-F(x))\}^{n-m-1}(1-F(y))dy$$

upon using the relation in (4.2.3). Integrating now by parts treating y^s for integration and the rest of the integrand for differentiation, we obtain when n=m+1 that

$$I(x) = \frac{1}{s+1}\left[-x^{s+1}(1-F(x)) + \int_{y>x} y^{s+1} f(y)dy\right],$$

and when $n \geq m+2$ that

$$I(x) = \frac{1}{s+1}\left[-(n-m-1)\int_{y>x} y^{s+1}\{-\ln(1-F(y))+\ln(1-F(x))\}^{n-m-2} f(y)dy\right.$$
$$\left. + \int_{y>x} y^{s+1}\{-\ln(1-F(y))+\ln(1-F(x))\}^{n-m-1} f(y)dy\right].$$

Upon substituting the above expressions of I(x) in Eq. (4.2.9) and simplifying the resulting equations, we obtain when n = m+1 that

$$E\left(X_{U(m)}^r X_{U(m+1)}^s\right) + \beta E\left(X_{U(m)}^r X_{U(m+1)}^{s+1}\right)$$
$$= \frac{1}{s+1}\left[-E\left(X_{U(m+1)}^{s+1}\right) + E\left(X_{U(m)}^r X_{U(m+1)}^{s+1}\right)\right]$$

and when $n \geq m+2$ that

$$E\left(X_{U(m)}^r X_{U(n)}^s\right) + \beta E\left(X_{U(m)}^r X_{U(n)}^{s+1}\right)$$
$$= \frac{1}{s+1}\left[-E\left(X_{U(m)}^r X_{U(n-1)}^{s+1}\right) + E\left(X_{U(m)}^r X_{U(n)}^{s+1}\right)\right]$$

The relations in (4.2.7) and (4.2.8) are derived simply by rewriting the above two equations.

Remark 4.2.2: The recurrence relations presented in Theorem 4.2.2 can be used in a simple recursive manner to compute all the product moments of all record values. It is known that the generalized Pareto distribution in (4.2.1) has finite variance if $\beta < \frac{1}{2}$. In this case, by setting r=1 and s = 0 in (4.2.7) we get

$$E\left(X_{U(m)} X_{U(m+1)}\right) = \frac{1}{1-\beta}\left[E\left(X_{U(m)}\right) + E\left(X_{U(m)}^2\right)\right]$$

which, together with (4.2.6), immediately yields

$$Cov(X_{U(m)}, X_{U(m+1)}) = \frac{1}{1-\beta} Var(X_{U(m)}) \quad (4.2.10)$$

Similarly, by setting r = 1 and s = 0 in (4.2.8) we get for n>m+2

$$E(X_{U(m)} X_{U(n)}) = \frac{1}{1-\beta}[E(X_{U(m)}) + E(X_{U(m)} X_{U(n-1)})]$$

which, together with (4.2.6), readily implies

$$Cov(X_{U(m)}, X_{U(n)}) = \frac{1}{1-\beta} Cov(X_{U(m)}, X_{U(n-1)})$$
$$= \frac{1}{(1-\beta)^{n-m}} Var(X_{U(m)}) \quad (4.2.11)$$

Remark 4.2.3. Upon letting the shape parameter β tend to 0 in the recurrence relations presented in Theorems 1 and 2, we simply deduce the relations for the single and product moments of upper record values from the standard exponential distribution established in chapter 2.

Theorem 4.2.3

For m≥1 and r,s=0,1,2,....,

$$E(X_{U(m)}^{r+1} X_{U(m+1)}^{s}) = \frac{1}{(r+1)\beta}[E(X_{U(m)}^{r+s+1}) - E(X_{U(m-1)}^{r+1} X_{U(m)}^{s})$$
$$-(r+1)E(X_{U(m)}^{r} X_{U(m+1)}^{s})]; \quad (4.2.12)$$

and for $1 \leq m \leq n-2$ and r,s = 0,1,2,....,

$$E(X_{U(m)}^{r+1} X_{U(n)}^{s})$$
$$= \frac{1}{(r+1)\beta}[E(X_{U(m)}^{r+1} X_{U(n-1)}^{s}) - E(X_{U(m-1)}^{r+1} X_{U(n-1)}^{s}) - (r+1)E(X_{U(m)}^{r} X_{U(n)}^{s})]$$

(4.2.13)

Proof.

From (4.2.6), let us consider for $1 \leq m \leq n-1$ and r,s = 0,1,2,....

$$E\left(X_{U(m)}^r X_{U(n)}^s\right) + \beta E\left(X_{U(m)}^{r+1} X_{U(n)}^s\right)$$

$$= \iint_{x<y} \left(x^r y^s + \beta x^{r+1} y^s\right) f_{m,n}(x,y) dx\, dy$$

$$= \frac{1}{(m-1)!(n-m-1)!} \int_y y^s f(y) J(y) dy,$$

(4.2.14)

where

$$J(y)$$
$$= \int_{x<y} x^r (1+\beta x) \{-\ln(1-F(x))\}^{m-1} \{-\ln(1-F(y)) + \ln(1-F(x))\}^{n-m-1} \cdot$$

$$\frac{f(x)}{1-F(x)} dx \int_{x<y} x^r \{-\ln(1-F(x))\}^{m-1} \{-\ln(1-F(y)) + \ln(1-F(x))\}^{n-m-1} dx$$

upon using the relation in (4.2.3). Integrating now by parts treating x^r for integration and the rest of the integrand for differentiation, we obtain when n=m+1 that

$$J(y)$$
$$= \frac{1}{r+1}\left[\begin{array}{l} y^{r+1}\{-\ln(1-F(y))\}^{m-1} - \\ (m-1)\int_{x<y} x^{r+1}\{-\ln(1-F(x))\}^{m-2} \frac{f(x)}{1-F(x)} dx \end{array}\right]$$

and when n≥m+2 that

$$J(y)$$
$$= \frac{1}{r+1}\left[(n-m-1)\int_{x<y} x^{r+1}\{-\ln(1-F(x))\}^{m-1} \cdot I_1 \right.$$
$$\left. -(m-1)\cdot I_2 \right.$$

Where $I_1 = \{-\ln(1-F(y)) + \ln(1-F(x))\}^{n-m-2} \frac{f(x)}{1-F(x)} dx$

and

$$I_2 = \int_{x<y} x^{r+1} \{-\ln(1-F(x))\}^{m-2} \{-\ln(1-F(y))+\ln(1-F(x))\}^{n-m-1}$$
$$\cdot \frac{f(x)}{1-F(x)} dx$$

Upon substituting the above expressions for $J(y)$ in Eq. (4.2.14) and simplifying the resulting equations, we obtain when $n = m+1$ that

$$E\left(X^r_{U(m)} X^s_{U(m+1)}\right) + \beta E\left(X^{r+1}_{U(m)} X^s_{U(m+1)}\right)$$
$$\frac{1}{r+1}\left[E\left(X^{r+s+1}_{U(m)}\right) - E\left(X^{r+1}_{U(m-1)} X^s_{U(m)}\right)\right]$$

and when $n \geq m+2$ that

$$E\left(X^r_{U(m)} X^s_{U(n)}\right) + \beta E\left(X^{r+1}_{U(m)} X^s_{U(n)}\right)$$
$$\frac{1}{r+1}\left[E\left(X^{r+1}_{U(m)} X^s_{U(n-1)}\right) - E\left(X^{r+1}_{U(m-1)} X^s_{U(n-1)}\right)\right]$$

The relations in (4.2.12) and (4.2.13) are derived simply by rewriting the above two equations.

Remark 4.2.4. The recurrence relations presented in Theorem 4.2.3 will also enable one to obtain all the product moments of all record values in a simple recursive manner.

Proceedings similarly, one may derive recurrence relations for higher order product moments of record values as well. For example, by proceeding in a manner analogous to Theorem 4.2.2, we may establish the following two relations:

For $1 \leq m_1 < m_2 < ... < m_k$ and $r_1, r_2, ..., r_{k+1} = 0,1,2,...,$

$$E\left(\prod_{i=1}^{k} X^{r_i}_{U(m)} X^{r_{k+1}+1}_{U(m_k+1)}\right)$$
$$= \frac{1}{1-(r_{k+1}+1)\beta}[(r_{k+1}+1)E(\prod_{i+1}^{k} X^{r_i}_{U(m)} X^{r_{k+1}}_{U(m_k+1)})$$
$$+ E\left(X^{r_i}_{U(m)} X^{r_k+r_{k+1}+1}_{U(m_k)}\right)], \quad (4.2.15)$$

and for $1 \leq m_1 < m_2 < \cdots < m_k < m_{k+1}-1$ and $r_1, r_2, ... r_{k+1} = 0,1,2,...,$

$$E\left(\prod_{i=1}^{k} X_{U(m_i)}^{r_i} X_{U(m_{k+1})}^{r_{k+1}+1}\right)$$

$$= \frac{1}{1-(r_{k+1}+1)\beta}\left[(r_{k+1}+1)E\left(\prod_{i=1}^{k+1} X_{U(m_i)}^{r_i}\right) + E\left(\prod_{i=1}^{k} X_{U(m_i)}^{r_i} X_{U(m_{k+1}-1)}^{r_{k+1}+1}\right)\right],$$

(4.3.16)

when $\beta < \dfrac{1}{r_{k+1}+1}$.

4.3. ESTIMATION OF PARAMETERS

We will consider the estimators of μ and σ when β is known. Minimum Variance Linear Unbiased Estimators of μ and σ.

Theorem 4.3.1.

The minimum variance linear unbiased estimators $\hat{\mu}$ and $\hat{\sigma}$ of μ and σ based on the observed record values $r_1, r_2, \ldots, r_m$ are

$$\hat{\mu} = r_1 - (1-\beta)^{-1}\hat{\sigma}$$

$$\hat{\sigma} = (1-\beta)(\beta - D^{-1}(1-2\beta)^3 r_1 + D^{-1}\beta(1-\beta)\sum_{i=2}^{m-1}(1-2\beta)^{i+1} r_i$$

$$+ D^{-1}(1-\beta)^2 (1-2\beta)^{m+1} r_m$$

where

$$D = \sum_{l=2}^{m}(1-2\beta)^{i+1} \text{ and } \beta < 1/2.$$

Proof.

We assume $GP(\mu,\sigma,\beta)$ with $\beta \neq 0$ and with finite variance. Let R be the m × 1 vector corresponding to $X_{U(i)}$, i = 1,2, ..., m, then we can write

$$E(R) = \mu L + \sigma \delta$$

where

$$R' = (X_{U(1)}, X_{U(2)}, ..., X_{U(m)})$$
$$L' = (1,1,....,1), \delta' = (\alpha_1, \alpha_2, ..., \alpha_m)$$
$$\alpha_i = \beta^{-1}(1-\beta)^{-i},$$

and $\alpha_i = \beta^{-1}(1-\beta)^{-i}$, $i = 1,2,..., m$.

We can write
$V(R) = \sigma^2 V, V = (V_{i,j}), V_{i,j} = \beta^{-2} a_i b_j, 1 \le i \le j \le m$ and $V_{i,j} = V_{j,i}$.

We can express the inverse of V as V^{-1} ($= V^{i,j}$),

$$V^{i+1,i} = V^{i,i+1} = -\frac{1}{a_{i+1}b_i - a_i b_{i+1}} = -(1-2\beta)^{i+1}(1-\beta), i = 1,2, ..., m-1,$$

$$V^{i,i} = \frac{a_{i+1}b_{i-1} - a_{i-1}b_{i+1}}{(a_i b_{i-1} - a_{i-1}b_i)(a_{i+1}b_i - a_i b_{i+1})}, i = 1,2,...,n, V^{i,j} = 0, \text{ for } |i-j| > 1,$$

where $a_o = 0 = b_{n+1}$ and $b_o = 1 = a_{n+1}$.

On simplification, we obtain
$$V^{i,i} = (1-2\beta)^i (2 - 4\beta + \beta^2), i = 1, 2, ..., m-1$$
and
$$V^{m,m} = (1-2\beta)^m (1-\beta).$$

The minimum variance linear unbiased estimators (MVLUE) $\hat{\mu}, \hat{\sigma}$ of μ and σ are respectively based on the observed record values $r_1, r_2, ..., r_m$ are

$$\hat{\mu} = -\delta' V^{-1}(L\delta' - \delta L')V^{-1} r/\Delta, \text{ and}$$

$$\hat{\sigma} = L'V^{-1}(L\delta' - \delta L')V^{-1} r/\Delta,$$

where
$$\Delta = (L'V^{-1}L)(\delta'V^{-1}\delta) - (L'V^{-1}\delta)^2$$

and r is the observed value of R. On substituting the values for δ and V^{-1} and subsequent simplification, it can be shown that

$$\hat{\mu} = r_1 - \hat{\sigma}(1-\beta)^{-1} \text{ and}$$

$$\hat{\sigma} = (1-\beta)(\beta - D^{-1}(1-2\beta)^3 r_1) + D^{-1}\beta(1-\beta) \sum_{i=2}^{m}(1-2\beta)^{i+1} r_i$$

where

$$D = \sum_{i=2}^{m}(1-2\beta)^{i+1}.$$

The corresponding variances and the covariance of the estimates are

$$Var(\hat{\mu}) = \sigma^2 \frac{T}{D}$$

$$Var(\hat{\sigma}) = \sigma^2 \frac{\beta T - (1-2\beta)}{D}$$

$$Cov(\hat{\mu},\hat{\sigma}) = \sigma^2 \frac{\{(1-2\beta)^2 + \beta^2 T\}}{D}$$

and

$$T = \sum_{i=2}^{m} (1-2\beta)^i .$$

(b) Best Linear Invariant Estimators (BLIE)

Thereom 4.3.2

The best linear invariant (in the sense of minimum mean squared error and invariance with respect to the location parameter μ) estimators $\tilde{\mu}, \tilde{\sigma}$ of μ and σ are respectively

$$\tilde{\mu} = \hat{\mu} - \frac{\beta T - (1-2\beta)}{T(1-\beta)^2} \hat{\sigma} \text{ and}$$

$$\tilde{\sigma} = \frac{D}{T(1-\beta)^2} \hat{\sigma}, \text{ where}$$

$$D = \sum_{i=2}^{m} (1-2\beta)^{i+1}, T = \sum_{i=1}^{m} (1-2\beta)^i$$

and $\hat{\mu}$ and $\hat{\sigma}$ are MVLUE of μ and σ.

Proof.

The BLIE $\tilde{\mu}$ and $\tilde{\sigma}$ can be written as

$$\hat{\mu} = \hat{\mu} - \frac{E_{12}}{1 + E_{22}} \hat{\sigma}$$

and

$$\tilde{\sigma} = \frac{1}{1+E_{22}} \hat{\sigma},$$

where

$$\begin{pmatrix} Var(\hat{\mu}) & Cov(\hat{\mu},\hat{\sigma}) \\ Cov(\hat{\mu},\hat{\sigma}) & Var(\hat{\sigma}) \end{pmatrix} = \sigma^2 \begin{pmatrix} E_{11} & E_{12} \\ E_{12} & E_{22} \end{pmatrix}.$$

The mean squared errors of $\tilde{\mu}$ and $\tilde{\sigma}$ are

$$MSE(\tilde{\mu}) = \sigma^2 (E_{11} - \frac{E_{12}^2}{1+E_{22}}),$$

$$MSE(\tilde{\sigma}) = \sigma^2 (\frac{E_{22}}{1+E_{22}}).$$

Substituting the values of E_{11}, E_{12} and E_{22} in terms of β, T and D, we get the result.

(c) Estimator of β for known μ and σ.

    Maximum Likelihood Estimastor of β.

    Without any loss of generality we will assume $\mu = 0$ and $\sigma = 1$.
The log likelihood function of $r_1, r_2, \ldots, r_m$ can be written as

$$\ln L = -\sum_{i=1}^{m-1} \ln(1+\beta r_i) - (1+\beta^{-1})\ln(1+\beta r_m)$$

Differentiating ln L with respect to β and equating to zero, we have

$$\beta(m - \sum_{i=1}^{m} \frac{1}{1+\beta r_i}) = \frac{1}{1+\beta r_m} - 1 + \ln(1+\beta r_m).$$

The exact solution of the above equation is difficult to find.

A Moment Estimator of β.

    We have seen that for $\mu = 0$ and $\sigma = 1$.

$$E(X_{U(m)}) = \beta^{-1} \{(1-\beta)^{-m} - 1\}. \text{ Thus}$$

$$E(\overline{X}) = E\{(X_{U(1)} + X_{U(2)} + \ldots + X_{U(m)})/m\} = \frac{1}{m\beta^2}\{(1-\beta)^{-m} - 1\} - \frac{1}{\beta}$$

$$= \frac{X_{U(m)} - m}{m\beta}$$

Thus we can take $\tilde{\beta}$ as an estimator of β where

$$\tilde{\beta} = \frac{r_m - m}{r_1 + r_2 + \ldots + r_m}, \text{ for } r_1 + r_2 + \ldots + r_m \neq 0$$

4.4. PREDICTION OF RECORD VALUES

We will consider the predictor of $X_{U(s)}$ based on m record values for m < s.

Theorem 4.4.1

Let $H' = (h_1, h_2, \ldots, h_m)$, where $\sigma^2 h_i = \text{Cov}(X_{U(i)}, X_{U(s)})$, $i = 1, 2, \ldots, m$ and $\sigma^* = \sigma^{-1} E(X_{U(s)} - \mu)$. Then the best (in the sense of minimum mean squared error) linear unbiased predictor (BLUP) of $X_{U(s)}$ is

$$\hat{X}_{U(s)} = \hat{\mu} + \hat{\sigma}\alpha_s + H'V^{-1}(r - \hat{\mu}L - \hat{\sigma}\delta),$$

Proof.

It can be shown easily that

$$H'V^{-1} = (0, 0, \ldots, (1-\beta)^{n-2}),$$

$$H'V^{-1}(r - \hat{\mu}L - \hat{\sigma}\delta) = (1-\beta)^{n-s}(r_n - \hat{\mu} - \hat{\sigma}\alpha_n).$$

Thus

$$\hat{X}_{U(s)} = (1 + \beta\alpha_{s-m})r_m - \alpha_{s-n}(\beta\hat{\mu} - \hat{\sigma})$$

with

$$\alpha_{s-n} = \frac{1}{\beta}\{(1-\beta)^{n-s} - 1\}.$$

The best (unrestricted) least squares predictor $X^*_{U(s)}$ of $X_{U(s)}$ is

$$X^*_{U(s)} = E(X_{U(s)} | X_{U(1)}, X_{U(2)}, \ldots, X_{U(m)}).$$

By using (4.2.6), we have

$$X^*_{U(s)} = \mu + \frac{\sigma}{\beta}\{(1-\beta)^{s-m}(1+(r_m-\mu)\beta\sigma^{-1})-1\}$$

where r_m is the observed value of $X_{U(m)}$. It is evident that $X^*_{U(s)}$ depends on the unknown parameters. If we substitute the MVLUE estimators $\hat{\mu}$ and $\hat{\sigma}$ of μ and σ in $X^*_{U(s)}$, then $X^*_{U(s)}$ becomes equal to $\hat{X}_{U(s)}$. Let $\tilde{X}_{U(s)}$ be the best linear invariant predictor of $X_{U(s)}$. Then it can be shown that $\tilde{X}_{U(s)} = \hat{X}_{U(s)} - c^*_{12}(1+E_{22})^{-1}\hat{\sigma}$,

$$c^*_{12}\sigma^2 = Cov(\hat{\sigma}, (1-W'V^{-1}L)\hat{\mu} + (\alpha_s - W'V^{-1}\delta)\hat{\sigma}$$

$$c^*_{12}\sigma^2 = Cov(\hat{\sigma}, (1-W'V^{-1}L)\hat{\mu} + (\alpha_s - W'V^{-1}\delta)\hat{\sigma},$$

and

$$E_{22}\sigma^2 = Var(\hat{\sigma}).$$

Now

$$1 - H'V^{-1}L = 1 - (1-\beta)^{m-s} = -\beta\alpha_{s-m}$$

$$\alpha_s - H'V^{-1}\delta = \alpha_s - (1-\beta)^{m-s}\alpha_m = \alpha_{s-m}$$

Thus

$$c^*_{12}(1+E_{22})^{-1} = \frac{\alpha_{s-n}(1-2\beta)}{T(1-\beta)}$$

and hence

$$\tilde{X}_{U(s)} = \hat{X}_{U(s)} - \frac{\alpha_{s-n}(1-2\beta)}{T(1-\beta)}.$$

$$MSE(\tilde{X}_{U(s)}) = MSE(\hat{X}_{U(s)}) - c^*_o\sigma^2, \quad c^*_o =$$

$$(c^*_{12})^2 (1+E_{22})^{-1}.$$

4.5. CLASSICAL PARETO DISTRIBUTION

In this section we will consider the record values of the classical Pareto distribution whose cumulative distribution function, F(x), is of the form

$$F(x) = 1- \left(\frac{\theta}{x}\right)^v, 0<\theta\leq x< \infty, v> 0. \quad (4.5.1)$$

This distribution was labelled as Pareto(I)(θ, v) by Arnold(1983). It is well known that a Pareto distribution of the form (4.5.1) provides reasonably good fit to distributions of income and property values.

Let $f_n(x)$ be the pdf of $X_{U(n)}$, then

$$f_n(x) = \frac{1}{\Gamma(n)}(v\ln(x/\theta))^{n-1}\frac{v}{\theta}\left(\frac{\theta}{x}\right)^{v+1} \quad (4.5.2)$$

Using (4.5.2), we can write

$$X_{U(n)} \stackrel{d}{=} \theta \prod_{i=1}^{n} U_i, \, n\geq 1, \quad (4.5.3)$$

where $\stackrel{d}{=}$ denotes the equality in distribution and $U_1, U_2, \ldots, U_n$ are independent and identically distributed as Pareto (I) (1,v) with the pdf $f(x)$ as

$$f(x) = v x^{-(v+1)}, x\geq 1.$$

Consequently the consecutive ratios of the record values $X_{U(n)}/X_{U(n-1)}$ are independent and identically distributed as Pareto (I) (1,v).

$$P\left(\frac{X_{U(r)}}{X_{U(r-1)}}\geq x\right) = P(U_r \geq x)$$
$$= x^{-v}, v>0, 1<x<\infty.$$

The product moments of $X_{U(m)}$ and $X_{U(n)}$ can be obtained as follows:

$$X^r_{U(m)} X^s_{U(n)} \stackrel{d}{=} \prod_{i=1}^{m} U_i^{r+s} \left(\prod_{i=m1}^{n} U_i^s\right)$$

and thus

$$E(X^r_{U(m)} X^s_{U(n)}) \stackrel{d}{=} \theta^{r+s}\left(\frac{v}{v-r-s}\right)^m \left(\frac{v}{v-s}\right)^{n-m}, \text{ for } v > r+s.$$

Hence

$$E(X_{U(m)} X_{U(n)}) = \theta^2 \left(\frac{v}{v-2}\right)^m \left(\frac{v}{v-1}\right)^{n-m}, v>2$$

and

$$Cov(X_{U(m)} X_{U(n)}) = \theta^2 \left(\frac{v}{v-1}\right)^{n-m} Var(X_{U(m)})$$

Generalized Pareto Distribution

$$\text{Var}(X_{U(m)}) = \theta^2 \left(\frac{v}{v-2}\right)^m - \left(\frac{v}{v-1}\right)^{2m}.$$

$$\text{Cov}(X_{U(m)} X_{U(n)}) = \theta^2 c_{n-m} d_n,$$

where
$$c_k = v^k (v-1)^{-k}, \; d_k = v^k (v-2)^{-k} - v^{2k}(v-1)^{-2k}, \; v > 2.$$

Let $x_1, x_2, \ldots, x_n$ be the observed values of $X_{U(1)}, X_{U(2)}, \ldots, X_{U(n)}$, then considering the log likelihood function, it can be shown that the maximum likelihhod estimators of θ and v are respectively:

$$\hat{\theta} = x_1,$$

and

$$\hat{v} = n / \ln(x_{U(n)} / x_{U(1)}).$$

It is evident that $\hat{\theta}$ is distributed as Pareto(I)(θ, v). Therefore

$$E(\hat{\theta}) = \theta v / (v-1), \; v > 1$$

and

$$\text{MSE}(\hat{\theta}) = \frac{2\theta^2}{(v-1)(v-2)}, v > 2.$$

considering the joint distribution of $X_{U(n)}$ and $X_{U(1)}$ and using the transformations

$$T = \ln(X_{U(n)} / X_{U(1)})$$
$$V = X_{U(1)},$$

it can be shown that T is distributed as Gamma distribution with pdf f(t) as

$$f(t) = \frac{v^{n-1}}{\Gamma(n-1)} t^{n-2} e^{-t}.$$

Thus we can write

$$\hat{v} = n / T.$$

Since

$$E(T^{-k}) = \frac{\Gamma(n-1-k)}{\Gamma(n-1)} v^2,$$

$$E(\hat{v}) = \frac{nv}{n-2}, \; n > 2.$$

The Mean squared error $\hat{v}$ is

$$\text{MSE}(\hat{v}) = \frac{n+6}{(n-2)(n-3)}, n > 3.$$

Table 4.5.1. Variances and Covariances of $X_{U(m)}$ and $X_{U(n)}$.

M	n	2.5	3.0	3.5	4.0	4.5	5.0
1	1	2.2222	0.7500	0.3733	0.2222	0.1469	0.1042
1	2	3.7037	1.1250	0.5227	0.2963	0.1889	0.1302
2	2	17.2840	3.9375	1.6028	0.8395	0.5074	0.3364
1	3	6.1728	1.6875	0.7317	0.3951	0.2429	0.1628
2	3	28.8066	5.9062	2.2440	1.1193	0.6525	0.4205
3	3	103.5665	15.6094	5.1742	2.3813	1.3148	0.8149
1	4	10.2881	2.5312	1.0244	0.5267	0.3123	0.2035
2	4	48.0110	8.8594	3.1416	1.4925	0.8387	0.5256
3	4	172.6109	23.4141	7.2438	3.1751	1.6905	1.0187
4	4	565.4626	55.3711	14.8841	6.0113	3.0304	1.7556

4.6. LOMAX DISTRIBUTION.

A random variable X is said to belong to the Lomax distribution ($X \in L(\mu,\sigma,v)$ if its probability density function f(x) is as follows:

$$f(x) = \frac{v}{\sigma}\left(1 + \frac{x-\mu}{\sigma}\right)^{-(v+1)}, x \geq \mu, \sigma > 0 \text{ and } v > 0. \quad (4.6.1)$$

The corresponding cumulative probability distribution function F(x) can be written as

$$F(x) = 1 - (1 + \frac{x-\mu}{\sigma})^{-v}, x \geq \mu, \sigma > 0 \text{ and } v > 0.$$

We say $X \in L(\mu,\sigma,v)$ if the pdf of X is given by (4.6.1) This distribution has been used in connection with studies of income, size of cities, reliability modelling. The Lomax distribution is also known as Pareto II distribution. The graph of the pdf X when $X \in L(0,1,1)$ is given below.

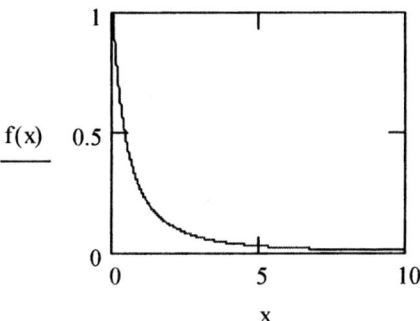

Figure $.6.1. The pdf of X when $X \in L(0,1,1)$

Considering the marginal distribution of $X_{U(n)}$, it can be easily be shown that

$$E(X_{U(n)}) = \mu - \sigma + \sigma(\frac{\nu}{\nu-1})^n, n > 1,$$

$$Var(X_{U(n)}) = \sigma^2 \{(\frac{\nu}{\nu-2})^n - (\frac{\nu}{\nu-1})^{2n}\}, n > 2.$$

From the joint pdf of $X_{U(m)}$ and $X_{U(n)}$, it can be derived that the

$$Cov(X_{U(m)}, X_{U(n)}) = (\frac{\nu}{\nu-1})^{n-m} Var(X_{U(m)}).$$

Let $V_{ij} = Cov(X_{U(i)}, X_{U(j)})$, $V = (V_{ij})$ and $\Omega = (V)^{-1} = (V^{i,j})$, $i,j = 1, 2, ..., n$, then

$$V^{i,i} = (2\nu^2 - 4\nu + 1) c^i, i = 1, 2, ..., n-1$$
$$V^{i+1,i} = -(\nu^2 - 3\nu + 2) c^i = V^{i,i+1}, i = 1, 2, ..., n-1$$
$$V^{n,n} = (\nu^2 - 2\nu + 1) c^n$$
$$V^{i,j} = 0, |i-j| > 1$$

and $c = \dfrac{\nu}{\nu - 2}$.

(1) Estimators of μ and σ for known ν.

Using Lloyd's(1952) method for deriving the minimum variance linear unbiased estimator (MVLUE), it can be shown that the

MVLUE $\hat{\mu}$ and $\hat{\sigma}$ of μ and σ respectively based on the first n record values are

$$\hat{\mu} = \sum_{j=1}^{n} p_j X_{U(j)}$$

and

$$\hat{\sigma} = \sum_{j=1}^{n} q_j X_{U(j)},$$

where

$$p_1 = (\nu(\nu-1)T_1 - (\nu-2))/(\nu(\nu T_1 - \nu + 2))$$

$$p_j = -\left(\frac{\nu-2}{\nu}\right)^j /(\nu T_1 - \nu + 2), j=2,...,n-1$$

$$p_n = \{(\nu-1)T_1 - \frac{(\nu-1)^2(\nu-2)}{\nu}\}/(\nu T_1 - \nu + 2)$$

$$q_1 = p_1 \frac{(\nu-2)^2}{\nu T_1 - \nu + 2}$$

$$q_j = (\nu-1)p_j, j=2,...,n$$

and

$$T_1 = \sum_{j=1}^{n} \left(\frac{\nu-2}{\nu}\right)^j.$$

Further we have

$$Var(\hat{\mu}) = \sigma^2 \frac{T_1}{T_2}$$

$$Var(\hat{\sigma}) = \sigma^2 \frac{T_1 + (\nu-2)^2}{T_2}$$

$$Cov(\hat{\mu}, \hat{\sigma}) = -\sigma^2 \frac{T_1 - \nu + 2}{T_2}$$

where

$$T_2 = (\nu-2)(\nu T_1 - \nu + 2).$$

For example with n = 4 and

$$\hat{\mu} = 1.4065\, X_{U(1)} - 0.3226\, X_{U(2)} - 0.0645\, X_{U(3)} - 0.0194\, X_{U(4)}$$

$\hat{\sigma}$ = -0.6097 $X_{U(1)}$ + 0.4839 $X_{U(2)}$+ 0.0968 $X_{U(3)}$ +0.0290 $X_{U(4)}$.

The corresponding varances and covariance of $\hat{\mu}$ and $\hat{\sigma}$ are

$$Var(\hat{\mu}) = 4.0258\ \sigma^2$$
$$Var(\hat{\sigma}) = 8.0581\ \sigma^2$$

and

$$Cov(\hat{\mu}, \hat{\sigma}) = -4.0387\ \sigma^2.$$

Similarly as in other cases, smaller mean squared errors for the estimators of μ and σ can be obtained by dropping the requirements of unbiasedness. Based on the first n record values the best linear invariant (in the sense of minimum mean squared error and invariance with respect to the location parameter μ) estimators (BLIE) $\tilde{\mu}, \tilde{\sigma}$ of μ and σ are

$$\tilde{\mu} = \hat{\mu} + \hat{\sigma}\frac{T_1 - v + 2}{T_1(v-1)^2},$$

and

$$\tilde{\sigma} = \hat{\sigma}\frac{T_2}{T_1(v-1)^2}.$$

The mean squared errors of $\tilde{\mu}, \tilde{\sigma}$ are

$$MSE(\tilde{\mu}) = \sigma^2[\frac{T_1}{T_2} - \frac{(T_1 - v + 2)^2}{T_1 T_2 (v-1)^2}]$$

and

$$MSE(\tilde{\sigma}) = \sigma^2 \frac{T_1 + (v-2)^2}{(v-1)^2 T_1}.$$

For example with n = 4 and v -2.5, we have

$\tilde{\mu}$ = 1.6784 $X_{U(1)}$ - 0.5584 $X_{U(2)}$ - 0.1077 $X_{U(3)}$ - 0.0323 $X_{U(4)}$

$\tilde{\sigma}$ = - 0.0673 + 0.0534 $X_{U(2)}$ + 0.0107 $X_{U(3)}$ + 0.0032 $X_{U(4)}$.

The corresponding mean squared errors of $\tilde{\mu}, \tilde{\sigma}$ are respectively

$$MSE(\tilde{\mu}) = 2.2251\ \sigma^2$$

and

$$MSE(\tilde{\sigma}) = 0.8896\ \sigma^2.$$

Table 4.6.1 gives the variances and the mean squared errors of MVLUE and BLIE respectively for some selected values of v and for n = 4.

Table 4.6.1 Variances and Mean squred errors of $\hat{\mu}, \hat{\sigma}, \tilde{\mu}$ and $\tilde{\sigma}$.

v	Var($\hat{\mu}$)	Var($\hat{\sigma}$)	MSE($\tilde{\mu}$)	MSE($\tilde{\sigma}$)
2.1	100.0107	120.0130	17.3556	0.9917
2.5	4.0258	8.0581	2.2251	0.8898
3.0	1.0256	3.1026	0.7563	0.7563
8.0	0.3248	0.6994	0.0304	0.3787
10.0	0.0189	0.5312	0.0176	0.0347
20.0	0.0039	0.4139	0.0037	0.2927

It is obvious from the table 4.6.1 that the mean squared errors of BLIE are cosiderably smaller than those of the MVLUE. The differences in the MSE of the estimators are large for small values of v, they decrease with increase in v.

(2) Estimator of v for known μ and σ.
It can be shown that $\{1+\frac{X_{U(n)}-\mu}{\sigma}\}$ is a suuficient statistic for v when μ and σ are known It is also complete. Now

$$E(\ln(1+\frac{X_{U(n)}-\mu}{\sigma}))^{-1} = \int_0^\infty \frac{v}{\Gamma(n)} u^{n-2} e^{-u} du$$

$$= \frac{v}{n-1}.$$

Thus the minimum variance unbiased estimator $\hat{v}$ of v is

$$\hat{v} = (n-1)\{\ln(1+\frac{X_{U(n)}-\mu}{\sigma})\}^{-1}.$$

The variance of $\hat{v}$ is $v^2(n-2)^{-1}$. Here also a smaller mean squared error estimator v^* for v can be obtained by dropping the unbiasedness requirement.
The estimator is given by

$$v^* = \frac{n-2}{n-1}\hat{v}.$$

The expected value and the variance of the estimator are

$$E(v^*) = \frac{n-2}{n-1}v \text{ and } MSE(v^*) = \frac{v^2}{n-1} \text{ repectively.}$$

CHAPTER 5

POWER FUNCTION DISTRIBUTION

5.0 INTRODUCTION

A random variable (rv) X is said to have the three parameter power function distribution if its probability density function (pdf) is of the following form:

$$f(x,\alpha,\beta,\gamma) = \gamma \beta^{-\gamma} (\alpha + \beta - x)^{\gamma-1},$$
$$\text{for } \alpha < x < \alpha + \beta, \beta > 0, \gamma > 0,$$
$$= 0, \text{ otherwise.}$$
(5.0.1)

We will say a rv $X \in PF(\alpha,\beta,\gamma)$ if its pdf is given by (5.0.1). This is a Pearson's Type I distribution. If $\gamma=1$, then f(x, α,β,γ) as given by (5.0.1) coincides with the uniform distribution in the interval (α, $\alpha + \beta$). If we take $Y = (\alpha + \beta)^\gamma$, the Y has the uniform distribution in (0,1). If γ is an integer, then the pdf of X as given in (5.0.1) can be consider as the pdf of ξ, where $\xi = \max(X_1, X_2,\ldots, X_\gamma)$.

The following figures 1.0.1 and 1.0.2 of f(x) and g(x) are the graphs of the pdfs of PF (α,β,γ) for $\alpha = 0$, $\beta = 1$, $\gamma = 1/2$ and $\alpha = 0$, $\beta = 1$, $\gamma = 4$ respectively.

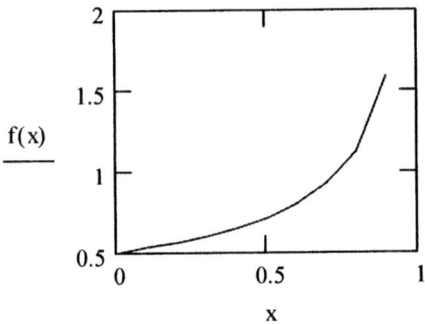

Figure 5.0.1. Pdf of GP(0,1,1/2)

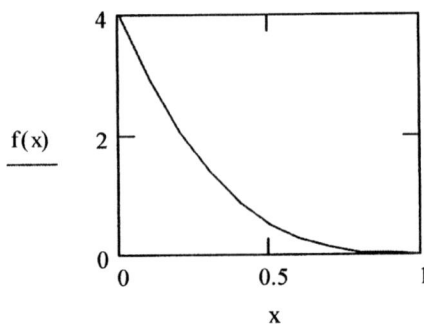

Figure 5.0.1. Pdf of GP(0,1,4)

5.1. Distributional Properties

The joint pdf of $X_{U(1)}, X_{U(2)}, ..., X_{U(m)}$ can be written as

$$f(r_1, r_2, ..., r_m) = \beta^{-m\gamma} \gamma(\alpha+\beta-r_m) \prod_{i=1}^{m-1} (\alpha+\beta-r_i),$$

$$\alpha < r_1 < ... < r_m < \alpha+\beta$$

= 0, otherwise. (5.1.1)

The marginal pdf of $X_{U(m)}$ is

$$f_m(x) = \frac{1}{\Gamma(m)} \gamma^n \beta^{-\gamma} (\alpha+\beta-x)^{\gamma-1} (\ln\beta - \ln(\alpha+\beta-x))^{m-1},$$

$$\alpha < x < \alpha+\beta,$$

Now
$$= 0, \text{ otherwise.} \qquad (5.1.2)$$

$$E(X_{U(m)}) = \int_\alpha^{\alpha+\beta} f_m(x)\,dx, \text{ letting } \alpha+\beta-x = \beta e^{-t/\gamma},$$

$$= \int_0^\infty \frac{1}{\Gamma(m)} t^{m-1} e^{-t} (\alpha+\beta-\beta e^{-t/\gamma})\,dt$$

$$= \int_0^\infty \frac{1}{\Gamma(m)} t^{m-1} e^{-t} (\alpha+\beta-\beta e^{-t/\gamma})\,dt.$$

$$= \alpha + \beta - \beta \left(\frac{\gamma}{\gamma+1}\right)^m. \qquad (5.1.3)$$

Similarly

$$E(X_{U(m)})^2 = \int_0^\infty \frac{1}{\Gamma(m)} t^{m-1} e^{-t} (\alpha+\beta-\beta e^{-t/\gamma})^2\,dt$$

$$= (\alpha+\beta)^2 - 2\beta(\alpha+\beta)\left(\frac{\gamma}{\gamma+1}\right)^m + \beta^2\left(\frac{\gamma}{\gamma+1}\right)^m$$

and

$$\text{Var}(X_{U(m)}) = E(X_{U(m)})^2 - \{E(X_{U(m)})\}^2$$

$$= \beta^2 \left\{\left(\frac{\gamma}{\gamma+2}\right)^m - \left(\frac{\gamma}{\gamma+1}\right)^{2m}\right\}. \qquad (5.1.4)$$

The joint pdf of $X_{U(m)}$ and $X_{U(n)}$ is

$$f_{m,n}(x,y) = c_{mn} \gamma^n \beta^{-\gamma} (\alpha+\beta-y)^{\gamma-1} \{\ln\beta - \ln(\alpha+\beta-x)\}^{m-1}$$

$$\cdot \{\ln\beta - \ln(\alpha+\beta-x)\}^{n-m-1}$$

for $\alpha < x < y < \alpha + \beta,$

$$= 0, \text{ otherwise,} \qquad (5.1.5)$$

where

$$c_{mn} = \frac{1}{\Gamma(m)\Gamma(n-m)}, \quad n > m \geq 1.$$

The conditional pdf of $X_{U(n)} \mid X_{U(m)} = x$ is

$$f(y \mid X_{U(m)} = x)$$

$$= \frac{\gamma^{n-m}}{\Gamma(n-m)} \left(\frac{\alpha+\beta-y}{\alpha+\beta-x}\right)^{\gamma-1} \{\ln \frac{\alpha+\beta-x}{\alpha+\beta-y}\}^{n-m-1},$$

$$\alpha < x < y < \alpha+\beta.$$

The conditional expectation of $X_{U(n)} \mid X_{U(m)} = x$ is

$$E(y \mid X_{U(m)} = x)$$

$$= \int_\alpha^{\alpha+\beta} \frac{\gamma^{n-m}}{\Gamma(n-m)} \left(\frac{\alpha+\beta-y}{\alpha+\beta-x}\right)^{\gamma-1} \{\ln \frac{\alpha+\beta-x}{\alpha+\beta-y}\}^{n-m-1} dy$$

$$= \int_0^\infty \frac{\gamma^{n-m}}{\Gamma(n-m)} (\alpha+\beta - (\alpha+\beta-x\,e^{-t})) \, t^{n-m-1} \, e^{-\gamma t} \, dt$$

$$= \alpha+\beta - (\alpha+\beta-x)\left(\frac{\gamma}{\gamma+1}\right)^{n-m}.$$

For $m < n$,

$$\text{Cov}(X_{U(m)}, X_{U(n)}) = \left(\frac{\gamma}{\gamma+1}\right)^{n-m} \text{Var}(X_{U(m)}).$$

The correlation coefficient $\rho_{m,n}$ of $X_{U(m)}$ and $X_{U(n)}$ is given by

$$\rho_{m,n} = \sqrt{\left(\frac{\gamma^2+2\gamma+1}{\gamma^2+\gamma}\right)-1} \Big/ [\sqrt{\left(\frac{\gamma^2+2\gamma+1}{\gamma^2+\gamma}\right)^n -1}] \quad (5.1.6)$$

As $\gamma \to \infty$, $\quad \rho_{m,n} \to \sqrt{\frac{m}{n}}$.

5.2. RECURRENCE RELATION BETWEEN MOMENTS

We will consider in this section without any loss of generality $\alpha = 0$ and $\beta = 1$ i.e.

$$f(x) = \gamma(1-x)^{\gamma-1}, \qquad 0 < x < 1, \qquad (5.2.1)$$

Power Function Distribution

The cdf is
$$=0, \text{ otherwise.}$$
$$F(x) = 1 - (1-x)^{\gamma-1}, 0 < x < 1.$$
It is easy to see in this case that

$$\gamma(1 - F(x)) - (1-x) f(x). \qquad (5.2.2)$$

The relation (5.2.2) will be used to derive some simple recurrence relations for the single and the product moments of the upper record values from the power function distribution.

In this section some recurrence relations satisfied by the single and product moments of upper record values from the power function distribution. These recurrence relations will enable one to obtain all the single and product moments of all record values in a simple recursive manner.

(a) Relations for single moments

Let $X_{U(1)} < X_{U(2)} < \ldots$ be the sequence of upper record values from (5.3.1). For convenience, we shall also take $XU(0) = 0$. Then the pdf of $X_{U(n)}$, n=1,2,..., is given by

$$f(x) = \frac{1}{\Gamma(n)} (H(x))^{n-1} f(x), \qquad (5.2.3)$$

for $-\infty < x < \infty$.

Theorem 5.2.1

For $n \geq 2$, and $r = 0,1,2,\ldots$

$$E\left(X_{U(n)}^{r+1}\right) = \frac{r+1}{\gamma+r+1} E\left(X_{U(n)}^{r}\right) + \frac{\gamma}{\gamma+r+1} E(X_{U(n-1)}^{r+1})$$

$$(5.2.4)$$

Proof.

From (5.2.3), for $n > 2$ and $r = 0,1,\ldots$,

$$E\left(X_{U(n)}^{r} - X_{U(n)}^{r+1}\right) = \int_0^\infty \left(x^r - x^{r+1}\right) f_n(x) dx$$

$$= \frac{\gamma}{(n-1)!} \int_0^\infty x^r \{-\ln(1-F(x))\}^{n-1} \{1-F(x)\} dx \quad \text{(using (5.2.2))}$$

$$= \frac{\gamma}{r+1} \left[\int_0^\infty x^{r+1} \frac{1}{(n-1)!} \{-\ln(1-F(x))\}^{n-1} f(x) dx \right.$$

$$\left. - \int_0^\infty x^{r+1} \frac{1}{(n-2)!} \{-\ln(1-F(x))\}^{n-2} f(x) dx \right]$$

$$= \frac{\gamma}{r+1} \left[E\!\left(X_{U(n)}^{r+1}\right) - E\!\left(X_{U(n-1)}^{r+1}\right) \right]$$

where the last but one step follows by integrating by parts. The recurrence relation in equation (5.2.4) is derived simply by rewriting the above equation.

Corollary 5.2.1.

By repeatedly applying the recurrence relation in (5.2.4), we get for $n > 2$, $1 < m < n-1$ and $r = 0,1,2,\ldots$

$$E\!\left(X_{U(n)}^{r+1}\right) = \left(\frac{r+1}{\gamma+r-1}\right) \sum_{p=0}^{n-m-1} \left(\frac{\gamma}{\gamma+r+1}\right)^p E\!\left(X_{U(n-p)}^r\right)$$

$$+ \left(\frac{\gamma}{\gamma+r+1}\right)^{n-m} E\!\left(X_{U(m)}^{r+1}\right) \qquad (5.2.5)$$

Corollary 5.2.2.

Write $(r+1)^{(-p)} = 1$ for $p = 0$, $= (r+1) r \ldots (r-p+2)$, for $p \geq 1$. By repeated application of the recurrence relation in (5.2.4), we obtain for $n > 2$, $r = 0,1,2,\ldots$

$$E\!\left(X_{U(n)}^{r+1}\right) = \gamma \sum_{p=0}^{r+1} \frac{(r+1)^{(p)}}{(\gamma+1+p)^{(p+1)}} E\!\left(X_{U(n-1)}^{r+1-p}\right) \qquad (5.2.6)$$

Next, we have the joint density function of $X_{U(m)}$ and $X_{U(n)}$, $1 < m < n$, as

$$f_{m,n}(x,y) = \frac{1}{(m-1)!(n-m-1)!} \{-\ln(1-F(x))\}^{m-1} \frac{f(x)}{1-F(x)}$$

Power Function Distribution 161

$$\bullet \{-\ln(1-F(y))+\ln(1-F(x))\}^{n-m-1} f(y),$$

(5.2.7)

Once again, upon using the relation in (5.2.2), we can derive some simple recurrence relations for the product moments of record values.

Theorem 5.2.2

For $m \geq 1$ and $r,s = 0,1,2,...$

$$E\left(X^r_{U(m)} X^{s+1}_{U(m+1)}\right) = \frac{s+1}{\gamma+s+1} E\left(X^r_{U(m)} X^s_{U(m+1)}\right) + \frac{\gamma}{\gamma+s+1} E\left(X^{r+s+1}_{U(m)}\right)$$

(5.2.8)

and for $1 < m < n-2$ and $r,s = 0,1,2,...$,

$$E\left(X^r_{U(m)} X^{s+1}_{U(n)}\right) = \frac{s+1}{\gamma+s+1} E\left(X^r_{U(m)} X^s_{U(n)}\right) + \frac{\gamma}{\gamma+s+1} E\left(X^r_{U(m)} X^{s+1}_{U(n-1)}\right)$$

(5.2.9)

Proof:

From (5.2.7), let us consider for $1 < m < n-1$ and $r,s = 0,1,2...$

$$E\left(X^r_{U(m)} X^s_{U(n)} - X^r_{U(m)} X^{s+1}_{U(n)}\right)$$

$$\iint_{0 \leq x < y < 1} \left(x^r y^s - x^r y^{s+1}\right) f_{m,n}(x,y) dy\, dx$$

$$= \frac{1}{(m-1)!(n-m-1)!} \int_0^1 x^r \{-\ln(1-F(x))\}^{m-1} \cdot \frac{f(x)}{1-F(x)} I(x) dx$$

(5.2.10)

$$I(x) = \int_x^1 y^s (1-y)\{-\ln(1-F(y))+\ln(1-F(x))\}^{n-m-1} f(y) dy$$

$$= \gamma \int_x^1 y^s \{-\ln(1-F(y))+\ln(1-F(x))\}^{n-m-1} \{1-F(y)\} dy$$

(upon using (5.2.2))

$$= \frac{\gamma}{s+1}\left[\int_x^1 y^{s+1} f(y)dy - x^{s+1}\{1-F(x)\}\right], \text{ for } n = m+2$$

$$= \frac{\gamma}{s+1} \left[\int_x^1 y^{s+1} \{-\ln(1-F(y)) + \ln(1-F(x))\}^{n-m-1} f(y) dy \right.$$

$$\left. - (n-m-1) \int_x^1 y^{s+1} \{-\ln(1-F(y)) + \ln(1-F(x))\}^{n-m-2} f(y) dy \right],$$

for $n > m + 2$.

The last two equations are derived by integrating by parts. Upon substituting the above expressions of $I(x)$ in Eq. (5.2.10) and simplifying the resulting equations, we obtain when $n = m+1$ that

$$E(X^r_{U(m)} X^s_{U(m+1)}) - E(X^r_{U(m)} X^{s+1}_{U(m+1)})$$
$$= \frac{\gamma}{s+1} \{E(X^r_{U(m)} X^{s+1}_{U(m+1)}) - E(X^{r+s+1}_{U(m)})\},$$

and when $n - m \geq 2$ that

$$E(X^r_{U(m)} X^s_{U(n)}) - E(X^r_{U(m)} X^{s+1}_{U(n)})$$
$$= \frac{\gamma}{s+1} \{E(X^r_{U(m)} X^{s+1}_{U(n)}) - E(X^r_{U(m)} X^{s+1}_{U(n-1)})\}.$$

The recurrence relations in (5.2.8) and (5.2.9) are derived simply by rewriting the above equations.

Corollary 5.2.3

For $m > 1$

$$Cov(X_{U(m)}, X_{U(m+1)}) = \frac{\gamma}{\gamma+1} Var(X_{U(m)}) \qquad (5.2.11)$$

$$Cov(X_{U(m)}, X_{U(n)}) = \frac{\gamma}{\gamma+1} Cov(X_{U(m)}, X_{U(n-1)}), \qquad (5.2.12)$$

Consequently, for $1 < m < n-1$

$$Cov(X_{U(m)}, X_{U(n)}) = \left(\frac{\gamma}{\gamma+1}\right)^{n-m} Var(X_{U(m)}) \qquad (5.2.13)$$

Proof:

(5.2.11) follows from (5.2.4) and (5.2.7), and (5.2.12) from (5.2.4) and (5.2.9). Repeated application of (5.2.12) yields (5.2.13).

Corollary 5.2.4.

By repeated application of the recurrence relations in (5.2.9) and (5.2.10), we get from m > 1, r,s = 0,1,2,....

$$E\left(X_{U(m)}^r X_{U(m+1)}^{s+1}\right) = \gamma \sum_{p=0}^{s+1} \frac{(s+1)^{(p)}}{(\gamma+s+1+p)^{(p+1)}} E\left(X_{U(m)}^{r+s+1-p}\right)$$

(5.2.14)

and for 1 < m < n - 2 and r,s = 0,1,2,...

$$E\left(X_{U(m)}^r X_{U(n)}^{s+1}\right) = \gamma \sum_{p=0}^{s+1} \frac{(s+1)^{(p)}}{(\gamma+s+1+p)^{(p+1)}} E\left(X_{U(m)}^r X_{U(n-1)}^{s+1-p}\right)$$

(5.2.15)

Theorem 5.2.3

For m > 2 and r,s = 0,1,2,...,

$$E\left(X_{U(m)}^{r+1} X_{U(m+1)}^{s}\right) = \frac{\gamma}{r+1}\left\{E\left(X_{U(m)}^{r+s+1}\right) - E\left(X_{U(m-1)}^{r+1} X_{U(m)}^{s}\right)\right\}$$
$$- E\left(X_{U(m)}^r X_{U(m+1)}^s\right); \quad (5.2.16)$$

and for $2 \leq m \leq n-2$ and r,s = 0,1,2,......

$$E\left(X_{U(m)}^{r+1} X_{U(n)}^{s}\right) = \frac{\gamma}{r+1}\left\{E\left(X_{U(m)}^{r+1} X_{U(n-1)}^{s}\right) - E\left(X_{U(m-1)}^{r+1} X_{U(n-1)}^{s}\right)\right\}$$
$$- E\left(X_{U(m)}^r X_{U(n)}^s\right) \quad (5.2.17)$$

Proof:

From (5.2.7), let us consider for 2 < m < n-1 and r,s = 0,1,2,...

$$E\left(X_{U(m)}^r X_{U(n)}^s - X_{U(m)}^{r+1} X_{U(n)}^s\right)$$

$$= \frac{1}{(m-1)!(n-m-1)!} \int_0^d y^s f(y) J(y) dy, \qquad (5.2.18)$$

where
$J(y)$
$$= \int_0^y x^r (1-x) \{-\ln(1-F(x))\}^{m-1} \{-\ln(1-F(y)) + \ln(1-F(x))\}^{n-m-1}$$
$$\cdot \frac{f(x)}{1-F(x)} dx$$
$$= \gamma \int_0^y x^r \{-\ln(1-F(x))\}^{m-1} \{-\ln(1-F(y)) + \ln(1-F(x))\}^{n-m-1} dx$$

(using (5.2.2))

$$= \frac{\gamma}{r+1} \Big[y^{r+1} \{-\ln(1-F(y))\}^{m-1}$$
$$- (m-1) \int_0^y x^{r+1} \{-\ln(1-F(x))\}^{m-2} \frac{f(x)}{1-F(x)} dx \Big], \text{ for } n = m+1$$

$$= \frac{\gamma}{r+1} \Big[(n-m-1) \int_0^y x^{r+1} \{-\ln(1-F(x))\}^{m-1}$$
$$\cdot \frac{f(x)}{1-F(x)} \{-\ln(1-F(y)) + \ln(1-F(x))\}^{n-m-2} dx$$
$$- (m-1) \int_0^y x^{r+1} \{-\ln(1-F(x))\}^{m-2}$$
$$\cdot \frac{f(x)}{1-F(x)} \{-\ln(1-F(y)) + \ln(1-F(x))\}^{n-m-1} dx \Big], \text{ for } n = m+2.$$

As before, the last two equations are obtained by integration by parts. Upon substituting the above expressions of $J(y)$ in Eq. (5.2.18) and simplifying the resulting equations, we obtain when $n = m+1$ that
$$E\big(X_{U(m)}^r X_{U(m+1)}^s - X_{U(m)}^{r+1} X_{U(m+1)}^s\big)$$
$$= \frac{\gamma}{r+1} \Big\{ E\big(X_{U(m)}^{r+s+1}\big) - E\big(X_{U(m-1)}^{r+1} X_{U(m)}^s\big) \Big\}$$

and when $n > m+2$ that
$$E\big(X_{U(m)}^r X_{U(n)}^s - X_{U(m)}^{r+1} X_{U(n)}^s\big)$$
$$= \frac{\gamma}{r+1} \Big\{ E\big(X_{U(m)}^{r+1} X_{U(n-1)}^s\big) - E\big(X_{U(m-1)}^{r+1} X_{U(n-1)}^s\big) \Big\}$$

Power Function Distribution

$$E\left(X_{U(m)}^r X_{U(n)}^s - X_{U(m)}^{r+1} X_{U(n)}^s\right)$$
$$= \frac{\gamma}{r+1}\left\{E\left(X_{U(m)}^{r+1} X_{U(n-1)}^s\right) - E\left(X_{U(m-1)}^{r+1} X_{U(n-1)}^s\right)\right\}$$

The recurrence relations in (5.2.16) and (5.2.17) are derived simply by rewriting the above equations.

Corollary 5.2.5.

By repeated application of the recurrence relation in (5.2.16) and (5.2.17), we obtain for m > 1, r,s = 0,1,2,.....

$$E\left(X_{U(m)}^{r+1} X_{U(m+1)}^s\right) = \sum_{p=0}^{m-1} (-1)^p \left(\frac{\gamma}{r+1}\right)^p \left\{\frac{\gamma}{r+1} E\left(X_{U(m-p)}^{r+s+1}\right) - E\left(X_{U(m-p)}^r X_{U(m-p+1)}^s\right)\right\}$$

and for $1 \leq m \leq n - 2$ and r,s, = 0,1,2,.....

$$E\left(X_{U(m)}^{r+1} X_{U(n)}^s\right) = \sum_{p=0}^{m-1} (-1)^p \left(\frac{\gamma}{r+1}\right)^p \left\{\frac{\gamma}{r+1} E\left(X_{U(m-p)}^{r+1} X_{U(n-p-1)}^s\right) - E\left(X_{U(m-p)}^r X_{U(n-p)}^s\right)\right\}$$

5.3. Estimation of the Parameters

Case 1: The minimum variancet linear unbiased estimate of α and β when γ is known.

Let $W_k = c_k(X_{U(k)} \frac{\gamma}{\gamma+1} X_{U(k-1)}), k=1,2....,m,$

with $X_{U(o)} = 0$, and $c_k = (\gamma+1)(\frac{\gamma+2}{\gamma})^{k/2}, k=1,2,....,m.$

Now

$$E(W_1)=(\frac{\gamma+2}{\gamma})^{1/2}\{(\gamma+1)\alpha+\beta\},$$

$$E(W_k)=(\frac{\gamma+2}{\gamma})^{k/2}(\alpha+\beta),\ k=2,3,\ldots,m.$$

Var(W_k) = β^2, k = 1, 2, ..., m

Cov($W_i W_j$) = 0, $i \neq j$, $1 \leq i, j \leq m$.

Let $W' = (W_1, W_2, \cdots, W_n)$, then $E(W) = X\theta$, where

$$X = \begin{bmatrix} ((\gamma+2/\gamma)^{1/2})(\gamma+1) & ((\gamma+2)/\gamma)^{1/2} \\ (\gamma+2)/\gamma & (\gamma+2)/\gamma \\ \vdots & \vdots \\ ((\gamma+2/\gamma)^{n/2}) & ((\gamma+2/\gamma)^{n/2}) \end{bmatrix}, \theta = \begin{bmatrix} \alpha \\ \beta \end{bmatrix}$$

We can write X'X as

$$X'X = \begin{pmatrix} (\gamma+2)^2 + T & \gamma+2+T \\ \gamma+2+T & T \end{pmatrix}$$

$$T = \sum_{k=1}^{m} (\frac{\gamma+2}{\gamma})^k$$

$$(X'X)^{-1} = D_o^{-1} \begin{pmatrix} T & -(\gamma+2+T) \\ -(\gamma+2+T) & (\gamma+2)^2 + T \end{pmatrix}$$

$$D_0 = (\gamma+2)(\gamma T - \gamma - 2)$$

$$X'W = \begin{pmatrix} V_1 \\ V_2 \end{pmatrix}$$

$$V_1 = (\gamma(\gamma+2))^{1/2} W_1 + V_2$$

$$V_2 = \sum_{k=1}^{m} (\frac{\gamma+2}{\gamma})^{k/2} W_k$$

Theorem 5.3.1

The minimum variance unbiased estimates $\hat{\alpha}, \hat{\beta}$ of α and β respectively based on $Y_1,..., Y_n$ (assuming γ as known) are

$$\begin{bmatrix} \hat{\alpha} \\ \hat{\beta} \end{bmatrix} = (X'X)^{-1} X'W$$

On simplification, we get

$$\hat{\alpha} = \frac{1}{D_o} \left[(\gamma(\gamma+2))^{1/2} W_1 - \sum_{k=1}^{n} ((\gamma+2)/\gamma)^{k/2} W_k \right]$$

$$\hat{\beta} = \frac{1}{D_o} \left[-(T+\gamma+2)(\gamma(\gamma+2))^{1/2} W_1 + (\gamma+2)(\gamma+1) \sum_{k=1}^{n} ((\gamma+2)/\gamma)^{k/2} W_k \right]$$

The variances and covariance of $\hat{\alpha}$ and $\hat{\beta}$ are given by

$$\text{Var}(\hat{\alpha}) = \beta^2 T D_o^{-1},$$

$$\text{Var}(\hat{\beta}) = \beta^2 ((\gamma+2)^2 + T) D_o^{-1}$$

and

$$\text{Cov}(\hat{\alpha}, \hat{\beta}) = -\beta^2 (\gamma+2+T) D_o^{-1}$$

(b) Invariant Estimators

Theorem 5.3.2

The best linear invariant (in the sense of minimum mean squared error and invariance with respect to the location parameter α) estimators $\tilde{\alpha}$ and $\tilde{\beta}$ of α and β are respectively

$$\tilde{\alpha} = \hat{\alpha} - \frac{\gamma+2+T}{(\gamma+1)\{(\gamma+1)T - (\gamma+2)\}} \hat{\beta}$$

$$\text{and } \tilde{\beta} = \frac{D_o}{(\gamma+1)\{(\gamma+1)T - (\gamma+2)\}} \hat{\beta}$$

where

$$D_o = (\gamma+2)\{\gamma T - (\gamma+2)\}, T = \sum_{i=1}^{m} (\frac{\gamma+2}{\gamma})^i$$

and $\hat{\alpha}$ and $\hat{\beta}$ are MVLUEs of α and β.

Proof.

The BLIE $\tilde{\alpha}$ and $\tilde{\beta}$ of α and β can be written as

$$\tilde{\alpha} = \hat{\alpha} - \frac{E_{12}}{1+E_{22}}\hat{\beta}$$

and

$$\tilde{\beta} = \frac{1}{1+E_{22}}\hat{\beta},$$

where

$$\begin{pmatrix} Var(\hat{\alpha}) & Cov(\hat{\alpha},\hat{\beta}) \\ Cov(\hat{\alpha},\hat{\beta}) & Var(\hat{\beta}) \end{pmatrix} = \gamma^2 \begin{pmatrix} E_{11} & E_{12} \\ E_{12} & E_{22} \end{pmatrix}.$$

The mean squared errors of $\tilde{\alpha}$ and $\tilde{\beta}$ of α and β are

$$MSE(\tilde{\alpha}) = \gamma^2 (E_{11} - \frac{E_{12}^2}{1+E_{22}}),$$

$$MSE(\tilde{\beta}) = \gamma^2 (\frac{E_{22}}{1+E_{22}}).$$

Substituting the values of E_{11}, E_{12} and E_{22} in terms of γ, we get the results.

(c) Estimator of β for known μ and σ.

    Maximum Likelihood Estimator of β.

    Without any loss of generality we will assume $\mu = 0$ and $\sigma = 1$.

The log likelihood function of $r_1, r_2, \ldots, r_m$ can be written as

$$\ln L = n\ln\gamma - \sum_{i=1}^{m} \frac{1}{1-r_i} + \gamma \ln(1-r_m)$$

Power Function Distribution

Differentiating with respect γ and equating to zero, we get $\breve{\gamma}$ as the maximum likelihood estimator of γ as

$$\breve{\gamma} = -\frac{m}{\ln(1-r_m)}$$

A moment Estimator of γ.

Taking α = 0 and β = 1, we get $E(X_{U(m)}) = (\frac{\gamma}{\gamma+1})^m - 1$ and

$$E(X_{U(1)} + X_{U(2)} + \ldots + X_{U(m)}) = \gamma\{(\frac{\gamma}{\gamma+1})^m - 1\} - m.$$

Thus we can a moment estimator based on the m record values $r_1, r_2, \ldots, r_m$ as

$$\breve{\gamma} = \frac{r_1 + r_2 + \ldots + r_m + m}{r_m}$$

5.4. Predictor of Record Values

We will consider the predictor of $X_{U(s)}$ based on m record values for m < s. Let $R = (X_{U(1)}, X_{U(2)}, \ldots, X_{U(m)})$. Then we can write $E(R) = \alpha L + \beta \delta$, $L' = (1,1,\ldots,1)$, $\delta' = (\delta_1, \delta_2, \ldots, \delta_m)$ and $\delta_i = (\frac{\gamma}{\gamma+1})^i - 1$.

$Var(R) = \beta^2 V$, $V = (V_{ij})$, $V_{ij} = a_i b_j$, $a_i = (\frac{\gamma+1}{\gamma})^i [(\frac{\gamma}{\gamma+2})^i - (\frac{\gamma}{\gamma+1})^{2i}]$

and $b_j = (\frac{\gamma}{\gamma+1})^j$. Let $V^{-1} = (V^{ij})$, then it can shown that

$$(V^{ij}) = \begin{cases} -(\frac{\gamma+2}{\gamma})^{\min(i,j)}(\gamma+2)(\gamma+1), |i-j|=1, i,j=1,2,\ldots,m \\ (\frac{\gamma+2}{\gamma})^{i+1}(2\gamma^2+4\gamma+1)\frac{\gamma(\gamma+2)}{(\gamma+1)^2}, i=1,2,\ldots,m-1 \\ (\frac{\gamma+2}{\lambda})^{n-1}(\gamma+2)(\gamma+1)(\frac{\gamma+1}{\gamma}), i=n \\ 0, |i-j|>1 \end{cases}$$

Theorem 5.4.1

Let $H' = (h_1, h_2, \ldots, h_m)$, where $\beta^2 h_i = \text{Cov}(X_{U(i)}, X_{U(s)})$, $i = 1, 2, \ldots, m$ and $\delta_s = \beta^{-1} E(X_{U(s)} - \alpha)$. Then the best (in the sense of minimum mean squared error) linear unbiased predictor (BLUP) of $X_{U(s)}$ based on the observed record values $r_1, r_2, \ldots, r_m$ is

$$\left(\frac{\gamma}{\gamma+1}\right)^{s-m}[r_m - \hat{\alpha} - \delta_m \hat{\beta}] + \hat{\alpha} + \delta_s \hat{\beta}$$

where $\hat{\alpha}$ and $\hat{\beta}$ are MVLUEs of α and β.

Proof.

The best (in the sense of minimum mean squared error) linear unbiased predictor (BLUP) of $X_{U(s)}$ based on the observed record values $r_1, r_2, \ldots, r_m$ is $\hat{X}_{U(s)} = \hat{\alpha} + \hat{\beta}\delta_s + H'V^{-1}(r - \hat{\alpha}L - \hat{\beta}\delta)$, where $r' = (r_1, r_2, \ldots, r_m)$ and $\hat{\alpha}$ and $\hat{\beta}$ are MVLUE of α and β. It can be shown easily that

$$H'V^{-1} = \left(0, 0, \ldots, \left(\frac{\gamma}{\gamma+1}\right)^{s-m}\right),$$

$$H'V^{-1}(r - \hat{\alpha}L - \hat{\beta}\delta) = \left(\frac{\gamma}{\gamma+1}\right)^{s-m}(r_m - \hat{\alpha} - \hat{\beta}\delta_m).$$

Substituting these values in the expression of $\hat{X}_{U(s)}$, we get the result. The best (unrestricted) least squares predictor $X^*_{U(s)}$ of $X_{U(s)}$ is

$$X^*_{U(s)} = E(X_{U(s)} \mid X_{U(1)}, X_{U(2)}, \ldots, X_{U(m)}).$$

By using (5.1.5), we have

$$X^*_{U(s)} = \alpha + \beta - (\alpha + \beta - r_m)\left(\frac{\gamma}{\gamma+1}\right)^{s-m}$$

where r_m is the observed value of $X_{U(m)}$.

It is evident that $X^*_{U(s)}$ depends on the unknown parameters α and β. If substitute the MVLUEs of α and β in the above expression, then this will be equal to BLUPs.

Theorem 5.4.2

The best linear invariant (minimum MSE and invariant with respect to the location parameter α) predictor $\tilde{X}_{U(s)}$ is

$$\tilde{X}_{U(s)} = \hat{X}_{U(s)} \frac{E^*_{12}}{1+E_{22}} \hat{\beta}$$

where $E^*_{12} \beta^2 = Cov(\hat{\beta}, (1 - H'V^{-1}L)\hat{\alpha} + (\alpha_s - H'V^{-1}\delta)\hat{\beta})$ and $\hat{\alpha}$ and $\hat{\beta}$ are MVLUE of α and β.

Proof.

Now

$$1 - H'V^{-1}L = 1 - (1-\beta)^{m-s} = -\beta \alpha_{s-m}$$

$$\alpha_s - H'V^{-1}\delta = \alpha_s - (1-\beta)^{m-s}\alpha_m = \alpha_{s-m}$$

Thus

$$c^*_{12}(1 + E_{22})^{-1} = \frac{\alpha_{s-n}(1-2\beta)}{T(1-\beta)}$$

and hence

$$\tilde{X}_{U(s)} = \hat{X}_{U(s)} - \frac{\alpha_{s-n}(1-2\beta)}{T(1-\beta)}.$$

5.5. ONE PARAMETER UNIFORM DISTRIBUTION.

Suppose $\gamma = 1$ and $\alpha = 0$, i.e. when X is distributed uniformly in the interval $(0, \beta)$, We have in this case the pdf $f_n(x)$ of $X_{U(n)}$ as

$$f_n(x) = \frac{1}{\Gamma(n)}[\ln\frac{\beta}{x}]^{n-1}, \quad 0 < x < \beta. \tag{5.5.1}$$

Using (5.5.1), we have

$$E(X_{U(n)}) = (1 - 2^{-n})\beta$$

$$Var(X_{U(n)}) = (3^{-n} - 4^{-n})\beta^2$$

The joint pdf of $X_{U(m)}$ and $X_{U(n)}$ is

$$f_{m,n}(x,y) = \frac{1}{\Gamma(m)}\frac{1}{\Gamma(n-m)}\frac{1}{\beta}\frac{1}{\beta-x}[\ln\frac{\beta}{\beta-x}]^{m-1}[\ln\frac{\beta}{\beta-y}]^{n-m-1}, \tag{5.5.2}$$

$$n > m > 0, \; 0 < x < y < \beta.$$

It follows from (5.5.2) that

$$E(X_{U(n)} | X_{U(m)} = x_m) = 2^{m-n} x_m + (1 - 2^{m-n})\beta.$$

and

$$Cov(X_{U(m)}, X_{U(n)}) = 2^{m-n} Var(X_{U(m)}), \; m < n, \; 1 \leq m \leq n$$

The correlation coefficient $\rho_{m,n}$ of $X_{U(m)}$ and $X_{U(n)}$

$$\rho_{m,n} = \left(\left(\frac{4}{3}\right)^m - 1\right)^{\frac{1}{2}} \left(\left(\frac{4}{3}\right)^n - 1\right)^{-\frac{1}{2}}, \; m < n$$

Using the following transformation

$$W_1 = X_{U(1)}$$

$$W_i = 3^{(i-1)/2} (X_{U(i)} - \frac{1}{2} X_{U(i-1)}), \; i = 2,3,\ldots,n.$$

$$E(W_i) = (1/2)(3)^{(i-1)/2} \beta$$

$$Var(W_i) = \frac{\beta^2}{12},$$

$$Cov(W_i, W_j) = 0, \; i \neq j, \; i,j = 1,2,\ldots,n.$$

Let

$$X' = (\frac{1}{2}, \frac{1}{2}(3)^{1/2}, \frac{1}{2}(3), \ldots, \frac{1}{2}(3)^{n-1})$$

and

$$W' = (W_1, W_2, \ldots, W_n),$$

then the best linear unbiased estimator $\hat{\beta}$ of β based on the first n record values is

$$\hat{\beta} = (X'X)^{-1} X'W$$

$$= \frac{4}{3^n - 1} (\sum_{i=1}^{n} (3)^{(i-1)/2} W_i$$

$$= \frac{4}{3^n - 1} (3^{n-1} y_n - \frac{1}{2}(3)^{n-2} y_{n-1} - \ldots - \frac{1}{2} y_1),$$

where y_i is the observed value of $X_{U(i)}$, $i = 1, 2, \ldots, n$.

The following table gives the coefficients of the MVLUE $\hat{\beta}$ for some selected values n.

Table 5.5.1. Coefficients of y_n's in MVLUE $\hat{\beta}$

n	y_1	y_2	y_3	y_4	y_5	y_6
2	-1/4	3/2				
3	-1/13	-3/13	18/13			
4	-1/40	-3/40	-9/40	27/20		
5	-1/121	-3/121	-9/121	-27/121	162/121	
6	-1/364	-3/364	-9/364	-27/364	-81/364	243/182

where $y_1, y_2, \ldots, y_n$ are the observed values of $X_{U(1)}, X_{U(2)}, \ldots, X_{U(n)}$.

Since $X'X = \frac{3^n - 1}{8}$ and $Var(W_i) = \frac{\beta^2}{12}$, we have $Var(\hat{\beta})$

$$= (X'X)^{-1} \frac{\beta^2}{12}$$

$$= \frac{2\beta^2}{3} (3^n - 1)^{-1}.$$

If we drop the condition of unbiasedness, then the estimator $\tilde{\beta}$, where

$$\tilde{\beta} = \frac{3(3^n - 1)}{3^{n+1} - 1} \hat{\beta}$$

has minimum mean squared error.

Bias of $\tilde{\beta} = E(\tilde{\beta}) - \beta = -\dfrac{2}{3^{n+1}-1}\beta$

and

$$\text{MSE}(\tilde{\beta}) = \dfrac{2}{3^{n+1}-1}.$$

Writing

$$Y_{n+s} = Y_{n+s} - \dfrac{1}{2}Y_{n+s-1} + \dfrac{1}{2}(Y_{n+s-1} - \dfrac{1}{2}Y_{n+s-2}) + \cdots + \dfrac{1}{2^{n+s-2}}(Y_2 - \dfrac{1}{2}Y_1) + \dfrac{1}{2^{n+s-1}}Y_1,$$

it can be shown that

$$\text{Cov}(Y_{n+s}, W_i) = \dfrac{\text{Var}(W_i)}{2^{n+s-i} \cdot 3^{(i-1)/2}}, \quad i = 1, 2, \ldots, n.$$

It can be shown that the best linear unbiased predictor (BLUP) of Y_{n+s} is $\hat{Y}_{n+s}$, where

$$\hat{Y}_{n+s} = (1 - \dfrac{1}{2^{n+s}})\hat{\beta} + c'V^{-1}(W - X\hat{\beta}),$$

where
$c' = (c_1, c_2, \ldots, c_n)$, $V^{-1} = (X'X)^{-1}$ and $c_i \text{Var}(W_i) = \text{Cov}(Y_{n+s}, W_i)$, $s \geq 1$.

Thus

$$\hat{Y}_{n+s} = (1 - \dfrac{1}{2^{n+s}})\hat{\beta} + \dfrac{8}{3^n - 1}[\sum_{i=1}^{n} \dfrac{1}{2^{n+s-i}} \cdot \dfrac{W_i}{3^{(i-1)/2}} \cdot \dfrac{\hat{\beta}}{2^s}(1 - \dfrac{1}{2^n})]$$

The best linear (unrestricted) least square predictor of Y_{n+s} is $\tilde{Y}_{n+s}$, where

$$\tilde{Y}_{r+s} = E(Y_{n+s} | Y_1, Y_2, \ldots, Y_n)$$

$$= \dfrac{y_n}{2^s} + (1 - \dfrac{1}{2^s})\beta,$$

Substituting $\hat{\beta}$ for β, we get the best linear least squares predictor as

$$\dfrac{y_n}{2^s} + (1 - \dfrac{1}{2^s}) \cdot \dfrac{4}{3^n - 1}(3^{n-1}y_n - \dfrac{1}{2}(3)^{n-2}y_{n-1} - \cdots - \dfrac{1}{2}y_1).$$

Arslan, Ahsanullah and Bairamov (2003) presented the following characterization of the unifrm distribution based on the lower record values.

Theorem 5.5.1.
Let $X_1, X_2, \ldots$, be a sequence of independent and identically distributed nonnegative absolutely bounded continuos random variables and V_i be uniformly distributed on $(0,1)$ and independent of X_i's. Without any loss of generality we assume that the distribution function of X.'s is such that $F(0) = 0$ and $F(1)$. Then the relation $X_{L(n)} \stackrel{d}{=} X_{L(n-1)} V_1$ holds for some fixed $n > 1$ if and only if $X_i \in U(0,1)$.

Proof.
It can easily be shown that if $X_i \in U(0,1)$, then $X_{L(n)} \stackrel{d}{=} X_{L(n-1)} V_1$.
Suppose that $X_{L(n)} \stackrel{d}{=} X_{L(n-1)} V_1$, then

$$F_{(n)}(x) = P(X_{L(n)} \leq x) = \int_0^1 F_{(n-1)}(x/u)\,du$$

$$= \int_0^{x1} du + \int_x^1 F_{(n-)}(x/u)\,du$$

$$= x + x \int_x^1 F_{(n-1)}(t) t^{-2} dt \qquad (5.5.3)$$

Differentiating (5.5.3) with respect to x we obtain

$$f_{(n)}(x) = 1 - \frac{1}{x} F_{(n-1)}(x) + \int_0^1 f_{(n-1)}(t) t^{-2}\, dt$$

i.e. $\quad x f_{(n)}(x) = x - F_{(n-1)}(x) + x \int_x^1 f_{(n-1)}(t) t^{-2}\, dt$

$$- x - F_{(n-1)}(x) + F_{(n)}(x) - x \qquad (5.5.4)$$

Now it is easy to show that

$$F_{(n)}(x) - F_{(n-1)}(x) = F(x)\frac{(h(x))^{n-1}}{\Gamma(n)} = F(x)\frac{f_{(n)}(x)}{f(x)} \quad (5.5.5)$$

Sustituting (5,5,5) in (5.5.4), we have

$$\frac{f(x)}{F(x)} = \frac{1}{x} \quad (5.5.6)$$

for all x, 0<x<1. Hence

$$F(x) = x, \quad 0 \le <x \le 1.$$

CHAPTER 6

DISCRETE DISTRIBUTION

In this chapter we will consider the record values of discrete distribution..

6.0. INTRODUCTION

Let $X_1, X_2, ..., X_n, ...$ be a sequence independent and identically distributed random variables taking values on $0,1,2,...$ such that $F(n) < 1$ for all n $n=0,1,2,...$ We define the upper record times, $U(n)$ as $U(1) = 1$, $U(n+1) = \min\{j > U(n), X_j > X_{U(n)}\}$, $n=1,2,....$ The nth upper record value is defined as $X_{U(n)}$. Let $p_k = P(X_1=k)$, $P(k) = \sum_{j=0}^{k} p(j)$, $k \geq 0$ and $\overline{P}(k) = 1 - P(k)$ with and $P(\infty) = 1$ The joint probability mass function (pmf) of the $X_{U(1)}, X_{U(2)}, ... X_{U(n)}$ is defined as
$$P_{1,2,...,n}(x_1,x_2,..x_n) = P(X_{U(1)}=x_1, X_{U(2)}=x_2, ..., X_{U(n)}=x_n)$$
$$= \frac{p(x_1)}{\overline{P}(x_1)} \cdot \frac{p(x_2)}{\overline{P}(x_2)} \cdots \frac{p(x_{n-1})}{\overline{P}(x_{n-1})} p(x_n)$$
$$0 \leq x_1 < x_2 < ... < x_n < \infty,$$
$$= 0, \text{ otherwise.} \tag{6.0.1}$$

The marginal pmf's of the upper record values are given as
$p_1(x_1) = P(X_{U(1)} = x_1) = p(x_1)$, $x_1 = 0,1,2,...$,
$p_2(x_2) = P(X_{U(2)} = x_2) = R_1(x_2) p(x_2)$,
where

$$R_1(k) = \sum_{0 \le x_1 < x_2} B(x_1), \quad B(x) = \frac{p(x)}{\bar{P}(x)}, \quad x_2 = 1, 2, \ldots$$

$$P_n(x_n) = P(X_{U(n)} = x_n) = R_{n-1}(x_n) \, p(x_n),$$

where

$$R_{n-1}(x_n) = \sum_{0 \le x_1 < x_2 < \ldots < x_{n-1} < x_n} B(x_1) B(x_2) \ldots B(x_{n-1}), \quad x_n = n-1, n, \ldots$$

(6.0.2)

The joint pmf of $X_{U(m)}$ and $X_{U(n)}$, $m < n$ is given by

$$P_{m,n}(x_m, x_n) = P(X_{U(m)} = x_m, X_{U(n)} = x_m)$$
$$= R_{m-1}(x_m) A(x_m) R_{m+1,n}(x_m, x_n) p(x_n), \quad m \le x_m \le x_n - n + m < \infty,$$

(6.0.3)

where

$$R_{m+1,n}(x,y) =$$

$$\sum_{x_m < x_{m+1} < x_{m+2} < \ldots < x_n} B(x_{m+1}) \ldots B(x_{n-1}), \quad m < n-1$$

$$= 1 \text{ if } m = n-1$$

The conditional pmf of $X_{U(n)}$ given $X_{U(m)} = x_m$ is given by

$$P_{n|m}(x_n | X_{U(m)} = x_m) = R_{m,n}(x_m, x_n) \frac{p(x_n)}{\bar{P}(x_m)}, \quad x_m \le x_n - n + m < \infty.$$

(6.0.4)

$$P_{n|n-1}(x_n | X_{U(n-1)} = x_{n-1}) = \frac{p(x_n)}{\bar{P}(x_{n-1})}, \quad x_{n-1} < x_n.$$

(6.0.5)

Using (6.0.1) and (6.0.4) it follows that the sequence of upper record values $X_{U(1)}, X_{U(2)} \ldots$ forms a Markov chain. Let $I_n = n$ if n is a record value i.e. $X_{U(m)} = n$, for $m = 1, 2, \ldots$ and $I_n = 0$ if $X_{U(1)}, X_{U(2)}, \ldots$ does not contain the value n. The following Theorem is due to Shorrock (1972).

Theorem 6.0.1.

The random variables $I_1, I_2, \ldots$ are mutually independent and

$$P(I_n = 1) = P\{X = n \mid X \ge n\} = \frac{P(X = n)}{P(X \ge n)}, \quad n = 0, 1, 2, \ldots$$

Proof.

Discrete Distributions

$P(I_n = n)$
$= P(X_1=n) + P(X_1<n, X_2=n) + P(X_1<n, X_2<n, X_3=n)+...$
$= P(X_1=n) (P(X<n) + P^2(X<n) +....)$
$= \dfrac{P(X=n)}{1-P(X<n)} = \dfrac{P(X=n)}{P(X \geq n)}$. (6.0.6)

Let $0 \leq \alpha(1) < \alpha(2)$, then
$P(I_{\alpha(1)} = 1, I_{\alpha(2)} = 1)$
$= \sum_m P(I_{\alpha(1)} = 1, I_{\alpha(2)} = 1), t(1) = m)$, t(1) is time when $\alpha(1)$ occurs.

$\sum_m \sum_{r=1}^{\infty} P\{I_{\alpha(1)} = 1, t(1)$
$= m, X_{m+1} < \alpha(1), ... X_{m+r-1} < \alpha(1), X_{m+r} = \alpha(2)\}$

$\sum_m P\{I_{\alpha(1)} = 1, t(k) = m\} \sum_{r=1}^{\infty} P(X_{m+1}<\alpha(1))$

$P(X_{m+r-1}<\alpha(1))P(X_{m+r} =\alpha(2))$
$= \sum_m P\{I_{\alpha(1)} = 1, t(k) = m\} \dfrac{P(X = \alpha(2))}{P(X \geq \alpha(1))}$
$= P(I_{\alpha(1)} = 1) P(I_{\alpha(2)} = 1)$, by (6.0.4).

(6.0.7)

By iteration the independence of $I_1, I_2,...$ follows.

The following result was proved by Aliev and Ahsanullah (2002).

Theorem 6.0.2.

Let $X_1, X_2,...$ be a sequence of independent and identically distributed random variables taking values on $0,1,2,...$ with common distribution function F such that $F(n) < 1$ for all n and $E(X_i^2) <\infty$. Suppose that $\{B_k, k= 0,1,...|$ be a sequence of numbers such that $2+2B_{n+1}-B_s -B_{s+2} \geq 0$. If there exits F(x) such that $E\{(X_{U(2)} -X_{U(1)})^2|X_{U(1)} =s\} = B_s$, s $=0,1,2..$ Then F(x) is unique.

Proof.
From (6.0.5), we obtain

$$E((X_{U(2)} - X_{U(1)})^2 | X_{U(1)} = s)$$

$$= \frac{\sum_{j=1}^{\infty} j^2 p_{s+j}}{\sum_{j=1}^{\infty} p_{s+j}},$$

where $p_j = P(X=J)$, $j = 0,1,2,\ldots$ \hfill (6.0.8)

Thus the condition $E\{(X_{U(2)} - X_{U(1)})^2 | X_{U(1)}\} = B_s$ implies

$$\sum_{j=1}^{\infty} j^2 p_{s+j} = B_s \sum_{j=1}^{\infty} p_{s+j}, \text{ for } s \geq 0, \quad (6.0.9)$$

Writing $s = s+1$ in (6.0.9), we get from (6.0.8) and (6.0.9),

$$\sum_{j=1}^{\infty} (j-1)^2 p_{s+j} = B_{s+1} \sum_{j=1}^{\infty} p_{s+j+1} \quad (6.0.10)$$

Subtracting (6.0,10) from (6.0.9) we obtain

$$\sum_{j=1}^{\infty} (2j-1) p_{s+j} = B_s \sum_{j=1}^{\infty} p_{s+j} - B_{s+1} \sum_{j=1}^{\infty} p_{s+1+j} \quad (6.0.11)$$

Now substituting $s = s+1$ in (6.0.11), we will have

$$\sum_{j=1}^{\infty} (2j-1) p_{s++1+j} = B_{s+1} \sum_{j=1}^{\infty} p_{s++1+j} - B_{s+2} \sum_{j=1}^{\infty} p_{s+2+j}$$

\hfill (6.0.12)

Subtracting (6.0.12) from (6.0.11) and on simplification, we obtain

$$P_{s+2} = \frac{1 + 2B_{s+1} - B_{s+2}}{B_{s+2}} p_{s+1}$$

$$- \frac{2 + 2B_{s+1} - B_s - B_{s+2}}{B_{s+2}} (1 - p_0 - p_1 - \ldots p_s) \quad (6.0.13)$$

Since the coefficients

$\dfrac{2 + 2B_{s+1} - B_s - B_{s+2}}{B_{s+2}}$ and $\dfrac{1 + 2B_{s+1} - B_{s+2}}{B_{s+2}}$ are positive, it means that P_{s+2} is increasing (decreasing) if p_{s+1} increases(decreases) for all s ≥ 0.. It means that for any p_0 all probabilities $p_2, p_3,\ldots$ increases when p_1

increases. Together with the condition $\sum_{i=0}^{\infty} p_i = 1$ we conclude that for any given p_0, we have only one F(x) which satisfy (6.0.13)

6.1 GEOMETRIC DISTRIBUTION

A discrete random variable X is said to have geometric distribution if its probability mass function pmf) is of the following form:
$$p(k) = P(X = k) = pq^{k-1},$$
$$0 < p < 1, q = 1-p, k \in A_0$$
$$= 0, \text{ otherwise}, \quad (6.1.1)$$
where A_n = is the set of integers n+1, n+2, ..., and $n \geq 0$. We say $X \in$ GE(p), if the pmf of X is as given in (6.0.1). For k > 0, we define $r(k) = P[X = k | X \geq k]$.

We choose to distinguish between GE(p) and the larger class of distributions having geometric tail (GET). We write $X \in$ GET(s, p) if the pmf of X is as follows:
$$p(k) = P[X = k] = cq^{k-1}, q = 1-p, k \in A_s,$$
$$= 0, \text{ otherwise}, \quad (6.1.2)$$
where c is such that $\sum_{k=s+1}^{\infty} p(k)=1$. If s = 0, then GET(s, p) = GE(p) with c = p

.The geometric distribution like the exponential distribution possesses the memory less property i.e.
$$\overline{p}(r + s) = \overline{p}(r) \, \overline{p}(s), \quad (6.1.3)$$
where r and s are positive integers and $\overline{p}(j) = \sum_{k=j+1}^{\infty} p(k)$.

Geometric distribution is said to a discrete analogue of the exponential distribution.

DISTRIBUTION OF RECORD VALUES

If $X \in$ GE(p), then $\overline{P}(x) = q^x$ and $p(x) = pq^{x-1}$, for $x \in A_0$.

Substituting the values of $\overline{P}(x_i)$ and $p(x_i)$ in (6.0.1), we get

$$p(x_1, x_2, \ldots, x_m) = p^n q^{x_m - m}, \quad 1 \le x_1 < x_2 < \ldots < x_m < \infty$$
$$= 0, \text{ otherwise.} \tag{6.1.4}$$

The conditional pmf of $X_{U(n)} | X_{U(n-1)} = x_{n-1}$ is

$$P(X_{U(n)} = x_n | X_{U(n-1)} = x_{n-1}) = pq^{x_n - x_{n-1} - 1}, \quad n-1 \le x_{n-1} < x_n < \infty,$$
$$= 0, \text{ otherwise.}$$

Thus $X_{U(n)} - X_{U(n-1)}$ is independent of $X_{U(n-1)}$ and $X_{U(n)} - X_{U(n-1)} \in$ GE(p), $n = 2, 3, \ldots$.

Let
$V_1 = X_{U(1)}$
$V_2 = X_{U(2)} - X_{U(1)}$
$V_n = X_{U(n)} - X_{U(n-1)}$.

Then V_i's are independent and $V_i \in$ GE(p).

We have
$$X_{U(n)} = V_1 + V_2 + \ldots + V_n.$$

Since $E(V_i) = \dfrac{1}{p}$, we obtain

$$E(X_{U(n)}) = \frac{n}{p}$$

and

$$E(X_{U(n)} | X_{U(m)} = x_m) = x_m + \frac{n-m}{p}, \quad n > m.$$

The sequence $S_n = X_{U(n)} - \dfrac{n}{p}$, $n = 1, 2, \ldots$ forms a martingale. Thus

$$E(S_{n+1} | S_1, S_2, \ldots, S_n) = S_n.$$

It is known that if $X. \in G\ E(p)$, then

$$E(s^X) = \sum_{x=1}^{\infty} s^x pq^{x-1} = \frac{ps}{1-qs}. \tag{6.1.5}$$

Using (6.1.5), We obtain

$$E(s^{X_{U(n)}}) = E(s^{V_1+V_2+\ldots V_n}) = \left(\frac{ps}{1-qs}\right)^n \tag{6.1.6}$$

The coefficient of s^x in $\left(\frac{ps}{1-qs}\right)^n$ is $\binom{x-1}{n-1} p^n q^{x-n}, x \geq n$.

Thus the marginal pmf of $X_{U(m)}$ can be written as

$$p_m(x) = p[X_{U(m)} = x] = \binom{x-1}{m-1} p^m q^{x-m}, x \in A_{m-1}, m \geq 1$$

$$= 0, \text{ otherwise.} \tag{6.1.7}$$

We see that $X_{U(m)}$ has a negative binomial distribution with parameters m and p.

We can write

$$X_{U(n)}|X_{U(m)} = x_m \stackrel{d}{=} U_{m+1} + \ldots + U_n + x_m, n > m.$$

and

$$E(s^{X_{U(n)}} | X_{U(m)} = x) = s^{x_m} \left(\frac{ps}{1-qs}\right)^{n-m}.$$

The coefficient of s^y in $s^{x_m} \left(\frac{ps}{1-qs}\right)^{n-m}$ is

$$\binom{y-x_m-1}{n-m-1} p^{n-m} q^{y-x_m-n+m},$$

Thus we obtain the conditional pmf of $X_{U(n)}$ given $X_{U(m)}$ as

$$P(X_{U(n)}=x_n|X_{U(m)}=x_m)= \binom{x_n-x_m-1}{n-m-1} p^{n-m} q^{x_n-x_m-n+m},$$

$$0 < m \leq x_m \leq x_n-n+m < \infty.$$

But we know that the marginal pmf of $X_{U(m)}$ is

$$p_m(x) = p[X_{U(m)}=x] = \binom{x-1}{m-1} p^m q^{x-m}, x \in A_{m-1}, m \geq 1$$

Thus the joint pmf of $X_{U(m)}$ and $X_{U(n)}$ is

$$p_{m,n}(x,y) = P[X_{U(m)}=x_m, X_{U(n)}=x_n] = \binom{x-1}{m-1}\binom{y-x-1}{n-m-1} p^n q^{y-n}$$

$$m \leq x < y-n+m < \infty$$

$$= 0, \text{ otherwise.}$$

Let $Z_{m,n} = X_{U(n)} - X_{U(m)}$, $0 < m < n < \infty$, then

$P(Z_{m,n} = z \mid X_{U(m)} = x) = P(X_{U(n)} = z+x \mid X_{U(m)} = x)$

$= \binom{z-1}{n-m-1} p^{n-m}(1-p)^{z-n+m}$, for $z \in A_{n-m-1}$,

$$= 0, \text{ otherwise.} \qquad (6.1.8)$$

Thus $Z_{n,m}$ and $X_{U(m)}$ are independent. Further $Z_{n,m}$ and $X_{U(n-m)}$ are identically distributed.

ESTIMATION OF PARAMETERS

Since $X_{U(m)} \stackrel{d}{=} V_1 + V_2 + \ldots + V_m$, where $V_1, \ldots, V_m$ are independent and identically distributed as $GE(p)$. Using this property, we get

$E(X_{U(n)}) = np^{-1}$, $Var(X_{U(n)}) = np^{-2}q$. $\qquad (6.1.9)$
$Cov(X_{U(n)}, X_{U(m)}) = Var(X_{U(m)}) = (n-m) p^{-2} q \qquad (6.1.10)$

Suppose we have observation the first m record value $r_1, r_2, \ldots, r_m$ and we wish to estimate a function of the unknown parameter p. It is evident from (6.1.3) that $X_{U(m)}$ is a sufficient statistic for p. Further $X_{U(m)}$ is a complete sufficient statistic.

Table 6.1.1 UMVUE for some selected functions of p

Function of p	UMVUE
$1/p$	r_m / m
$1/p^2$	$r_m (r_m +1) / (m(m+1))$
p	$(m-1)/ (r_m -1)$

CHARACTERIZATIONS

There are several characterizations of the geometric distributions based on the (i) independence of $X_{U(n)} - X_{U(m)}$ and $X_{U(m)}$ (ii) conditional distribution of $X_{U(n)} \mid X_{U(m)}$ and (iii) moment properties of some functions of $X_{U(n)}$ for n >m.

The following theorem (originally proved by Srivastava (1979)) is based on the probability of $X_{U(2)} - X_{U(1)} \mid X_{U(1)}$.

Theorem 6.1.1.

Suppose F(x) is the distribution function of the sequence of i.i.d. random variables $\{X_n, n \geq 1\}$ with positive mass function only at 1,2,... Then $P[X_{U(2)} - X_{U(1)} = 1 \mid X_{U(1)} = i] = P[X_{U(2)} - X_{U(1)} = 1]$ for i = 1,2,...,if and only if X_n has the geometric distribution with pmf as given by

$$p_j = P[X = j] = c\, p\, (1-p)^{j-2}, j = 2,3,\ldots \qquad (6.1.9)$$

and

$$p_1 = 1 - \sum_{j=2}^{\infty} p_j = 1 - c,\ 0 < p < 1,\ 0 < c < 1.$$

Proof.

We give here the original proof of Srivastasva.

$$P[X_{U(2)} - X_{U(1)} = 1 \mid X_{U(1)} = i]$$

$$= P[X_{U(2)} = i + 1, X_{U(1)} = i] / P[X_{U(1)} = i]$$

$$= \frac{p_{i+1}}{1-(p_1+\ldots+p_i)}.$$

Since this conditional probability is independent of i, we must have

$$p = \frac{p_{i+1}}{1-(p_1+\ldots+p_i)}, \text{ for } j = 1,2,\ldots$$

For $j = 1$, we get $p_2 = p(1-p_1) = cp$, say.
For $j = 2$, we get $p_3 = p(1-p_1-p_2) = (1-p_1)p(1-p) = cp(1-p)$.
Similarly for $j = k$, we have

$$p_k = cp(1-p)^{j-2}, \; k \geq 3. \quad (6.1.10)$$

If p_j is as given by (6.1.9), then
$$P[\, X_{U(2)} - X_{U(1)} = 1 \mid X_{U(1)} = i\,] = P[\, X_{U(2)} - X_{U(1)} = 1\,].$$
A generalization of the Theorem 6.1.9 is the following theorem.

Theorem 6.1.2

Let $\{X_n, n \geq 1\}$ be a sequence of independent and identically distributed discrete random variables with common distribution function F. Suppose X is concentrated on the positive integers and $a = \sup\{x \mid F(x) < 1\} = \infty$. Then $X_n \in GET(n,p)$ for some fixed n, $n \geq 1$, if and only $X_{U(n+1)} - X_{U(n)}$ and $X_{U(n)}$ are independent.

Proof.

The 'only if' part follows immediately from the from equation (6.1.5), so we need to established the 'if' part. For $x \in A_0$, let
$$c(u) = P[\, X_{U(n+1)} - X_{U(n)} = u \mid X_{U(n)} = x\,]$$
$$= \frac{p(u+x)}{\bar{p}(x)}$$

$$(6.1.11)$$

$$= \frac{\bar{p}(u+x-1) - \bar{p}(u+x)}{\bar{p}(x)}, u \in A_o, x \in A_n.$$

Summing both sides of (6.1.11) with respect to u from 1 to u_0, and writing

$$c_1(u_o) = \sum_{u=1}^{u_o} c(u) \text{ and } c_0 = 1 - c_1(u_o). \quad (6.1.12)$$

On simplification, we get
$$\bar{p}(x+u_o) = c_o(u_o)\bar{p}(x), \quad u \in A_o, x \in A_n \quad (6.1.13)$$
The general solution of (6.1.11) is
$$\bar{p}(x) = cq^x, x \in A_n \quad (6.1.14)$$
where c is independent of p.

Using the boundary condition $\bar{p}(\infty) = 0$, we get
$$\bar{p}(x) = cq^x, x \in A_n, 0 < p < 1, x \in A_n.$$

We have already seen that
$$P[X_{U(n+1)} - X_{U(n)} = u \mid X_{U(n)} = y] = pq^{u-1}, u \in A_o$$
$$= P[X_k = u].$$

Does the above condition characterize the geometric distribution? As an answer to that question we have the following theorem.

Theorem 6.1.3.

Let $\{X_n, n \geq 1\}$ be a sequence of independent and identically distributed random variables with common distribution function F. Suppose X is concentrated on the positive integers with $a = \sup\{x \mid F(x) < 1\} = \infty$. Further if $P[X_{U(n+1)} - X_{U(n)} = u \mid X_{U(n)} = y] = P[X_1 = u]$ for two fixed $y \in A_{n-1}$, y_1, y_2 relatively prime and all $u \in A_o$, then $X \in GET(n,p)$

Proof.

Suppose that
$$P[X_{U(n+1)} - X_{U(n)} = u \mid X_{U(n)} = y] = P[X_1 = u], \quad (6.1.15)$$
then from (6.0.4)
$$[X_{U(n+1)} - X_{U(n)} = u \mid X_{U(n)} = y] = \frac{p(u+y)}{\bar{p}(y)} = p(u) \quad (6.1.16)$$
for two relatively prime $y_1, y_2 \in A_{n-1}$ and all $u \in A_o$. Summing (6.4.8) with respect to u from $u_o + 1$ to ∞, we get
$$\frac{\bar{p}(u_o + y)}{\bar{p}(y)} = \bar{p}(u_o), \quad (6.1.17)$$
for two relatively prime $y_1, y_2 \in A_{n-1}$ and all $u \in A_o$. The general solution of (6.1.17) is
$$\bar{p}(x) = cp^x, x \in A_n,$$

and since $\bar{p}(\infty) = 0$, we must have
$$\bar{p}(x) = cp^x, 0 < p < 1, x \in A_n. \tag{6.1.18}$$
Srivastava (1979) gave a characterization of the geometric distribution using the condition $E(X_{U(2)}| X_{U(1)} = y) \alpha + y$. Ahsanullah and Holland (1984) proved the following theorem which is a generalization of Srivastava's result.

Theorem 6.1.4.

Let $\{X_n, n \geq 1\}$ be a sequence of independent and identically distributed discrete random variables with common distribution function F. Suppose X is concentrated on the positive integers with $a = \sup\{x| F(x) < 1\} = \infty$. Further suppose $E[X_{U(n+1)}]^2 < \infty$. If $E(X_{U(n+1)} | X_{U(n)} = y) = y + p^{-1}$ for all $y \in A_{n-1}$, then $X_1 \in GET(n,p)$ and $0 < p < 1$.

Proof.

Suppose
$$E(X_{U(n+1)} | X_{U(n)} = y] = p^{-1} + y, \text{ for all } y \in A_{n-1}.$$
It follows from (6.1.5) that
$$P[X_{U(n+1)} = u+y | X_{U(n)} = y] = \frac{p(u+y)}{\bar{p}(y)}, y \in A_{n-1},$$
and hence
$$E[X_{U(n+1)} | X_{U(n)} = y] = \sum_{u=y}^{\infty} (u+y) \frac{p(u+y)}{\bar{p}(y)}$$
$$= p^{-1} + y,$$
which implies that
$$\sum_{u=1}^{\infty} u \frac{p(u+y)}{\bar{p}(y)} = p^{-1}.$$
Thus we have
$$p^{-1} = \frac{\sum_{u=1}^{\infty} u[\bar{p}(u+y-1) - \bar{p}(u+y)]}{\bar{p}(y)}$$

$$= \sum_{j=0}^{\infty} \frac{\bar{p}(y+i)}{\bar{p}(y)}$$

$$= \frac{J(y)}{J(y+1)-J(y+1)},$$

where $J(y) = \sum_{i=0}^{\infty} \bar{p}(y+i)$. Thus

$$J(y+1) = q J(y), q = 1-p \qquad (6.1.19)$$

for all $y \in A_{n-1}$.

The general solution of (6.1.19) with the boundary condition, $J(n) = \theta, 0 < \theta < 1$, is

$$J(x) = \theta q^{x-n}, x \in A_{n-1}.$$

Therefore

$$\bar{p}(x) = J(x) - J(x+1) = \theta p q^{x-n}, x \in A_{n-1}.$$

i.e. $x \in GET(n,p)$.

We have seen that

$$P[X_{U(n+1)} - X_{U(n)} = u \mid X_{U(n)} = y] = p q^{u-1}, u \in A_0$$
$$= P[X_k = u].$$

Thus

$$E[(X_{U(n+1)} - X_{U(n)})^2 \mid X_{U(n)} = y] = \sum_{u=1}^{\infty} u^2 p q^{u-1}$$

$$= \frac{1+q}{p^2}.$$

Thus $E[(X_{U(n+1)} - X_{U(n)})^2 \mid X_{U(n)} = y]$ is independent of y. If fact it can be shown that $E[(X_{U(n+1)} - X_{U(n)})^k \mid X_{U(n)} = y]$, for any positive integer k, is independent of y. It will be interesting to know whether this is a characteristic property of the geometric distribution. As a partial solution to this question, we have the following theorem by Balakrishnan and Balasubramanian (1994).

Theorem 6.1.5.

Let $\{X_n, n \geq 1\}$ be a sequence of independent and identically distributed discrete random variables with common distribution function F. Suppose X is concentrated on the positive integers with $p(0) > 0$

and a = sup{ x| F(x) < 1} = ∞. Further suppose $E[X_{U(2)}]^2 < \infty$. Then $E([X_{U(2)} - X_{U(1)}]^2 | X_{U(1)} = y) = c$, where c is a constant independent of y, if and only if $X_r \in GE(p)$, $r \geq 1$ and $0 < p < 1$.

Proof.

If $X_r \in GE(p)$, $r \geq 1$ and $0 < p < 1$, then

$$E([X_{U(2)} - X_{U(1)}]^2 | X_{U(1)} = y) = \sum_{j=1}^{\infty} j^2 p q^{j-1}$$

$$= p[\sum_{j=1}^{\infty} j(j+1) - j] q^{j-1}$$

$$= p[\frac{2}{p^3} - \frac{1}{p^2}] = \frac{1+q}{p^2}$$

= c, where c is independent of u.

Now

$$P[X_{U(2)} = u+y | X_{U(1)} = y] = \frac{p(u+y)}{\overline{p}(y)}, y \in A_0,$$

The condition $E([X_{U(2)} - X_{U(1)}]^2 | X_{U(1)} = y) = c$, is equivalent to

$$\sum_{j=1}^{\infty} j^2 \frac{p(y+j)}{\overline{p}(y)} = c, \text{ i.e.}$$

$$\sum_{j=1}^{\infty} j^2 p(y+j) = c \sum_{j=}^{\infty} p(y+j). \tag{6.1.20}$$

Using difference operator Δ and noting $\Delta A(x) = A(x+1) - A(x)$ and $\Delta^2 A(x) = A(x+2) - 2A(x+1) + A(x)$, we have from (6.1.20)

$$\sum_{j=1}^{\infty} \Delta [j^2 p(y+j)] = c \sum_{j=}^{\infty} \Delta^2 [p(y+j)]. \tag{6.1.21}$$

On simplification, we obtain from (6.1.21), the following equation

$$p(y+1) + 2 \sum_{j=2}^{\infty} p(y+j) = c p(y+1) - c p(y+2). \tag{6.1.22}$$

Changing y to y+1, we get from (6.1.22)

Discrete Distributions

$$p(y+2) + \sum_{j=3}^{\infty} p(y+j) = cp(y+2) - cp(y+3). \quad (6.1.23)$$

Subtracting (6.1.23) from (6.1.22), we have the following difference equation

$$(c-1) p(y+1) - (2c+1) p(y+2) + c\, p(y+3) = 0 \quad (6.1.24)$$

We can write the solution of (6.1.24) as

$$P(y) = k_1 \alpha^y + k_2 \beta^y \quad (6.1.25)$$

where $y \in A_0$ and α and β are the roots of the quadratic equation

$$c\, t^2 - (2c+1)t + (c-1) = 0. \quad (6.1.26)$$

The two roots of (6.1.26) are

$$\alpha = \frac{2c+1+\sqrt{8c+1}}{2c} \text{ and } \beta = \frac{2c+1-\sqrt{8c+1}}{2c}. \quad (61.27)$$

Since $y \in A_0$ and $\alpha > 1$, we must have $k_1 = 0$ and thus

$$p(y) = k_2\, \beta^y, y \in A_0, \quad (6.1.28)$$

where $\beta < 1$.

Since $p(0) = k_2$, we have $X_k \in GE(p)$, $k \geq 1$ and $0 < p < 1$.
Balakrishnan and Balasubramanian proved (1994) proved the Theorem 6.1.5 without the assumption of infinite support of X_k. If in the Theorem 6.1.5, we replace the condition $E([\,X_{U(2)} - X_{U(1)}]^2 |\, X_{U(1)} = y\,) = c$, by $E([\,X_{U(n)} - X_{U(n)}]^2 |\, X_{U(n)} = y\,) = c$, $y \in A_r$, $r \geq n$, then we can obtain a characterization of $GET(p)$ with $0 < p < 1$.

Dembinska and Wesolowski (2000) proved the following Theorem.

THEOREM 6.1.6.

Let $\{X_n, n \geq 1\}$ be a sequence of independent and identically distributed discrete random variables with common distribution function F. Suppose X is concentrated on the positive integers and $a = \sup\{x\, |F(x) < 1\} = \infty$. If $E(X_{U(n+2)}) < \infty$ and $E(X_{U(n+2)} - X_{U(n)} |\, X_{U(n)}) = b$, then $X_n \in GET(n, b/2)$.

PREDICTION OF RECORD VALUES

Given observed values of $X_{U(1)}, X_{U(2)}, \ldots X_{U(m)}$, we are interested to predict $X_{U(s)}$ for $s > m$. It is easy to verify that

$$E(X_{U(s)} \mid X_{U(m)} = r_m, X_{U(m-1)} = r_{m-1}, \ldots, X_{U(1)} = r_1)$$
$$= E(X_{U(m)} \mid X_{U(m)} = r_m)$$
$$= (s-m)/p + r_m.$$

If p is known, then

$$r_m + (s-m)/p \qquad (6.1.29)$$

is the minimum variance unbiased predictor of $X_{U(s)}$. If p is unknown, then substituting the unbiased estimator of p^{-1}, we get $\tilde{X}_{U(s)}$ as a predictor of $X_{U(s)}$, where

$$\tilde{X}_{U(s)} = s\, r_m / m \qquad (6.1.30)$$

which is unbiased for $X_{U(s)}$. The non stochastic multiple of $\tilde{X}_{U(s)}$ with smallest mean square error for predicting $X_{U(s)}$ is

$$\overline{X}_{U(s)} = \frac{s\, r_m\, p^{-1}}{(m+1)\, p^{-1} - 1} \qquad (6.1.31)$$

Since P^{-1} is unknown, substituting MVLUE estimator for p^{-1} in (6.1.31), we get

$$\overline{X}_{U(s)} = \frac{s\, r_m^2}{(m+1)r_m - m}.$$

6.2. RECORDS OF NON IDETICALLY DISTRIBUTED RANDOM VARIABLES

Record values for non identically distributed discrete non-negative random variables are defined as follows: let $\{X_{nj}, n \geq 1\}$ be a double sequence of independent positive integer-valued rvs with the cdf F_n and the corresponding probability mass function (pmf) $p_n(.)$ for each $j = 1, 2, \ldots$ We take $X_{1,1}$ as the first record and write $X_{1,1} = X_{1,U(1)}$, with $U(1) = 1$. Once we observe a record value $X_{n,U(n)}$, we sample from $\{X_{n+1, j}\}$ beginning with $j = U(n) + 1$ until a new record is attained; the new record value is denoted as $X_{n+1,U(n+1)}$. Subsequent record value times are defined by

$$U(n+1) = \min\{j \mid j > U(n), X_{n+1,j} > X_{n,U(n)}\}, n \in A_0.$$

In the above setting we are permitting the probability mass function to change instantaneously following the occurrence of each new record. Such a change occurs in practical situations. For example, suppose $X_{n,j}$ with j > 1, correspond to random shocks attacking a component of a system which does not fail until the shock exceeds $X_{n,U(n)}$. Suppose $p_n(.)$ is the pmf of $X_{n,j}$, and that after each failure of a component a stronger modified component is used which sustains shocks of at most the magnitude of the last record shock $X_{n,U(n)}$. The subsequent random shocks are then $X_{n+1,j}, j \geq 1$ each having pmf $p_{n+1}(.)$.

The joint pmf of the first n (upper) record values in the non-identically distributed case is

$$P[X_{1,U(1)} = x_1, X_{2,U(2)} = x_2, ..., X_{n,U(n)} = x_n]$$
$$= \frac{p_1(x_1)}{\overline{p}_2(x_1)} \cdot \frac{p_2(x_2)}{\overline{p}_3(x_2)} \cdots \frac{p_{n-1}(x_{n-1})}{\overline{p}_n(x_{n-1})} \cdot p_n(x_n), \quad (6.2.1)$$
$$\text{for } 1 \leq x_1 < x_2 \cdots < x_n < \infty$$
$$= 0, \text{ otherwise,}$$

where
$$\overline{p}_k(x_k) = P[X_{n,j} > x_k] = 1 - F_k(x_k), k = 1, 2, ..., n.$$

Then
$$P[X_{n,U(n)} = x_n | X_{n-1,U(n-1)} = x_{n-1}, \cdots, X_{1,U(1)} = x_1]$$
$$\qquad\qquad\qquad\qquad\qquad\qquad\qquad\qquad (6.2.2)$$
$$= \frac{p_n(x_n)}{\overline{p}_n(x_{n-1})}, \quad 1 \leq x_{n-1} < x_n < \infty$$

Example 6.2.1 Let us consider the geometric distribution, $F_k \in GE(P_k)$, k=1,2,...,n, (6.2.1) becomes

$$\prod_{i=1}^{n}\left(\frac{p_i}{q_i}\right) \cdot \prod_{j=1}^{n-1}\left(\frac{q_j}{q_{j+1}}\right)^{x_j}, \text{ for } 1 \leq x_1 < x_2 \cdots < x_n < \infty,$$
$$0, \text{ otherwise.}$$

Then (6.2.2) is
$$p_n q_n^{x_n - x_{n-1} - 1}, 1 < x_{n-1} < x_n < \infty \qquad (6.2.3)$$
$$0, \text{ otherwise.}$$

It can be shown that (6.2.3) is also the conditional pmf
$$P[X_{n,U(n)} = x_n | X_{n-1,U(n-1)} = x_{n-1}]$$
Define

$$\eta_1 = X_{1,U(1)}$$
$$\eta_2 = X_{n,U(n)} - X_{n-1,U(n-1)}, n \geq 2 \qquad (6.2.4)$$

Then
$$X_{n,U(n)} = \eta_1 + \eta_2 + \cdots + \eta_n$$

where the η_i's are independent and $\eta_i \in GE(p_i)$.
The conditional Probability of $X_{n,U(n)} | X_{n-1,U(n-1)}$ can be calculated as follows:

$$P[\eta_n = z | X_{n-1,U(n-1)} = x_{n-1}]$$
$$= P[X_{n,U(n)} = z + x_{n-1} | X_{n-1,U(n-1)} = x_{n-1}]$$
$$= \eta p_n q_n^{z-1}, z = 1, 2, \ldots \qquad (6.2.5)$$
$$= 0, \text{ otherwise.}$$

Using the identity

$$\sum_{k=1}^{\infty} s^x q^{x-1} p = \frac{ps}{1-qs}, \text{ we have}$$

$$E(s^{X_{n,U(n)}}) = E(s^{\eta_1 + \eta_2 + \cdots + \eta_n}) = s^n \prod_{i=1}^{n} \frac{p_i}{1-sq_i}.$$

If the p_i's are distinct, then the partial fraction expansion yields

$$s^n \prod_{i=1}^{n} \frac{p_i}{1-zq_i} = c_o \sum_{j=1}^{n} \frac{sr_j}{1-sq_j} \qquad (6.2.6)$$

where

$$c_o = p_1 p_2 \ldots p_n \text{ and } r_j = \prod_{j=1, j \neq k}^{n} \frac{1}{q_j - q_k}.$$

$$p_n^* = P[X_{n,U(n)} = x], x > n$$
$$= \text{coefficient of } s^x \text{ in the right hand side of (6.2.6)}$$
$$= c_o \sum_{r=1}^{n} r_j q_j^{x-1}.$$

If $p_1 = p_2 = \cdots = p_n = p$, then the coefficient of s^x in the expression $(\frac{ps}{1-qs})^n$ is

$$\binom{x-1}{n-1} p^n q^{x-n}, x \geq n.$$

Hence for the i.i.d. case, we get the pmf of $X_{n,U(n)}$ as given in (6.1.7).

We can write
$$X_{n,U(n)} \mid X_{m,U(m)} = x_m \stackrel{d}{=} \eta_{m+1} + \cdots + \eta_n + x_m$$
and
$$E(z^{X_{n,U(n)}} \mid X_{m,U(m)} = x_m) = z^{x_m} \prod_{i=1}^{n-m} \frac{p_{m+j}}{1 - z q_{m+j}}.$$

If $p_1 = p_2 = \cdots = p_n = p$, then equating the coefficients of z^{x_n}, we obtain the pmf of $X_{n,U(n)} \mid X_{m,U(m)}$ as given in section 6.1

6.3. WEAK RECORDS

Vervaat (1973) introduced the concept of weak records of discrete distribution. Let $X_1, X_2, \ldots$ be a sequence of independent and identically distributed random variables taking values on $0, 1, \ldots$ with distribution function F such that $F(n) < 1$ for any n. The weak record times $U_w(n)$ and weak upper record values $X_{U_w(n)}$ are defined as follows: $U_w(1) = 1$
$U_w(n+1)$ min $\{j > L_w(n), X_j \geq \max(X_1, X_2, \ldots X_{j-1})\}$
and the corresponding weak upper record value is defined as $X_{U_w(n+1)}$. If in the above expression if we replace $\geq$ by $>$, then we obtain record times and record values instead of weak record times and weak record values.

The joint pmf of $X_{U_w(1)}, X_{U_w(2)}, \ldots, X_{U_w(n)}$ is given by

$$P_{w,1,2,\ldots,n}(x_1, x_2, \ldots, x_n) = \left(\prod_{i=1}^{n-1} \frac{p(x_i)}{\vec{P}(x_i - 1)}\right) p(x_n) \qquad (6.3.1)$$

for $0 \leq x_1 \leq x_2 \leq \ldots x_n < \infty$.

For any $m > 1$ and $n > m$, we can write
$$P(X_{U_w(n)} = x_n, \ldots X_{U_w(m+1)} = x_{m+1} \mid X_{U_w(m)} = x_m, \ldots$$
$$X_{U_w(1)} = x_1)$$
$$= \left(\prod_{i=m}^{n-1} \frac{p(x_i)}{\vec{P}(x_i - 1)}\right) \frac{p(x_n)}{\vec{F}(x_m - 1)} \qquad (6.3.2)$$

It follows easily from (6.3.1) and (6.3.2) that the weak records, $X_{U_W}(1), X_{U_W}(2), \ldots$ form a Markov chain.

The marginal pmf's of the upper weak records are given by

$$P(X_{U_W}(1) = x_1) = P_{w,1}(x_1) = p(x_1), \quad x_1 = 0, 1, 2, \ldots,$$

$$P(X_{U_W}(2) = x_2) = P_{w,2}(x_2) = R_{w,1}(x_2) p(x_2), \quad x_2 = 0, 1, 2, \ldots.$$

where

$$R_{w,1}(x_2) = \sum_{0 \leq x_1 \leq x_2} \frac{p(x_1)}{\vec{P}(x_1 - 1)} \qquad (6.3.3)$$

$$P(X_{U_W}(n) = x_n) = P_{w,n}(x_n) = R_{w,n-1}(x_n) p(x_n),$$

where

$$R_{w,n-1}(x_n) = \sum_{0 \leq x_1 \leq x_2 \leq \ldots x_{n-1}} \prod_{i=1}^{n-1} \frac{p(x_i)}{\vec{P}(x_i - 1)} p(x_n)$$

(6.3.4)

The joint pmf of $X_{U_W}(m)$ and $X_{U_W}(n)$, $m < n$ nd $X_{U(n)}, m < n$ is given by

$$P_{w,m,n}(x_m, x_n)$$
$$= R_{w,m}(x_m) A_w(x_m) R_{wm+1,n}(x_m, x_n) p(x_n),$$
$$m \leq x_m \leq x_n - n + m < \infty,$$

where

$$R_{w,m,n}(x,y) = \sum_{x_m \leq x_{m+1} \leq x_{m+2} \cdots \leq n} A_w(x_{m+1}) \ldots A_w(x_{n-1}),$$
$$m < n-1$$
$$= 1 \text{ if } m = n-1,$$

and $A_w(x) = \dfrac{p(x)}{\vec{P}(x-1)}$.

The conditional pmf of $X_{U_W}(m)$ given $X_{U_W}(n)$, is given by

$$P_{w,n|m}(X_{U_W}(n) = x_n | X_{U_W}(m) = x_m)$$
$$= R_{w,m+1,n}(x_m, x_n) \frac{p(x_n)}{\vec{P}(x_m - 1)}, \qquad (6.3.5)$$

for $m \leq \underline{x_m} \leq x_n < \infty$.

Thus the pmf of $X_{U_w(n)}$ given $X_{U_w(n-1)}$ is

$$P_{w, n|n-1}(X X_{U_w(n)} = x_n | X_{U_w(n-1)} = x_{n-1}$$
$$= \frac{p(x_n)}{p(x_{n-1})} \qquad (6.3.6)$$

$$P_{w, n|n-2}((X_{U_w(n)} = x_n | X_{U_w(n-1)} = x_{n-2})$$
$$= R_{w,n-2,n}(x_{n-2}, x_n) \frac{p(x_n)}{\bar{P}(x_{n-2}-1)}$$

Theorem 6.3.1

Let $\{X_i, i=1,2,...\}$ be sequence of independent and identically distributed random variables taking values on $0,1,2,...,n$, $n \leq \infty$, with distribution F such that $F(n) < \infty$ for $n < \infty$ and $E(X_1 \ln(1+X_1)) < \infty$. The for some continuous function ψ, the condition

$E(\psi (X_{U_w(n)}) | X_{U_w(n-1)} = j) = g(j)$ determines the distribution.

Proof.

We have from (6.3.6)

$$P(\psi(X_{U_w(n)}) = y | X_{U_w(n-1)} = x) = \frac{p_y}{q_x}, \qquad (6.3.7)$$

where $p_y = P(X=y)$ and $q_x = P(X \geq x)$.

Now

$$E(\psi(X_{U_{w_n}}) | X_{U_w(n-1)} = j) = \frac{1}{q_j} \sum_{k=j}^{N} \psi(k) p_k .$$

Using the condition as given in the theorem, we can write the above expression as

$$g(j) q_j = \sum_{k=j}^{n} \psi(k) p_k \qquad (6.3.8)$$

Taking first order difference, we obtain from (6.3.8)

$$g(j)q_j - g(j+1)q_{j+1} = \psi(j)p_j \qquad (6.3.9)$$

Thus
$$g(j)q_j - g(j+1)(q_j - p_j) = \psi(j)p_j \qquad (6.3.10)$$

i.e.
$$p_j = \frac{g(j+1) - g(j)}{g(j+1) - \psi(j)} q_j \qquad (6.3.11)$$

Since $q_j = \dfrac{q_j}{q_{j-1}} \cdot \dfrac{q_{j-1}}{q_{j-2}} \cdots \dfrac{q_1}{q_0}, q_0 = 1$, we have from (6.3.11)

$$p_j = \frac{g(j+1) - g(j)}{g(j+1) - \psi(j)} \prod_{k=0}^{j-1} \left(\frac{q_{k+1}}{q_k} \right) \qquad (6.3.12)$$

From (6.3.10)

$$g(j)q_j - g(j+1)q_{j+1} = \psi(j)(q_j - q_{j+1})$$

i.e.
$$\frac{q_{j+1}}{q_j} = \frac{g(j) - \psi(j)}{g(j+1) - \psi(j)} \qquad (6.3.13)$$

From (6.3.13), we can write
$$p_j = \frac{g(j+1) - g(j)}{g(j+1) - \psi(j)} \prod_{k=0}^{j-1} \left(\frac{g(k) - \psi(k)}{g(k+1) - \psi(k)} \right) \qquad (6.3.14)$$

Example 6.3..1. Geometric distribution

Suppose $X_1, X=2, \ldots$ be a sequence of independent and identically random variables with $p(k) = pq^k$ and $\vec{P}(k-1) = q^k$, $k=0,1,2,\ldots$

Here $R_{w,1}(x_2) = \displaystyle\sum_{1 \leq x_1 \leq x_2} \frac{p(x_1)}{\vec{P}(x_1 - 1)} = x_2 p$.

Thus

$P_{w,2}(k) = R_{w,1}(k) p(k) = (k+1) p^2 q^k$, $k = 0,1,2,\ldots$

Since $P_{w,n|n-1}((x_n | X_{U_w}(n-1) = x_m) = \dfrac{p(x_n)}{\vec{P}(x_{n-1}-1)} = p q^{x_n - x_m}$,

$x_n \geq x_{n-1}$,
we obtain

$$P_{w,3}(x_3) = \sum_{x_2=0}^{x_3} (x_2+1) p^2 q^{x_2} pq^{x_3-x_2}$$

$$= \sum_{x_2=0}^{x_3} (x_2+1) p^3 q^{x_3}$$

$$= \dfrac{(x_3+1)(x_3+2)}{2} p^3 q^{x_3}, \quad x_3 = 0,1,2,\ldots$$

By induction it can be proved that

$$P_{w,n}(x_n) = \dfrac{x_n(x_n+1)\ldots(x_n+n-1)}{(n-1)!} p^n q^{x_n-1}$$

$$= \binom{x_n+n-1}{n-1} p^n q^{x_n} \quad n \geq 2 \text{ and } \underline{x_n} = 0,1,2,\ldots$$

We can write

$$X_{U_w(n)} \stackrel{d}{=} V_{(1)} + V_{(2)} + \ldots + V_{(n)} \text{ where } V_{(i)} \ i=1,\ldots,n$$

are independent and identically distributed with $P(V_{(i)} = k) = pq^k$, $k = 0,1,2,\ldots$ We have $E(X_{U_w(n)}) = \dfrac{np}{q}$. Let $S_{(n)} = X_{U_w(n)} - \dfrac{np}{q}$, the sequence $\{S_{(n)}, n=1,2,\ldots\}$ forms a martingale. Hence

$E(S_{(n+1)} | S_{(1)}, \ldots, S_{(n)}) = S_{(n)}$.

$E(X_{U_w}(n) | X_{U_w}(n-1) = x_m)$

$= \sum\limits_{x_n = x_{n-1}}^{\infty} x_n \, p q^{x_n - x_{n-1}} = x_{n-1} + \dfrac{q}{p}$.

Further the sequence $S^*_{(n)} = \dfrac{X_{U_w(n)}}{n}, n=1,2,\ldots$ forms a backward martingales. $E((S^*_{(m)} | S^*_{(n)}) = S^*_{(n)}\}$, $m < n$.

The conditional pmf of $X_{U_w(n)}$ given $X_{U_w(n-2)}$, is given by

$$P_{w,\,n|,n-2}(X_{U_w(n)}\,|X_{U(n-2)}=x_{n-2})$$
$$= R_{w,n-2,n}(x_n, x_{n-2}) \frac{p(x_n)}{\bar{P}(x_{n-2}-1)},$$

For $0 \leq x_{n-2} \leq x_n < \infty$,

where

$$R_{w,n-2,n}(x,y) = \sum_{x_{n-2} \leq x_{n-1} \leq x} A_w(x_{n-1}) = (x - x_{n-2} + 1).$$

The conditional expectation of $X_{U_w(n)} | X_{U_w(n-2)} = x$ is

$$E(X_{U_w(n)} | X_{U_w(n-2)} = x_{n-2})$$
$$= \sum_{x=x_{n-2}}^{\infty} x(x - x_{n-2} + 1)] p^2 q^{x-x_{n-2}}$$
$$= x_{n-2} + \sum_{x=x_{n-2}}^{\infty} [x - x_{n-2})(x - x_{n-2} + 1)] p^2 q^{x-x_{n-2}}$$
$$= x_{n-2} + \frac{2q}{p}$$

Stepanov (1994) and Aliev (1998) proved that if $E(X_{U_w(n)} | X_{U_w(n-1)} = x_{n-1}) = x_{n-1} + b$, then X_i's $\in$ GT(1/(1+b)). This result follows from equation (6.3.14) if we take $\psi(x) = x$ nd $g(x) = x+b$.

A generalization of this is the following theorem due to Wesolowski and Ahsanullah (2001).

THEOREM 6.3.1.

Let $X_1, X_2, \ldots$ be a sequence of independent and identically distributed random variables taking values on $0, 1, \ldots, N$ with distribution function F such that $F(n) < 1$ for any $n < N$ and N need not be finite. If $E(X_{wU(n)} | X_{wU)n-2)}) = x) = x+b$, $n>2$, then X_i's $\in$ GE(b/(2+b))

Proof.

Let $p_k = P(X=k)$ and $q_k = p(X \geq k)$. Then

$$E(X_{wU(n)} | X_{wU(n-2)} = m)$$

$$= \frac{1}{q_m} \sum_{r=m}^{N} \frac{p_r}{q_r} \sum_{k=r}^{N} k p_k$$

$$= m + b, \text{ by assumption.}$$

We can write

$$\sum_{r=m}^{N} \frac{p_r}{q_r} \sum_{k=r}^{N} k p_k = (m+b) q_m, \qquad (6.3.15)$$

On taking first order differences, we obtain from (6.3.15)

$$(m+b)\frac{q_m^2}{p_m} - (m+1+b)\frac{q_m q_{m+1}}{p_m} = \sum_{k=m}^{N} k p_k, \qquad (6.3.16)$$

$$m=0,1,\ldots,N-1$$

Again taking the first order difference of (6.3.16), and taking $r(m) = q_m / q_{m+1}$, we obtain

$$\frac{(m+b)q_m^2 - (m+1+b)q_m q_m}{p_m} - \frac{(m+1+b)q_{m+1}^2 - (m+2+b)q_{m+1} q_{m+2}}{p_{m+1}}$$

$$= m\, p_m.$$

$$m = 0,1,2,\ldots, N-2$$

Dividing both sides of the above equation by q_{m+1} and writing $r(m) = q_m / q_{m+1}$, we obtain

$$\frac{(m+b)r^2(m) - (m+1+b)r(m)}{r(m)-1} - \frac{(m+1+b)r(m+1) - (r+2+b)}{r(m+1)-1}$$

$$= m(r(m)-1), \, m=0,1,\ldots,N \qquad (6.3.17)$$

Putting $h(m) = 1/(r(m) -1)$, we get from the above equation

$$h(m+1) = h(m) + 2 - b/h(m), \qquad (6.3.18)$$

$$m=0,1,2,\ldots, N$$

assuming $g(0)$, we get as the solution of (6.3.18) is $q_j = \left(\frac{b}{b+2}\right)^j$, $j = 0,1,\ldots N$,

Example 6.3.2. Beta- Binomial distribution

Suppose X_1, $X=2$, ... be a sequence of independent and identically random variables having Beta – Binomial distribution, ,BB(N, β) with pmf as

$$p(j) = P(X=j) = \binom{\beta+N-j-1}{N-j}\binom{\beta+N}{N}^{-1}, j = 0.1, 2, \ldots, N$$

(6.3.19).

and

$$\vec{P}(k-1) = q_k = \sum_{j=k}^{N} p_j,$$

$$= \sum_{j=k}^{N} \binom{\beta+N-j-1}{N-j}\binom{\beta+N}{N}^{-1}$$

$$= \sum_{j=0}^{N-k} \binom{\beta+N-j-1}{j}\binom{\beta+N}{N}^{-1}$$

$$= \binom{\beta+N-k}{N-k}\binom{\beta+N}{N}^{-1}.$$

Here $R_{w,1}(x_2) = \sum_{1 \leq x_1 \leq x_2} \dfrac{p(x_1)}{\vec{P}(x_1-1)} = \sum_{1 \leq x_1 \leq x_2} \dfrac{\binom{\beta+N-x_1-1}{N-x_1}}{\binom{\beta+N-x_1}{N-x_1}}$

$$= \sum_{1 \leq x_1 \leq x_2} \dfrac{\beta}{N+n-x_1}$$

Thus

$$P_{w,2}(j) = R_{w,1}(j)\,p(j) =$$

$$= \sum_{0 \leq x_1 \leq j} \dfrac{\beta}{N+n-x_1} \binom{\beta+N-j-1}{N-j}\binom{\beta+N}{N}^{-1}$$

j=k,...,N

$E(X_{wU(n)} | X_{wU(n-2)} = m)$

$$= \frac{1}{q_m} \sum_{r=m}^{N} \frac{p_r}{q_r} \sum_{k=r}^{N} k p_k$$

$$= \binom{\beta+N-m}{N-m}^{-1} \sum_{r=m}^{N} \frac{\beta}{\beta+N-r} \sum_{k=r}^{N} k \binom{\beta+N-k-1}{N-k}$$

Now

$$\sum_{k=r}^{N} k \binom{\beta+N-k-1}{N-k}$$

$$= \sum_{i=0}^{N-r} (N-i) \binom{\beta+i-1}{i}$$

$$= N \sum_{i=0}^{N-r} \binom{\beta+i-1}{i} - \sum_{i=0}^{N-r} i \binom{\beta+i-1}{i}$$

$$= N \binom{\beta+N-r}{n-r} - \binom{\beta+N-r}{N-r-1}$$

$$= N \binom{\beta+N-r}{N-r} - \frac{(N-r)\beta}{\beta+1} \binom{\beta+N-r}{N-r}$$

$$= \frac{N+r\beta}{\phi+1} \binom{\beta+N-r}{N-r}$$

Thus

$E(X_{wU(n)} | X_{wU(n-2)} = m)$

$$= \frac{\beta}{\phi+1}\binom{\beta+n-m}{n-m}^{-1} \sum_{r=m}^{N} \frac{N+r\beta}{\beta+N-r}\binom{\beta+N-r}{N-r}$$

Now

$$\sum_{r=m}^{N} \frac{N+r\beta}{\beta+N-r}\binom{\beta+N-r}{N-r} = \sum_{r=m}^{N} \frac{N+r\beta}{\beta}\binom{\beta+N-r-1}{N-r}$$

$$= \frac{N}{\beta}\binom{\beta+N-m}{N-m} - \sum_{r=m}^{N} r\binom{\beta+N-r-1}{N-r}.$$

It can easily be shown that

$$\sum_{r=m}^{N} r\binom{\beta+N-r-1}{N-r} = \sum_{t=0}^{N-m}(N-t)\binom{\beta+t-1}{t}$$

$$= N\binom{\beta+N-m}{N-m} - \sum_{t=0}^{N-m} t\binom{\beta+t-1}{t}$$

$$= N\binom{\beta+N-m}{N-m} - \frac{(N-m)\beta}{\beta+1}\binom{\beta+N-m}{N-m}$$

$$= \frac{N+m\beta}{\beta+1}\binom{\beta+N-m}{N-m}$$

Thus

$$E(X_{wU(n)} | X_{wU(n-2)} = m)$$

$$= (\frac{\beta}{\beta+1})(\frac{N}{\beta} + \frac{N+m\beta}{\beta+1})$$

$$= (\frac{\beta}{\beta+1})^2 m + (\frac{2\beta+1}{(\beta+1)^2}) N .$$

Wesolowski and Ahsanullah 2001) proved that if

$E(X_{wU(n)} | X_{wU(n-2)} = m) = a\, m + b$, where m<1, then the distribution of the X's is Beta-Binomial, BB(b/1-a, $\sqrt{a}/(1-\sqrt{a})$).

Example 6.3.3.

Beta- Negative Binomial distribution

Suppose X_1, X=2, ... be a sequence of independent and identically random variables having Beta –Negative Binomial distribution, ,BNB(β,γ) with pmf as

$$p(j) = P(X=j) = \frac{\gamma}{\gamma+j} \binom{\beta}{\gamma} \binom{\beta+j+1}{\gamma+j}^{-1}, j = 0.1,2,...,,$$

where $\beta > \gamma > 0$. (6.3.20)

$$\vec{P}(k-1) = q_k = \sum_{j=k}^{\infty} p_j$$

$$= \sum_{j=k}^{\infty} \frac{\gamma}{\gamma+j} \binom{\beta}{\gamma} \binom{\beta+j+1}{\gamma+j}^{-1},$$

$$= \sum_{i=0}^{\infty} \frac{\gamma}{\gamma+k+i} \binom{\beta}{\gamma} \binom{\beta+k+i+1}{\gamma+k+i}^{-1}$$

$$= \frac{\gamma}{\gamma+k} \binom{\beta}{\gamma} \binom{\beta+k}{\gamma+k}^{-1}, k=0,1,2,...$$

Here $\quad R_{w,1}(j) = \sum_{0 \le x_1 \le j} \frac{p(x_1)}{q_{x_1}} = \sum_{0 \le x_1 \le j} \frac{\binom{\beta+x_1}{\gamma+x_1}}{\binom{\beta+x_1+1}{\gamma+x_1}}$

$$= \sum_{0 \le x_1 \le j} \frac{\beta - \gamma + 1}{\beta + x_1 + 1}$$

Thus
$$P_{w,2}(j) = R_{w,1}(j)\, p(j) =$$

$$= \sum_{0 \le x_1 \le j} \frac{\beta - \gamma + 1}{\beta + x_1 + 1} \frac{\gamma}{\gamma + j} \binom{\beta}{\gamma} \binom{\beta + j + 1}{\gamma + j}^{-1}$$

$$j = 0, 1, \ldots,$$

Now

$$E(X_{wU(n)} \mid X_{wU(n-2)} = m)$$

$$= \frac{1}{q_m} \sum_{r=m}^{\infty} \frac{p_r}{q_r} \sum_{k=r}^{\infty} k p_k$$

We have

$$\sum_{k=r}^{\infty} k p_k = \sum_{j=0}^{\infty} \frac{\gamma(r+j)}{\gamma + r + j} \binom{\beta}{\gamma} \binom{\beta + r + j + 1}{\gamma + r + j}$$

$$= \frac{\gamma(r-1)}{\gamma + r} \binom{\beta}{\gamma} \binom{\beta + r}{\gamma + r}^{-1} \sum_{j=0}^{\infty} \frac{\gamma + r}{\gamma + r + j} \binom{\beta + r}{\gamma + r} \binom{\beta + r + j + 1}{\gamma + r + j}^{-1}$$

$$= \frac{\gamma(r-1)}{\gamma + r} \binom{\beta}{\gamma} \binom{\beta + r}{\gamma + r}^{-1} + \frac{\gamma}{\gamma + r} \binom{\beta}{\gamma} \binom{\beta + r - 1}{\gamma + r}^{-1}$$

$$= \frac{\gamma[r(\beta - \gamma - 1) + \gamma]}{(\gamma + r)(\beta - \gamma)} \binom{\beta}{\gamma} \binom{\beta + r}{\gamma + r}^{-1}.$$

Thus

$$E(X_{wU(n)} \mid X_{wU(n-2)} = m)$$

$$= \frac{1}{q_m} \sum_{r=m}^{\infty} \frac{(\beta - \gamma + 1)\gamma[r(\beta - \gamma - 1) + \gamma]}{(\beta + r + 1)(\gamma + r)(\beta - \gamma)} \binom{\beta}{\gamma} \binom{\beta + r}{\gamma + r}^{-1}$$

$$= \left(\begin{array}{c}\beta\\\gamma\end{array}\right)\frac{1}{q_m}[\frac{\beta-\gamma+1}{\beta-\gamma}\sum_{r=m}^{\infty}\frac{\gamma r}{\gamma+r}\left(\begin{array}{c}\beta+r+1\\\gamma+r\end{array}\right)^{-1}$$

$$+\frac{\gamma}{\beta-\gamma}\sum_{r=m}^{\infty}\frac{\gamma}{\gamma+r}\left(\begin{array}{c}\beta+r+1\\\gamma+r\end{array}\right)^{-1}]$$

$$\frac{1}{q_m}\frac{(\beta-\gamma+1)[m(\beta-\gamma+1)+\gamma]}{(\beta-\gamma)^2}\backslash q_m+$$

On simplifying we the obtain

$$E(X_{wU(n)}|X_{wU(n-2)}=m)$$

$$= \frac{(\beta-\gamma+1)[m(\beta-\gamma+1)+\gamma]}{(\beta-\gamma)^2}+\frac{\gamma}{\beta-\gamma}.$$

$$= \frac{(\beta-\gamma+1)^2 m}{(\beta-\gamma)^2}+\frac{\gamma\{2(\beta-\gamma)+1\}}{(\beta-\gamma)^2} \qquad (.3.21)$$

The relation given in (6.3.21) is a characteristic property of the Beta-Negative Binomial distribution.

Wesolowski and Ahsanullah (2001) proved that if

$E(X_{wU(n)}|X_{wU(n-2)}=m)=a\,m+b$, where m>1, then the distribution of the X's is Beta-Negative Binomial, BEB ($\frac{b+\sqrt{a}+1}{a-1},\frac{b}{a-1}$).

CHAPTER 7

SOME SELECTED DISTRIBUTIONS

7.0. INTRODUCTION

In this chapter record values of some selected distributions including logistic, normal, Raleigh and uniform are discussed. The means, variances and covariances of the record values are given. Inferences of some of the distributions based on record values are discussed.

7.1. LOGISTIC DISTRIBUTION

Let $\{X_n, n \geq 1\}$ be a sequence of i.i.d. rvs from the standard logistic distribution with pdf

$$f(x) = \frac{e^{-x}}{(1+e^{-x})^2}, \quad -\infty < x < \infty \tag{7.1.1}$$

and cdf

$$F(x) = \frac{1}{1+e^{-x}}, \quad -\infty < x < \infty. \tag{7.1.2}$$

The figure 7.1.1 gives the pdf of the logistic distribution as given by (7.1.1). The pdf is symmetric around zero.

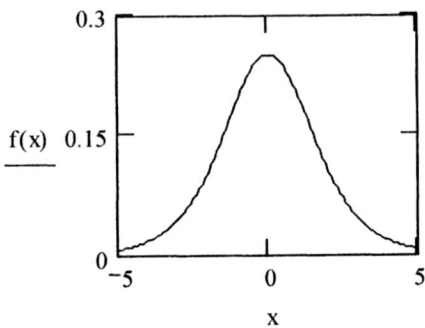

Fig. 7.1.1. pdf of X_i's.

Let $X_{U(1)}, X_{U(2)}, \ldots$ and $X_{L(1)}, X_{L(2)}, \ldots$ be the upper record and lower record values from the sequence $\{X_n\}$. Since $f(x)$ is symmetric around zero, $X_{U(n)} \stackrel{d}{=} -X_{L(n)}$ for all $n > 1$. We will consider here the upper record values.

Theorem 7.1.1

Let $\mu_n = E(X_{U(n)})$, $\mu_{m,n} = E(X_{U(m)}, X_{U(n)})$, then
$\mu_n = \mu_{n-1} + \zeta(n)$, $n > 1$, $\mu_1 = 0$,
$\mu_{m,n} = n\, E(X_{U(m)}) + m\, E(X_{U(n)}) + m\, \zeta(m+1) + m\, \zeta(n+1) - m(n+1)$
$$+ \sum_{k=1}^{\infty} \frac{1}{k(k+1)^{n-m}} \sum_{l=1}^{\infty} \frac{1}{l(l+1+k)^m},$$
where
$\zeta(.)$ is the Riemann zeta function.

Proof.

$$\mu_1 = E(X_1) = \int_{-\infty}^{\infty} \frac{xe^{-x}}{(1+e^{-x})^2} dx = 0.$$

The conditional pdf of $X_{U(n)} | X_{U(n-1)} = y$, for $n > 1$, is

$$f_{n,n-1,c}(x | X_{U(n-1)} = y) = \frac{e^{-x}(1+e^y)}{(1+e^{-x})^2}, \quad -\infty < y < x < \infty$$

(7.1.3)

Some Selected Distributions

The conditional expectation of $X_{U(n)} | X_{U(n-1)} = y$ is given by

$$E(X_{U(n)} | X_{U(n-1)} = y) = \int_y^\infty \frac{xe^{-x}(1+e^y)}{(1+e^{-x})^2} dx$$

$$= y + (1+e^y)\ln(1+e^{-y})$$

Thus

$$E(X_{U(n)}) = E(X_{U(n-1)})$$
$$+ \int_{-\infty}^\infty (1+e^y)\ln(1+e^{-y}) \frac{\{y+\ln(1+e^{-y})\}^{n-2}}{\Gamma(n-1)} \frac{e^{-y}}{(1+e^{-y})^2} dy$$

(7.1.4)

Substituting $t = e^{-y}(1+e^{-y})^{-1}$ and simplifying, we get

$$E(X_{U(n)}) = EX_{U(n-1)}) + \int_0^1 \frac{(-\ln t)(-\ln(1-t))^{n-2}}{(1-t)\Gamma(n-1)} dt$$

$$E(X_{U(n-1)}) + \zeta(n), \qquad (7.1.5)$$

where $\zeta(n)$ is the Riemann zeta function.
Since $\mu_1 = 0$, we have

$$\mu_n = \sum_{i=2}^n \zeta(i), \; n \geq 2. \qquad (7.1.6)$$

The expected values of the first ten upper record values are given in Table 7.1.1.

Table 7.1.1 $E(X_{U(n)})$, $1 \leq n \leq 10$

n	$E(X_{U(n)})$
1	0.0000
2	1.6449
3	2.8470
4	3.9293
5	4.9662
6	5.9836
7	6.9919
8	7.9960
9	8.9980
10	9.9990

$$\mu_{n,n} = E(X_{U(n)})^2 = \int_{-\infty}^{\infty} x^2 f_n(x)dx$$

$$= \int_{-\infty}^{\infty} x^2 \frac{(\ln(1+e^x))^{n-1}}{\Gamma(n)} \frac{e^{-x}}{(1+e^{-x})^2} dx$$

$$= \int_{0}^{1} [\ln t - \ln(1-t)]^2 \frac{\{-\ln(1-t)\}^{n-1}}{\Gamma(n)} dt$$

$$= \int_{0}^{1} \frac{\{-\ln(1-t)\}^{n+1}}{\Gamma(n)} dt - 2\int_{0}^{1} \frac{(\ln t)\{-\ln(1-t)\}^n}{\Gamma(n)} dt$$

$$+ \int_{0}^{1} \frac{\{\ln t\}^2 \{-\ln(1-t)\}^{n-1}}{\Gamma(n)} dt$$

Now

$$\int_{0}^{\infty} \frac{\{-\ln(1-t)\}^{n+1}}{\Gamma(n)} dt = n(n+1),$$

$$- \int_{0}^{\infty} \frac{\ln t \{-\ln(1-t)\}^n}{\Gamma(n)} dt = n[E(X_{U(n+1)}) - (n+1)]$$

and

$$\int_{0}^{1} \frac{\{\ln t\}^2 \{-\ln(1-t)\}^{n-1}}{\Gamma(n)} dt = \int_{0}^{\infty} \left\{ \sum_{k=1}^{\infty} \frac{e^{-tk}}{k} \right\}^2 \frac{1}{\Gamma(n)} t^{n-1} e^{-t} dt$$

$$= \sum_{j=2}^{\infty} B_j \int_{0}^{\infty} e^{-jt} \frac{1}{\Gamma(n)} t^{n-1} e^{-t} dt = \sum_{j+2}^{\infty} \frac{B_j}{(j+1)^n},$$

where B_j is the coefficient of e^{-jt} in $\left\{ \sum_{k=1}^{\infty} \frac{e^{-kt}}{k} \right\}^2$.

Thus

$$\mu_{n,n} = n(n+1) + 2n[E(X_{U(n+1)}) - (n+1)] + \sum_{j+2}^{\infty} \frac{B_j}{(j+1)^n}$$

$$= 2n\, E(X_{U(n+1)}) - n(n+1) + \sum_{l=2}^{\infty} \frac{B_l}{(l+1)^n},$$

$$= 2n \sum_{i=2}^{n+1} \zeta(i) - n(n+1) + \sum_{l=2}^{\infty} \frac{B_l}{(l+1)^n},$$

where

$$B_i = \frac{1}{i}(1 + \frac{1}{2} + \ldots + \frac{1}{i-1}), \, i \geq 2.$$

$$Var(X_{U(n)}) = 2n \sum_{i=2}^{n+1} \zeta(i) - n(n+1) + \sum_{l=2}^{\infty} \frac{B_l}{(l+1)^n} - \left(\sum_{i=2}^{n} \xi(i)\right)^2,$$

$$\mu_{m,n} = E(X_{U(m)} X_{U(n)}) = \int_{-\infty}^{\infty} \int_{y}^{\infty} xy f_{m,n}(y,x) dy dx$$

$$= \iint_{-\infty < y < x < \infty} \frac{(-\ln \overline{F}(y))^{m-1}}{\Gamma(m)\Gamma(n-m)} [\ln \overline{F}(x) - \overline{F}(y)]^{n-m-1} r(y) f(x) dy dx,$$

where

$r(y) = \frac{f(y)}{\overline{F}(y)}$, $\overline{F}(y) = 1 - F(y)$ and $f(y)$ and $F(y)$ are given by (7.1.1) and (7.1.2). Substituting $v = \frac{1}{1+e^{-x}}$ and $u = \frac{1}{1+e^{-y}}$ and simplification, we get

$$\mu_{m,n} = \int_0^1 \int_u^1 \frac{\{-\ln(1-u)\}^{m-1}}{\Gamma(m)\Gamma(n-m)} [-\ln(1-v) + \ln(1-u)]^{n-m-1}$$

$$[\ln u - \ln(1-u)][\ln v - \ln(1-v)] \frac{1}{1-u} dv du$$

Let $I_u = \int_u^1 [-\ln(1-v) + \ln(1-u)]^{n-m-1} [\ln v - \ln(1-v)] dv$

Substituting $w = -\ln(1-v) + \ln(1-u)$, we have

$$I_u = \int_0^{\infty} w^{n-m-1} [\ln\{1-(1-u)e^{-w}\} - \{w + \ln(1-u)\}](1-u)e^{-w} dw$$

$$=(1-u)[\sum_{k=1}^{\infty}\int_{0}^{\infty}(-1)(1-u)^k\frac{e^{-kw}}{k}e^{-w}w^{n-m-1}dw$$

$$+\Gamma(n-m+1)-\Gamma(n-m)\ln(1-u)]$$

$$=\Gamma(n-m)(1-u)[-\sum_{k=1}^{\infty}\frac{(1-u)^k}{k(k+1)^{n-m}}+(n-m)-\ln(1-u)]$$

Upon substituting I_u, we have

$$\mu_{m,n}=\int_{0}^{1}\frac{\{-\ln(1-u)\}^{m-1}}{\Gamma(m)}[n-m-\ln(1-u)-\sum_{k=1}^{\infty}\frac{(1-u)^k}{k(k+1)^{n-m}}]$$

$$\cdot[\ln u-\ln(1-u)]du$$

$$= (n-m)\, E(X_{U(m)}) + m\, E(X_{U(m+1)}) - m\sum_{k=1}^{\infty}\frac{1}{k(k+1)^{n+1}}$$

$$+\sum_{k=1}^{\infty}\frac{1}{k(k+1)^{n-m}}\sum_{l=1}^{\infty}\frac{1}{l(l+1+k)^m}$$

$$= n\, E(X_{U(m)}) + m\, E(X_{U(n)}) + m\, \zeta(m+1) + m\, \zeta(n+1) - m(n+1)$$

$$+\sum_{k=1}^{\infty}\frac{1}{k(k+1)^{n-m}}\sum_{l=1}^{\infty}\frac{1}{l(l+1+k)^m}$$

$\text{Cov}(X_{U(m)}, X_{U(n)}) = \mu_{m,n} - E(X_{U(m)})\, E(X_{U(n)})$.

Table 7.1.1 gives the variances and covariance of $X_{U(m)}$, $X_{U(n)}$, for $1 \leq m \leq n \leq 10$.

Table 7.1.2 Variances and Covariances of the upper record values

n \ m	1	2	3	4	5	6	7	8	9	10
1	3.2899									
2	2.4426	2.9882								
3	1.9701	2.6887	3.5414							
4	1.7913	2.5310	3.3885	4.3096						
5	1.7139	2.4636	3.3132	4.2258	5.1779					
6	1.6782	2.4327	3.2788	4.1853	5.1311	6.1016				
7	1.6612	2.4181	3.2625	4.1660	5.1084	6.0754	7.0576			
8	1.6530	2.4110	3.2546	4.1567	5.0974	6.0625	7.0429	8.0323		
9	1.6489	2.4075	3.2508	4.1522	5.0920	6.0563	7.0356	8.0241	9.0180	
10	1.6469	2.4058	3.2489	4.1500	5.0893	6.0532	7.0321	8.0200	9.0134	10.0100

7.2. NORMAL DISTRIBUTION

Let $\{X_n, n \geq 1\}$ be a sequence of i.i.d. random variables from standard normal distribution (N(0,1)) with pdf

$$\phi(x) = \frac{1}{\sqrt{2\pi}} e^{-x^2/2}, \quad -\infty < x < \infty. \tag{7.2.1}$$

and cdf

$$\Phi(x) = \int_{-\infty}^{x} \frac{1}{\sqrt{2\pi}} e^{-x^2/2} dx.$$

The graph of $\phi(x)$ is giben in gigure 7.2.1.

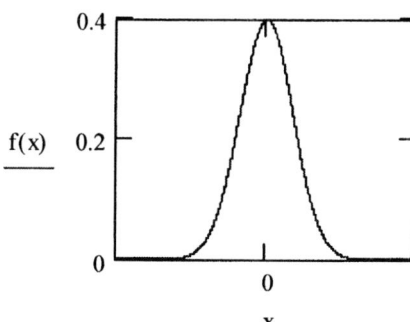

Figure 7.2.1. Pdf of X_i's.

Theorem 7.2.1

Let $\mu_{1,n} = E(X_{U(n)})$, $\mu_{n,n} = E(X_{U(n)})^2$ and $\mu_{m,n} = E(X_{U(m)} X_{U(n)})$, then

$$\mu_{n,n} = E(X_{U(n)})^2 = 1 + \mu_{n-1,n},$$

$$\mu_{1,n} = \frac{1}{\Gamma(n-1)} \int_{-\infty}^{\infty} \{-\ln(1-\Phi(x))\}^{n-2} (1-\Phi(x))^{-1} (\phi(x))^2 dx$$

and

$$\mu_{m,n} = \frac{1}{\Gamma(m)\Gamma(n-m)} \int_0^1 \int_0^1 \{\Phi^{-1}(u)\}\{\Phi^{-1}(v)\}$$

$$\frac{\{-\ln(1-u)\}^{m-1}}{1-u} \{\ln(1-u) - \ln(1-v)\}^{n-m-1} du\, dv.$$

Proof.

$$\mu_{n,n} = \frac{1}{\Gamma(n)} \int_{-\infty}^{\infty} x^2 [-\ln\{1-\Phi(x)\}]^{n-1} (\phi(x))\, dx$$

$$= -\frac{1}{\Gamma(n)} \int_{-\infty}^{\infty} x[-\ln\{1-\Phi(x)\}]^{n-1}\, d\phi(x)$$

since $-x\,\phi(x)\,dx = d\phi(x)$. Integrating the above expression by parts and simplifying, we have

$$\mu_{n,n} = \frac{1}{\Gamma(n)} \int_{-\infty}^{\infty} [-\ln\{1-\Phi(x)\}]^{n-1} (\phi(x))\, dx$$

$$+ \frac{1}{\Gamma(n-1)} \int_{-\infty}^{\infty} x[-\ln\{1-\Phi(x)\}]^{n-2} \frac{1}{1-\Phi(x)} (\phi(x))^2\, dx$$

$$= 1 + \frac{1}{\Gamma(n-1)} \int_{-\infty}^{\infty} x[-\ln\{1-\Phi(x)\}]^{n-2} \frac{1}{1-\Phi(x)} (\phi(x))^2\, dx.$$

We can write

$$\phi(x) = \int_x^{\infty} -\phi'(y)\, dy = \int_x^{\infty} y\phi(x)\, dy, \text{ thus}$$

$\mu_{n,n}$

$$= 1 + \frac{1}{\Gamma(n-1)} \int_{-\infty}^{\infty} \int_x^{\infty} xy[-\ln\{1-\Phi(x)\}]^{n-2} \frac{1}{1-\Phi(x)} \phi(x)(\phi(y))\, dx\, dy.$$

$= 1 + \mu_{n-1,n}$.

$\mu_{m,n}$

$$= \frac{1}{\Gamma(m)\Gamma(n-m)} \int_{-\infty}^{\infty} c \int_0^y \frac{y}{1-\Phi(y)} \frac{x}{1-\Phi(x)} [\ln\{1-\Phi(x)\} - \{\ln(1-\Phi(y))\}]^{n-m-1}$$

$\phi(x).\phi(y)\, dx\, dy$

On simplification, we get

Some Selected Distributions

$$\mu_{m,n} = \frac{1}{\Gamma(m)\Gamma(n-m)} \int_0^1 \int_0^{\Phi^{-1}} \{\Phi^{-1}(u)\}\{\Phi^{-1}(v)\}$$

$$\frac{\{-\ln(1-u)\}^{m-1}}{1-u} \{\ln(1-u) - \ln(1-v)\}^{n-m-1} du\,dv$$

The means, variances and covariances of the upper record values were obtained by numerical methods. The variances and covariances of the lower record values are the same. The means of the lower record values are the the negatives of the upper record values. The following tables give the means, variances and covariance of $X_{U(m)}$ and $X_{U(n)}$ for $1 \leq m \leq n \leq 10$.

Table 7.2.1. Mean of $X_{L(n)}$

n	$E(X_{L(n)})$
1	0.0000
2	0.9032
3	1.4990
4	1.9687
5	2.3667
6	2.7174
7	3.0339
8	3.3244
9	3.5942
10	3.8471

Table 7.2.2. Variances and Covariance of the upper record values

n	M									
	1	2	3	4	5	6	7	8	9	10
1	1.0000									
2	0.5956	0.7799								
3	0.4534	0.5953	0.7022							
4	0.3775	0.4964	0.5859	0.6611						
5	0.3292	0.4331	0.5115	0.5753	0.6353					
6	0.2951	0.3885	0.4589	0.5181	0.5702	0.6174				
7	0.2696	0.3550	0.4194	0.4735	0.5212	0.5643	0.6014			
8	0.2495	0.3286	0.3883	0.4385	0.4827	0.5226	0.5595	0.5938		
9	0.2332	0.3073	0.3631	0.4100	0.4514	0.4888	0.5233	0.5554	0.5856	
10	0.2197	0.2895	0.3421	0.3864	0.4253	0.4606	0.4931	0.5234	0.5519	0.5788

7.3. RAYLEIGH DISTRIBUTION

Let $\{X_n, n \geq 1\}$ be a sequence of i.i.d random variables from standard Rayleigh distribution with pdf

$$f(x) = x\, e^{-x^2/2}, \quad x > 0 \qquad (7.3.1)$$

and cdf

$$F(x) = 1 - e^{-x^2/2}, \quad x > 0. \qquad (7.3.2)$$

We say $X \in RH(0,1)$ if the pdf of X is given by (7.3.1)'Figure **7.3.1** gives the graph of f(x).

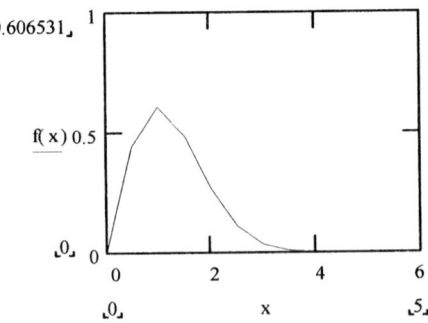

Figure 7.3.1. Pdf of X

Theorem 7.3.1

Let $\mu_n = E(X_{U(n)})$, $V_{n,n} = Var(X_{U(n)})$ and $V_{m,n} = Cov(X_{U(m)} X_{U(n)})$, then

$$\mu_n = \sqrt{2}\,\frac{\Gamma(n+\tfrac{1}{2})}{\Gamma(n)},\ V_{n,n} = 2\left[n - \left(\frac{\Gamma(n+1/2)}{\Gamma(n)}\right)^2\right] \text{ and }$$

$$V_{m,n} = 2\left[\frac{\Gamma(m+1/2)}{\Gamma(m)}\right]\left[\frac{\Gamma(n+1)}{\Gamma(n+1/2)} - \frac{\Gamma(n+1/2)}{\Gamma(n)}\right],\ \text{for } 1 \leq m < n.$$

Some Selected Distributions

Proof:

$$\mu_n = \frac{1}{\Gamma(n)}\int_0^\infty x\{-\ln(1-F(x))\}^{n-1} f(x)dx$$

$$= \frac{1}{\Gamma(n)}\int_0^\infty x\left(\frac{x^2}{2}\right)^{n-1} e^{-x^2/2} x\, dx$$

$$= \frac{1}{\Gamma(n)}\sqrt{2}\int_0^\infty u^{1/2} u^{n-1} e^{-u} du$$

$$= \sqrt{2}\frac{\Gamma(n+1/2)}{\Gamma(n)}.$$

Similarly it can be shown that

$$\mu_n^2 = E(X_{U(n)}^2) = 2\frac{\Gamma(n+1)}{\Gamma(n)} = 2n$$

$$\mu_{m,n} = $$

$$\frac{1}{\Gamma(m)\Gamma(n-m)}\int_0^\infty \int_0^y xy\left(\frac{x^2}{2}\right)^{m-1} x\left(\frac{y^2}{2}-\frac{x^2}{2}\right)^{n-m-1} y e^{-y^2/2} dx\, dy$$

$$= \frac{1}{\Gamma(m)\Gamma(n-m)}\frac{1}{2^{m-1}}\int_0^\infty y\left(\frac{y^2}{2}\right)^{n-m-1} y e^{-y^2/2} I_y\, dy,$$

where

$$I_y = \int_0^y (x^2)^m \left(1-\frac{x^2}{y^2}\right)^{n-m-1} dx$$

$$= \frac{1}{2} y^{2m+1} B(m+1/2, n-m),$$

with

$$B(a,b) = \frac{\Gamma(a)\Gamma(b)}{\Gamma(a+b)}.$$

On simplification we get

$$V_{n,n} = 2\left[n - \left(\frac{\Gamma(n+1/2)}{\Gamma(n)}\right)^2\right] \text{ and}$$

$$V_{m,n} = 2\left[\frac{\Gamma(m+1/2)}{\Gamma(m)}\right]\left[\frac{\Gamma(n+1)}{\Gamma(n+1/2)} - \frac{\Gamma(n+1/2)}{\Gamma(n)}\right], \text{ for } 1 \leq m < n.$$

$$= \left[\frac{\Gamma(m+1/2)}{\Gamma(m)}\right]\left[\frac{\Gamma(n)}{\Gamma(n+1/2)}\right]V_{n,n}$$

Table 7.3.1 gives the variances and covariances of $X_{U(m)}$ and $X_{U(n)}$ for $1 \leq m \leq n \leq 10$..

Table 7.3.1 Variances and Covariances of upper records

M									
1	2	3	4	5	6	7	8	9	10
.429204									
.310472	.465708								
.254757	.382135	.477669							
.221026	.331539	.414424	.483494						
.197860	.296791	.370988	.432820	.486922					
.180706	.271059	.338823	.395294	.444705	.489176				
.167348	.251023	.313778	.366075	.411834	.453018	.490769			
.156569	.234854	.293567	.342495	.385307	.423837	.459157	.491954		
.147634	.221450	.276813	.322948	.363317	.369649	.432953	.463878	.492870	
.140070	.210150	.262632	.306404	.344704	.39714	.410772	.440113	.467620	.493599

(N labels the rows)

The correlation coefficient $\rho_{m,n}$ between $X_{U(m)}$ and $X_{U(n)}$ is

$$\rho_{m,n} = \frac{\Gamma(n)}{\Gamma(m)} \cdot \frac{\Gamma(m+1/2)}{\Gamma(n+1/2)} \cdot \sqrt{\frac{V_{n,n}}{V_{m,m}}}$$

$$= \frac{\Gamma(m+\frac{1}{2})}{\Gamma(n+\frac{1}{2})} \cdot \frac{\Gamma(n)}{\Gamma(m)} \cdot \frac{\sqrt{n - \left(\frac{\Gamma(n+\frac{1}{2})}{\Gamma(n)}\right)^2}}{\sqrt{m - \left(\frac{\Gamma(m+\frac{1}{2})}{\Gamma(n)}\right)^2}}, \quad 1 \leq m \leq n.$$

We will consider the estimation of μ and σ based on the observed record values.of the two parameter Rayleigh distribution with the pdf

$$f(x,\mu,\sigma) = \frac{x-\mu}{\sigma} e^{-\frac{(x-\mu)^2}{2\sigma^2}}, \mu < x < \infty, \sigma > 0$$

(a) Minimum Variance Linear Unbiased Estimators of μ and σ.

Theorem 7.3.2

The minimum variance linear unbiased estimators $\hat{\mu}$ and $\hat{\sigma}$ of μ and σ based on the observed record values $r_1, r_2, \ldots, r_m$ are

$$\hat{\mu} = \sum_{i=1}^{m} c_i r_1, \text{ and } \hat{\sigma} = \sum_{i=1}^{m} d_i r_i,$$

where

$$c_1 = \frac{3 \alpha_m b_m}{2 D}, \quad c_i = \frac{1}{2i} \frac{\alpha_m b_m}{D}, i=2,3,\ldots,m-1,$$

$$c_m = 1 - \frac{\alpha_m b_m}{2D}\left[3 + \sum_{i=2}^{m-1} \frac{1}{i}\right], \quad d_1 = -\frac{3 b_m}{2 D}, \quad d_i = -\frac{1}{2i} \frac{b_m}{D}, i=2,3,\ldots,m-1,$$

$$d_m = \frac{1}{2} \frac{b_m}{D}\left\{3 + \sum_{i=2}^{m-1} \frac{1}{i}\right\},$$

where

$$D = \alpha_m b_m T - 1, \quad T = \left[\frac{3}{2} + \sum_{i=2}^{m-1} \frac{1}{2i} + (2m-1)(\frac{b_{m-1}}{b_m}-1)\right]$$

$$\alpha_k = \sqrt{2} \frac{\Gamma(k+\frac{1}{2})}{\Gamma(k)} = a_k \text{ and } b_k = \sqrt{2}\left\{\frac{\Gamma(k+1)}{\Gamma(k+\frac{1}{2})} - \frac{\Gamma(k+\frac{1}{2})}{\Gamma(k)}\right\},$$

$k = 1, 2, \ldots, m$.

Proof.

Let R be the $m \times 1$ vector corresponding to $X_{U(i)}$, $i = 1, 2, \ldots, m$, then we have

$$E(R) = \mu L + \sigma \delta$$

where

$R' = (X_{U(1)}, X_{U(2)}, \ldots, X_{U(m)})$
$L' = (1, 1, \ldots, 1), \delta' = (\alpha_1, \alpha_2, \ldots, \alpha_m)$

$$\alpha_i = \sqrt{2} \frac{\Gamma(i+1/2)}{\Gamma(i)}, i = 1, 2, \ldots, m.$$

We can write
$V(R) = \sigma^2 V$, $V = (V_{i,j})$, $V_{i,j} = a_i b_j$, $1 \le i \le j \le m$ and $V_{i,j} = V_{j,i}$.

The inverse V^{-1} ($= V^{i,j}$) can be expressed as

$$V^{i+1,i} = V^{i,i+1} = -\frac{1}{a_{i+1}b_i - a_i b_{i+1}} = -(2i+1), i = 1,2,...,m-1,$$

$$V^{i,i} = \frac{a_{i+1}b_{i-1} - a_{i-1}b_{i+1}}{(a_i b_{i-1} - a_{i-1} b_i)(a_{i+1}b_i - a_i b_{i+1})}, i = 1,2,...,n,$$

$V^{i,j} = 0$, for $|i-j| > 1$,
where $a_o = 0 = b_{n+1}$ and $b_o = 1 = a_{n+1}$.

On simplification, we obtain

$$V^{i,i} = \frac{8i^2 + 1}{2i}, i = 1,2,...,m-1,$$

and

$$V^{m,m} = (2m-1)\frac{b_{m-1}}{b_m}.$$

The minimum variance linear unbiased estimates (MVLUE) $\hat{\mu}, \hat{\sigma}$ of μ and σ respectively are

$$\hat{\mu} = -\delta'V^{-1}(L\delta' - \delta L')V^{-1}X/\Delta$$

$$\hat{\sigma} = L'V^{-1}(L\delta' - \delta L')V^{-1}X/\Delta,$$

where

$$\Delta = (L'V^{-1}L)(\delta'V^{-1}\delta) - (L'V^{-1}\delta)^2$$

and

$$Var(\hat{\mu}) = \sigma^2 L'V^{-1}\delta/\Delta,$$
$$Var(\hat{\sigma}) = \sigma^2 L'V^{-1}L/\Delta$$
$$Cov(\hat{\mu}, \hat{\sigma}) = -\sigma^2 L'V^{-1}\delta/\Delta.$$

On simplification, we obtain the MVLUE $\hat{\mu}, \hat{\sigma}$ of μ and σ. The corresponding variances and the covariance of the estimates are

Some Selected Distributions

$$Var(\hat{\mu}) = \sigma^2 \frac{\alpha_n b_n}{D}$$

$$Var(\hat{\sigma}) = \sigma^2 \frac{b_n^2 T}{D} \qquad (7.3.4)$$

$$Cov(\hat{\mu}, \hat{\sigma}) = -\sigma^2 \frac{b_n}{D}.$$

Best Linear Invariant Estimators (BLIEs) of μ and σ.

Theorem 7.3.2

The best linear invariant (in the sense of minimum mean squared error and invariance with respect to the location parameter μ) estimators (BLIEs) $\tilde{\mu}$ $\tilde{\sigma}$ of μ and σ are

$$\tilde{\mu} = \hat{\mu} - \hat{\sigma}\left(\frac{E_{12}}{1+E_{22}}\right)$$

and

$$\tilde{\sigma} = \hat{\sigma}/(1+E_{22}),$$

where $\hat{\mu}$ and $\hat{\sigma}$ are MVLUEs of μ and σ and

$$\begin{pmatrix} Var(\hat{\mu}) & Cov(\hat{\mu}, \hat{\sigma}) \\ Cov(\hat{\mu}, \hat{\sigma}) & Var(\hat{\sigma}) \end{pmatrix} = \sigma^2 \begin{pmatrix} E_{11} & E_{12} \\ E_{12} & E_{22} \end{pmatrix}.$$

The mean squared errors of these estimators are

$$MSE(\tilde{\mu}) = \sigma^2 \left(E_{11} - E_{12}^2 (1+E_{22})^{-1}\right)$$

and

$$MSE(\tilde{\sigma}) = \sigma^2 E_{22}(1+E_{22})^{-1}.$$

Using the values of E_{11}, E_{12} and E_{22} from (7.3.4), we obtain

$$\tilde{\mu} = \hat{\mu} + \hat{\sigma}\left(\frac{b_m}{D + b_m^2 T}\right)$$

and

$$\tilde{\sigma} = \hat{\sigma}\frac{D}{D + b_m^2 T}.$$

Remark 7.3.1. If $\mu = 0$, then $X_{U(m)}$ is a sufficient statistic for σ, MVLUE unbiased estimator of σ based on the observed records values $r_1, r_2, \ldots, r_m$ is

where
$$\hat{\sigma}_* = c r_m,$$
$$c = \frac{1}{E(X_{U(m)})} = \frac{1}{\sqrt{2}} \cdot \frac{\Gamma(n)}{\Gamma(n+\frac{1}{2})}.$$
$$Var(\hat{\sigma}_*) = \sigma^2 [n\{\frac{\Gamma(n)}{\Gamma(n+\frac{1}{2})}\}^2 - 1]$$

7.4. TWO PARAMETER UNIFORM DISTRIBUTION

Let $\{X_n, n \geq 1\}$ be a sequence of i.i.d. random variables from a uniform distribution with the following pdf

$$f(x) = \frac{1}{\theta_1 - \theta_2}, \theta_1 < x < \theta_2 \quad (7.4.1)$$

and cdf

$$F(x) = \frac{x - \theta_1}{\theta_2 - \theta_1}, \quad \theta_1 < x < \theta_2. \quad (7.4.2)$$

We will say $X \in U(\theta_1, \theta_2)$ if the pdf of X is as given in (7.4.2). The pdf $f_n(x)$ of $X_{U(n)}$ can be written as

$$f_n(x) = \frac{1}{\Gamma(n)} \frac{1}{\theta_2 - \theta_1} \{\ln \frac{\theta_2 - \theta_1}{\theta_2 - x}\}^{n-1}, \theta_1 < x < \theta_2 \quad (7.4.3)$$

Theorem 7.4.1

Let $\varsigma_1 = \frac{\theta_2 - X_{U(1)}}{\theta_2 - \theta_1}, \varsigma_i = \frac{\theta_2 - X_{U(i)}}{\theta_2 - X_{U(i-1)}}, i = 2,...,n$, then $\varsigma_1,...,\varsigma_n$ are i.i.d. $U(0,1)$.

Proof:

The joint pdf of $X_{U(1)}, X_{U(2)},..., X_{U(n)}$ can be written as

$$f(x_1, x_2, ..., x_n) = \frac{1}{\theta_2 - x_1} \cdot \frac{1}{\theta_2 - x_2} \cdots \frac{1}{\theta_2 - x_{n-1}} \frac{1}{\theta_2 - \theta_1},$$

$\theta_1 < x_1 < x_2 < ... < x_n < \theta_2$.

Let
$$X_{U(1)} = \theta_2 - (\theta_2 - \theta_1)\xi_1$$
$$X_{U(2)} = \theta_2 - (\theta_2 - \theta_1)\xi_1 \xi_2$$
$$X_{U(i)} = \theta_2 - (\theta_2 - \theta_1)\xi_1 \xi_2 ... \xi_i, i = 3, ..., n.$$

Some Selected Distributions

The Jacobian of the transformation is

$$J = \frac{\partial(X_{U(1)}, X_{U(2)}, \ldots, X_{U(n)})}{\partial(\xi_1, \xi_2, \ldots, \xi_n)} = (\theta_2 - \theta_1)^n \xi_1^{n-1} \xi_1^{n-2} \ldots \xi_{n-1}.$$

Using the transformation from $X_{U(i)}$'s to ξ_i's and using the Jacobian, we get the pdf of ξ_i's as

$f(e_1, e_2, \ldots, e_n) = 1$, $0 < e_i < 1$, $i = 1, 2, \ldots, n$.

Using the Theorem 7.4.1 or the distribution of $X_{U(n)}$ as given in (7.4.3), it can be shown that

$$E(X_{U(n)}) = 2^{-n} \theta_1 + (1 - 2^{-n}) \theta_2$$
$$Var(X_{U(n)}) = (3^{-n} - 4^{-n})(\theta_2 - \theta_1)^2. \qquad (7.4.4)$$

The joint pdf of $X_{U(m)}$ and $X_{U(n)}$ is

$$f_{m,n}(x,y) = \frac{1}{\Gamma(m)} \frac{1}{\Gamma(n-m)} \frac{1}{\theta_2 - \theta_1} \frac{1}{\theta_2 - x} \{\ln \frac{\theta_2 - \theta_1}{\theta_2 - x}\}^{m-1} \{\ln \frac{\theta_2 - \theta_1}{\theta_2 - y}\}^{n-m-1},$$

for $\theta_1 < x < y < \theta_2$ \qquad (7.4.5)

Thus, it follows that

$$E(X_{U(n)} | X_{U(m)} = y_m) = 2^{m-n} y_m + (1 - 2^{m-n}) \theta_2$$

and

$$Cov(X_{U(m)}, X_{U(n)}) = 2^{m-n} Var(X_{U(m)}). \qquad (7.4.6)$$

Let $\rho_{m,n}$ be the correlation coefficient of $X_{U(m)}$ and $X_{U(n)}$, then

$$\rho_{m,n} = 2^{m-n} \sqrt{Var(X_{U(n)} / X_{U(n)})} = \sqrt{\{(4/3)^m - 1\}\{(4/3)^n - 1\}^{-1}}. \qquad (7.4.7)$$

The follwing table gives the correlation coefficient between $X_{U(m)}$ and $X_{U(m)}$ for $1 \leq m \leq n \leq 10$.

Table 7.4.1. Correlation coefficients of upper records

n	\multicolumn{10}{c}{M}
	1	2	3	4	5	6	7	8	9	10
1	1									
2	.654654	1								
3	.493197	.753371	1							
4	.392792	.600000	.796421	1						
5	.322045	.491932	.652975	.819887	1					
6	.268647	.410365	.544705	.683941	.834189	1				
7	.226603	.346142	.459457	.576903	.703637	.843498	1			
8	.192571	.294157	.390454	.490261	.597962	.716818	.849816	1		
9	.164499	.251277	.333537	.418795	.510796	.612326	.725936	.854228	1	
10	.141037	.215437	.285964	.359062	.413794	.524989	.622395	.857369	1	

For fixed m, $\rho_{m,n}$ decreases as n increases. For fixed For fixed n, $\rho_{m,n}$ increases as mn increases.

(a) Relations of single moments

We will assume here without any loss of generality $\theta_1 = 0$ and $\theta_2 = 1$. For $n \geq 2$, and $r = 0,1,2,\ldots$

$$E\left(X_{U(n)}^{r+1}\right) = \frac{r+1}{r+2} E\left(X_{U(n)}^r\right) + \frac{1}{r+2} E(X_{U(n-1)}^{r+1}) \qquad (7.4.8)$$

Proof:

From (5.2.3), for $n \geq 2$ and $r = 0,1,\ldots,$

$$E\left(X_{U(n)}^r - X_{U(n)}^{r+1}\right) = \int_0^1 \left(x^r - x^{r+1}\right) f_n(x) dx$$

$$= \frac{1}{(n-1)!} \int_0^1 x^r \{-\ln(1-F(x))\}^{n-1} \{1 - F(x)\} dx$$

$$= \frac{1}{r+1} \left[\int_0^1 x^{r+1} \frac{1}{(n-1)!} \{-\ln(1-F(x))\}^{n-1} f(x) dx \right.$$

$$\left. - \int_0^1 x^{r+1} \frac{1}{(n-2)!} \{-\ln(1-F(x))\}^{n-2} f(x) dx \right]$$

$$= \frac{1}{r+1} \left[E\left(X_{U(n)}^{r+1}\right) - E\left(X_{U(n-1)}^{r+1}\right) \right]$$

where the last but one step follows by integrating by parts. The recurrence relation in equation 7.4.8) is derived simply by rewriting the above equation.

Corollary 7.4.1.

By repeatedly applying the recurrence relation in (7.4.8), we get for $n \geq 2$, $1 \leq m \leq n-1$ and $r = 0,1,2,\ldots$

$$E\left(X_{U(n)}^{r+1}\right) = \left(\frac{r+1}{r+2}\right)^{n-m-1} \sum_{p=0}^{n-m-1} \left(\frac{1}{r+2}\right)^p E\left(X_{U(n-p)}^r\right)$$

$$+ \left(\frac{1}{r+2}\right)^{n-m} E\left(X_{U(m)}^{r+1}\right) \qquad (7.4.9)$$

Some Selected Distributions 227

Corollary 7.4.2.
Write $(r+1)^{(p)} = 1$ for $p = 0$, $= (r+1)r...(r-p)$ for $p \geq 1$. By repeated application of the recurrence relation in (5.2.4), we obtain for $n \geq 2, r = 0,1,2,...$

$$E\left(X_{U(n)}^{r+1}\right) = \sum_{p=0}^{r+1} \frac{(r+1)^{(p)}}{(\gamma+1+p)^{(p+1)}} E\left(X_{U(n-1)}^{r+1-p}\right) \quad (7.4.10)$$

Next, we have the joint density function of $X_{U(m)}$ and $X_{U(n)}$, $1 \leq m < n$, as

$$f_{m,n}(x,y) = \frac{1}{(m-1)!(n-m-1)!} \{-\ln(1-F(x))\}^{m-1} \frac{f(x)}{1-F(x)}$$
$$\cdot \{-\ln(1-F(y)) + \ln(1-F(x))\}^{n-m-1} f(y),$$

Once again, upon using the relation $x\, f(x) = F(x)$, we can derive some simple recurrence relations for the product moments of record values.

Theorem 7.4.3
For $m \geq 1$ and $r, s = 0,1,2,...$

$$E\left(X_{U(m)}^{r} X_{U(m+1)}^{s+1}\right) = \frac{s+1}{s+2} E\left(X_{U(m)}^{r} X_{U(m+1)}^{s}\right) + \frac{1}{s+2} E\left(X_{U(m)}^{r+s+1}\right)$$
$$(7.4.11)$$

and for $1 \leq m \leq n-2$ and $r,s = 0,1,2,...,$

$$E\left(X_{U(m)}^{r} X_{U(n)}^{s+1}\right) = \frac{s+1}{s+2} E\left(X_{U(m)}^{r} X_{U(n)}^{s}\right) + \frac{1}{s+2} E\left(X_{U(m)}^{r} X_{U(n-1)}^{s+1}\right)$$
$$(7.4.12)$$

Proof:
Let us consider for $1 \leq m \leq n-1$ and $r,s = 0,1,2...$
$$E\left(X_{U(m)}^{r} X_{U(n)}^{s} - X_{U(m)}^{r} X_{U(n)}^{s+1}\right)$$
$$\iint_{0 \leq x < y < 1} \left(x^r y^s - x^r y^{s+1}\right) f_{m,n}(x,y) dy\, dx$$

$$= \frac{1}{(m-1)!(n-m-1)!} \int_0^1 x^r \{-\ln(1-F(x))\}^{m-1} \cdot \frac{f(x)}{1-F(x)} I(x) dx$$
$$(7.4.13)$$

$$= \int_x^1 y^s \{-\ln(1-F(y)) + \ln(1-F(x))\}^{n-m-1} \{1-F(y)\} dy \ y$$

$$= \frac{1}{s+1}\left[\int_x^1 y^{s+1} f(y)dy - x^{s+1}\{1-F(x)\}\right], \text{ for } n = m+1$$

$$= \frac{1}{s+1}\left[\int_x^1 y^{s+1}\{-\ln(1-F(y)) + \ln(1-F(x))\}^{n-m-1} f(y)dy \right.$$

$$\left. -(n-m-1)\int_x^1 y^{s+1}\{-\ln(1-F(y)) + \ln(1-F(x))\}^{n-m-2} f(y)dy\right],$$

for $n \geq m+2$.

The last two equations are derived by integrating by parts. Upon simplifying the expressions of I(x) in Eq. (7.4.13) and simplifying the resulting equations, we obtain when $n = m+1$ that

$$E\left(X^r_{U(m)} X^s_{U(m+1)}\right) - E\left(X^r_{U(m)} X^{s+1}_{U(m+1)}\right)$$

$$= \frac{1}{s+1}\left\{E\left(X^r_{U(m)} X^{s+1}_{U(m+1)}\right) - E\left(X^{r+s+1}_{U(m)}\right)\right\},$$

and when $n - m \geq 2$ that

$$E\left(X^r_{U(m)} X^s_{U(n)}\right) - E\left(X^r_{U(m)} X^{s+1}_{U(n)}\right)$$

$$= \frac{1}{s+1}\left\{E\left(X^r_{U(m)} X^{s+1}_{U(n)}\right) - E\left(X^r_{U(m)} X^{s+1}_{U(n-1)}\right)\right\}.$$

The recurrence relations in (7.4.11) and (7.4.12) are derived simply by rewriting the above equations.

Corollary 7.4.3

For $m \geq 1$

$$Cov\left(X_{U(m)}, X_{U(m+1)}\right) = \frac{1}{2} Var\left(X_{U(m)}\right) \qquad (7.4.13)$$

$$Cov(X_{U(m)}, X_{U(n)}) = \frac{1}{2} Cov(X_{U(m)}, X_{U(n-1)}) \qquad (7.4.14)$$

Consequently, for $1 \leq m \leq n-1$

$$Cov\left(X_{U(m)}, X_{U(n)}\right) = \left(\frac{1}{2}\right)^{n-m} Var\left(X_{U(m)}\right) \qquad (7.4.15)$$

Proof:

Some Selected Distributions

$$Cov(X_{U(m)}, X_{U(n)}) = \left(\frac{1}{2}\right)^{n-m} Var(X_{U(m)}) \qquad (7.4.15)$$

Proof:

(7.4.13) follows from (7.4.8) and (5.4.14) from (5.4.8) and (5.4.11). Repeated application of (5.4.14) yields (5.4.15).

Corollary 7.4.4,

By repeated application of the recurrence relations in (5.4.11) and (5.4.12), we get from $m \geq 1$, $r,s = 0,1,2,....$

$$E\left(X_{U(m)}^r X_{U(m+1)}^{s+1}\right) = \sum_{p=0}^{s+1} \frac{(s+1)^{(p)}}{(s+2+p)^{(p+1)}} E\left(X_{U(m)}^{r+s+1-p}\right) \qquad (5.4.15)$$

and for $1 \leq m \leq n-2$ and $r,s = 0,1,2,.....$

$$E\left(X_{U(m)}^r X_{U(n)}^{s+1}\right) = \sum_{p=0}^{s+1} \frac{(s+1)^{(p)}}{(s+2+p)^{(p+1)}} E\left(X_{U(m)}^r X_{U(n-1)}^{s+1-p}\right) \qquad (5.4.16)$$

(a) Estimation of θ_1 and θ_2.

We will consider here the estimation of θ_1 and θ_2 based on m upper record values $X_{U(1)}, X_{U(2)}, ..., X_{U(m)}$.
Consider the following transformation

$$W_1 = X_{U(1)}$$
$$W_i = (3)^{(i-1)/2} (X_{U(i)} - \frac{1}{2} X_{U(i-1)}), \; i = 2,3,......,m \qquad (7.4.7)$$

It can easily be verified that

$$E(W_1) = \frac{\theta_1 + \theta_2}{2}$$

$$E(W_i) = 3^{\frac{i-1}{2}} \frac{\theta_2 - \theta_1}{2}, i = 2,3,...,m, \qquad (7.4.8)$$

$$Var(W_i) = \frac{\sigma^2}{12}, i = 1,2,...,m,$$

and

$$Cov(W_i, W_j) = 0, \; i \neq j.$$

Let $W' = (W_1, W_2, ..., W_m)$, then $E(W) = H\theta$, where

$$H = \begin{bmatrix} \frac{1}{2} & \frac{1}{2} \\ 0 & \frac{1}{2^i}(3)^{\frac{1}{2}} \\ & \ddots \\ 0 & \frac{1}{2^n}(3)^{(n-1)/2} \end{bmatrix}, \quad \theta = \begin{bmatrix} \theta_1 \\ \theta_2 \end{bmatrix}.$$

We have

$$(H'H)^{-1} = \frac{32}{3(3^{m-1}-1)} \begin{bmatrix} \frac{3^m-1}{8} & -\frac{1}{4} \\ -\frac{1}{4} & \frac{1}{4} \end{bmatrix}$$

Thus, expressing W's in terms of the observed record values $r_1, r_2, ..., r_m$, we get

$$\hat{\theta}_1 = 2r_1 - \hat{\theta}_2 \text{ and}$$

$$\hat{\theta}_2 = \frac{4}{3(3^{m-1}-1)} \{3^{m-1} r_m - \frac{3^{m-2}}{2} r_{m-1} - .... - \frac{3}{2} r_1\}.$$

The variances covariance of these estimates are

$$Var(\hat{\theta}) = \frac{1}{9} \frac{3^m-1}{3^{m-1}-1} (\theta_2 - \theta_1)^2,$$

$$Var(\hat{\theta}_2) = \frac{2}{9} \frac{1}{3^{n-1}-1} (\theta_2 - \theta_1)^2$$

and

$$Cov(\hat{\theta}_1, \hat{\theta}_2) = \frac{2}{9} \frac{1}{3^{m-1}-1} (\theta_2 - \theta_1)^2.$$

The generalized variance $\hat{\Sigma} (\hat{\Sigma} = var\theta_1 \cdot var\theta_2 - (cov(\theta_1\theta_2))^2)$ is

$$\frac{2}{27} \cdot \frac{1}{3^{n-1}-1} (\theta_2 - \theta_1)^2.$$

Considering two records $X_{U(p)}$ and $X_{U(q)}$ ($q > p$), it follows from (7.4.4) and (7.4.6) that the best linear unbiased estimates $\hat{\theta}_1^*, \hat{\theta}_2^*$ of θ_1

and θ_2 based on the observed values r_p and r_q of these two record values are

$$\theta_1^* = 2^p r_p - (2^p - 1)\theta_2^*,$$

and

$$\theta_2^* = (r_q - 2^{p-q} r_p)/(1 - 2^{p-q}).$$

The variances and covariance of θ_1^* and θ_2^* are

$$\text{Var}(\theta_2^*) = (1 - 2^{p-q})^2 \frac{3^{p-q} - 4^{p-q}}{4 \cdot 3^{p+1}} (\theta_2 - \theta_1)^2,$$

$$\text{Var}(\theta_1^*) = (2^p - 1)^2 \text{Var}(\theta_2^*) + \frac{4^p - 3^p}{4 \cdot 3^{p+1}} (\theta_2 - \theta_1)^2$$

and

$$\text{Cov}(\theta_1^*, \theta_2^*) = -(2^r - 1) \text{Var}(\theta_2^*).$$

It can be shown that the generalized variance $\hat{\Sigma}^*$ of θ_1^* and θ_2^* ($\hat{\Sigma}^* =$ $\text{Var}(\theta_1^*) \cdot \text{Var}(\theta_2^*) - (\text{Cov}(\theta_1^*, \theta_2^*))^2$) is minimum when q = m and p = 1. Thus the best linear unbiased estimates $\tilde{\theta}_1, \tilde{\theta}_2$ of θ_1 and θ_2 based on the first and the m th record value is

$$\tilde{\theta}_1 = 2 r_1 - \tilde{\theta}_2$$

and

$$\tilde{\theta}_2 = \frac{r_m - 2^{1-m} r_1}{1 - 2^{1-m}},$$

where r_m and r_1 are the observed values of $X_{U(m)}$ and $X_{U(1)}$. The variances and covariance of these two estimates are as follows:

$$\text{Var}(\tilde{\theta}_1) = \{\frac{1}{3} + \frac{4^{m-1} - 3^{m-1}}{3^m (2^{m-1} - 1)^2}\}(\theta_2 - \theta_1)^2,$$

$$\text{Var}(\tilde{\theta}_2) = \{\frac{4^{m-1} - 3^{m-1}}{3^{m-1}(2^{m-1} - 1)^2}\}(\theta_2 - \theta_1)^2$$

and

$$\text{Cov}(\tilde{\theta}_1, \tilde{\theta}_2) = -\text{Var}(\tilde{\theta}_2).$$

Let $e_i = \dfrac{Var(\hat{\theta}_i)}{Var(\tilde{\theta}_i)}$, i = 1,2 and $e_{12} = \dfrac{Cov(\hat{\theta}_1, \hat{\theta}_2)}{Cov(\tilde{\theta}_1, \tilde{\theta}_2)}$.

The generalized variance $\tilde{\Sigma}$ $\tilde{\theta}_1, \tilde{\theta}_2$ is $\dfrac{1}{3} \dfrac{4^{m-1} - 3^{m-1}}{3^m (2^{m-1} - 1)^2} (\theta_2 - \theta_1)^4$. It can be shown that $e_{12} = e_2 = \dfrac{\hat{\Sigma}}{\tilde{\Sigma}}$.

Table 7.4.1 gives the values of e_1 and e_2, for m = 2,4,5,10,20 and 30. It can be seen from the table that the efficiency of the best linear unbiased estimate of θ_1 based on two record values are very high compared to the estimate based on the complete set on m records. However the efficiency of $\tilde{\theta}_2$ based on two records varies between 2/3 and 1. For m = 5,

$$\hat{\theta}_1 = 2r_1 - \hat{\theta}_2,$$

$$\hat{\theta}_2 = \dfrac{4}{3(3^4 - 1)}[3^4 r_5 - \dfrac{27}{2} r_4 - \dfrac{9}{2} r_3 - \dfrac{3}{2} r_2 - \dfrac{3}{2} r_1],$$

$$\tilde{\theta}_1 = 2 r_1 - \tilde{\theta}_2$$

and

$$\tilde{\theta}_2 = \dfrac{r_5 - \dfrac{r_1}{16}}{1 - \dfrac{1}{16}}$$

Table 1: Values of e_1 and e_2 (e_1 = .999 and e_2 = .868).

M	e_1	e_2
2	1.000	1.000
4	0.998	0.917
5	0.999	0.868
10	1.000	0.718
20	1.000	0.669
30	1.000	0.667

Remark 7.4.1: Though θ_2 can be accurately estimated based on two record values, the estimate for θ_1 based on two records is poor if m is large.

7.5. WEIBULL DISTRIBUTION

Let $\{X_n, n \geq 1\}$ be a sequence of i.i.d random variables from standard Weibull distribution with pdf

$$f(x) = x^{\gamma-1} e^{-x^\gamma/\gamma}, x > 0, \gamma > 0, \quad (7.5.1)$$

and cdf

$$F(x) = 1 - e^{-\frac{1}{\gamma}x^\gamma}, x > 0, \gamma > 0, \quad (7.5.2)$$

The pdf of the Weibull distribution as given by (7.5.1) becomes identical with the pdf of Raleigh distribution as given in (7.1.1) for $\gamma = 2$. The pdf of Weibull distribution for $\gamma = 1$ coincides with that of $E(0,1)$. Figure (7.3.1) gives the pdf of Weibull distribution for $\gamma = 1.5$.

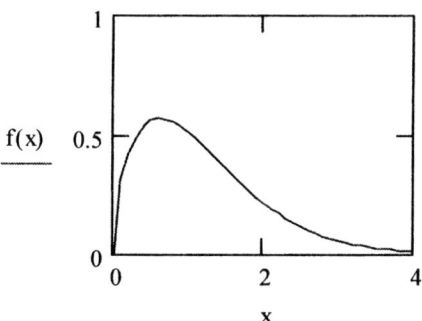

Figure 7.5.1 Pdf of X when $\gamma = 1.5$.

Theorem 7.5.1

Let $i = 1, 2, ..., m-1$, $\xi_i = \dfrac{X_{U(i)}}{X_{(i+1)}}$ then ξ_i, $i = 1, 2, ..., m-1$, are independent.

Proof:

The joint pdf of $X_{U(1)}, X_{U(2)}, ..., X_{U(m)}$ is

$$f(x_1, x_2, ..., x_m) = \gamma^m (x_1 x_2 .. x_m)^{\gamma-1} e^{-\frac{x_m^\gamma}{m}}, 0 < x_1 < x_2 < ... < x_m < \infty.$$

$\xi_o = X_{U(1)}$, and $\xi_i = \dfrac{X_{U(i)}}{X_{(i+1)}}$, $i = 2, ..., m-1$.

The Jacobian of the transformation

$$J = \left| \frac{\partial(X_{U(1)}, X_{U(2)}, ..., X_{U(m)})}{\partial(\xi_o, \xi_1, ..., \xi_{m-1})} \right| = \frac{\xi_o^{m-1}}{\xi_1^m \xi_2^{m-1} ... \xi_{m-1}^2}$$

We can write the pdf of ξ_i, $i = 0, 1, ..., m-1$, as

$$f(e_o, e_1, ..., e_{m-1}) = \frac{\gamma^m e_o^{m\gamma - 1}}{e_1^{(m-1)\gamma+1} e_2^{(m-2)\gamma+1} ...... e_{m-1}^{\gamma+1}} e^{-\frac{1}{\gamma}(\frac{e_o}{e_1 e_2 ... e_{m-1}})^{\gamma}}.$$

Now integrating the above expression with respect to e_0, we obtain the joint pdf of ξ_i, $i = 1, ..., m-1$, as

$$f(e_1, ..., e_{m-1}) = \Gamma(m) \gamma^{m-1} e_1^{\gamma-1} e_2^{2\gamma-1} ... e_{m-1}^{(m-1)\gamma-1}.$$

Thus ξ_i, $i = 1, 2, ..., m-1$ are independent and

$P(\xi_k \leq x) = x^{k\gamma}$, $1 \leq k \leq m$.

We have already seen similar results for ratios of the record values of the exponential distribution.

Theorem 7.5.2

Let $\mu_n = E(X_{U(n)})$, $V_{n,n} = Var(X_{U(n)})$ and $V_{m,n} = Cov(X_{U(m)} X_{U(n)})$, then

$$\mu_n = \gamma^{\frac{1}{\gamma}} \frac{\Gamma(n+\frac{1}{\gamma})}{\Gamma(n)}, \quad V_{n,n} = \gamma^{\frac{2}{\gamma}} \left\{ \frac{\Gamma(n+\frac{2}{\gamma})}{\Gamma(n)} - \left(\frac{\Gamma(n+\frac{1}{\gamma})}{\Gamma(n)} \right)^2 \right\}$$

and

$$V_{m,n} = \frac{\Gamma(m+\frac{1}{\gamma})}{\Gamma(m)} \cdot \gamma^{\frac{2}{\gamma}} \left\{ \frac{\Gamma(n+\frac{2}{\gamma})}{\Gamma(n+\frac{1}{\gamma})} - \frac{\Gamma(n+\frac{1}{\gamma})}{\Gamma(n)} \right\}, \text{ for } 1 \leq m < n.$$

Proof.

The pdf $f_n(x)$ of $X_{U(n)}$ can be written as

$$f_n(x) = \frac{1}{\Gamma(n)}\{\frac{x^{\gamma n-1}}{\gamma^{n-1}}\}e^{-x^\gamma/\gamma}, x>0, \gamma>0. \qquad (7.5.3)$$

$$E(X_{U(n)}) = \int_0^\infty \frac{1}{\Gamma(n)} \frac{x^{n\gamma}}{\gamma^{n-1}} e^{-(1/\gamma)x^\gamma} dx,$$

Substituting $t = \dfrac{x^\gamma}{\gamma}$, we obtain

$$E(X_{U(n)}) = \int_0^\infty \frac{\gamma^{1/\gamma}}{\Gamma(n)} e^{-t} (t)^{n+\frac{1}{\gamma}-1} dt$$

$$= \gamma^{\frac{1}{\gamma}} \frac{\Gamma(n+\frac{1}{\gamma})}{\Gamma(n)}$$

Similarly

$$E(X^2_{U(n)}) = \int_0^\infty \frac{1}{\Gamma(n)} \frac{x^{n\gamma+1}}{\gamma^{n-1}} e^{-(1/\gamma)x^\gamma} dx,$$

Substituting $t = \dfrac{x^\gamma}{\gamma}$, we get

$$E(X^2_{U(n)}) = \int_0^\infty \frac{\gamma^{2/\gamma}}{\Gamma(n)} e^{-t} (t)^{n+\frac{2}{\gamma}-1} dt$$

$$= \gamma^{2/\gamma} \frac{\Gamma(n+\frac{2}{\gamma})}{\Gamma(n)}$$

The joint pdf of $X_{U(m)}$ and $X_{U(n)}$ can be written as

$$f_{m,n}(x,y) = \frac{x^{\gamma-1}}{\Gamma(m)\Gamma(n-m)} (\frac{y^\gamma - x^\gamma}{\gamma})^{n-m-1} y^{\gamma-1} e^{-(1/\gamma)x^\gamma}$$

for $0<x<y<\infty$ and $m<n$,

$E(X_{U(m)} X_{U(n)})$
=
$$\int_0^\infty \int_0^y \frac{xy}{\Gamma(m)\Gamma(n-m)} \cdot \frac{x^{m\gamma-1}}{\gamma^{n-2}} [y^\gamma - x^\gamma]^{n-m-1} y^{\gamma-1} e^{-(1/\gamma)y^\gamma} dy\,dx$$

$$= \int_0^\infty \frac{y}{\Gamma(m)\Gamma(n-m)} \cdot \frac{I_y}{\gamma^{n-2}} y^{\gamma-1} e^{-(1/\gamma)y^\gamma} dy,$$

where

$$I_y = \int_0^y x^{m\gamma} (y^\gamma - x^\gamma)^{n-m-1} dx$$

$$= \int_0^1 \frac{y^{n\gamma-\gamma+1}}{\gamma} t^{m+\frac{1}{\gamma}-1} (1-t)^{n-m-1} dt$$

$$= \frac{y^{n\gamma-\gamma+1}}{\gamma} B(m+\frac{1}{\gamma}, n-m)$$

Thus

$E(X_{U(m)} X_{U(n)})$

$$= \int_0^\infty \frac{B(m+\frac{1}{\gamma},n-m)}{\Gamma(m)\Gamma(n-m)} \cdot \frac{y^{n\gamma+1}}{\gamma^{n-1}} e^{-(1/\gamma)y^\gamma} dy$$

$$= \frac{\Gamma(m+\frac{1}{\gamma})\Gamma(n+\frac{2}{\gamma})}{\Gamma(m)\Gamma(n-m)} \cdot \gamma^{2/\gamma}$$

$$\text{Var}(X_{U(n)}) = \gamma^{2/\gamma} \left\{ \frac{\Gamma(n+\frac{2}{\gamma})}{\Gamma(n)} - \left(\frac{\Gamma(n+\frac{1}{\gamma})}{\Gamma(n)}\right)^2 \right\}$$

and

$$\text{Cov}(X_{U(m)} X_{U(n)}) = \frac{\Gamma(m+\frac{1}{\gamma})}{\Gamma(m)} \cdot \gamma^{2/\gamma} \left\{ \frac{\Gamma(n+\frac{2}{\gamma})}{\Gamma(n+\frac{1}{\gamma})} - \frac{\Gamma(n+\frac{1}{\gamma})}{\Gamma(n)} \right\}, \quad 1 \le m \le n.$$

Suppose the first m records are from a two parameter (assuming the shape parameter γ as known) Weibull distribution with the pdf

Some Selected Distributions

$$f(x,\mu,\sigma) = \frac{(x-\mu)^{\gamma-1}}{\sigma^{\gamma}} e^{-\frac{(x-\mu)^{\gamma}}{\gamma \sigma^{\gamma}}}, \quad \mu < x < \infty, \sigma > 0$$

We will consider the estimation of μ and σ based on the observed record values.

(a) Minimum Variance Linear Unbiased Estimators of μ and σ.

Theorem 7.5.2

The minimum variance linear unbiased estimators $\hat{\mu}$ and $\hat{\sigma}$ of μ and σ based on the observed record values $r_1, r_2, \ldots, r_m$ are

$$\hat{\mu} = \sum_{i=1}^{m} c_i r_1, \text{ and } \hat{\sigma} = \sum_{i=1}^{m} d_i r_i ,$$

where

$$c_1 = \frac{\alpha_m b_m (\gamma+1) \gamma^{2/\gamma}}{D} \frac{1}{\Gamma(1+\frac{1}{\gamma})}, \quad c_i = \frac{\alpha_m b_m}{D} \gamma^{-2/\gamma}(\gamma-!) \frac{\Gamma(i)}{\Gamma(i+\frac{2}{\gamma})}, i=2,3,\ldots,m-1,$$

$$c_m = 1 - \frac{\alpha_m b_m}{D} \gamma^{-\frac{2}{\gamma}} \left[\frac{\gamma+1}{\Gamma(1+\frac{2}{\gamma})} + (\gamma-1)\sum_{i=2}^{m-1} \frac{\Gamma(i)}{\Gamma(i+\frac{2}{\gamma})} \right],$$

$$d_1 = -\frac{b_m (\gamma+1) \gamma^{-2/\gamma}}{D},$$

$$d_i = -\frac{b_m}{D}(\gamma-1)\gamma^{-2/\gamma} \frac{\Gamma(i)}{\Gamma(i+\frac{2}{\gamma})}, i=2,3,\ldots,m-1,$$

$$d_m = \frac{b_m}{D} \gamma^{-\frac{2}{\gamma}} \left[\frac{\gamma+1}{\Gamma(1+\frac{2}{\gamma})} + (\gamma-1)\sum_{i=2}^{m-1} \frac{\Gamma(i)}{\Gamma(i+\frac{2}{\gamma})} \right],$$

where

$D = \alpha_m b_m T - 1$,

$$T = \gamma^{-2/\gamma} \left[\frac{\gamma+1}{\Gamma(1+\frac{2}{\gamma})} + (\gamma-1) \sum_{i=2}^{m-1} \frac{\Gamma(i)}{\Gamma(i+\frac{2}{\gamma})} + \frac{\Gamma(m)}{\Gamma(m+\frac{2}{\gamma})} (m\gamma-\gamma+1)(m\gamma-\gamma+2)(\frac{b_{m-1}}{b_m} - 1) \right]$$

$$\alpha_m = \gamma^{1/\gamma} \frac{\Gamma(m+\frac{1}{\gamma})}{\Gamma(m)}, \text{ and } b_m = \gamma^{1/\gamma} \left\{ \frac{\Gamma(n+\frac{2}{\gamma})}{\Gamma(n+\frac{1}{\gamma})} \frac{\Gamma(n+\frac{1}{\gamma})}{\Gamma(n)} \right\}.$$

We can write
$V(R) = \sigma^2 V$, $V = (V_{i,j})$, $V_{i,j} = a_i b_j$, $1 \leq i \leq j \leq m$ and $V_{i,j} = V_{j,i}$.

The inverse V^{-1} ($= V^{i,j}$) can be expressed as

$$V^{i+1,i} = V^{i,i+1} = -\frac{1}{a_{i+1}b_i - a_i b_{i+1}}$$

$$= -\gamma^{-2/\gamma} i\gamma(i\gamma+1) \frac{\Gamma(i)}{\Gamma(i+\frac{2}{\gamma})}, i = 1, 2, ..., m-1,$$

$$V^{i,i} = \frac{a_{i+1}b_{i-1} - a_{i-1}b_{i+1}}{(a_i b_{i-1} - a_{i-1}b_i)(a_{i+1}b_i - a_i b_{i+1})}, i = 1, 2, ..., n, V^{i,j} = 0, \text{ for } |i-j| > 1,$$

where $a_o = 0 = b_{n+1}$ and $b_o = 1 = a_{n+1}$.

On simplification, we obtain

$$V^{i,i} = \gamma^{-2/\gamma} \frac{\Gamma(i)}{\Gamma(i+\frac{2}{\gamma})} [\gamma^2(2i^2 - 2i+1) + \gamma(4i-2)+1], i = 1, 2, ..., m-1$$

$$V^{m,m} = \gamma^{-2/\gamma} \frac{\Gamma(n)}{\Gamma(n+\frac{2}{\gamma})} \frac{b_{n-1}}{b_n} [(n\gamma-\gamma+1)(n\gamma-\gamma+2).$$

The minimum variance linear unbiased estimates (MVLUE) $\hat{\mu}, \hat{\sigma}$ of μ and σ respectively are

$$\hat{\mu} = -\delta' V^{-1} (L\delta' - \delta L') V^{-1} X / \Delta$$

$$\hat{\sigma} = L' V^{-1} (L\delta' - \delta L') V^{-1} X / \Delta,$$

where

$$\Delta = (L'V^{-1}L)(\delta'V^{-1}\delta) - (L'V^{-1}\delta)^2$$

and

$$Var(\hat{\mu}) = \sigma^2 L'V^{-1}\delta / \Delta$$
$$Var(\hat{\sigma}) = \sigma^2 L'V^{-1}L / \Delta$$
$$Cov(\hat{\mu}, \hat{\sigma}) = -\sigma^2 L'V^{-1}\delta / \Delta.$$

On simplification, we obtain the MVLUEs $\hat{\mu}, \hat{\sigma}$ of μ and σ. The corresponding variances and the covariances of the estimates are

$$Var(\hat{\mu}) = \sigma^2 \frac{a_n b_n}{D}$$

$$Var(\hat{\sigma}) = \sigma^2 \frac{b_n^2 T}{D} \quad (7.5.4)$$

$$Cov(\hat{\mu}, \hat{\sigma}) = -\sigma^2 \frac{b_n}{D}$$

Best Linear Invariant Estimators (BLIEs) of μ and σ.

Theorem 7.5.2

The best linear invariant (in the sense of minimum mean squared error and invariance with respect to the location parameter μ) estimators (BLIEs) $\tilde{\mu}$ $\tilde{\sigma}$ of μ and σ are

$$\tilde{\mu} = \hat{\mu} - \hat{\sigma}\left(\frac{E_{12}}{1+E_{22}}\right)$$

and

$$\tilde{\sigma} = \hat{\sigma}/(1+E_{22}),$$

where $\hat{\mu}$ and $\hat{\sigma}$ are MVLUEs of μ and σ and

$$\begin{pmatrix} Var(\hat{\mu}) & Cov(\hat{\mu}, \hat{\sigma}) \\ Cov(\hat{\mu}, \hat{\sigma}) & Var(\hat{\sigma}) \end{pmatrix} = \sigma^2 \begin{pmatrix} E_{11} & E_{12} \\ E_{12} & E_{22} \end{pmatrix}$$

The mean squared errors of these estimators are

$$MSE(\tilde{\mu}) = \sigma^2 \left(E_{11} - E_{12}^2 (1+E_{22})^{-1}\right)$$

and

$$MSE(\tilde{\sigma}) = \sigma^2 E_{22} (1+E_{22})^{-1} .$$

Using the values of E_{11}, E_{12} and E_{22} from (7.5.4), we obtain

$$\tilde{\mu} = \hat{\mu} + \hat{\sigma}\left(\frac{b_m}{D + b_m^2 T}\right)$$

and

$$\tilde{\sigma} = \hat{\sigma} \frac{D}{D + b_m^2 T} .$$

Remark 7.5.1. If $\mu = 0$, then $X_{U(m)}$ is a sufficient statistic for σ, thus MVLUE estimator of σ based on the observed record values $r_1, r_2, \cdots, r_m$ is
$$\hat{\sigma}_* = c_0\, r_n,$$
where
$$c_0 = \frac{1}{E(X_{U(m)})} = \gamma^{-1/\gamma}\,\frac{\Gamma(n)}{\Gamma(n+\frac{1}{\gamma})}.$$

$$\text{Var}(\hat{\sigma}_*) = \sigma^2 \left[\frac{\Gamma(n)\Gamma(n+\frac{2}{\gamma})}{\{\Gamma(n+\frac{1}{\gamma})\}^2} - 1\right].$$

7.6. DISTRIBUTIONS WHERE CONSECUTIVE RECORD VALUES HAVE LINEAR REGRESSION

The conditional p.d.f. f_{1c} of $Z_{U(n)}$ given $Z_{U(n-1)} = y$ can be written as $f_{1c}(z) = z\, f(z) / (1 - F(y))$.
For many distributions including exponential, Pareto and power function

$$E(X_{U(n)} \mid X_{U(n-1)} = y) = a + b\,y \qquad (7.6.1)$$

for some constants a and b . We will say a rv X with distribution function F belongs to the class C if its n th record value satisfy the condition (7.6.1).. In this paper, we will consider the record values of random variables belonging to class C.

Theorem 7.6.1
If the sequence of rvs $X_1, X_2, \ldots$, belong to class C with finite variance, then $\text{cov}(X_{U(n)}, X_{U(m)}) = b^{n-m}\,\text{var}(X_{U(m)})$, $n > m$.

Proof:
$$E(X_{U(m+2)}) = EE(X_{U(m+2)} \mid X_{U(m+1)} = t)$$
$$= EE(a + b\,t \mid X_{U(m)} = y)$$
$$= E(a + b(a + b\,y))$$
$$= a + a\,b + b^2\, E(X_{U(m)}).$$

Some Selected Distributions

In general

$$E(X_{U(n)}) = a + ab + ab^2 + ab^3 + \ldots + ab^{n-m-1} + b^{n-m} E(X_{U(m)}).$$
$$= a \frac{b^{n-m}-1}{b-1} + b^{n-m} E(X_{U(m)}), \text{ if } b \neq 1,$$
$$= (n-m) a + E(X_{U(m)}), \text{ if } b = 1.$$

Thus
$$\text{Cov}(X_{U(m)}, X_{U(n)}) = b^{n-m} \text{Var}(X_{U(m)}), \text{ if } b \neq 1$$
$$\text{For } m<n, = \text{Var}(X_{U(m)}), \text{ if } b = 1.$$

Theorem 7.6.2

If the sequence of i.i.d. rvs $X_1, X_2, \ldots$ has finite expectation with an absolutely continuous distribution function F with support on [c, d), where c is finite and d may be infinite. Further we assume that $d < \infty$ if $b \geq 1$ and $d = \frac{a}{b-1}$ for $b < 1$. Then

$$1 - F(x) = \left(\frac{a+(b-1)c}{a+(b-1)x} \right)^{\frac{b}{b-1}} \text{ for } b \neq 1$$

and

$$1 - F(x) = e^{-x/a} \text{ for } b = 1,$$

if and only if $E(X_{U(n)} | X_{U(n-1)} = y) = a + by$.

Proof:

Writing the conditional expectation of $X_{U(n+1)} | X_{U(n)} = y$ and simplifying we get

$$a + by = y + \int_y^d \frac{1-F(x)}{1-F(y)} dx$$

Differentiating both sides of the above equation with respect to y, we obtain
$$b = (a + (b-1)y)(f(y)/(1-F(y))) \qquad (7.6.3)$$

Now integrating with respect to y from c to x, we get

$$1-F(x) = \left(\frac{a+(b-1)c}{a+(b-1)x}\right)^{\frac{b}{b-1}} \text{ for } b \neq 1 \tag{7.6.4}$$

and

$$1 - F(x) = e^{-x/a} \text{ for } b = 1,$$

It can be shown that
$E(X) = a + bc$ and $Var(X) = (b(a+(b-1)c)^2)/(2-b)$

For various results of the rv X based record values for the case b=1, see Ahsanullah ((1988),(1980)). Let f_n be the probability density function of the n th record value, $X_{U(n)}$, then

for $b \neq 1$,
$$f_n(x) = \frac{\left(\frac{b}{b-1} \ln \frac{a+(b-1)c}{a+(b-1)x}\right)^n}{n!} \cdot \frac{b(a+(b-1)c)^{\frac{b}{b-1}}}{(a+(b-1)x)^{\frac{2b-1}{b-1}}} \tag{7.6.5}$$

It can be shown from (7.6.5) that
$$E(X_{U(n)}) = (1/(b-1))(b^n(a+(b-1)c) - a)$$

$$Var(X_{U(n)}) = (b-1)^{-2}(a+(b-1)c)^2 b^n ((2-b)^{-n} - b^n).$$

and
$$Cov(X_{U(m)}, X_{U(n)}) = b^{n-m} Var(X_{U(m)}).$$

We will assume without the loss generality the lower bound, c of the rv X as zero and $(Y - \mu)/\sigma = X$, then
$E(Y) = \mu + a\sigma$, $\alpha = E(X)$ and $var(Y) = a^2 b(2-b)^{-1} \sigma^2$.
For the finite variance, b must be less than 2.
Let $T_1, T_2, ..., T_n$ be the record values of Y corresponding to $X_{U(1)}, X_{U(2)}, ..., X_{U(n)}$. It can be shown that

$$T_n = \mu - \frac{a\sigma}{b-1} + \frac{a\sigma}{b-1} \prod_{i=1}^{n} U_i$$

where $U_1, U_2, ..., U_n$ are independent and identically distributed with $P(U_i \leq x) = 1 - x^{-b/(b-1)}$
Thus
$$E(T_n) = \mu + a \frac{b^n - 1}{b-1} \sigma$$

and
$$Var(T_n) = a^2(b-1)^{-2} b^n \{(2-b)^{-n} - b^n\} \sigma^2.$$

$$\text{Cov}(T_m, T_n) = b^{n-m} \text{Var}(T_m), m < n.$$

We can write the variances and covarinces of T's as
$$\text{Var}(T_r) = a_r b_r \sigma_1^2$$
and
$$\text{Cov}(T_r, T_s) = a_r b_s \sigma_1^2, r \le s$$
where
$$a_r = [(2-b)^{-r} - b^r], b_r = b^r, r = 1, 2, \ldots, \text{ and } \sigma_1^2 = a^2(b-1)^{-2}\sigma^2.$$

Estimators of μ and σ.

Theorem 7.6.3

The minimum variance linear unbiased estimators (MVLUEs) of $\hat{\mu}, \hat{\sigma}$ of μ and σ are
$$\hat{\mu} = T_1 - a\hat{\sigma}$$
and
$$\hat{\sigma} = a^{-1}[(\frac{b-1}{b} - D^{-1}(\frac{2-b}{b})T_1 -$$
$$- D^{-1}\frac{b-1}{b}\sum_{i=2}^{n-1}(\frac{2-b}{b})^{i+1}T_i + D^{-1}(\frac{2-b}{b})^{n+1}T_n$$

where
$$D = \sum_{i=2}^{n}(\frac{2-b}{b})^{i+1}.$$

Proof.

Let $T' = (T_1, T_2, \ldots, T_n)$, then we can write
$E(T) = \mu L + d \sigma_1$
$L' = (1, 1, \ldots, 1), d' = (d_1, d_2, \ldots, d_n)$
and
$d_i = b^n - 1, i = 1, 2, \ldots, n.$
Let $\text{Var}(T) = \sigma_1^2 \Sigma, \Sigma^{-1} = (V^{i,j})$
It can be shown that

$$V^{i+1,i} = V^{i,i+1} = -\frac{b}{(1-b)^2}(\frac{2-b}{b})^{i+1}$$

$$V^{ii} = \frac{1+2b-b^2}{(1-b)^2}(\frac{2-b}{b})^i, \ 1 \leq i \leq n$$

$$V^{nn} = \frac{1}{(1-b)^2}(\frac{2-b}{b})^n$$

$V^{i,j} = 0$, if $|i-j| > 1$

Let

$W_i = a^{-1}((2-b)/b)^{i/2}(T_i - b\,T_{i-1})$, $i = 1, 2, \ldots, n$ and $T_0 = 0$.

Then $\text{Var}(W_i) = \sigma^2$ and $\text{Cov}(W_i, W_k) = 0$, $i \neq k$, $1 \leq i, k \leq n$.
Suppose $W' = (W_1, W_2, \ldots, W_n)$ and $E(W) = Aq$, where $q' = (\mu, \sigma)$
$A' = [A_1\ A_2]$, $A_1' = (d_1, d_2, \ldots, d_n)$, $A_2' = (e_1, e_2, \ldots, e_n)$,
$d_i = ((2-b)/b)^i (1-b)$, $e_i = d_i/(1-b)$, $i = 2, 3, \ldots, n$, $d_1 = (1/a)((2-b)/b)^{1/2}$
and $e_1 = a\,d_1$.

Using least squares estimation method, we get on simplification
$\hat{\mu} = T_1 - a\hat{\sigma}$
and

$$\hat{\sigma} = a^{-1}[(\frac{b-1}{b})D^{-1}(\frac{2-b}{b})T_1 - D^{-1}\frac{b-1}{b}\sum_{i=2}^{n-1}(\frac{2-b}{b})^{i+1}T_i + D^{-1}(\frac{2-b}{b})^{n+1}T_n]$$

where

$$D = \sum_{i=2}^{n}(\frac{2-b}{b})^{i+1}.$$

$$\text{Var}(\hat{\mu}) = (\frac{a^2 T}{b^2 D})\sigma^2,$$

$$\text{Var}(\hat{\sigma}) = \{(\frac{2-b}{b})^2 + (\frac{b-1}{b})^2 T\}D^{-1}\sigma^2$$

and

$$\text{Cov}(\hat{\mu}, \hat{\sigma}) = \{(\frac{b-1}{b})T - (\frac{2-b}{b})\}b^{-1}D^{-1}a\sigma^2$$

where

$$T=\sum_{i=1}^{n} (\frac{2-b}{b})^i \text{ and } D= \sum_{i=1}^{n} (\frac{2-b}{b})^{i+1}.$$

Let $a = 2$ and $b = 1.5$, then
$$\hat{\mu} = (17/12) T_1 - (1/4) T_2 - (1/12) T_3 - (1/12) T_4$$
and
$$\hat{\sigma} = -(5/8) T_1 + (1/8)T_2 + (1/24)T_3 + (1/24)T_4.$$
The corresponding variance and covariances are
$$\text{Var}(\hat{\mu}) = \frac{160}{9}\sigma^2,$$
$$\text{Var}(\hat{\sigma}) = \frac{40}{81}\sigma^2 \text{ and } \text{Cov}(\hat{\mu},\hat{\sigma}) = \frac{41}{9}\sigma^2.$$

Theorem 7.6.4

The best linear invariant (in the sense of minimum mean squared error and invariance with respect to the location parameter) estimators are
$$\tilde{\mu} = \hat{\mu} \frac{b\{(b-1)t - 2+b)\}}{T}\hat{\sigma}$$
and
$$\tilde{\sigma} = \hat{\sigma}\frac{Db^2}{T}, \text{ where}$$
$$\hat{\sigma} = a^{-1}[(\frac{b-1}{b} - D^{-1}(\frac{2-b}{b})T_1 -$$
$$D^{-1}\frac{b-1}{b}\sum_{i=2}^{n-1}(\frac{2-b}{b})^{i+1}T_i + D^{-1}(\frac{2-b}{b})^{n+1}T_n$$

where
$$D = \sum_{i=2}^{n} (\frac{2-b}{b})^{i+1}.$$

MSE($\tilde{\mu}$)

$$= \frac{\sigma^2 a^2}{Db^2}[T - \frac{\{(b-1)T-(2-b)\}^2}{T}] \text{ and MSE}(\tilde{\sigma})$$

$$= \frac{\sigma^2 a}{T}[(b-1)T-(2-b)].$$

$$\text{Var}(\hat{\mu}) = (\frac{a^2 T}{b^2 D})\sigma^2,$$

and

$$\text{Var}(\hat{\sigma}) = \{(\frac{2-b}{b})^2 + (\frac{b-1}{b})^2 T\} D^{-1} \sigma^2$$

$$\text{Cov}(\hat{\mu}, \hat{\sigma}) = \{(\frac{b-1}{b})T - (\frac{2-b}{b})\} b^{-1} D^{-1} a \sigma^2$$

where

$$T = \sum_{i=1}^{n} (\frac{2-b}{b})^i \text{ and } D = \sum_{i=1}^{n} (\frac{2-b}{b})^{i+1}.$$

Example 7.6.1

With $n = 4$ and $b = 1.5$, we have

$$\tilde{\mu} = \frac{2105}{1920}T_1 - \frac{37}{640}T_2 - \frac{37}{1920}T_3 - \frac{37}{1920}T_4$$

$$\tilde{\sigma} = -\frac{1125}{1200}T_1 + \frac{9}{160}T_2 + \frac{3}{160}T_3 + \frac{3}{160}T_4$$

$$\text{MSE}(\tilde{\mu}) = \frac{127413}{10800}\sigma^2$$

$$\text{MSE}(\tilde{\sigma}) = \frac{121}{160}\sigma^2$$

Predictors of T_S

We shall consider the prediction of T_S based on n observed record values for s > n. Let $H' = (h_1, h_2,...., h_n)$, where $\sigma^2 h_i = \text{cov}(T_i, T_S)$, i = 1,2,...,n. It follows from the results of Goldberger(1962) that the best linear unbiased predictor (BLUP) of T_S is $\hat{T}_s$, where

$$\hat{T}_s = \hat{\mu} + \hat{\sigma}\gamma_s + H'V^{-1}(T - \hat{\mu}L - \hat{\sigma}\gamma)$$

and
$$H'V^{-1} = (0, 0, ..., b^{s-n})$$

$$\hat{T}_s = \hat{\mu} + \hat{\sigma}\gamma_s + b^{s-m}(T_m - \hat{\mu} - \hat{\sigma}\gamma_s)$$
$$= b^{s-m} T_n + (1 - b^{s-m})(\hat{\mu} - \hat{\sigma}\gamma_s)$$

The best (unrestricted) least squares predictor of T_S is $T_S^* = E(T_S | T_1, T_2, ..., T_n)$.
Thus

$$T_s^* = \mu + a \frac{b^{s-n} - 1}{b - 1} \sigma + ab^{s-n}(T_n - \mu)$$

If we substitute the MVLUE of μ and σ, then T_S^* becomes $\hat{T}_s$.

Let $\tilde{T}_s$ be the best linear invariant predictor of T_S. From the results of Mann (1969) it follows that

$$\tilde{T}_s = \hat{T}_s - \frac{c^*_{12}}{1 + E_{22}} \hat{\sigma}$$

where
$$c^*_{12} = \text{cov}(\hat{\sigma}, (1 - H'V^{-1}L)\hat{\mu} + (\gamma_s - H'V^{-1}\delta)a\hat{\sigma})$$

and
$$1 - H'V^{-1}L = 1 - b^{s-n} \text{ and } \gamma_s - H'V^{-1}\delta = \gamma_{s-n}$$

Thus
$$\tilde{T}_s = \hat{T}_s - \gamma_{s-n} \frac{2 - b}{b^2}$$

Considering the MSE of the predictor, it can be shown that
$$MSE(T_s^*) \le MSE(\tilde{T}_s) \le MSE(\hat{T}_s).$$

CHAPTER 8

ADDITIONAL TOPICS

8.0. INTRODUCTION

In this chapter, we will consider the limiting distributions and some other results of record values, record times and inter record times. Unless stated otherwise, we will restrict ourselves to the case when the distribution function F is continuous and has probability density function.

8.1. LIMITING DISTRIBUTION OF INTER-RECORD TIMES

We will discuss here the inter-record times corresponding to the upper record values. The corresponding results related to inter-record values of the lower records are similar.

We know (see Theorem 1.4.4) that

$$P(\Delta_n \geq s) = \frac{1}{s}\sum_{j=1}^{s} P(\Delta_{n-1} \geq j) \qquad (8.1.1)$$

Let $G_n(s) = P(\Delta_n \geq s)$, then
$P(\Delta_n = s) = G_n(s) - G_n(s+1)$ and
$$G_n(s) = \frac{1}{s}\sum_{j=1}^{s} G_{n-1}(j).$$

Now

$$P(\Delta_n = s) = \frac{1}{s}\sum_{j=1}^{s} G_{n-1}(j) - \frac{1}{s+1}\sum_{j=1}^{s+1} G_{n-1}(j)$$

$$= \frac{1}{s(s+1)}\sum_{j=1}^{s} G_{n-1}(j) - \frac{G_{n-1}(s+1)}{s+1}$$

$$= \frac{1}{s+1}\left[\sum_{j=1}^{s-1} G_{n-1}(j) + \frac{1}{s}\sum_{j=1}^{s} G_{n-1}(j) - \sum_{j=1}^{s} G_{n-1}(j) + G_{n-1}(s) - G_{n-1}(s+1)\right]$$

$$= \frac{1}{s+1}\left[(s-1)P(\Delta_n = s-1) + P(\Delta_{n-1} = s)\right] \quad (8.1.2)$$

The relation (8.1.2) can be used to calculate $P(\Delta_n = s)$ by the method of iteration.

Example 8.1.1.
Using Theorem 1.4.1, we have

$$P(\Delta_2 = 5) = \sum_{i=0}^{4} \binom{4}{i}(-1)^i \frac{1}{(2+i)^2} = 0.0484$$

$$P(\Delta_3 = 4) = \sum_{i=0}^{3} \binom{3}{i}(-1)^i \frac{1}{(2+i)^3} = 0.0528$$

Using the formula (8.1.2), we get

$$P(\Delta_3 = 5) = \frac{1}{6}[4P(\Delta_3 = 4) + P(\Delta_2 = 5)] = \frac{4(0.0528) + 0.0484}{6} = 0.0433$$

Using the Theorem 1.4.1, we get

$$P(\Delta_3 = 5) = \sum_{i=0}^{4} \binom{4}{i}(-1)^i \frac{1}{(2+i)^3} = 0.0433.$$

From Theorem 1.4.4, we have

$$P(\Delta_1 \geq n) = \frac{1}{n} \text{ and } P(\Delta_2 \geq n) = \frac{1}{n}\sum_{i=1}^{n} P(\Delta_1 \geq i) = \frac{1}{n}\sum_{i=1}^{n} \frac{1}{i}.$$

Since for large n,

$$\sum_{j=1}^{n} \frac{1}{j} \cong \upsilon + \ln n,$$ where υ is the Euler's constant, we can write

Additional Topics

$$P(\Delta_2 \geq n) = \frac{1}{n}(\ln n). \tag{8.1.3}$$

Using (8.1.3), Theorem 1.4.2 and approximation for large n, we obtain

$$P(\Delta_3 \geq n) = \frac{1}{n} \cdot \frac{1}{2!}(\ln n)^2$$

and

$$P(\Delta_m \geq n) = \frac{1}{n} \cdot \frac{1}{(m-1)!}(\ln n)^{m-1}, \quad m > 1. \tag{8.1.4}$$

$$= \frac{|s(m-1,n)|}{n!},$$

where $|s(m,n)|$ is the absolute value of s(m,n) and s(m,n) is the Stirling's number of the first kind (see Appendix A).

Example 8.1.2.

For m = 4, $P(\Delta_4 \geq 5000) = \frac{1}{5000} \frac{(\ln 5000)^3}{3!} = .0206$.

Using Table 1.4.2, we get $P(\Delta_4 \geq 5000) = 1 - .9734 = .0266$.
The following Theorem is due to Tata (1969).

Theorem 8.1.1.

$$\lim_{n \to \infty} \frac{\ln \Delta_n - n}{\sqrt{n}} \underset{=}{d} N(0,1),$$

where $N(0,1)$ is the standard normal distribution.

Proof.

$$P[\frac{\ln \Delta_n - n}{\sqrt{n}} \geq k] = P[\Delta_n \geq e^{n+k\sqrt{n}}]$$

$$= \int_0^\infty \frac{y^{n-1} e^{-y}}{\Gamma(n)}(1-e^{-y})^{e^{n+k\sqrt{n}}} dy, \quad \text{by (1.4.8)}$$

$$= \int_n^\infty \frac{(n+\sqrt{n})^{n-1}}{\Gamma(n)} e^{-(n+x\sqrt{n})}(1-e^{-(n+x\sqrt{n})})^{e^{n+k\sqrt{n}}} \sqrt{n}\, dx.$$

Now

$$\lim_{n\to\infty} (1-e^{-(n+x\sqrt{n})})^{e^{n+k\sqrt{n}}} = 0, \text{ if } x < k$$
$$= 1, \text{ if } x > k$$
$$= e^{-1} \text{ if } x = k$$

and

$$\lim_{n\to\infty} \frac{(N+\sqrt{n})^{n-1}}{\Gamma(n)} e^{-(n+x\sqrt{n})} \cdot n = \frac{1}{\sqrt{2\pi}} e^{-\frac{1}{2}x^2}$$

Hence

$$\lim_{n\to\infty} P[\frac{\ln \Delta_n - n}{\sqrt{n}} \geq k] = \int_k^\infty \frac{1}{\sqrt{2\pi}} e^{-\frac{1}{2}x^2} dx.$$

Thus

$$E(\ln \Delta_n) \cong n \text{ and } Var(\ln \Delta_n) \cong n.$$

8.2. LIMITING DISTRIBUTION OF RECORD VALUES

We will discuss here the limiting distribution of the upper record values. The distribution of $R(X_n)$ is exponential, $E(0,1)$. It follows from (2.1.1) that

$$R(X_{U(n)}) \stackrel{d}{=} W_1 + W_2 + \cdots + W_n \qquad (8.2.1)$$

where $W_1, W_2, \ldots, W_n$ are i.i.d. $E(0,1)$.

Hence

$$P[\frac{R(X_{U(n)}) - n}{\sqrt{n}} \leq x] = \int_{-\infty}^x \frac{1}{\sqrt{2\pi}} e^{-\frac{1}{2}u^2} du. \qquad (8.2.2)$$

From (8.2.1), it follows that

$$\frac{R(X_{U(n)})}{n} \to 1 \text{ with probability one.} \qquad (8.2.3)$$

From the relation (8.2.1), we have the following result of the law of iterated logarithm for $R(X_{U(n)})$.

Result 8.2.1. With probability one

$$\limsup_{n\to\infty} \frac{R(X_{U(n)}) - n}{(2n \ln \ln n)^{1/2}} = 1$$

$$\liminf_{n\to\infty} \frac{R(X_{U(n)})-n}{(2n\ln\ln n)^{1/2}} = -1. \qquad (8.2.4)$$

Tata (1969) proved the following theorem.

Theorem 8.2.1.

Let R(x) be is convex and twice differentiable with

$$\lim_{x\to\infty} \frac{R(x)}{x} = \infty$$

$$\lim_{x\to\infty} \frac{R(x)}{x^2} = 0.$$

Then there exists constants $a_n > 0$ and b_n such that

$$\lim_{n\to\infty} P\left[\frac{X_{U(n)} - b_n}{a_n} \le x\right] = \int_{-\infty}^{x} \frac{1}{\sqrt{2\pi}} e^{-\frac{1}{2}t^2} dt.$$

Proof:
We will give here the original proof of Tata (1969).
Let $R(b_n) = n$ and $R(b_n + a_n) = n + \sqrt{n}$.
Therefore, we get

$$n + \sqrt{n} = R(b_n + a_n) = R(b_n) + a_n r(b_n + \theta a_n), \quad 0 < \theta < 1,$$
$$= n + a_n r(b_n + \theta a_n).$$

$$P\left[\frac{X_{U(n)} - b_n}{a_n} \le x\right] = P\left[\frac{R(X_{U(n)}) - n}{\sqrt{n}} \le \frac{R(b_n + xa_n) - n}{\sqrt{n}}\right]. \qquad (8.2.5)$$

Now

$$\lim_{n\to\infty} \frac{a_n}{b_n} = 0,$$

$$\lim_{n\to\infty} \frac{r(b_n + \eta a_n x)}{r(b_n + \theta a_n)} = 0$$

and

$$\lim_{n\to\infty} \frac{R(b_n + xa_n) - n}{\sqrt{n}} = x.$$

Taking limit of (8.2.5) as $n \to \infty$ and using (8.2.2), we obtain

$$\lim_{n\to\infty} P\left[\frac{X_{U(n)} - b_n}{a_n} \leq x\right] = \int_{-\infty}^{x} \frac{1}{\sqrt{2\pi}} e^{-\frac{1}{2}t^2} dt.$$

The conditions given in Theorem 8.2.1 is sufficient condition.

Example 8.2.1.
Suppose that { X_i, i=1,2,... } is a sequence of i.i.d. random variable with cdf F(x) = . Here R(x) = x^α, $1 < \alpha < 2$ Thus R(x) satisfies the conditions of the Theorem 8.2.1 and for some suitable a_n and b_n, we have

$$\lim_{n\to\infty} P\left[\frac{X_{U(n)} - b_n}{a_n} \leq x\right] = \int_{-\infty}^{x} \frac{1}{\sqrt{2\pi}} e^{-\frac{1}{2}t^2} dt$$

Suppose $\alpha = 1$, then R(x) = x and R9x) does not satisfy the conditions of Theorem 8.2.1.. However we have seen that in this case

$$P \lim_{n\to\infty} P\left[\frac{X_{U(n)} - n}{\sqrt{n}} \leq x\right] = \int_{-\infty}^{x} \frac{1}{\sqrt{2\pi}} e^{-\frac{1}{2}t^2} dt$$

8.3. LIMITING DISTRIBUTION OF RECORD TIMES

We will consider here the limiting distribution of U(n). The corresponding results for L(n) are similar.
We have seen in section 1.4 that {U(n), n ≥ 1} forms a Markov chain with the probabilities

$$P(U(2)=k) = \frac{1}{k(k-1)}, \quad k > 1.$$

$$P(U(n+1) = k | U(n) = j) = \frac{j}{k(k-1)}, \quad k > j \geq 1, n > 1$$

and

$$P(U(n+1) > k | U(n) = j) = \min\left(\frac{j}{k}, 1\right), \quad k > j \geq 1, n > 1.$$

$$P\left(\frac{U(n)}{U(n+1)} < \frac{x}{y} \mid U(n)=x\right) = P(U(n+1) > \frac{y}{x} \mid U(n)=x)$$

$$= \frac{x}{y}.$$

Since any real x in the interval can be approximated by the rational m/n, we have the following Theorem. The Theorem was originally proved by Tata (1969).

Theorem 8.3.1.

The distribution of $\frac{U(n)}{U(n+1)}$ is asymptotically uniform over the unit interval, i.e. $\lim_{n\to\infty} P\left(\frac{U(n)}{U(n+1)} < x\right) = x, 0 < x < 1$.

Proof:

$$P\left(\frac{U(n)}{U(n+1)} < x \mid U(n)=y\right) = P\left(U(n+1) > \frac{y}{x} \mid U(n)=y\right)$$

$$= \frac{y}{\|\frac{y}{x}\|} \to x$$

as n → ∞, independent of U(n). Here ||t|| denotes the largest integer ≤ t. Thus as n → ∞, the sequence { $\frac{U(n)}{U(n+1)}$ } is independently and identically distributed as U(0,1).

Since $\frac{U(n)}{U(n+k)} = \frac{U(n)}{U(n+1)} \cdot \frac{U(n+1)}{U(n+2)} \cdots \frac{U(n+k-1)}{U(n+k)}$, we can consider $\frac{U(n)}{U(n+k)}$ as n→ ∞ as the product of k independent U(0,1) random variables. Hence we have the following Theorem.

Theorem 8.3.2.

As $n \to \infty$, $P\left[\dfrac{U(n)}{U(n+k)} \leq x\right] = \int_0^x \dfrac{(-\ln w)^{k-1}}{\Gamma(k)} dw = x \sum_{j=0}^{k-1} \dfrac{(-\ln x)^j}{\Gamma(j+1)}$.

8.4. REPRESENTATION OF RECORDS

Let $Y_1, Y_2,\ldots, Y_n,\ldots$ be a sequence of independent and identically distributed random variable with the cdf as $F_0(x) = 1-\exp(-x)$, $x>0$. Further suppose that $X_1, X_2,\ldots$ be a sequence i.i.d. r.v.'s with continuous cdf F. Then one has

$$= lm(1 - F(x)) \stackrel{d}{=} Y_1.$$

The following theorem (Bairamov and Ahsanullah (2000)) gives the representation of the nth record as sum on n independent random variables.

Theorem 8.4.1.

$X_{U(n)} \stackrel{d}{=} g_F^{-1}(g_F(X_1) + g_F(X_2) + \ldots + g_F(X_n))$, where $g_F(x) = -\ln(1-F(x))$ and $g_F^{-1}(x) = F^{-1}(1-e^{-x})$..

Using the result of example 1.2.1, we obtain

$P(X_{U(n)} \leq x) = P(Y_1+Y_2+\ldots+Y_n \leq -\ln(1-F(x)))$

$= P(-\ln(1-F(x_1)) + (-\ln(1-F(X_2))) + \ldots + (-\ln(1-F(x_n))) \leq -\ln(1-F(x))$

$= P(g_F(X_1) + g_F(X_2) + \ldots + g_F(X_n) \leq x)$, where $g_F(x) = -\ln(1-F(x)$,

$= P(g_F^{-1}\{g_F(X_1) + g_F(X_2) + \ldots + g_F(X_n)\} \leq x)$ where $g_F^{-1}(x) = F^{-1}(1-e^{-x})$.

$$X_{U(n)} \stackrel{d}{=} g_F^{-1}(g_F(X_1) + g_F(X_2) + \ldots + g_F(X_n)) \quad (8.4.1)$$

Using (8.4.1) we will give here the representation of nth record values of several well known distribution.

Example 8.4.1.

For the two parameter exponential distribution, $E(\mu, \sigma)$, with cdf $F(x)$ as

$$F(x) = 1 - e^{-(x-\mu)/\sigma}, \ x \geq 0, \ \text{we obtain}$$

$$X_{U(n)} \stackrel{d}{=} X_1 + X_2 +,,, + X_n - (n-1)\mu$$

Example 8.4.2.

Consider the Webull Distribution, $W(\alpha, \beta)$ with

$$F(x) = 1 - e^{-\beta x^\alpha}, \ x \geq 0, \ \alpha > 0, \ \beta > 0,$$
$$= 0, \ \text{for } x < 0.$$

Using Theorem 8.4.1, we obtain

$$X_{U(n)} \stackrel{d}{=} (X_1^\alpha + X_2^\alpha +,,, + X_2^\alpha)^{\frac{1}{\alpha}}.$$

Example 8.4.3

Consider the Power Function Distribution, POW (δ, α, β) with cdf $F(x)$ as

$$F(x) = \begin{cases} 0, x < 0 \\ 1 - \left(\frac{\beta - x}{\beta - \alpha}\right)^\theta, \alpha \leq x \leq \beta, \delta > 0, -\infty < \alpha < \beta < \infty, \\ 1, x \geq \beta. \end{cases}$$

For this distribution, the following representation is true

$$X_{U(n)}' \stackrel{d}{=} \beta - (\beta - \alpha)^{\frac{1}{\delta}} (\beta - X_1)(\beta - X_2)\ldots(\beta - X_n).$$

Example 8.4.4.

Consider the Pareto distribution, $P(\delta,\alpha,\beta)$ with $F(x)$ as

$$F(x) = \begin{cases} 1 - \left(\dfrac{\alpha+\beta}{x+\beta}\right)^{\delta}, & x \geq \alpha \\ 0, & x < \alpha. \end{cases}$$

It can easily be shown the following representation of $X_{U(n)}$

$$X_{U(n)} \stackrel{d}{=} \dfrac{1}{(\alpha+\delta)^{n-1}}(X_1+\delta)(X_2+\delta)\ldots(X_n+\delta).-\alpha.$$

The following Theorem can be proved following the same procedure as given in Theorem 8.4.1 (for details see Ahsanullah and Nevzorov (2001 p. 242).

Theorem 8.4.2

Suppose that $\{X_1, X_2, \ldots\}$ and $\{Y_1, Y_2, \ldots, \}$ are to sequence of i.i.d. r.v.'s with continuous distribution functions F and H respectively. Then

$$\{X_{U(1)}, X_{U(2)}, \ldots\} \stackrel{d}{=} \{G(H((Y_{U(1)}, Y_{U(2)}, \ldots\} \qquad (8.4.2)$$

where G is the inverse function of F.

8.5. LIMITING DISTRIBUTIONS OF NUMBER OF RECORDS

We have seen in Theorem 1.5.1 that

$$E(M_n) = \sum_{j=1}^{n} \dfrac{1}{j}$$

and

$$Var(M_n) = \sum_{i=1}^{n} \dfrac{i-1}{i^2},$$

where $M_n = \sum_{i=1}^{n} Z_i$. Considering the joint and the marginal densities, it can be shown easily that the random variables Z_i's are independent.

Additional Topics

Considering one-sided Chebyshev inequality

$$P[M_n \geq t] \leq \frac{\text{var}(M_n)}{\text{var}(M_n)+\{(t-E(M_n)\}^2},$$

we get

$P[M_n \geq 20] \leq 0.036.$

As n→ ∞,

$E(M_n) \to \upsilon + \ln n$

$\text{Var}(M_n) \to \upsilon + \ln n - \frac{\pi^2}{6}$, υ is the Euler's constant = .5772...

The table 8.4.1 gives the exact and approximate values of $E(M_n)$ and $\text{Var}(M_n)$ for some selected values of n.

Table 8.5.1 Exact and approximate values of $E(M_n)$ and $\text{Var}(M_n)$

N	$E(M_n)$	$\upsilon + \ln n$	$\text{Var}(M_n)$	$\upsilon + \ln n - \frac{\pi^2}{6}$
5	2.28	2.19	0.82	0.54
10	2.93	2.88	1.38	1.23
20	3.60	3.57	2.00	1.93
50	4.50	4.48	2.87	2.84
100	5.19	5.18	3.55	3.54
200	5.88	5.87	4.24	4.23
500	6.79	6.79	5.15	5.15
1000	7.49	7.48	5.84	5.84

$E(M_n) \to \infty$ as n → ∞ and $\sum_{n=1}^{\infty} \left(\frac{\text{var}(M_n)}{\sum_{i=1}^{n} E(Z_i)} \right) < \infty$. We have

$\frac{M_n}{\ln n} \to 1$ with probability one as n → ∞. It can be shown that the random variables Z_i's satisfy the Liapunov condition, i.e.

$$\frac{1}{\{\mathrm{var}(M_n)\}^{\frac{2+\delta}{2}}} \sum_{j=1}^{n} E|Z_j - E(Z_j)|^{2+\delta} \to 0, \text{ as } n \to \infty. \text{ Thus}$$

$$\frac{M_n - \ln n}{\sqrt{\ln n}} \xrightarrow{d} N(0,1) \text{ as } n \to \infty.$$

$P[M_{bn} = M_{an}]$ = Probability that there is no records between the x_i's with index i between an+1 and bn, i.e. an + 1 $\leq$ i $\leq$ bn = a/b.

Using the Z's as defined in section 1.5, we have

$$Z_i = 0, \ i = an+1, an+2, \ldots bn.$$

and $E(S^{Z_i}) = 1 + \dfrac{s-1}{i}$.

Let

$$\eta(s) = \prod_{i=an+1}^{bn} E(s^{Z_i}), \text{ then}$$

$$\eta(s) = \prod_{i=an+1}^{bn} (1 + \frac{s-1}{i}).$$

Now taking logarithms of both sides and using Taylor series expansion, we have as n $\to \infty$

$$\ln \eta(s) = (s-1) \sum_{i=an+1}^{bn} \frac{1}{i} \cong (s-1) \ln \frac{b}{a}.$$

Thus as n $\to \infty$, $\ln \eta(s)$ is the logarithm of a Poisson generating function with mean $\ln \dfrac{b}{a}$. Hence as n $\to \infty$,

$$P[M_{bn} - M_{an} = j] = \frac{(\ln \frac{b}{a})^j}{j!} \cdot \frac{a}{b}.$$

8.6. RANDOM RECORD MODEL

Suppose P be a point process on $[0,\infty)$ with counting measure $N(.)$ and the interval sequence $\{Y_j\}, j = 1,2,...$. We assume P has a point at $t = 0$ and $N(t)$ be the number of points of P in the interval $(0, t]$. The jth point of P can be denoted as S_j, where $S_j = \sum_{i=1}^{j} Y_i, j =1,2,...$. We associate with S_j is an independent random variable X_j. We assume $\{X_j\}, j = 0,1,2,...$ as i.i.d with continuous cumulative distribution function F. In this section we will consider the upper record values of $\{X_j\}$. We will consider the observation X_0 at $t = 0$ as the first upper record value. In addition we assume $p_k(t) = P\{N(t)=k\}$ and $P\{N(t)<\infty\}=1$ for all $t < \infty$.

The indices at which the upper record values occur are given by the record times $\{U^*(n)\}, n \geq 1$, where $U^*(n) = \min\{j| j > U^*(n-1), X_j > X_{U^*(n-1)}, n \geq 1\}$, with $U^*(0) = 0$. We define the upper inter record counts as $\Delta_r^* = U^*(r) - U^*(r-1), r \geq 1$. Since $U^*(0) = 0$, we have $U^*(r) = U^*(r-1) + ... + U^*(1)$. Let $M^*(t)$ be the number of records to occur in $(0,t]$. This type of record model is called random record model. Random record model was first formulated by Pickands(1971) for the homogeneous Poisson process. Gaver (1976) considered the record values, record times and inter record times for several different point processes P. Bunge and Nagaraja (1992) gave an infinite series representation for the joint characteristic function of the first n record times for general P.

$\tau_1 = \inf\{t \mid n \leq N(t), X_n > X_0\}$, $X_{U^*(1)} = X_{N(\tau_1)}$,

$\tau_1+\tau_2 = \inf\{t|n\leq N(t), X_n > X_{U^*(1)}\}$, $X_{U^*(2)} = X_{N(\tau_1+\tau_2)}$,

....

$\tau_1+\tau_2+......+\tau_m = \inf\{t|n\leq N(t), X_{U^*(m)} = X_{N(\tau_1+\tau_2+...+\tau_m)}$.

If $P(Y_j = 1) = 1$ for all $j \geq 1$, then this record process reduces to the classical record model discussed before. The following theorem is due to Gaver(1976)

Theorem 8.6.1.

Suppose P is Poisson with time dependent rate $\lambda(t)$ and cumulative time dependent rate $\Lambda(t) = \int_0^t \lambda(u)du$, then, $E(\tau_1) < \infty$ iff $\int_h^\infty \frac{dt}{\Lambda(t)} < \infty$ or some $h > 0$.

Proof:

$$P(\tau_1 > t | X_0 = x) = \sum_{n=0}^{\infty} P(\tau_1 > t | X_0 = x, N(t) = n) P(N(t) = n)$$

$$= \sum_{n=0}^{\infty} F^n(x) \frac{e^{-\Lambda(t)}(\Lambda(t))^n}{n!}$$

$$= e^{-\Lambda(t)[1-F(x)]}$$

Thus

$$P(\tau_1 > t) = \int_{-\infty}^{\infty} e^{-\Lambda(t)[1-F(x)]} dF(x) = \frac{1-e^{-\Lambda(t)}}{\Lambda(t)}.$$

Now

$$E(\tau_1) = e^{-\Lambda(h)} \int_h^\infty \frac{dt}{\Lambda(t)} \leq E(\tau_1) \leq h + \int_h^\infty \frac{dt}{\Lambda(t)}, \text{ for some } h > 0.$$

Hence

$$(1 - e^{-\Lambda(h)}) \int_h^\infty \frac{dt}{\Lambda(t)} \leq E(\tau_1) \leq h + \int_h^\infty \frac{dt}{\Lambda(t)},$$

and

$$E(\tau_1) < \infty \text{ iff } \int_h^\infty \frac{dt}{\Lambda(t)} < \infty.$$

For time homogeneous Poisson process $\Lambda(t) = \mu t$, $E(\tau_1)$ is infinite and $P(\tau_1 > t) = \frac{1-e^{-\mu t}}{\mu t}$ and $P(\tau_1 > t | X_0 = x) = 1 - e^{-\mu t(1-F(x))}$.

The following table gives the values of $P(\tau_1 > t)$ for some selected values of μ and t.

Additional Topics 263

Table 8.6.1. P($\tau_1 > t$)

T	μ 1	2	5	10
1	0.632121	0.432332	0.198652	0.099995
2	0.432332	0.245421	0.099995	0.050000
3	0.316738	0.166254	0.066667	0.033333
4	0.245421	0.124958	0.050000	0.025000
5	0.198652	0.099995	0.040000	0.020000
6	0.166354	0.083333	0.033333	0.016667
7	0.142727	0.071429	0.028571	0.014286
8	0.124958	0.062500	0.250000	0.012500
9	0.111097	0.055560	0.022222	0.011111
10	0.099995	0.050000	0.020000	0.010000

P ($\tau_1 > t$) decreases as μ increases. E(τ_1) is infinite but E(τ_1| $X_0 = x$)

$= \dfrac{1}{\mu(1-F(x))}$. Thus for absolute large values of x $\lim_{x \to \infty}$ E(τ_1| $X_0 = x$)

$= \infty$

and $\lim_{x \to -\infty}$ E(τ_1| X_0) $= \dfrac{1}{\mu}$.

In general for homogeneous Poisson process

P($\tau_k > t | X_{U^*(k-1)} = x) = e^{-\mu t(1-F(x))}$.

Hence

$$P(\tau_k > t) = \int_{-\infty}^{\infty} e^{-\mu t(1-F(x))} (R(x))^{k-1} \dfrac{f(x)}{(k-1)!} dx .$$

Theorem 8.6.2.

For a homogeneous Poisson process with $\Lambda(t) = \mu t$

$$P(\tau_k > t) = \sum_{j=0}^{\infty} \sum_{i=0}^{\infty} \dfrac{(-\mu t)^j}{j!(k-1)!} c_j B(i+k, j+1) ,$$

where

B(i,j) is the Beta function, $c_0 = 1$ and $c_m = \dfrac{1}{m}\sum_{r=0}^{m}(rk-m)\dfrac{c_{m-r}}{r+1}$.

Proof:

$$P(\tau_k > t) = \int_{-\infty}^{\infty} e^{-\mu t(1-F(x))}(R(x))^{k-1}\dfrac{f(x)}{(k-1)!}dx$$

$$= \int_{-\infty}^{\infty}[\sum_{j=0}^{\infty}\dfrac{\{-\mu t(1-F(x))\}^j}{j!(k-1)!}][\sum_{i=0}^{\infty}\dfrac{(F(x))^{i+1}}{i+1}]^{k-1}$$

Now using the relation (see Gradshteyn and Ryzhik (1980))

$(\sum_{m=0}^{\infty} a_m x^m)^{k-1} = \sum_{m=0}^{\infty} c_m x^m$, where $c_0 = 1$ and $c_m = \dfrac{1}{m}\sum_{r=0}^{m}(rk-m)\dfrac{c_{m-r}}{r+1}$,

we have

$$P(\tau_k > t) = \sum_{j=0}^{\infty}\sum_{i=0}^{\infty}\dfrac{(-\mu t)^j}{j!(k-1)!}c_j \int_{-\infty}^{\infty}\{1-F(x)\}^j (F(x))^{i+k-1} f(x)dx.$$

Putting $w = F(x)$, we get

$$P(\tau_k > t) = \sum_{j=0}^{\infty}\sum_{i=0}^{\infty}\dfrac{(-\mu t)^j}{j!(k-1)!}c_j \int_{-\infty}^{\infty}\{1-w\}^j (w)^{i+k-1} dw.$$

Writing the integral in terms of the Beta function, we obtain the result.

Theorem 8.6.3.

For a homogeneous Poisson process with $\Lambda(t) = \mu t$,

$$E(M(t)) = \sum_{n=1}^{\infty}\sum_{j=1}^{\infty}\dfrac{e^{-\mu t}(\mu t)^n}{jn!}$$

and

$$Var(M(t)) = \sum_{n=1}^{\infty}\sum_{j=1}^{n}\dfrac{(j-1)e^{-\mu t}(\mu t)^n}{j^2 n!} + \sum_{n=1}^{\infty}[\sum_{j=1}^{n}\dfrac{1}{j}]^2 \dfrac{e^{-\mu t}(\mu t)^n}{n!}$$

$$- e^{-2\mu t}[\sum_{n=1}^{\infty}\sum_{j=1}^{n}\dfrac{(\mu t)^n}{j\,n!}]^2.$$

Proof:

$$E(M(t)) = E[E(M(t)|N(t))] = E[\sum_{j=1}^{N(t)} \frac{1}{j}]$$

$$= \sum_{n=1}^{\infty} \sum_{j=1}^{\infty} \frac{e^{-\mu t}(\mu t)^n}{jn!}.$$

Considering the conditional variance formula,
$$\text{Var}[M(t)] = E[\text{Var}(M(t)|N(t)] + \text{Var}[E[M(t)|N(t)]]$$

$$\text{Var}(M(t)) = E[\sum_{j=1}^{N(t)} \frac{j-1}{j^2}] + \text{var}[\sum_{j=1}^{N(t)} \frac{1}{j}]$$

$$= \sum_{n=1}^{\infty} \sum_{j=1}^{n} \frac{(j-1)e^{-\mu t}(\mu t)^n}{j^2 n!} + \sum_{n=1}^{\infty} [\sum_{j=1}^{n} \frac{1}{j}]^2 \frac{e^{-\mu t}(\mu t)^n}{n!}$$

$$- e^{-2\mu t} [\sum_{n=1}^{\infty} \sum_{j=1}^{n} \frac{(\mu t)^n}{j n!}]^2.$$

Theorem 8.6.4.

Let $T_0 = 0$, $T_1 = \tau_1$, $T_2 = \tau_1 + \tau_2, \ldots, T_k = \tau_1 + \tau_2 + \ldots + \tau_k$, then the sequence $T_1, T_2, \ldots$ forms a Markov process.

Proof.

$$P(T_k > t_k | T_1 = 0, T_1 = t_1, \ldots, T_{k-1} = t_{k-1})$$
$$= P(T_{k-1} + \tau_k > t_k | T_0 = 0, T_1 = t_1, \ldots, T_{k-1} = t_{k-1})$$
$$= P(\tau_k > t_k - t_{k-1} | T_0 = 0, T_1 = t_1, \ldots, T_{k-1} = t_{k-1})$$

Since the waiting time for the next record depends on the value of the present record and does not depend on the occurrence time, we have
$$P(T_k > t_k | T_0 = 0, T_1 = t_1, \ldots, T_{k-1} = t_{k-1})$$
$$= P(\tau_{k-1} > t_k - t_{k-1}).$$
$$= P(\tau_{k-1} > t_k - t_{k-1} | X_{U^*(k-1)} = x) f_{U^*(k-1)}(x)$$
$$= e^{-\Lambda(t)}(1 - F(x)) f_{U^*(k-1)}(x),$$

where $t = t_k - t_{k-1}$.

Theorem 8.6.5.

For a homogeneous Poisson process with $\Lambda(t) = \mu t$, $(\mu \tau_n)^{1/n} \to e$ in probability as $n \to \infty$.

Proof:

The characteristic function of $\varphi_1(s)$ of $\frac{1}{n}(\ln \mu \tau_n)$ is

$$\varphi_1(s) = E[\exp(\frac{s}{n}(\ln \mu \tau_n))] = E[(\mu \tau_n)^{s/n}]$$

Since τ_n, the time between the nth and (n+1)th records does not depend on tthe distribution of X, we will assume the distribution of X as exponential.
Now

$$E[\exp(\frac{is}{n}(\ln \mu \tau_n)) \mid \{U^*(n) = x\}] = \int_0^\infty (\mu t)^{\frac{is}{n}} e^{-\mu t e^{-x}} \mu e^{-x} dt$$

$$= \int_0^\infty e^{\frac{isx}{n}} u^{\frac{s}{n}} e^{-u} du.$$

Using the probability density function of the nth record value from exponential distribution, we get

$$\varphi_1(s) = \int_0^\infty e^{i\frac{sx}{n}} \frac{x^{n-1} e^{-x}}{\Gamma(n)} dx \int_0^\infty u^{\frac{s}{n}} e^{-u} du$$

$$= \frac{1}{(1 - \frac{is}{n})^n} \int_0^\infty u^{\frac{is}{n}} e^{-u} du$$

$$\frac{\Gamma(1 + \frac{s}{n})}{(1 - \frac{is}{n})^n} \to e^{is} \text{ as } n \to \infty.$$

Thus by the continuity theorem of the characteristic function, the result follows.

8.7, RECORDS OF DEPENDENT SEQUENCE

We will consider in this section the record values of non identically distributed random variables. Yang (1975) considered the records of the sequence $\{Y_k, k = 1,2,...\}$ where

$$Y_k = \max\{X_{k,1},...,X_{k,n(k)}\}, k = 1,2,...$$

and

$$\{X_{ij}\} j = 1,...,n(i), i = 1,2,....$$

He assumed the distributions of $X_{i,j}$ as independent and identically with a common distribution function F and n(k) takes the value $\lambda^{k-1} n(1), n = 1,2,....$ Yang studied this model for the olympic records. He assumed that n(k) is the size of the world population at the kth record and λ is the rate of increase of the world population per year. Yang's model can be considered as records in a sequence of independent observations $Y_1, Y_2,...$ with cdf of Y_k as

$$F_k(x) = (F(x))^{n(k)}, k = 1,..., \text{ with } n(k) = \lambda^{k-1} n(1).$$

Yang's model is a special case of F^α model introduced by Nevzorov (1990).

Definition. A sequence of independent random variables $X_1, X_2,...$ with cdf's $F_1, F_2,...$ forms an F^α - scheme if

$$F_k = F^{\alpha(k)}, k = 1,2,...$$

where F is a continuous distribution function and $\alpha(1), \alpha(2)...$ are some positive constants.

Without any loss of generality, we can take $F_1 = F$ and $\alpha(1) = 1$. Let $I_j, i \geq 1$ be the record indicator in the sequence $\{Y_k\}, k = 1,2,...$
Let $s(k) = \alpha(1) + ... + \alpha(k)$.
Theorem 8.7.1.

$$P(I_n = 1) = 1 - P(I_n = 0) = \frac{\alpha(n)}{s(n)}, \text{ F is continuous..}$$

Proof

$$P(I_n = 1) = P(X_n > X_1, X_2, \ldots, X_{n-1})$$
$$= \int_{-\infty}^{\infty} F(x)^{s(n-1)} dF^{\alpha(n)}(x) dx = \int_0^1 x^{s(n-1)} dx^{\alpha(n)}$$
$$= \frac{\alpha(n)}{s(n+1) + \alpha(n)} = \frac{\alpha(n)}{s(n)}$$

Theorem 8.7.2.
The indicators $I_1, I_2, \ldots, I_n$ are independent.

Proof
For any $1 = k(1) < k(2) < \ldots < k(n))$
$$P[I_{k(1)} = 1, I_{k(2)} = 2, \ldots I_{k(n)} = 1]$$
$$= PL^- X_{k(1)} > M(k(1) - 1), X_{k(2)} > M(k(2) - 1), \text{ where}$$
$$M(n) = \max(Y_1, \ldots, Y_n)$$
$$= \int_0^1 u_1^{s(k(1)-1)} du_1^{\alpha(k)} \cdot \int_0^1 u_2^{s(k(2))-s(k(1))} du_2^{\alpha(k(2))}$$
$$\ldots \cdot \int_{u_{n-1}}^1 u_n^{s(k(n)-1)-s(r-1)} d\left(u_n^{\alpha k(n)}\right)\right\}$$
$$= \prod_{r=1}^n \frac{\alpha(k(r))}{s(\alpha(k(r)))} = \prod_{j=1}^n P(I(k(j)) = 1)$$

Theorem 8.7.3.
The record indicators $I_1, I_2, \ldots I_n$ and $M(n) = \max(Y_1, Y_2, \ldots, Y_n)$ are independent.

Proof
For any n and $1 \leq k(1) < k(2) < -k(n)$, we obtain
$$PL^- I_{\alpha(1)} = 1, I_{\alpha(2)} = 1, \ldots, I_{\alpha(n)} = 1_2 M(n) \leq x\} = \int_0^x u_1^{s(k(1)-1)} d\left(u_1^{\alpha(k(1))}\right)$$
$$\cdot \int_{u_1}^w u_2^{s(k(2))-1-s(k(1))} d\left(u_2^{\alpha(x(2))}\right)$$
$$\cdot \int_{u_{n-1}}^x u_n^{s(k(n)-1)-s(k(n-1)-1)} \cdot x^{s(n)-s(k/r)} \cdot$$
$$= \prod_{i=1}^{n-1} -\frac{\alpha(k(i))}{s(k(n))} x^{s(n)}$$
$$= P(I_{k(1)} = 1, \ldots I_{k(n)} = 1) P(M_n \leq x),$$

Ballerini (1994) considered the F^α scheme when Y_n's are dependent. He assumed that

$$P(Y_1 \le y_1, Y_2 \le y_2, \ldots, Y_n \le y_n)$$
$$= A\left(\sum_{i=1}^{n} A^{-1} F_i(y_i)\right), n \ge 1, \qquad (8.7.1)$$

where A is a completely monotone function mapping $(0, \infty)$ onto $(0,1)$, with $A(0) = 1$. The expression given in (8.8.1) is known as Archimedian copula. Assume $A(\mu) = \exp\left(-s^\beta\right), 0 < \beta \le 1$, Ballerini showed that the Theorem 8.8.3 is true for Y's and

$$P(I_r = j) = \frac{(\alpha(j))^{\beta^{-1}}}{\sum_{i=1}^{\infty}(\alpha(j))^{\beta^{-1}}}.$$

The following result was given byNevzozrov (2001 p.110),

Theorem 8.7.4.

Let $X_1, X_2, \ldots$ be independent random variables which form an F^α-scheme with cdf F and exponents $\alpha(1), \alpha(2), \ldots$ Then

$$F(X_{U(n)} < x) = E(F(x))^{S(U(n))}.$$

Proof. Let $X_{n,n} = \max\{X_1, X_2, \ldots, X_n\}$.

$$P(X_{U(n)} < x) = \sum_{m=n}^{\infty} P\{X_{U(n),U(n)} < x \mid U(n) = m\} P(U(n) = m\}$$

$$= \sum_{m=n}^{\infty} P\{X_{U(n),U(n)} < x \mid I_1 + \ldots + I_{m-1} = n-1, I_m = 1\}. P(U(n) = m\}$$

$$= \sum_{m=n}^{\infty} P\{X_{U(n),U(n)} < x \mid . P(U(n) = m\}$$

$$= \sum_{m=n}^{\infty} \{F(x)\}^{s(m)}. P(U(n) = m\} = E\{F(x)\}^{U(m)}$$

8.8. CONCOMITANTS

Let $\{X_i, Y_i, i = 1,2, \}$ be a sequence of i.i.d. bivariate random variables with cdf $F_{12}(x,y)$ and pdf $f_{12}(x,y)$. Let $X_{U(1)} = X_1$,

$X_{U(2)}$, ... be the upper record values of the X's and Y(1), Y(2), ... be the corresponding values of Y's in the sequence { X_i, Y_i, i = 1,2, ...}. Then we will call Y(r) as the rth upper concomitant of the rth upper record value. Similarly, we can define lower concomitant corresponding to the lower record values. We will mention here the word concomitant to mean upper concomitant.

The conditional distribution of $Y(k) | X_{U(k)}$ is the same as the conditional pdf of $Y_i | X_i$.
Hence the joint pdf f_{12}^* of $X_{U(k)}$ and Y(k) is

$$f_{12}^*(x,y) = f_{12}(x,y) \frac{\{-\ln(1-F_1(x))\}^{k-1}}{\Gamma(k)},$$

where $F_1(x)$ is the marginal cdf of X.
The marginal pdf of $f_2^*(y,k)$ of Y(k) can be written as

$$f_2^*(y,k) = \int_{-\infty}^{\infty} f_{12}(x,y) \frac{\{-\ln(1-F(x)\}^{k-1}}{\Gamma(k)} dx. \tag{8.8.1}$$

The rth moment Y(k) is given by

$$E(Y(k))^r) = \int_{-\infty}^{\infty} y^r f_{12}(x,y) \frac{\{-\ln(1-F(x)\}^{k-1}}{\Gamma(k)} dx$$

$$= \int_{-\infty}^{\infty} E(y^r \mid x) f_k(x) dx = \mu_y^r(k), \text{ say.} \tag{8.8.2}$$

The variance of Y(k) = $\mu_y^2(k) - (\mu_y^1(k))^2$. (8.8.3)
The joint pdf of Y(1),Y(2), ..., Y(m) can be written as

$$f_2^*(y_1, y_2,..., y_m) = \prod_{i=1}^{m-1} \frac{f(x_i, y_i)}{1-F_1(x_i)} f(x_m, y_m) dx_i \tag{8.8.4}$$

for $-\infty < y_1 < y_2 < ..... < y_m < \infty$.
The covariance between Y(p) and Y(q) is
Cov(Y(p),Y(q)) = Cov [E{ Y| $X_{U(p)} = x_p$) , E{ Y| $X_{U(q)} = x_q$}]

Example 8.8.1.
Suppose we consider the bivariate exponential distribution (see, Gumbel (1960); Johnson and Kotz(1977)) with following joint cdf
$F(x,y) = (1 - e^{-x})(1 - e^{-y}) \{ 1 + c e^{-x-y} \}$, $0 < x,y < \infty$, $-1 < c < 1$.
Then corresponding pdf of X and Y is
$f(x,y) = e^{-(x+y)} \{ 1 + c(2 e^{-x} -1)(2e^{-y} -1\}$, $0 < x,y < \infty$, $-1 < c < 1$.
The conditional probability $P(Y \leq y \mid X = x)$ is

$P(Y \leq y | X = x) = \{1-c(2e^{-x} -1)\}(1 - e^{-y}) + c(2e^{-x} -1)(1 - e^{-2y})$
Since the marginal distribution of X and Y are exponential with mean unity. The conditional mean and variance are

$$E(Y|X=x) = 1 + \frac{c}{2} - ce^{-x}$$

$$Var(Y|X=x) = 1 + \frac{c}{2} - \frac{c^2}{4} - (c-c^2)e^{-u} - c^2 e^{-2u}.$$

Using the distribution Of the kth record value of X as given in (2.1.1), the pdf of Y(k) is given by

$$f_2^*(y,k) = \int_0^\infty e^{-y}[1+c\{(2e^{-x}-1)(2e^{-y}-1)\}\frac{x^{k-1}}{\Gamma(k)}e^{-x}dx$$

$$= e^{-y}\{1+c - 2ce^{-y} - \frac{c}{2^{k-1}} + \frac{ce^{-y}}{2^{k-2}}\}. \qquad (8.8.5)$$

The mean and variance of the concomitant is

$$E(Y(k)) = 1 + \frac{c}{2} - \frac{c}{2^k},$$

and

$$Var(Y(k)) = 1 + \frac{c}{2} - \frac{c^2}{4} - \frac{c-c^2}{2^k} - \frac{c^2}{4^k}.$$

As $k \to \infty$, $E(Y(k)) \to 1 + c/2$ and $Var(Y(k)) \to 1 + c/2 - c^2/4$.
The covariance between Y(p) and Y(q) is

$$Cov(Y(p), Y(q)) = c^2 Cov(e^{-x_p}, e^{-x_q}) = \frac{c^2}{2 \cdot 3^k} - \frac{c^2}{2 \cdot 4^k}.$$

Example 8.8.2.
Suppose (X_i, Y_i), $i=1,2,\ldots$ be i.i.d. bivariate normal distribution with the following pdf

$$f(x,y) = \frac{1}{2\pi\sigma_1\sigma_2\sqrt{1-\rho^2}} e^{-\frac{1}{2}H(x,y)}, -\infty < x, y < \infty,$$

with $H(x,y) = \frac{1}{1-\rho^2}[(\frac{x-\theta_1}{\delta_1})^2 - 2\rho(\frac{x-\theta_1}{\delta_1})(\frac{y-\theta_2}{\delta_2}) + (\frac{y-\theta_2}{\delta_2})^2$. The conditional expectation and variance of $Y|X = x$ is

$$E(Y \mid X = x) = \theta_2 + \rho \delta_2 \frac{x - \theta_1}{\delta_1}$$

$\text{Var}(Y \mid X=x) = (1 - \rho^2)\delta_2^2$. Thus the expectation and the variance of Y(k) is

$$E(Y(k)) = E(E(Y \mid X_{U(k)})) = \theta_2 + \rho \delta_2 \frac{E(X_{U(k)} - \theta_1)}{\delta_1},$$

and

$$\text{Var}(Y(k)) = (1 - \rho^2)^2 \delta_2^2 + (\frac{\rho \delta_2}{\delta_1})^2 . \text{Var}(X_{U(k)}).$$

The expectation and the variance of $X_{U(k)}$ are given in section 7.2.

Theorem 8.8.4.

Let $X_1, X_2,...$ be independent random variables which form an F^α-scheme with cdf F and exponents $\alpha(1), \alpha(2),......$ Then

$$F(X_{U(n)} < x) = E(F(x))^{s(U(n))}.$$

Proof.

Let $X_{n,n} = \max\{X_1, X_2, ..., X_n\}$.

$$P(X_{U(n)} < x) = \sum_{m=n}^{\infty} P\{X_{U(n),U(n)} < x \mid U(n) = m\} P(U(n) = m)$$

$$= \sum_{m=n}^{\infty} P\{X_{U(n),U(n)} < x \mid I_1 + .. + I_{m-1} = n-1, I_m = 1\}. P(U(n) = m)$$

$$= \sum_{m=n}^{\infty} P\{X_{U(n),U(n)} < x \mid. P(U(n) = m)$$

$$= \sum_{m=n}^{\infty} \{F(x)\}^{s(m)}. P(U(n) = m) = E\{F(x)\}^{U(m)}$$

APPENDIX

A.1. Stirling numbers of the first kind

The Stirling number of the first kind $S(m,n)$ may be defined as the coefficient of x^m in the expression $P(x,n)$, where

$$P(x,n) = x(x-1)(x-2)\ldots(x-n+1) \tag{A.1.1}$$

$$= \sum_{m=0}^{n} s(m,n)x^m.$$

Thus
$$s(0,n) = 0,$$
$$s(n,n) = 1$$
$$s(n-1, n) = -\frac{n(n-1)}{2}$$

and
$$s(1,n) = (-1)^{n-1}(n-1)!$$

Putting $x = 0$, we get

$$\sum_{m=0}^{n} s(m,n) = 0, n > 1.$$

The followings can easily be deduced

$$|s(m,n)| = (-1)^{m+n} s(m,n),$$

$$\sum_{m=0}^{n} |s(m,n)| = n!,$$

$$s(m, n+1) = s(m-1, n) - n\, s(m,n), n \geq m \geq 1 \tag{A.1.2}$$

and

$$s(m+1,n) = \sum_{j=0}^{n} \binom{n}{j} s(m-1, n-j)(-1)^j j!. \tag{A.1.3}$$

For large n

$$|s(m,n)| \approx \frac{(\upsilon + \ln n)^{m-1}}{(m-1)!} \cdot (n-1)!, \text{ where } \upsilon \text{ is the Euler's constant.}$$

$$\lim_{n \to \infty} \frac{1}{n} \frac{s(m, n+1)}{s(m, n)} = -1.$$

Let $M_n(t)$ be the generating function of s(m,n), then

$$M_n(t) = \sum_{j=0}^{\infty} s(m, j) \frac{t^j}{j!}, \quad |t| \leq 1$$

$$= \frac{(\ln(1+t))^j}{j!}.$$

Table A.1 gives the absolute values of the Stirling numbers for $1 \leq r \leq n \leq 10$.

Table A.1 |S(m,n)|

n/r	1	2	3	4	5	6	7	8	9	10
1	1									
2	1									
3	2	3	1							
4	6	11	6	1						
5	24	50	35	10	1					
6	120	274	225	85	15	1				
7	120	1764	1624	735	175	21	1			
8	5040	13068	13132	6769	1960	322	28	1		
9	40320	109584	118124	67284	22449	4536	546	26	1	
10	362880	1026576	1172700	723680	269324	63273	9450	870	45	1

A.2. Bernoulli numbers

The Bernoulli number B_n is defined as the coefficient of X^n in the expression $P_1(t)$, where

$$P_1(t) = \frac{t}{e^t - 1} = \sum_{n=0}^{\infty} B_n \frac{t^n}{n!}. \quad (A.2.1)$$

Writing $\frac{t}{e^t - 1} = \frac{\ln\{1 + (e^t - 1)\}}{e^t - 1}$, and substituting $e^t - 1 = u$, we have

$$\frac{\ln(1+u)}{u} = \sum_{j=0}^{\infty} B_j \frac{[\ln(1+u)]^j}{j!}. \quad (A.2.2)$$

From (A.2.2), we have

$$\frac{\ln(1+u)}{u} = \sum_{j=0}^{\infty} B_j \frac{[\ln(1+u)]^j}{j!} \qquad (A.2.2)$$

From (A.2.2), we have
$B_0 = 1$, $B_1 = -1/2$ and the successive values of B_n's can be obtained from the equation

$$B_n = \sum_{j=0}^{\infty} \binom{n}{j} B_j \qquad (A.2.3)$$

The first ten Bernoulli numbers are

B_0	B_1	B_2	B_3	B_4	B_5	B_6	B_7	B_8	B_9
1	-1/2	1/6	0	-1/30	0	1/42	0	1/30	0

It can be shown that
$$B_{2n+1} = 0, \ n = 1, 2, 3, \ldots \qquad (A.2.4)$$
and
$$B_{2n} = (-1)^{n+1} \frac{2(2n)!}{(2\pi)^{2n}} \sum_{j=1}^{\infty} \frac{1}{j^{2n}} \qquad (A.2.5)$$

For large n,
$$B_{2n} \cong (-1)^{n+1} \pi^{-2n+\frac{1}{2}} e^{-2n} n^{2n+\frac{1}{2}} \qquad (A.2.6)$$
and
$$\frac{B_{2n}}{B_{2n-2}} \approx \frac{n^2}{\pi^2}. \qquad (A.2.7)$$

A.3. Cauchy type functional equations

Let $F(x)$ be a distribution function with $F(0) = 0$. We have already used the following two equations using $F(x)$ in the characterization problems.

$$\overline{F}(x+y) = \overline{F}(x)\overline{F}(y), \ x, y \geq 0 \qquad (A.3.1)$$
and
$$\int_0^{\infty} \{\frac{\overline{F}(x+y)}{\overline{F}(x)} - \overline{F}(y)\} dH(x) = 0 \qquad (A.3.2)$$

The equation (A.3.1) is one of the four type of equations that are known as Cauchy functional equations (CFU). The equation (A.3.2) is known as integrated Cauchy functional equation (ICFE). By induction, we obtain from (A.3.1)

$$\bar{F}(x_1+x_2+...+x_n)=\bar{F}(x_1)\bar{F}(x_2)...\bar{F}(x_n) \quad (A.3.3)$$

for $x_i \geq 0$, $i = 1,2,...,n$.

Now by substitution $x_1 = x_2 = ... = x_n = x \geq 0$, we have

$$\bar{F}(nx)=(\bar{F}(x))^n \quad (A.3.4)$$

If $\bar{F}(x)$ is continuous at a point $x = x_0 > 0$, then by (A.3.4) it can be shown that $\bar{F}(x)$ is continuous at every point $x \geq 0$. Since F(x) is the distribution function and $\bar{F}(x) = 1 - F(x)$, $\bar{F}(x)$ is a right continuous, non decreasing function with $\bar{F}(0)=1$ and $\bar{F}(\infty)=0$. If $x > 0$, and m is a positive integers, the by (A.3.1)

$$\bar{F}(x)=(\bar{F}(\tfrac{x}{m}))^m \quad (A.3.5)$$

If $\bar{F}(x) = 1$, for some $x > 0$, then $\bar{F}(nx) = (\bar{F}(x))^n = 1$, which contradicts $\bar{F}(\infty)=0$. if $\bar{F}(x) = 0$ for some $x = x_0 > 0$, then by (A.3.4) it follows that $\bar{F}(x) = 0$ for all $x > 0$, and by right continuity $\bar{F}(0)=0$, a contradiction. Thus $0 < \bar{F}(x) < 1$, for all x, $0 < x < \infty$. Suppose $\bar{F}(1)=e^{-\lambda}$ for some λ, $0 < \lambda < \infty$. Then by (A.3.4) and (A.3.5), $\bar{F}(\tfrac{1}{m})=e^{-\lambda/m}$ and $\bar{F}(\tfrac{n}{m})=e^{-\lambda n/m}$. Thus $\bar{F}(x)= e^{-\lambda x}$ for all rational number x. By right continuity of $\bar{F}(x)$, it follows that

$$\bar{F}(x) = e^{-\lambda x}, \text{ for all } x > 0. \quad (A.3.5)$$

If a non degenerate distribution function satisfies the equation for all values of y_1 and y_2 such that $\ln y_1 (\ln y_2)^{-1}$ is irrational, then $\bar{F}(x) = e^{-\lambda x}$, $x \geq 0$, where λ is a real positive number. This result was established by Marsaglia and Tubilia(1975) and Sethuraman (1965).

The functional equation

$$G(x+y) = G(x) G(y) \quad (A.3.6)$$

for all x, y = a, a+ b, a+2b,...., a+nb, b $\neq$ 0 and n is a non negative integer, has been used by several authors in connection with the conditional distributions and the characterizations of the discrete distributions (see Patil and Seshadri (1964)).

The solutions of (A.3.6) can be summarized as follows:

Case (a), $n < \infty$.

If $a = 0$, then the solutions of the equation (A.3.6) are

(i) $G(x) = 0$,

(ii) $G(x) = 1$, if $x = 0$
$= 0$, otherwise,

(iii) $G(x) = e^{dx}$, $x = b, 2b, ..., nb$,

where d is an arbitrary number.

If $a \neq 0$ and $G(a) = 0$, then the solution of (A.3.6) is

$G(x) = 0$, for $x = a, a+b, ..., a+ (2n-1)b$,
$= c$, for $x = a + nb$,
$= c^2$, for $x = 2a + 2nb$.

If $a \neq 0$ and $G(a) \neq 0$, then the solution of (A.3.6) is

$G(x) = c\, e^{dx}$, for $x = a, a+b, ..., a+ nb$
$= c^2\, e^{dx}$, for $x = 2a, 2a+b, ..., 2a+2nb$,

where c and d are arbitrary numbers except that $c \neq 0$.

Case (b), $n = \infty$.

The solutions of (A.3.6) are

for $a \neq 0$,

(i) $\quad G(x) = c\, e^{dx}$, for $x = a, a+b, ...$,
$= c^2\, e^{dx}$, for $x = 2a, 2a+b, ...$,
$= 0$, otherwise,

where c and d are arbitrary numbers and if $\{ a, a+b, ...\} \cap \{ 2a, 2a+b, ...\} = \phi$. Otherwise for $a = 0$,

(ii) $\quad G(x) = e^{cx}$, for $x = mb, (m+1)b, (m+2)b,....$,

(iii) $\quad G(x) = 1$, for $x = 0$
$= 0$, otherwise

(iv) $\quad G(x) = 0$, $x = mb, (m+1)b, (m+2)b$,

where c is an arbitrary number and m is an arbitrary non negative integer or zero.

Equation (A.3.2) has occurred in the literature in several connections. Ahsanullah (1976),(1977), (1978) and (1991) used this equation in the characterizations of exponential distribution using order statistics and record values. He showed that if F(x)) has monotone hazard rate then the equation has (A.3.2) has a unique solution and it is exponential. Grossward and Kotz (1980) under a different set of conditions which include the absolute continuity of F(x) showed that the exponential distribution is the unique solution of (A.3.2).

Klebanov and Melamed (1983) proved that the unique solution (A.3.2) is exponential i.e. $F(x) = 1 - e^{-\lambda x}$, $x \geq 0$, $\lambda > 0$ and $F(0) = 0$ for $x < 0$, if

$$f(x) \geq 0, \quad \int_{-\infty}^{\infty} f(x)dx = 1 \text{ and}$$

(i) $\bar{F}(x) = e^{-\rho x} \varphi(x), \rho > 0,$

where $\varphi(x)$ satisfies the following conditions

(ii) $f(x) / \varphi(x) \leq M e^{-\alpha x}$, for some positive constants M and α,

(iii) $f(x) / \varphi(x)$ is differentiable and

(iv) $\int_0^\infty \dfrac{d}{dx} [f(x) / \varphi(x)] \, dx < \infty.$

Lau and Rao (1982) gave a general solution of (A.3.2). For various solutions of (A.3.2) under different set of conditions, see Ramachandran and Lau (1991).

COMPLEMENTS AND PROBLEMS

1. Using the inequality $\sum_{s=1}^{\infty} s^{-\frac{1}{2}} t^{s-1} < 2(1-t)^{-\frac{1}{2}}$, show that
$$E(\Delta_n^{-\frac{1}{2}}) < 3\left(\tfrac{2}{3}\right)^n.$$

2. Let F be a continuous distribution function of a sequence of i.i.d. random variable $\{X_n, n \geq 1\}$ with $E|x|^{1+\delta} < \infty$ for $\delta > 0$. Then F is uniquely determined by the sequence $E\{X_{U(n)}, n \geq N > 0\}$.
(Kirmani and Beg, 1984)

3. Show that the equality of the expectations of Z_n and Z_{n-1} characterizes the exponential distribution (Ahsanullah, 1981a)

4. Suppose that $\{X_n, n \geq 1\}$ is a sequence of independent and identically distributed random variables with continuous distribution function $F(x)$. If for some constants p and q, $E(X_{U_{n+k}} | X_{U(n)} = y) = py + q$ a.s., than except for change of location and scale, we have
   (1) $F(x) = 1 - (-x)^\theta$, $-1 < x < 0$, $\theta > 0$, if $0 < p < 1$,
   (2) $F(x) = 1 - e^{-x}$, $x > 0$, if $p = 1$,
   (3) $F(x) = 1 - x^\theta$, if $p > 1$, where $\theta = \dfrac{p}{1-p}$.
   Dembinska and Wesolowski (2000)

5. If $Z_{n,m} = X_{U(n)} - X_{U(m)}$, $n > m$, then the conditional distribution of $Z_{n,m} | X_{U(m)} = x_m$, is the same as the n-m th record value from

the distribution
$$F_c = \frac{F(x) - F(x_m)}{1 - F(x_m)} \quad \text{for } x \geq x_m$$
$$= 0, \quad \text{otherwise.}$$

6. Suppose the sequence $\{X_n, n \geq 1\}$ is i.i.d. with distribution function
   F(x), where
   $$F(x) = 1 - (\frac{\alpha}{x})^\beta, \quad x \geq \alpha, \beta > 0$$
   $$= 0, \text{ otherwise.} \quad \text{(Pareto Law)}$$
   Show that $X_{U(n)} / X_{U(m)}$ and $X_{U(m)}$, $0 < m < n$, are independent.

7. If the sequence $\{X_n, n \geq 1\}$ is i.i.d. and has continuous distribution function, then does the independence of $X_{U(n)} / X_{U(m)}$ and $X_{U(m)}$, $0 < m < n$, imply that $\{X_n, n \geq 1\}$ is distributed according to Pareto Law?

8. Suppose the sequence $\{X_n, n \geq 1\}$ is i.i.d. with probability density function f(x), where
   $$f(x) = \frac{\alpha}{\beta} x^{\alpha-1} e^{-(1/\beta)x^\alpha}, x > 0, \alpha, \beta > 0,$$
   $$= 0, \text{ otherwise,} \quad \text{(Weibull Law)}$$
   then $X_{U(m)} / X_{U(n)}$ and $X_{U(n)}$, $(0 < m < n)$ are independent.

9. Suppose the sequence $\{X_n, n \geq 1\}$ is i.i.d. with probability density function f(x), where
   $$f(x) = \frac{a}{k}\left(\frac{k}{x}\right)^{a+1}, x \geq k, a, k > 0 \quad \text{(Pareto distribution)}$$
   then $H_n(x) = \ln\Gamma(n) + \ln\frac{k}{a} + \frac{a+1}{a} + (n-1)\psi(n)$.

10. Suppose the sequence $\{X_n, n \geq 1\}$ is i.i.d. with probability density function f(x), where

$$f(x) = \frac{1}{\sigma\sqrt{2\pi}} e^{-x^2/(2\sigma^2)}, -\infty<x<\infty, \sigma>0 \quad \text{(normal distribution)}$$

then $H_n(x) = \ln\Gamma(n)-(n-1)\psi(n)+\frac{1}{2}\ln(2\pi)+\ln\sigma+\frac{1}{2}\alpha_n^2$,

$\alpha_n^2 = E(X_{U(n)}^2)$.

11. Suppose the sequence $\{X_n, n \geq 1\}$ is i.i.d. with probability density function f(x), where

$f(x) = \sigma^{-1} e^{x/\sigma} e^{-e^{x/\sigma}}$ (Gumbel distribution),

let $H_{(n)}(x)$ be the entropy corresponding to the nth lower record values, then

$H_{(n)}(x) = \ln\Gamma(n)+(n-2)\psi(n)+n+\ln\sigma$.

12. If the sequence $\{X_n, n \geq 1\}$ is i.i.d. and has continuous distribution function, then does the independence of $X_{U(m)} / X_{U(n)}$ and $X_{U(n)}$, $0 < m < n$, imply that $\{X_n, n \geq 1\}$ is distributed according to Weibull Law?

To prove the problems 13 to 16. assume F as continuous.

13. $\lim_{n\to\infty} (\Delta_n)^{1/n} = e$

Thus the inter record times foe a sequence of observations $X_1, X_2, \ldots$ from an arbitrary continuous distribution will give a precise estimate of e.

14. $\limsup_{n\to\infty} \frac{\ln\Delta_n - n}{(2n\ln\ln n)^{1/2}} = 1 \ a.s.$

$\liminf_{n\to\infty} \frac{\ln\Delta_n - n}{(2n\ln\ln n)^{1/2}} = -1 \ a.s.$

(Strawderman and Holmes, 1970)

15. $$\limsup_{n\to\infty} \frac{\ln U(n) - n}{(2n \ln \ln n)^{1/2}} = 1 \ a.s.$$
$$\liminf_{n\to\infty} \frac{\ln U(n) - n}{(2n \ln \ln n)^{1/2}} = -1 \ a.s. \qquad \text{(Renyi, 1962)}.$$

16. $E(\ln \Delta_n) = n - \gamma + O(\frac{n}{2^n})$, γ is the Euler Constant, and
$$\text{Var}(\ln \Delta_n) = n + \frac{\pi^2}{6} + O(\frac{n^2}{2^n}). \qquad \text{(Pfeifer, 1984)}$$

17. Suppose that $\{X_n, n \geq 1\}$ is a sequence of independently distributed random variables with cumulative distribution function $F_n(x)$ and probability density function $f_n(x)$, such that
$$f_1 = \sum_{0}^{\infty} a_n \, 1_{[n, n+1)},$$
where $\{a_n ; n \geq 0\}$ is a sequence of positive real numbers with $\sum_{n=0}^{\infty} a_n = 1$ and let
$F_n(x) = 1 - e^{-x}$, $x \geq 0$, $n = 2, 4, 5, \ldots$
$F_3(x) = 1 - \exp\{-(2\pi x + \sin 2\pi x)\}$, $x \geq 0$.
Then $X_{U(2)} - X_{U(1)}$ and $X_{U(1)}$ are independent as well as $X_{U(n+1)} - X_{U(n)}$ and $X_{U(n)} - X_{U(n-1)}$, $n > 3$.
(Pfeifer, 1982)

18. If P is a renewal process with i.i.d. interval sequence Y_n, $n \geq 1$ with $E(Y_i^{1+\delta}) < \infty$, for some $\delta > 0$, and $E(Y_i) = \mu < \infty$, then $P(\tau_1 > t) \to \mu / t$ as $t \to \infty$.

19. Suppose that $X_1, X_2, \ldots$ is a sequence of i.i.d. random variables with probability density function $f(x) = 1$, $0 < x < 1$. Prove that for $m \geq 2$ and $r, s = 0, 1, 2, \ldots,$

$$E\left(X_{U(m)}^{r+1} X_{U(m+1)}^{s}\right) = \frac{1}{r+1}\left\{E\left(X_{U(m)}^{r+s+1}\right) - E\left(X_{U(m-1)}^{r+1} X_{U(m)}^{s}\right)\right\}$$
$$- E(X_{U(m)}^{r} X_{U(m+1)}^{s}).$$

20. For the uniformly distributed random variables ($F(x) = (x-a)(b-a)^{-1}$), $a < b < \infty$, prove that
$$E[(X_{U(2)} - X_{U(1)})^2 | X_{U(1)} = y] = \frac{(b-y)^2}{3}.$$

21. Let $\{X_n, n \geq 1\}$ be a sequence of independent and identically distributed random variables with continuous distribution function $F(x)$. Then $F(x) = 1 - e^{-x}$ if and only if $E(X_{U(2)}) = E(X^2) = 2$.

22. Suppose the cdf $F(x)$ of an i.i.d. sequence $\{X_n, n \geq 1\}$ has the density $f(x)$ which is continuous and $F(x) > 0$ for $x > 0$. Let G be a non-decreasing function such that for every $x > 0$, G has a point of increase in $(0,x)$ and $G(0) = 0$. If for some fixed integers $1 \leq i \leq j$, $E[G(X_{U(i)} - X_{U(i-1)}) | X_{U(j)} = x)] = E[G(X_{U(i-1)} - X_{U(i-2)}) | X_{U(i)} = x]$, $\forall x > 0$, then $X_n \in E(0,\sigma)$, where σ is an arbitrary positive number.

(Huang and Li, 1993)

23. If $E[(X_{U(n)} - X_{U(n-1)})^r | X_{U(n-1)} = x] = c$ (independent of x) for some fixed n and r, $r \geq 1$, then $F \in E(0,\sigma)$, $0 < \sigma < \infty$

(Gupta, 1984)

24. Let $X_1, X_2, \ldots$, be i.i.d. random sequence from a distribution with cdf $F(x)$ and pdf $f(x)$ with $\inf\{x | F(x) > 0\} = 0$. Let $F(x)$ be strictly increasing for $x > 0$ and F be NBU (NWU). Then $X \in E(0,\sigma)$, if and only if $E(X_{U(n)} - X_{U(m)}) = E(X_{U(n-m)})$.

(Gajek and Gather, 1989)

25. For a random record model with P as homogeneous Poisson Process with $\Lambda(t) = \mu t$, prove that
$$\frac{\ln \mu \tau_n - n}{\sqrt{n}} \to N(0,1), \text{ as } n \to \infty. \qquad \text{(Gaver, 1976)}$$

26.. Let $X_1, X_2, \ldots$, be a sequence of i.i.d. rvs with positive mass at $1, 2, \ldots$ with distribution function F such that $a = \text{Sup}\{x|F(x) < 1\} = \infty$. Define $Y_{k,n}$ as in problem # 32. Let $Z(k,n,m) = Y_{k,n} - Y_{k,m}$. $n > m$. If $P[Z(k,n,n-1) > r| Y_{k,n-1} = s] = p^k\{X_1 > r\}$ for some fixed $n \geq 2$, arbitrary $s \in \{n-1, n, \ldots\}$ and all $r = 1, 2, \ldots$, then $F \in GE(p)$, $0 < p < 1$.
(Stepanov, 1989)

27. Let $\{X_{i,j}\}$, $j = 1, 2, \ldots, n_i$, $i = 1, 2, \ldots$ be a double sequence of independent and identically distributed random variables with a continuous distribution function $F(x)$. Suppose $Y_i = \max\{X_{i1}, X_{i2}, \ldots, X_{in_i}\}$, $i = 1, 2, \ldots$

Set
$V_0 = 1$
$V_i = \min\{n: Y_n > Y_1\}$,
$V_{n+1} = \min\{Y_n > Y_{V_n}\}$,
$\Delta_n = V_n - V_{n-1}$, $n = 1, 2, \ldots$, $S(k) = n_1 + n_2 + \cdots + n_k$.
Prove that
$$P(\Delta_1 > j) = \frac{n_1}{S(j+1)}$$
and
$$P(\Delta_n > j) = \sum_{k_1=2}^{\infty} \sum_{k_2=k_1+1}^{\infty} \cdots \sum_{k_{n-1}=k_{n-2}+1}^{\infty} \frac{n_1 n_{k_1} \ldots n_{k_{n-1}}}{S(k_1-1) \ldots S(k_{n-1}-1) S(k_{n-1}+j)}.$$
(Yang, 1975)

28. Suppose $\{X_n, \geq 1\}$ is i.i.d. with common continuous distribution function F with E $(X_1^+) < \infty$ and $Y_i = X_i + c\,i$, $c > 0$, $j \geq 1$. Further let

$$1_i = \begin{cases} 1 & \text{if } Y_i \text{ is a upper record,} \\ 0, & \text{otherwise} \end{cases}$$

and $N_n = \sum_{j=1}^{n} 1_j$. Prove that as $n \to \infty$, $N_n / n \to p$ almost surely and in L_2, where $p = \int_{-\infty}^{\infty} G_\infty(y) F(dy)$ and

$$G_\infty(x) = \prod_{j=1}^{\infty} F(x+cj).$$

(Ballerini and Resnick, 1985)

29. If $X_{U(n+1)}$ has an IFR(increasing failure rate) distribution, then so does $X_{U(n)}$. (Kochar, 1990)

30. A distribution F with $F(0) = 0$ and $\mu = E(X_1) = \int_0^\infty \overline{F}(x) dx < \infty$ is said to be harmonic new better (worse) than used in expectation, abbreviated HNBUE (HNWUE), if

$\int_t^\infty \overline{F}(x) dx \leq (\geq) \mu e^{-t/\mu}, t \geq 0$. Let $\{X_n, n \geq 1\}$ be a sequence of i.i.d. random variables with cdf F and F(0)= 0. Let N is the rv defined as $N = \min \{ i > 1: X_i < X_1\}$. Suppose F is either HNBUE or HNWUE. Then $E(NX_N) = E(X_1)$ iff $\overline{F}(x) = e^{-x/\mu}, x > 0$.

(Ahsanullah and Kirmani, 1991)

31. Suppose $\{X_n, n \geq 1\}$ be a sequence of independent and identically distributed random variables with cdf $F(x) = 1 - e^{-x}$ then show that for

$1 \leq m_1 < m_2 < ... < m_k$ and $r_1, r_2, ..., r_{k+1} = 0, 1, 2, ...$

$$E\left(\prod_{i=1}^{k} X_{U(m_i)}^{r_i} X_{U(m_k+1)}^{r_{k+1}+1}\right) = E\left(\prod_{i=1}^{k-1} X_{U(m_i)}^{r_i} X_{U(m_k)}^{r_k+r_{k+1}+1}\right)$$

$$+(r_{k+1}+1)E(\prod_{i+1}^{k} X_{U(m_i)}^{r_i} X_{U(m_k+1)}^{r_{k+1}})$$

and that for $1 \leq m_1 < m_2 < ... < m_{k+1} - 2$ and $r_1, r_2, ..., r_{k+1} = 0, 1, 2, ...$

$$E\left(\prod_{i=1}^{k} X_{U(m_i)}^{r_i} X_{U(m_k+1)}^{r_{k+1}+1}\right) = E\left(\prod_{i=1}^{k} X_{U(m_i)}^{r_i} X_{U(m_{k+1})}^{r_{k+1}+1}\right) +$$

$$+(r_{k+1}+1)E(\prod_{i=1}^{k+1} X_{U(m_i)}^{r_i})$$

(Balakrishnan and Ahsanullah, 1993)

32. Let $\{X_n, n \geq 1\}$ be a sequence of i.i.d random variables from standard Weibull distribution with pdf

$$f(x) = x^{\gamma-1} e^{-x^{\gamma}/\gamma}, x > 0, \gamma > 0.$$

Let $X_{U(m)}$ be the mth (upper) record value from this distribution. Show that

$$E(X_{U(m)})^k = \frac{\Gamma(m+\frac{k}{\gamma})}{\Gamma(m)} \gamma^{k/\gamma}, k = 1, 2, ...$$

33. Suppose that $X_1, X_2, ...$ is a sequence of i.i.d. random variables with distribution function $F(x) = x$, $0 < x < 1$. Prove that $X_{L(n)} \stackrel{d}{=} X X_{L(n-1)}$, $n \geq 1$, where X is independent as $X_{L(n)}$ and $X_{L(n-1)}$ and is distributed as $U(0,1)$.

34. Let $\{X_n, n \geq 1\}$ be a sequence of i.i.d. random variable with continuous cdf F such that $F(0) = 0$. Assume that G is a nondecreasing function having non-lattice support on $x > 0$ with

$G(0) = 0$ and $E(G(X_1)) < \infty$. If, for some fixed non-negative integers j and k,
$$E(G(R_{j+k+1} - R_{j+k})| R_j = x) = c$$
for every $x > 0$, where $c > 0$ is a constant, and if for some ξ,
$$c < \int_0^\infty e^{-\zeta x} dG(x) < \infty,$$
then $c = E(G(X_1))$ and X_1 is exponentially distributed.

(Huang and Li, 1993)

35. Let $\{X_n, n \geq 1\}$ be a sequence of independent and identically distributed non-negative random variables with cumulative distribution function $F(x)$ and the probability density function $f(x)$. If F belongs to the class c_2, then the conditional cumulative distribution function of $Z_{n+1,n}$ given $X_{U(n)}$ belongs to the class c_2.

(Ahsanullah, 1981)

36. Let $(X_n, n \geq 1)$ be a sequence of i.i.d. rvs from the standard Rayleigh distribution with pdf $f(x)$ as
$$f(x) = xe^{-\frac{x^2}{2}}, \ 0 < x < \infty, \text{ then prove that}$$
$$E(X_{U(n)})^k = 2^{\frac{k}{2}} \frac{\Gamma(n+\frac{k}{2})}{\Gamma(n)}.$$

37. Let $\{X_n, n \geq 1\}$ be a sequence of i.i.d. random variable with continuous cdf f such that $F(0) = 0$. We define the process $N_{(0,t]}$ for $0 < t < \infty$ as
$$N_{(0,t]} = \#\{m: X_{U(m)} \leq t\}.$$
Show that $P(N_{(0,b]} - N_{(0,a]} = 0) = \dfrac{\overline{F}(b)}{\overline{F}(a)}$, $b > a > 0$.

38. Suppose $\{X_n, n \geq 1\}$ is a sequence of i.i.d. random variable with cdf $F(x)$, $F(x) = x^\gamma$, $0 < x < 1$, $\gamma > 0$. Show that the MLE $\hat{\lambda}$ of γ is $n / \ln [1- X_{U(n)}]$,

$E(\hat{\lambda}) = n\gamma / (n-1)$ and $Var(\hat{\lambda}) = \dfrac{n^2}{(n-1)^2} \cdot \dfrac{\gamma^2}{n-2}$, $n > 2$.

39. Suppose $\{X_n, n \geq 1\}$ be a sequence of i.i.d. random variables with cdf F and $F(0) = 0$. Let N is the rv defined as $N = \min \{ i > 1: X_i < X_1\}$. Suppose that $\lim_{x \to 0+} \dfrac{F(x)}{x} = \lambda, 0 < \lambda < \infty$. Then X_1 has the exponential distribution (with mean $= 1/\lambda$) iff, for $n \geq 2$, the conditional distribution of NX_N given $N = n$ is identical with the unconditional distribution of NX_N.

(Ahsanullah and Kirmani, 1991)

40. Suppose $\{X_n, n \geq 1\}$ be a sequence of i.i.d. random variables with pdf f, where

$f(x,\sigma) = \dfrac{x}{\sigma^2} e^{-\dfrac{x^2}{2\sigma^2}}$, $x > 0$, $\sigma > 0$.

Let $X_{U(1)}$, $X_{U(2)}$, ..., $X_{U(m)}$ be first m record values of the sequence. Then considering the joint pdf of these record values, it is easy to show that $X_{U(m)}$ is the sufficient statistics for σ. Thus the MVLUE estimator $\hat{\sigma}$ of σ is

$\hat{\sigma} = c\, X_{U(m)}$, where $1/c = E(X_{U(m)})$. $Var(\hat{\sigma}) = \sigma^2 \left[n(\Gamma(n))(\Gamma(n+1/2))^{-2} - 1\right]$.

Show that the best linear unbiased predictor of σ is $c\hat{\sigma}$.

41. Let $X_{U(1)}, X_{U(2)},...$ be record values based on a sequence of independent random variables with a continuous d.f. F ane $Z_{U(1)}, Z_{U(2)},...$ be the record values from an exponential distribution with $F(x) = 1-e^{-x}$, $x>0$, then $\{X_{U(1)}, ..., X_{U(n)}\} \stackrel{d}{=} \{H(Z_{U(1)}),..., H(Z_{U(n)})\}$, $H(x)$

Complements and Problems 291

$= G(1-e^{-x})$ and G is the inverse of F. (Ahsanullah and Nevzorov (2000))

42. Let $\{X_{n,k}, n,k \geq 1\}$ be a double sequence of independent random variables. For all $k \geq 1$, suppose F_n is the cumulative distribution function of $X_{n,k}$. Let $L^*(0) = 1$ and $L^*(n) = \min \{ j \mid j > L^*(n-1), X_{n+1,j} > X_{n,L^*(n-1)} \}$. Then we have $X_{n,L^*(n-1)}$ as the record values of $X_{n,k}$, $n, k \geq 1$. Suppose $F_n \in GE(p_n)$, then $X_{n,L^*(n-1)} \stackrel{d}{=} U_1 + U_2 + ... + U_n$,
where $U_i = GE(p_i)$, $i = 1, 2, ..., n$ and $n \geq 1$.
(Ahsanullah, 1988)

43. Suppose that $\{X_n \ n \geq 1\}$ be a of independent random variables with $f(x) = 1$, $0 < x < 1$,
    $= 0$. otherwise.
    Show that $Z_i = \dfrac{1 - X_{U(i)}}{1 - X_{U(i)}}$, $i = 1, 2, ...$ ($X_{U(0)} = 0$) are i.i.d. with $F(x) = 1 - 1/x$, $x \geq 1$.
    (Bairamov and Ahsanullah (2000)).

43. Assume that $X_{U(1)}, X_{U(2)}, ..., X_{U(n)}$ are n record values from the uniform, $U(0,\sigma)$, distribution. Show that $X_{U(1)}, X_{U(2)} - \dfrac{1}{2} X_{U(1)}$, $X_{U(3)} - \dfrac{1}{2} X_{U(2)}, ..., X_{U(n)} - \dfrac{1}{2} X_{U(n-1)}$ are all uncorrelated with
$E(.X_{U(i)} - \dfrac{1}{2} X_{U(i-1)}) = \dfrac{\sigma}{2}$ and
$Var(X_{U(i)} - \dfrac{1}{2} X_{U(i-1)}) = \dfrac{\sigma^2}{4(3)^i}$.

44. Assume $\{X_i, i \geq 1\}$ is a sequence of identically distributed continuous random variables and $E|X_1|^{2+\delta}$ is finite for some $\delta > 0$. Show that

(a) $\{E(X_{U(n)})\}^2 \leq \dfrac{n+1}{n} E(X_{U(n)})^2$, $n \geq 1$

(b) The equality in (a) holds if X_1 has exponential distribution.

(Lin 1988))

45. Prove that for a continuous random variable prove that

$$E(\ln U(n)) = n - v - \dfrac{1}{2^{n+1}} - \dfrac{5}{24} \cdot \dfrac{1}{3^n} - \dfrac{5\delta}{4^n},$$

where $0 < \delta < 1$ and $v = 0.57722\ldots$ is the Euler's constant.

(Nevzorov (1988))

REFERENCES

Abramowitz, M. and I. Stegan (Eds.). Handbook of Mathematical Functions.New York, NY: Dover, 1972.

Aczel, J. Lectures on Functional Equations and Their Applications. New York, NY: Academic Press, 1966.

Adke, S.R. "Records generated by Markov sequence", Statistics & Probability Letters 18 (1997): 257-263.

Agarwal, M.L. and A. Nagabhushanam. " Coverage of a Record Value and Related Distribution Problems, Bulletin Calcutta Statistical association 20 (1971): 99-103.

Ahsanullah, M. "A Characteristic Property of the Exponential Distribution", Annals of Statistics 5 (1977): 580-582.

-----------------"Record Values and the Exponential Distribution", Annals of the Institute of Statistical Mathematics, 30 (1978):429-433.

--------------- "Characterization of the Exponential Distribution by Record Values", Sankhya, 41, B (1979): 116-121.

----------------- ".Linear Prediction of Record Values for the Two Parameter Exponential Distribution", Annals of the Institute of Statistical Mathematics 32, a (1980): 363-368.

------------------ "Record Values of the Exponentially Distributed Random Variables", Statistiche Hefte, 2 (1981a):121-127.

------------------. "On a Characterization of the Exponential Distribution by Weak Homoscedasticity of Record Values", Biometrical Journal 23 (1981b): 715-717.

---------------== "Record Values of the Exponentially Distributed Random Variables", Statistiche Hefte 21 (1981c):121-127.

------------------ "Charectizatons the Exponential Distribution by Some Properties of Record Values", Statistiche Hefte 23(1982):326-332.

------------------ " Record values from a rectangular distribution", Pakistan Journal of Statistics. 2, no.1 (1986 a): 1-6.

-------------------- " Estimation of the Parameters of a Rectangular Distribution by Record Values", Computational Statistics Quarterly 2 (1986 b): 119-125.

-------------------- ."Two Characterizations of the Exponential Distribution", Communications in Statistics-Theory and Methods 16, no.2 (1987a): 375-381.

-------------------- " Record Statistics and the Exponential Distribution", Pakistan Journal of Statistics. 3, A (1987b):17-40.

-------------------- Introduction to Record Statistics. Needham Height, MA: Ginn Press, 1988.

----------------. " Estimation of the Parameters of the Gumbel Distribution Based on m Record Value", Computational Statistics Quarterly.3 (1990): 231- 239.

---------------- " Some Characteristic Properties of the Record Values from the Exponential Distribution", Sankhya B, 53 (1991a): 403-408.

---------------- " Record Values of the Lomax Distribution", Statistica Neerlandica 45, no. 1 (1991b): 21 - 29.

---------------- " On Record Values from the Generalized Pareto Distribution", Pakistan Journal of Statistics. 7, no. 2 (1991b): 129-136.

---------------- ".Inference and Prediction Problems of the Gunbel Distributions based on Record Values", Pakistan Journal of Statistics, 2 (1991 c): 53-62.

------------------ "Inference and Perdition Problems of the Generalized Pareto Distribution Based on Record Values". (1992 a):. 49-57 in Non Parametric Statistics: Order Statistics and Non Parametrics -.Theory and Applications. Edited by P.K. Sen and I.A. Salama. New York. NY: North Holland,1992.

---------------- ".Record Values of Independent and Identically Distributed Continuous Random Variables", Pakistan Journal of Statistics 8 no. 2 (1992 b): 9-34.

---------------- "Records of the Generalized Extreme Value Distribution", Pakistan Journal of Statistics 10, no.1, A (1994a): 147-170.

----------------. "Record Values from Univariate Continuous Distributions".(1994):.1-12. In. Proceedings of the Extreme Value of the Extreme Value Theory and Applications. 1994.

----------------. " Some Inferences of Uniform Distribution based on Record Values", Pakistan Journal of Statistics. 9, no.2 (1994d): 27-33.

----------------. " Records of Univariate Distributions", Pakistan Journal of Statistics 9, no.3 (1994d): 49-72.

----------------. " Records Values, Random Record Models and Concomitants", Journal of Statistical Research 28 (1994e): 89-109.

---------------- Record Statistics. New York, NY, Nova Science Publishers Inc,, 1995.

---------------- " Some Inferences of the Generalized Extreme Value Distribution Based on Record Values", Journal of Mathematical Sciences 78, no,1(1996): 2-10..

---------------------- "Concomitants of Record Values", Pakistan Journal of Statistics. 16, no. 2 (2000):207-215.

---------------------- "K-Record Values of the Type I Extreme Value Distribution', Journal of Statistical Studies,. Special Volume 2002:283-292.

---------------- "Some Inferences Based on K-Record Values of Uniform Distribution", Stochastic Modelling and Applications, 2003: (to appear)

Ahsanullah, M and D. Bhoj. "Record Values of Extreme Value Distributions and a Test for Domain of Attraction of Type I Extreme Value Distribution", Sankhya 58, B (1008):151-158.

Ahsanullah, M. and B. Holland.. " Some Properties of the Distribution of Record Values from the Geometric Distribution", Statische Hefte 25 (1984): 319-327.

------------------ "Distributional Properties of Record Values from the Geometric Distribution", Statistica Neerlandica 41 (1987):129-137.

-------------------- "On the Use of Record Values to Estimate the Location and Scale Parameters of the Generalized Extreme Value Distribution", Sankhya 36 , A (1991):480-499.

Ahsanullah, M. and M.Z. Raqab. "Recurrence Relations for the Moment Gnerating Functions from Pareto and Gumbel Distribution", Stochastic Modelling and Applications. 2, No.2 (2000):35-48.

Ahsanullah, M and V.B. Nevzorov. Ordered Random Variables. New York: Nova Science Publishers Inc.,2001.

Ahsanullah, M and J. Wesolowski. "Linearity of Best Non-adjacent Record Values" ,Sankhya ,B (1998): 231-237

Aliev, F.A. "Characterizations of Discrete Distributions through Weak Records:, Journal of Applied Statistical Science 8, no.,1 .(1998): 13-16.

---------------- " New Characterizations of Discrete Distributions through Weak Records", Theory of Probability and Applications. 44, no.4 (1999): 756-761.

------------------ "A Comment on Unimodality of the distribution of Record Statistics." Statistics & Probability Letters. 64(2003): 39-40.

Aliev, F.A and M. Ahsanullah. "On Characterizations of Discrete Distributions through Regressions of Record Values", Pakistan Journal of Statistics. 18, no. 3 (2002) 415-421.

Alpuim, T.M. ":Record Values in Populations with Increasing or Random Dimensions", Metron, 43, No.3-4 (1985):145-155.

AlZaid, A.A. and M. Ahsanullah "A Characterization of the Gumbell Distribution Based on Record Values". Communications in Statistics, 32, NO.11 (2003):2101,2108.

Arnold, B.C. Pareto Distributions. Fairland, Maryland. International Co-operative Publishing House.1983.

Arnold, B.C. and N. Balakrishnan, Relations, Bounds and Approximations for Order Statistics, Lecture Notes in Statistics No. 53. New York, NY. Springer-Verlag, 1989.

Arnold, B.C , N. Balakrishnan, and H.N. Nagaraja Records. New York, NY: John Wiley and Sons Inc. 1998.

Arslan,G. M.Ahsanullah and I.G.Bairamov ." On characterization properties of the uniform distribution.2003: (unpublished).

Azlarov, T. A. and N.A.Volodin, Characterization Problems Associated with the Exponential Distribution. New York, NY. Springer-Verlag, 1986.

Bairamov, I.G . ". Some Distribution Free Properties of Statistics Based on Record Values and Characterizations of the Distributions Through a Record", Journal of Applied Statistical Science. 5, no.1 (1997):17-25.

Bairamov, I.G and M. Ahsanullah, "Distributional Relations Between Order Statistics and the Sample itself and Characterizations of Exponential Distribution." Journal of Applied Statistical Science.10, no.1 (2000): 1-16.

Bairamov, I.G and S. Kotz,. "On Distributions of Exceedances Associated with Order Statistics and Record Values for Arbitrary Distributions". Statistical Papers 42 (2001): 171-185.

Balakrishnan, N and M. Ahsanullah. "Recurrence Relations for Single and Product Moments of Record Values from Generalzed Pareto Distribution", Communications in Statistics- Theory and Methods.23 (1994a):2841-2852.

.--------------------.." Relations for Single and Product Moments of Record Values from Lomax Distribution", Sankhya B,56,no.2 (1994b): 140-146..

--------------------. "Relations for Single and Product Moments of Record Values from Exponential Distribution", Journal of Applied Statistical Science 2 (1995):73-87..

Balakrishnan, N., M. Ahsanullah, and P.S.Chan. "Relations for Single and Product Moments of Record Values from Gumbel Distribution", Statistics & Probability Letters 15 (1992):223-227.

---------------------- "On the Logistic record Values and Associated Inference", Journal of Applied Statistical Science 2 (1995):233-248..

Balakrishnan, N, K. Balasubramanian, "A Characterization of Geometric Distribution Based on Record Values", Journal of Applied Statistical Science 2,no.3 (1995): 277-282.

Balakrishnan, N, P.S. Chan and M. Ahsanullah. " Recurrence relations for moments of record values from generalized extreme value distribution", Communications in Statistics-Theory and Methods 22 (1993):1471-1482.

Ballerini, R. and S.I..Resnick,. "Records from Improving Populations", Journal of Applied Probability 22 (1985):487-502.

---------------------- "Records in presence of a Linear Trend", Advances in Applied Probability 19 (1995):801-828.

Barton, D. E. and C. L Mallows "Some Aspects of the Random Sequence", Annals of Mathematical Statistics 36,(1965): 236-260.

Basak, P. "Lower Record Values and Characterization of Exponential Distribution". Calcutta Statistical Association Bulletin, 46 (1996): 1-7.

Blaquez, F.L., J.L.Rebollo "A Characterization of Distributions Based on Linear Regression of Order Statistics and Record Values", Sankhya 59,A (1997): 311-323.\

Blom,G. D.Thorburn, and T. Vessey. "The Distribution of the Record Position and its Applications". American Statistician 44 (1990):152-153.

Bruss , F.T. "Invariant Record Processes and Applications to Best Choice Modeling", Stochastic Processes and Applications 17 (1988): 331-338.

Bunge, J.A. and H.N. Nagaraja.. "Exact Distribution Theory for Some Point Process Record Models". Advances in Applied Probability 24(1992):20-44.

Chandler, K. N. "The Distribution and Frequency of Record Values". Journal of Royal Statistical Society,14,B (1952): 220-228.

Cinlar, E. Introduction to Stochastic Processes. New Jersey: Prentice-Hall, 1975.

Dallas, A.C. "Record Values and the Exponential Distribution", Journal of Applied Probability 18 (1981a): 959-951.

-------------. "A Characterization Using Conditional Variance", Metrika 28 (1981b): 151-153.

David, H.A. Order Statistics. Second Edition. New York: John Wiley and Sons, Inc., 1981..

DeHaan, L. and S.I. Resnick.. "Almost Sure Limit Points of Record Values", Journal of Applied Probability 10, (1973):528-542.

Deheuvels, P. " The Complete Characterization of the Upper and Lower Class of Record and Inter - Record Times of i.i.d. Sequence", Zeitschrift fuer Wahrschcinlichkeits theorie und Verwandte Gabiete 6 (1983):1-6.

-------------." The Characterization of Distributions by Order Statistics and Record Values - an Unified Approach.", Journal of Applied Probability 21 (1984): 326-334.

Deken, J.G. "Record Values, Scheduled Maxima Sequences", Journal of Applied Probability 15 (1978): 491-496.

Dembinska, A. and J. Wesolowski. "Linearity of Prediction for Non-adjacent Record Values", Journal of Statistical Planning and Inference 90 (2000): 195-205.

---------------- " Constancy of Regression for size two record spacings:.Pakistan Journal of Statistics 19 no.1 (2003):143-149.

Dunsmore, J.R. "The Future Occurrence of Records", Annals of the Institute of Statistical Mathematics 35 (1983): 267-277.

Dwass, M. "External Processes", Annals of Mathematical Statistics 35 (1964): 1718-1725.

Embrechts, P. and E. Omey. "On Subordinated Distributions and Random Record Processes", Mathematical Proceedings of the Cambridge Philosophical Society 93 no.3(1983):339-353.

Feller, W. An Introduction to Probability Theory and its Applications. Volume II. New York, NY. John Wiley & Sons.,1966.

Forteet, F.G. and A. Stuart. " Distribution - Free Tests in Time Series Based on the Breaking of Records",.Journal of Royal Statistical Society 16, B,(1954):2-22..

Forteet, F.G. and D. Teichroew . "A Sampling Experiment on the Powers of the Record Tests for a Trend in a Time Series", Journal of Royal Statistical Society 17,B (1955):115-121.

Franco, M. and J.M.Ruiz. (2001). "On Characterizations of Distributions by Expected Values of Order Statistics and Record Values with Gap", Metrika, 45 (1955):107-119.

-------------------------.."Characterization of Discrete distributions based on conditional expectations of Record Values", Statistical Papers 42,(2001):101-110.

Galambos, J. The Asymptotic Theory of Extreme Order Statistics.. Second Edition. Malabar, Florida. Robert E. Krieger Publishing Co, ,1987.

Galambos, J. and S. Kotz Characterizations of Probability Distributions. Lecture Notes in Mathematics. No. 675, New York, NY : Springer Verlag , 1978.

Galambos, J and E. Seneta. " Record Times", Proceedings of the American Mathematical Society 50 (1975):383-387.

Galambos, J and I. Simonelli. Bonferroni-type Inequalities with Applications. New York, NY :Springer Verlag. 1996.

Gajek, L. and U. Gather "Characterizations of the Exponential Distribution by Failure Rate and Moment Properties of Order Statistics" .in Lecture Notes in Statistics, 51. Extreme Value Theory Proceedings 1996:114-124. J. Husler, R.D. Reiss(Eds).. Berlin, Germany: Springer- Verlag, 1996.

Gaver, D. "Random Record Models", Journal of Applied Probability 13 (1976): 538-547.

Gaver, D. and Jacobs, P.A.. "Non Homogeneously Paced Random Records and Associated Extremal Processes", Journal of Applied Probability 15 (1978): 543-551.

Glick N. "Breaking Records and Breaking Boards". American Mathematical Monthly 85, no. 1 (1978): 2-26.

Gnedenko, B. "Sur la Distribution Limite du Terme Maximum d'une Serie Aletoise", Ann. Math. 44 (1943): 423-453.

Goldburger, A. S. " Best Linear Unbiased Predictors in the Generalized Linear Regression Model", Journal of American Statistical Association 57 (1962):369-375.

Goldie, C.M.. "Records, Permutations and Greatest Convex Minorants", Mathematical Proceedings of the Cambridge Philosophical Society 106 (1989):169-177.

Goldie, C.M. and S.I. Resnick, "Records in Partially Ordered Set". Annals of Probability. 17 (1989): 675-689.

-------------------------- "Many Multivariate Records", Stochastic Processes and Their Applications. 59 (1995): 185-216..

Goldie, C.M. and , L.C.G , Rogers "The k - Record Processes are i.i.d", Zeitschrift fuer Wahrschcinlichkeitstheorie und Verwandte Gabiete. 67 (1984): 97-211.

Gradshteyn, I.S. and I.M. Ryzhik. Tables of Integrals, Series, and Products, New York, NY: Academic Press Inc..Corrected and Enlarged Edition.,1980.

Grosswald, E. and S. Kotz, "An Integrated Lack of Memory Property of the Exponential Distribution", Annals of the Institute of Statistical Mathematics 33, A (1980):205-214.

Grudzien, Z. and D. Szynal "On the Expected Values of kth Record Values and Characterizations of Distributions" in Probability and Statistical Decision Theory A.,1985:119-127.(F. Konecny , J. Mogyorodi and W. Wertz, Eds.), Budapest, Hungary: Dordrecht – Reidel, 1985.

Gulati, S. and W.J Padgett. "Nonparametric Quantile Estimation from Record Breaking Data", Australian Journal of Statistics 36(1994a):211-223.

-------------------"Smooth Nonparametric Estimation of Distribution and Density Function from Record Breaking Data", Communications in Statistics-Theory and Methods 23 (1994b): 1259-1274.

--------------------- "Smooth nonparametric Estimation of the Hazard and Hazard Rate Functions from Record Breaking Data", Journal of Statistical Planning and Inference 42 (1994c): 331-341.

Gumbel, E.J.. Statistics of Extremes. New York, NY: Columbia Univ. Press, 1958.

-------------- ". Bivariate Exponential distributions", Journal of American Statistical Association 55 (1960):698-707.

Gupta, R. C. " Relationships between Order Statistic and Record Values and Some characterization Results", Journal of Applied Probability 21, (1984):425-430.

Gupta, R.C. and S..N.U.A. Kirmani "Closures and Monotonicity Prpperties of Non-Homogenious Poisson Processes and Record Values.",Probability in Engineering and Informational Sciences 2, (1988): 475-484.

Gut, A. "Convergence rates for Record Times and the Associated Covering Processes", Stochastic Processes and Their Applications 36, (1990 a):135-152.

Guthrie, G. L. and Holmes, P. T. "On Record and Inter-Record Times of a Sequence of Random Variables Defined on a Markov Chain", Advances in Applied Probability 7 (1975): 195-214.

Haghighi- Tabab, D. and Wright, E "On the Distribution of Records in a Finite Sequence of Observations, with an Application to a Road Traffic Problem "Journal of Applied Probability 10, (1973):556-571.

Haiman, G. "Almost Sure Asymptotic Behavior of the Record and Record Time Sequences of a Stationary Time Series". New Perspective in Theoretical and Applied Statistics,1987: 459-466. M.L. Puri, J.P. Vilaplana and W. Wertz, Eds. New York, NY:John Wiley,1987. New York,

Haiman, G, Mayeur, N.,and Nevzorov, V.B. and Puri, M.L. "Records and 2-Block Records of 1- dependent Stationary Sequences under Local Dependence", Annals Institute . Henri poincare 34 (1998): 481-503.

Haimann,G. and V.B.Nevzorov. "Stochastic Ordering of the Number of Records" Stochastic Theory and Applications. Papers in Honor of H.A. David, 1996: 105-116. H.N. Nagaraja, P.K. Sen and D.F. Morison, eds, Berlin, Germany: Springer Verlag, 1996.

Hall, P. "Representations and Limit Theorems for Extreme Value Distributions", Journal of Applied Probability. 15 (1975):639-644.

Hill, B.M. "A Simple General Approach to Inference about the Tail of a Distribution", Annals of Statistics. 3 (1975): 1163-1174.

Holmes, P.T. and W. Strawderman, "A Note on the Waiting Times between Record Observations", Journal of Applied Probability 6 (1969):. 711-714.

Horwitz, J. "Extreme Values from a Non Stationary Stochastic Process: an Application to Air Quality Analysis (with discxussion)", Technometrics 22 (1980):469-482.

Huang, Wen-Jang and Shun-Hwa Li, "Characterization Results Based on Record Values", Statistica Sinica, 3 (1993):583-599.

Jenkinson, A.F. (1955)."The Frequency Distribution of the Annual Maximum (or minimum) values of Meteorological Elements", Quarterly Journal of Meteorological 87 (1955):158-171.

Johnson, N.L. and S. Kotz. Distributions in Statistics: Continuous Multivariate Distributions. New York, NY: John Wiley Inc.,1977.

Kakosyan, A. V., L.B. Klebanov and J.A.Melamed. Characterization of Distribution by the Method of Intensively Monotone Operators. Lecture Notes Math. 1088. New York, N.Y. Springer Verlag ,1984.

Karlin, S.. A First Course in Stochastic Processes. New York, NY: Academic Press, 1966.

Kirmani, S.N.U.A. and M.I.Beg. "On Characterization of Distributions by Expected Records", Sankhya 48 A (1983): 463-465.

Klebanov, L. B. and J.A.Melamed.. "A Method Associated with Characterizations of the exponential distribution", Annals of the Institute of Statistical Mathematics 35,A (1983):105-114.

Korwar, R.M. "On Characterizing Distributions for which the Second Record has a Linear Regression on the First ", Sankhya B 46 (1984): 108-109.

\-\-\-\-\-\-\-\-\-\-\-\-\-\- "Some Partial Ordering Results on Record Values". Communications in Statistics-Theory and Methods.19 no. 1, (1990):299-306.

Lau, Ka-sing and C.R.Rao "Integrated Cauchy Functional Equation and Characterization of the Exponential", Sankhya A, 44 (1962): 72-90.

Leadbetter, M.R.,G.Lindgreen and H.Rootzen. Extremes and Related Properties of Random Sequences and Series, New York, 1983.

Lin, G.D. "On Characterizations of Distributions Via Moments of Record Values", Probability Theory and the Related Fields 74 (1987):479-483.

\-\-\-\-\-\-\-\-\-\-\-\-\- " Characterizations of uniform distributions and of exponential distributions. Sankhya, A, 49, 272-273.

Lloyd, E.H. "Least Squares Estimation of Location and Scale Parameters Using Order Statistics", Biometrika 39 (1952): 88-95.

Malov, S.V. "Sequential τ-ranks", Journal of Applied Statistical Science 5 (1997): 211-224.

Mann, N.R. "Optimum Estimators for Linear Functions of Location and Scale Parameters", Annals of Mathematical Statistics 40 (1969) :2149-2155.

Marsglia,G. and A. Tubilla.. "A Note on the Lack of Memory Property of the Exponential Distribution.", Annals of Probability 3 (1975): 352-354.

Mellon, B. The Olympic Record Book. New York, NY: Garland Publishing, Inc. ,1988.

Mohan, N.R. and S.S. Nayak. "A Characterization Based on the Equidistribution of the First Two Spacings of Record Values", "Zeitschrift fuer Wahrschcinlichkeitstheorie und Verwandte Gabiete Z. 60 (1982) : 219-221.

Nagaraja, H. N. "On a Characterization Based on Record Values", Australian Journal of Statistics. 19, (1977):70-73.

-------------- "On the Expected Values of Record Values", .Australian Journal of Statistics. 20 (1978): 176-182.

-------------- "Record Values and Related Statistics -- a Review", Communications in Statistics-Theory and Methods 17 (1988): 2223-2238.

Nagaraja, H. N, and V. B, Nevzorov. "On characterizations Based on Record Values and Order Statistics", Journal of statistical Planning and Inference. 61 (1977) : 271-284.

Nagaraja, H. N, P. Sen, and R. C. Srivastava, "Some Characterizations of Geometric Tail Distributions Based on Record Values", Statistical Papers 30 (1989).:147-155.

Nayak, S.S. "Characterizations Based on Record Values", Journal of Indian Statistical Association. 19 (1981). 123-127.

--------------. "Record Values for and Partial Maxima of a Dependent Sequence", Journal of Indian Statistical Association 23 (1985): 109-125.

Neuts, M.F. "Waiting Times Between Record Observations", Journal of Applied Probability 4 (967). 206-208.

Nevzorova, L,,V.B. Nevzorov and N. Balakrishnan, "Characterizations of distributions by extreme and records in Archimedian copula processes." (1997):469-478. In Advances in the Theory and Pratice of Statisttics- A volume in Honor of Samuel Kotz (Eds. N.L. Johnson and N. Balakrishnan), New York: John Wiley and Sons. 1997.

Nevzorov, V. B. " Records", Theoretical Probability and Applications. l. 32 (1988):201-228.

--------------. "A Characterization of Exponential Distributions by Correlation between Records". Mathematical Methods of Statistics. 1 (1992): 49-54.

--------------. "Asymptotic distributions of Records in Non –stationary Schemes", Journal of Statistical Planning and Inference 45 (1995): 261-273.

----------. Records: Mathematical Theory. Translation of Mathematical Monographs, Volume 194. Providence, RI: American Mathematical Society, 2001.

Nevzorov, V.B. and M. Ahsanullah "Some Distributions of Induced Records", Biometrical Journal 42, no.8 (2000):1069-1081.

-----------------------"Extremes and Records for Concomitants of Order Statistics and Record Values." , Journal Of Applied Statistical Science 10 , no,3 (2001):181-190.

Oncel.S.Y., M. Ahsanullah, M,Gebizlioglu and F.A. Aliev. "Characterization of Geometric Distribution through Normal and Weak Record Values". Stochastic Modelling and Applications. 4, no.1 (2001): 53-58.

Pawlas, P. and D. Szynal. "Recurrence Relations for Single and Product Moments of K-th Record Values From Pareto, ,Generalized Pareto and Burr Distributions", Communications in Statistics-Theory and Methods 28 no.7 (1999): 1699-1701.

Pfeifer, D. "Asymptotic Expansions for the Mean and Variance of Logarithmic Inter-Record Times", Methods in Oprations.39, (1981).113-121.

-------------- "Characterizations of Exponential Distributions by Independent Non Stationary Increments", Journal of Applied Probability 19 (1982): 127-135.

--------------. ".Limit Laws for Inter-Record Times for Non Homogeneous Markov chains". Journal of Operational Behavior and Statistics 1 (1988):69-74.

Pickands III, J. "The Two Dimensional Poisson Process and Extremal Processes", Journal of Applied Probability 8 (1971): 745-756.

Rahimov, I. "Record Values of a family of Branching Processes", IMA Volumes in Mathematics and its Application. 84 (1995): 285-295.

Rahimov, I and M. Ahsanullah, "Records Generated by the total Progeny of Branching Processes", Far East Journal of Theoretical Statistics. 5 no.10 (2001): 81-84.

-----------------------------"Records Related to Sequence of Branching Stochastic Process", Pakistan Journal of Statistics 19 (2003): 73-98.

Ramachandran, B. and R.S.Lau,). Functional Equations in Probability Theory. Boston, MA: Academic Press,1991.

Rao, C.R. and D.N Shanbhag,. "Recent Approaches for Characterizations Based on Order Statistics and Record Values" .In Handbook of Statistics, (N. Balakrishnan and C.R. Rao eds.) 10 (1998): 231-257.

Raqab, M.Z. "Bounds Based on Greatest Convex Minorants for Moments of Record Values", Statistics and Probability Letters 36 (1997): 35-41.
---------------.." Characterizations of Distributions Based on Conditional Expectations of Record Values", Statistics and Decisions. 20 (2002): 309-319.

Raqab, M. Z. and M. Ahsanullah. "Relations for Marginal and Joint Moment Generating Functions of Record Values From Power Function Distribution". Journal of Applied Statistical Science 10, NO.1 (2000): 27-36.,

--------------."On Moment Generating Functions of Records from Extreme Value Distributions", Pakistan Journal of Statistics 19 no.1,(2003): 1-13.

Raqab, M. Z. and M. Ahsanullah and V.B. Nevzorov. " Concomitants of Ordered Random Variables. Journal of Statistical Theory and Applications 1, no.1 (2002):15-26..

Raqab, M.Z. and Amin, W.A. "A Note on Reliability Properties of k Record Statistics", Metrika 46 (1997): 245-251.

Reiss, R.D. Approximate Distributions of Order Statistics., New York, N.Y: Springer-Verlag. 1989.

Renyi, A. "Theorie des Elements Saillants d'une Suit d'observations", Colloquium on Combinatorial Methods in Probability Theory. . Aarhus University (1962): 104-115.

Resnick, S. Extreme Values , Regular Variation and Point Processes. New York: Springer Verlag, 1987..

---------------- " Limit laws for record values. Stochastic Processes and Their Applications 1, no.1, (1973 a): 67-82.

--------------." Record Values and Maxima". Annals of Probability 1, (1973 b): 650-662.

Roberts, E.M. "Revew of Statistics of Extreme Values with Application to Air Quality Data. Part II. Application". J. Air Pollution Control Assoc.29, (1979): 733-740.

Rohtagi,V.K. and G.I. Szekely. "On the background of some correlation inequalities". Journal of Statistical Computation and Simulation, 49,(1992):220-226..

Shah, B.K. "Note on Moments of a Logistic Order Statistics", Annals of Mathematical Statistics. 41, (1970): 2151-2152.

Salamingo, F.J. and L.D. Whitaker "On Estimating Population Characteristics from Record Breaking Observations .I. Parametric Results", Naval Research logistic Quarterly 5, . (1986):.531-543.

Sen, P.K. "On Moments of the Sample Quantiles", Calcutta Statistical association Bulletin. 9(1959):1-19.

Sethuramann, J. "On a Characterization of the Three Limiting Types of Extremes". Sankhya, A. 27 (1965): 357-364.

Shorrock, S. " Record Values and Record Times", Journal of Applied Probability 9 (1972): 316-326.

--------------. " Record Values and Maxima", Annals of Probability 1.(1973a): 650-662.

-------------. " Record Values and Inter-Record Times", Journal of Applied Probability 10 (1973) : 543-555.

Siddiqui, M.M. and R.W. Biondini. " The Joint Distribution of Record Values and Inter-Record Times". Annals of Probability 3 (1975): 1012-1013.

Singpurwala, N.D. "Extreme Values from a Lognormal Law with Applications to Air Population Problems", Technometrics 14, (1972): 703-711.

Smith, R.L. "Extreme Value Theory Based on the r Largest Annual Events", Journal of Hydrology. 86 (1986): 27-43.

------------- and I. Weissman. "Large Deviations of Tail Estimators based on the Pareto Approximations", Journal of Applied Probability 24. (1987): 619-630.

Srivastava, R.C. "Two Characterizations of the Geometric Distribution by Record Values". Sankhya B, 40, (1978): 276-278..

Stam, A.J. "Independent Poisson Processes by Record Values and Inter-Record Times", .Stochastic Processes and Their Applications 19, (1985): 315-325.

Stepanov, A. V. "Characterizations of a Geometric Class of Distributions", Theory of Probability .and Mathematical Statistics, 41, (1990). 133-136 (English Translation)

------------------ ".Limit Theorems for Weak Records", Theory of Probability . and Applications. 37 (1992):579-574 (English Translation).

--------------. "A Characterization Theorem for Weak Records". Theory of Probability and Applications. 38 (1994):762-764 (English Translation)..

-------------- "Records when the Last Point of Increase is an atom", Journal of Applied Statistical Science 9, no. 2, (2001): 161-167..

--------------. "Conditional Moments of Record Times", Statistical Papers. 44 (2003):131-140.

Strawderman, W. and P.T.Holmes. "On the Law of Iterated Logarithm for Inter Record Times", Journal of Applied Probability 7 (1970): 432-439.

Tallie, C. "A Note on Srivastava's Characterization of the Exponential Distribution Based on Record Values". In Statistical Distributions in Scientific Work. Eds. C. Tallie, G.P. Patil and B. Boldessari, Reidel, Dordrecht, 4, (1981): 417-418.

Tata, M.N. "On Outstanding Values in a Sequence of Random Variables", Zeitschrift fuer Wehrscheinlichkeitsththeorie und Verwandte Gebiete 12, (1969):9-20.

Teugels, J.L.). "On Successive Record Values in a Sequence of Independent and Identically Distributed Random Variables".In Statistical Extremes and Applications. (Tiago de Oliveira, Ed.). Dordrecht-Reidel, (1984): 639-650.

Tippett, L.H.C. " On the Extreme Individuals and the Range of Samples Taken from a Normal Population", Biometrika, 17, (1925):364- 387.

Vervaat, W. "Limit Theorems for Records from Discrete Distributions", Stochastic Processes and Their Applications 1 (1973): 317-334.

Weissman, I. "Estimations of Parameters and Large Quantiles Based on the k Largest Observations", Journal of American Statistical Association 73 (1978): 812-815.

Wesolowski, J, and M. Ahsanullah, "Linearity of Regression for Non-adjacent weak Records", Statistica Sinica, 11 (2000): 30-52.

Westcott, M. "The Random Record Model", Proceedings of the Royal Society of London Series A 356 .(1977): 529-547.

-------------- "On the Tail Behavior of Record Time Distributions in a Random Record Process", Annals of Probability 7 (1979): 868-237.

Williams, D. "Renyi's Record Problem and Engel's Series", Bulletin

of the London Mathematical Society 5, (1973): 235-237.

Wu, J. "Characterization of Generalized Mixtures of Geometric and Exponential Distributions Based on Upper Record Values", Statistical Papers, 42, (2001): 123-133.

Yang, M. "On the Distribution of Inter-Record Times in an Increasing Population", Journal of Applied Probability 12, (1975):148-154.

INDEX

Bernoulli Numbers 20,30,282-283
Best Linear Invariant Estimator
  118-120,144-145,153-
  154,167-168,171,174,245-
  247
Best linear Invariant Predictor 98,
Cauchy Functional Equation
  277-280
Distributions
  Beta binomial 202-203
  Beta negative binomial 205-207
  Exponential
    7,13,14,19,20,30,45,61,64,
    75,76,81,83,88,90,98,99,1
    04,106,239,253,266,269,
    290
  Geometric
    181-194,189,193,198-201
  Gumbel 8,10,24,26, 61,102,
    103,111,125,124-126
  Logistic 209-214
  Normal 215-217,248,249,267
  Pareto 12,134,147,148,282
  Power Function 155-176,254
  Rayleigh 218,224-232
  Uniform 175-176,248,250,251
  Weibull 8,61,282,283
  F^α Scheme 269-274
Generalized Extreme Value
  103,107,110,263
Hazard Rate 3,24
k-records 33-59

Limiting Distributions of
  Inter-record Times 249-252
  Record Times 254-256
  Record Values 254-256
  Number of Records 19,38,39
MarkovChain
  34,45,49,180,181,200,
Maximum Likelihood Estimator
  120-122,145-146,168-169
Minimum variance linear unbiased
  Estimator   123-124,,146-
  147,170-171,174,192
Minimum variance linear
  unbiased Estimate
  74,75,98,113- 118,123,
  128,142,147,152, 164-
  167,243
New Better Than Used 13,23,24,29
New Worse Than Used 13,23,24,29
Number of Records 19,38,39
Record Values
  1,2,4,5,7,8,15,27,44,59,60,
  61,62,71,74,97,99,109,110
  ,134,243,246,253,257,258,
  263,335,159
Record Times
  1,25,27,28,33,42,48,94,24
  3,2647,250,257,258
Stirling's number
  35,40,42,245,274-
  277,281,282
Weak Records 195-199

ADELPHI PAPERS 211

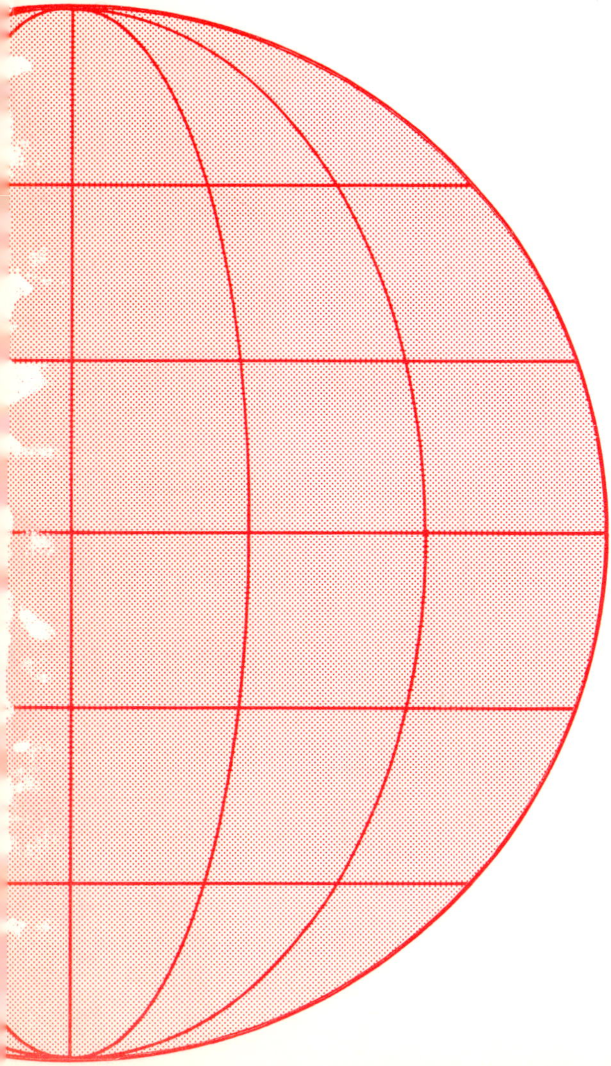

NATO's Out-of-Area Problem

MARC BENTINCK

AUTUMN 1986

ADELPHI PAPER 211

Marc Bentinck wrote this Paper while a Research Associate at the IISS in 1984—5. He is a member of the Netherlands Foreign Service.

The views expressed in this Paper are the author's own and should not be taken to represent the views of the Institute or its members.

First published Autumn 1986 by
the International Institute for Strategic Studies
23 Tavistock Street, London WC2E 7NQ

ISBN 0 86079 105 X
ISSN 0567-932X

©The International Institute for Strategic Studies 1986

All rights reserved. No parts of this publication may be reproduced, stored in a retrieval system, or transmitted in any form or by any means, electronic, mechanical, photo-copying, recording or otherwise, without the prior permission of the International Institute for Strategic Studies.

The International Institute for Strategic Studies was founded in 1958 as a centre for the provision of information on and research into the problems of international security, defence and arms control in the nuclear age. It is international in its Council and Staff, and its membership is drawn from over 80 countries. It is independent of governments and is not the advocate of any particular interest.
The Institute is concerned with strategic questions — not just with the military aspects of security but with the social and economic sources and political and moral implications of the use and existence of the armed force: in other words with the basic problems of peace.
The Institute's publications are intended for a much wider audience than its own membership and are available to the general public on subscription or singly.

Printed in Great Britain by Henry Ling Ltd, The Dorset Press, Dorchester

Contents

Introduction   3
I. The Historical Experience   6
II. Global Dimensions of Western Security: Interests and Vulnerabilities   25
III. Managing Out-of-Area Challenges Inside and Outside NATO   44
Conclusions   63
Notes   67

NATO's-Out-of-Area Problem

INTRODUCTION

The out-of-area issue presents members of the North Atlantic Treaty Organization with the difficulty of balancing their collective interest in North Atlantic security with their variously shared and perceived commitments in other parts of the world. The contest between the demands of NATO and extra-European security needs has been a perennial breeding-ground for intra-Alliance disputes. This competition is known to have complicated the Washington negotiations which led to the signature of the North Atlantic Treaty in 1949. Subsequently, the out-of-area issue arose mainly in the context of the rearguard struggles of particular European NATO Allies to preserve their fading colonial empires. The apparent absence at present of a serious extra-European crisis between the Allies does not necessarily mean that all is well. Certainly, in the eyes of American policy-makers out-of-area challenges remain an unresolved issue within NATO. Under the pressure of unforeseen events outside Europe, the possibility of a serious transatlantic crisis of confidence, which persists behind the out-of-area language of NATO communiqués, could erupt suddenly to the surface. This is apparent in two ways.

First, while more recent out-of-area crises tended to question the present organization of Western security, joint and visible policy responses on the part of the Allies seem to be slow to materialize. The Soviet invasion of Afghanistan in December 1979, unresolved Middle Eastern conflicts, continuing concerns about Western oil security, increasing turmoil in Central America and the rise of state-sponsored terrorism are taking place against a background of growing interdependence of conflicts. In the past, the effects of such conflicts tended to remain localized. Because the Soviet Union is seen today as having a global role, political and economic instability in third-world countries is perceived to be acquiring wider, international dimensions. This instability is often regarded (particularly in the US) as permitting the advancement of Soviet interests. The concerns which these developments have raised within the Western Alliance are indicative of the realization that the deterioration of the West's global security environment could affect critical Allied interests beyond Europe. Although the principal threat to the Western Alliance is still felt to lie in the North Atlantic region, the perceived increase of actual or potential extra-regional vulnerabilities has drawn attention again to the limits of NATO's constitutional area of operations. From the ensuing debate, the view has been emerging that events beyond the formal geographical boundaries stipulated by Article VI of the North Atlantic Treaty may increasingly have implications for Western security. Some member governments have always argued so, and the Allies acknowledged this view officially in their 1982 Bonn Summit Declaration, as well as in recent communiqués following ministerial sessions of NATO's North Atlantic Council and the Defence Planning Committee. However, any amendment to Article VI which might broaden NATO's military purview is ruled out. An initiative to that effect would be tantamount to opening a Pandora's box of Allied disputes, from which NATO might never recover.

Second, the reaffirmation under the first Reagan Administration of the United States' global security commitments has redirected the out-of-area debate towards the forms of support which the European NATO Allies could or should give to American planning for out-of-area contingencies. The latter issue is not likely to be resolved easily in view of the persistent transatlantic, as well as intra-European, divergencies in reactions to the following dilemmas. Can the members of a pluralistic political alliance generate common views of, and co-ordinated responses to, a wide array of out-of-area vulnerabilities which do not amount to a single, overriding and unifying threat? To what extent should the out-of-area dynamics of the global super-power contest be allowed to undermine the management of East-West relations in Europe and the privileged nature of Western Europe's relations with many third-world countries? Can NATO or its members realistically plan for out-of-area contingencies, at a time when the transatlantic debate on 'division of labour' and 'burden-sharing' is calling into question the organization and adequacy of the common defence effort in Europe?

These are dilemmas whose existence the Allies cannot deny but nor can they be easily solved. On the one hand, the idea that Allied co-operative reflexes should halt at NATO's formal treaty boundaries conveys a sense of dangerous arbitrariness, at a time when global interdependence militates against the continued insulation of North Atlantic security from developments elsewhere in the world. On the other hand, out-of-area issues also constitute the field where Allied interests are certain to be least in line and where co-operation appears most difficult to achieve. Both unilateral actions undertaken by particular Allies and attempts to evolve Alliance-wide viewpoints and responses thus present the risk of dividing the Alliance.

NATO's out-of-area problem is not unmanageable, however. There is scope for practical, *ad hoc* co-operation between those Allies which possess both the political will and capabilities to protect essential Western out-of-area interests, as the regular US, British and French naval presence in and close to the Persian Gulf demonstrates. Moreover, out-of-area interventions directly or indirectly in support of Western interests need not be an exclusively American security burden. British and French defence activities outside the NATO area are already significant enough to lend credibility to the notion of a European military contribution to the management of out-of-area contingencies. Also, it can at least be argued that Western – and especially Western European – aid provided to developing countries is helping to address some of the socio-economic factors contributing to third-world instability.

This implies that NATO's out-of-area problem might require not so much a net increase of extra-regional involvement on the part of the Allies, but rather the elaboration of some ground rules to enable the Allies to co-ordinate better the efforts which they are already making. Yet, even this modest goal will be hard to attain. The out-of-area issue brings into sharp relief the whole question of the readjustment of intra-Alliance relationships. Thus the US currently expects its European Allies to devote greater resources to the execution of what they perceive as essentially American out-of-area policies, at a time when attempts are being made to reinforce both the European identity within NATO and the process of European Political Cooperation (EPC). Both the feasibility and the effects of such measures as Allied intelligence sharing and crisis consultation with respect to out-of-area questions are, in other words, likely to reflect the uncertainties surrounding the substantive and institutional aspects of an expanded European security role within the Western Alliance.

This Paper will focus on the Alliance, as well as on the national factors bearing upon the out-of-area problem, with a view to the better political management of an issue which is inherent in the nature of the Treaty underlying the North Atlantic Alliance. By seeking to identify judicious forms of extra-European security co-operation, some of which are in fact already taking place, this Paper will help to dispel claims that NATO Allies are unwilling or unable – or both – to take combined action outside the area of formal treaty commitments. Not only do such claims tend to have little basis in reality, but they are also largely responsible for the sterile quality of recurrent out-of-area recriminations between the Allies, especially in the transatlantic context. Chapter I will look back at some past examples of out-of-area contingencies, in order to outline the basic dilemmas which have shaped Allied discussions of, and reactions to the problem. Chapter II will examine the present and, where possible, future dimensions of the issues which the out-of-area problem raises for particular Allies and for the Alliance as a whole. More specifically, Chapter II will seek to assess the relative weight of the various economic, political and military vulnerabilities which are often cited as evidence of the West's deteriorating security posture out-of-area.

The final Chapter will suggest ways to manage the out-of-area problem, taking into account both the distinct perceptions, vulnerabilities and capabilities of NATO's diverse membership and the interests of the Alliance itself.

I. THE HISTORICAL EXPERIENCE

The North Atlantic Pact is more than a traditional alliance within the zone of the military blocs, it is less than a traditional alliance outside that zone.
(*RAYMOND ARON*)[1]

What limits to the Alliance?
The global connotations of the term 'Western Alliance' are not well supported by the nature of the commitments which have bound North America and Western Europe since 1949. Both the formulation of the key provisions of the North Atlantic Treaty, and their actual significance in international life, reveal the rather limited and one-sided nature of the arrangements underlying the Western Alliance. This is true in the functional and in the geographical sense.

Although the Treaty contains language about the promotion of 'stability and well-being' and the encouragement of economic collaboration (Article II), in fact the Alliance was designed for the overriding purpose of maintaining security. While the vagueness of these non-military goals reassured some of the signatories, especially the United States, they disappointed others.[2] Although the security guarantee established in Article V of the Treaty is of a multilateral and mutual nature, this was done in deference to the wounded pride of its European signatories. The real guarantee was – and continues to be – a unilateral American pledge to secure Western Europe against Soviet aggression. Moreover, the implementation of the security guarantee, whether unilateral or not, was subjected to 'consultations' on the express wish of the American Congress which did not want to see the US dragged automatically into yet another intra-European war. In turn, this reflects how, from the very beginning, varying estimates of national self-interest qualified the core provisions of the Treaty. Although some European signatories to the Treaty possessed distant and still important colonial interests, which in 1949 had already come under pressure, American insistence that the area of Treaty commitments remain limited prevailed. Thus the geographical purview of the Alliance in 1949 was restricted essentially to the territories of its members in Europe and North America and to that portion of the Atlantic Ocean lying north of the Tropic of Cancer. Despite US objections, Algeria was also included under the terms of Article VI, only because France was able to point out that it constituted an integral part of its metropolitan territory. But, significantly British, French and US *bases* in Cyprus, Algeria and Libya were not included.

Studies of the preliminary talks in Washington which led to the signature of the North Atlantic Treaty reveal substantial differences of opinion between the participants as to the functional and geographical scope of the kind of Alliance which they had in mind.[3] Albeit muted in form, these differences found their way into the Treaty. From them ambiguities emerged, which have attended NATO's subsequent existence and foiled repeated attempts to broaden NATO's limited premise into a truly political alliance of equal partners geared to the management of Western global interests. Among other issues, the geopolitical limits of the Alliance have been – and continue to be – both cause and effect of the failure to transform NATO into something which manifestly it is not.

NATO's geographical limits?
If the Alliance was to be conceived regionally, the precise delimitation of its geographical scope did not appear to be self-evident. By agreeing to the two-phased extension of the Atlantic security concept into the Mediterranean, the Allies in fact tackled their first 'out-of-area problem'. Fear of Anglo-Saxon dominance in NATO prompted France to insist on inviting Italy to accede to the North Atlantic Treaty in 1949. The original Atlantic identity of the Alliance was further diluted by the admission, despite initial Danish and Norwegian objections, of Greece and Turkey in October 1951 at the initiative of the United States. Greece and Turkey had been the first two countries to benefit from the 1947 Truman Doctrine, in the form of direct American financial and political support for the struggle against Communist subversion and Soviet pressure. Although the Western counter-attack in both countries is usually identified with the US relieving Britain of its imperial commitments in the Eastern Mediterranean, the British government at the time hoped to sustain these commitments with the United States 'providing the cash but not the strategy'.[4] By 1950, however, Anglo-American rivalry in the Eastern Mediterranean was largely at an end. Increasingly Greece and Turkey became integrated into NATO's planning for the defence of what came to be known as the Southern Flank. Subsequently, the establishment of US naval and air bases in Greece and Turkey, from which nuclear strikes could be carried out against the Soviet Union, reflected the role of these two NATO allies in America's global containment strategy of the 1950s.

Judging by the intractable nature of the disputes between Greece and Turkey, the extension of NATO membership beyond the Atlantic area has been a mixed blessing. A more recent example of the same phenomenon can be found in the temporary uncertainties created by Spain's accession to the North Atlantic Treaty in May 1982, in the light of the subsequent decision of the Socialist government in Madrid to freeze the process of military integration in NATO, pending the outcome of a referendum on Spain's membership. These uncertainties were only lifted in March 1986 when, against most predictions, a convincing majority of the Spanish voters were in favour of continued Spanish membership in NATO. While the outcome of the referendum barred full integration of the Spanish armed forces under NATO command, nevertheless it cleared the way for a subsequent agreement on the terms under which Spain will co-operate militarily with the Alliance.[5]

Both these developments should at last settle a number of issues raised by Spain's presence in the Alliance. These include the adjustment of bilateral military relations between Spain and the US, as well as Spain's wish to involve NATO in the defence of its North African enclaves of

Ceuta and Melilla – a wish to which the other NATO allies are not likely to accede. In a more general sense, the confirmation of Spanish membership of NATO, apart from giving the Alliance a greater Mediterranean and North African focus, can be expected to add to the diversity of Allied reactions towards out-of-area events, as Spain's reactions to the Falklands War seemed to suggest.

The geographical limits of the Alliance were also brought into focus by NATO's maritime contingency planning for the southern hemisphere.[6] As the number of African ports from which Western naval forces could operate was dwindling rapidly in the wake of decolonization, Portugal's base facilities in West Africa and Mozambique – as well as South Africa's location – acquired greater strategic importance. Yet, from the early 1960s, Portugal faced increasing political isolation in NATO for its attempts to hang on to its African possessions. Although Portuguese Africa seems to have been included at one time in NATO's contingency plans, Portugal's wish to secure a NATO role for its naval bases in Africa was never translated into policy.[7] A similar episode was NATO's alleged naval co-operation with South Africa. In October 1972 NATO's Defence Planning Committee (DPC) authorized the Supreme Allied Commander Atlantic (SACLANT) to investigate the growing threat which the Soviet Navy was perceived to pose to Allied shipping using the Cape route.[8] Speculations that contacts existed between NATO and the South African Navy could be explained in part by the fact that, at the time, Britain still had access to the South African naval base of Simonstown. Moreover, South Africa had made no secret, for obvious reasons, of its interest in military co-operation with NATO. Yet the alleged contacts did not take place, in view of the growing sensitivity within the Alliance to international criticisms of apartheid. Thus, the political implications of NATO's maritime contingency planning tended to become an intra-Alliance issue in itself.

Both episodes illustrate the contrast between the global retreat of Western power since the late 1950s and the growing unwillingness of the Alliance to contemplate any expansion of the NATO area, even for the limited purposes of joint maritime contingency planning. While out-of-area issues have turned the 'limits-of-alliance' problem into an almost permanent theme for discussion within the Alliance, their practical effect has been, if anything, to confirm NATO's existing geographical boundaries. To all intents and purposes the area covered by the mutual security guarantee of Article V of the North Atlantic Treaty now includes the following territories and seas: the territories of the signatory states in Europe and North America; Turkey; the European waters – the Channel, North Sea, Baltic Sea (in practice as far as the Danish island of Bornholm) – Norwegian Sea (in practice as far as the 25th degree of longitude) and the Mediterranean, minus the territorial waters of non-NATO members; the Atlantic Ocean north of the Tropic of Cancer and, within that zone, the islands under jurisdiction of the signatory states, and ships and aircraft of the signatory states when in or over the above-mentioned areas.

How far does Allied solidarity extend?
Strictly speaking, out-of-area events fall within the national competence of those allied governments which happen or wish to be involved. From an Alliance point of view, they are expected to manage their respective extra-regional interests on the strength of their own political and military resources. Nevertheless, some Allies at times have felt the need to enlist NATO support for their national out-of-area involvements. Thus attempts have been made by nations to establish a requirement for allied solidarity beyond the NATO area. The record of consensus-building is distinctly mixed. The timing, form and origins of these attempts reflect the quite baffling interaction of changes within the global, transatlantic, Western European and domestic environments of the Alliance. This conclusion is suggested by the fluctuating, at times converging, at times diverging, objectives of NATO's three main out-of-area actors – Britain, France and the United States.

BRITAIN
Britain's out-of-area role reflects its gradual but inexorable retreat from an imperial power to the interests and capabilities of a medium-rank European state. In practice, several factors have influenced both the pace and direction of that process. First, until the late 1960s out-of-area interventions, such as those in Jordan (1958), Kuwait (1961), Cyprus (1963), Malaysia (1963–66) and East Africa (1964), seemed to sustain Britain's claim to a global role, albeit a diminished one. By the mid-1970s, however, years of financial duress at home had left little of Britain's extra-European security role, both in terms of overseas military presence and interventionary capabilities. British forces had been, or were being, withdrawn from Singapore and Malaysia, as well as from the Persian Gulf. British units available for out-of-area interventions, as well as airlift capabilities, had become quite modest.[9] While the sequence of events which threatened regional stability in South-west Asia in 1978–80 led Britain to reaffirm the need for a British contribution to American contingency planning to counter Soviet out-of-area threats,[10] Britain seemed less well placed than France by the 1980s to project military power out-of-area. This applied particularly to the Gulf region and to the Indian Ocean where, as late as 1967, Britain had possessed some key strategic assets for the protection of Western interests in the area.

Second, Britain's out-of-area policies have been shaped by the prospects, the limitations and the later erosion of the 'special relationship' with the United States. The undisputable intimacy of the Anglo-American partnership, with respect to the build-up of NATO and bilateral defence co-operation,[11] encouraged British policy-makers during the 1950s to believe that the special relationship would also work in matters of global strategy. More moderately, Britain assumed that Anglo-American co-operation was the best way to further Western interests in the Third World. The special relationship actually worked both ways. On the one hand it favoured the revival of a genuine Anglo-American partnership in arms – as had occurred during the Korean War.[12] On the other, the very intimacy of the special relationship could also accentuate existing policy differences with regard to global strategy. Thus Britain's traditional policy of diplomatic realism and its Commonwealth commitments clashed with both the spirit and the purpose of American containment policies over the issue of granting recognition to Communist China.[13] Conversely, America's growing absorption in the imperatives of the worldwide anti-Communist struggle led it to dissociate itself from British policies, when these were perceived to alienate client states and dependencies. This was particularly the case in the Middle East, an area where US and British policies had never been in real accord.[14] American efforts since the end of World War II to develop close ties with a number of Middle Eastern states could only take place at the expense of British influence in the region. The US deliberately refrained from backing its political and commercial penetration of Iran, Iraq, Libya and Saudi Arabia with significant military presences, thereby leaving the overstretched British garrisons in the area to bear the brunt of Arab nationalism. The limits of the special relationship manifested themselves when the US, in contrast to Britain, decided not to adhere to the 1955 Baghdad Pact after having initially encouraged its formation.[15] Latent Anglo-American tensions over the Middle East degenerated into open confrontation during the 1956 Suez Crisis. Close collaboration was soon restored, however, as demonstrated by the co-ordinated intervention of Britain and the US in Jordan and Lebanon respectively in July 1958.[16] The special relationship was virtually disregarded in the Pacific area, where Britain found itself excluded from the 1951 ANZUS Pact between Australia, New Zealand and the US. This also pointed to the more general process of rapidly loosening defence ties between Britain and the Commonwealth, and the corresponding contraction of British post-colonial security commitments.

In terms of military partnership beyond Europe, the Anglo-American relationship dwindled in later years to what has been termed a 'residual relationship',[17] as symbolized by Britain's decisions in 1969 and 1975 respectively no longer to designate British ground forces for the contingency plans of the 1954 South-East Asia Treaty Organization (SEATO)[18] and any forces to the Central Treaty Organization (CENTO). Britain's eventual entry into the European Economic Community (EEC) in 1973 politically confirmed the erosion of the special relationship with America and, correspondingly, the Eurocentric security policies which Britain has tended to pursue since the late 1960s. Yet, although there is no longer much durable substance to the military partnership, it is still easy for Britain and the US to talk the same language and sometimes, as in the South Atlantic in 1982 or in the Red Sea in 1984, to work closely together.

FRANCE

French security policy, on the other hand, has sought persistently to maintain or promote conditions for the preservation of an autonomous, and thereby distinctively French, role within the overall context of the Western Alliance. Translated into the terms of the changing global arena and the fluctuating patterns of intra-Alliance relations, this objective has led French security policy alternately to support and to oppose NATO's strategy. This has been most visible with respect to Allied defence concepts in the European theatre but, to a certain degree, it has also manifested itself out-of-area. As in the case of Britain, French out-of-area policies have been shaped to a considerable extent by decolonization and receding post-imperial security commitments. Unlike the British experience, however, the French retreat from empire was often a bitter process, marked by protracted colonial wars in Indochina and Algeria. In the absence of a special relationship with the US as a means of cushioning the loss of global power, successive French governments during the 1950s saw decolonization as a threat and sought to prevent it. France was inclined therefore to view its attempts to enlist Allied political support for its actions – as well as US bilateral assistance for its colonial war efforts – as tests of its relations with its main security partners. In doing so, French policy-makers argued that France was holding the line in Indochina against the advance of Communism, and that continued French control over North Africa was essential to Allied security in Europe.[19] But while the French engagement in Indochina indeed did generate Allied (and especially US) financial support,[20] the subsequent Algerian War contributed to the deterioration of French relations with the Alliance.[21] French mistrust of American attitudes towards decolonization, which manifested itself in an unwillingness to involve the US in French operations in Indochina, was heightened by the Suez crisis. Resentment over US dominance in the Alliance at the expense of French out-of-area interests played a large part in de Gaulle's call for tripartite decision-making on NATO strategy and Western global policy.[22] For de Gaulle, the international situation in 1958 no longer justified unfettered American leadership of the Alliance and, as he saw it, American determination of French security policy. The subsequent reshaping of French security policy outside NATO's military structure was designed to confer on the French government a margin of manoeuvre from which French international influence and prestige would directly benefit, both in Europe and elsewhere in the world. Apart from the accelerated build-up of an independent nuclear deterrent, this also meant restructuring relations with its former (especially African) colonies on the basis of bilateral defence and economic co-operation agreements,[23] as well as on the reorganization of French interventionary capabilities.[24]

By establishing an independent French out-of-area role, the renewal of France's privileged and exclusive relations with francophone Africa especially enabled it to turn colonial disengagement to its political advantage, and to criticize US global policies openly, especially with respect to Vietnam.[25] However, the limits of that approach became clear after 1975 when Soviet-Cuban penetration in Angola, southern Africa and the Horn came to threaten French interests in Africa.[26] Although France reacted with a series of interventions in Chad, the Western Sahara (Mauritania) and Zaire,[27] French activism in Africa[28] also revealed the inherent limitations of an independent French role. From a political standpoint, the avowed anti-Soviet purpose of some French actions in Africa, by tending to realign France with the Western Alliance in the eyes of French domestic and international public opinion, put into question the autonomy of French security policy. Meanwhile, the Alliance itself refrained from giving France unequivocal support.[29] From a military standpoint, the shortcomings of French logistic and long-range power projection capabilities turned the two interventions in Zaire in 1977 and 1978 into joint Franco-American operations, with the US providing airlift and supplies but *not* combat forces. Once the interventions had achieved their immediate goals, French units withdrew quickly in favour of African peace-keeping forces. The intensification of French military involvement in Africa constitutes a quite severe economic drain on French resources, at the relative expense of economic development aid for Africa. In a more general sense, the belated transformation of Africa into a theatre of East-West competition has revealed the increasing problems for Western security in the area, to which the traditional French presence will only be able to offer partial solutions.[30]

THE UNITED STATES
American attitudes towards the issue of NATO out-of-area solidarity have been influenced by the globalism of America's security policies, the credibility of which remains under constant international scrutiny. Furthermore, three factors have affected the ways in which the US has sought to strike a balance between the expectations generated by its leading position in NATO and other competing strategic priorities: American global power and influence; the evolution of the super-power relationship; and the out-of-area concerns of the European NATO Allies themselves.

During the early years of the Alliance, the US found itself confronted with various attempts by the European powers to make their beleaguered colonial positions a source of concern for the Alliance as a whole. American responses had to balance such conflicting considerations as America's traditional opposition to colonialism, the search for gradual and peaceful change in the Third World in accord with Western interests,[31] the priority of Western European reconstruction, and the need to accommodate Britain and France as two its chief NATO Allies. In practice, the question of American involvement in decolonization struggles came to depend on the perceived source and urgency of a colonial contingency, the degree of engagement of the colonial power (as well as the relative weight of that power in NATO), Congressional opinion and the Western position in the United Nations (UN). American material support for the French in Indochina illustrates this. From the start, US policy-makers saw the French position as precarious, if not untenable in the long run.[32] The Viet Minh posed no threat to NATO and Indochina could not be described as a vital strategic asset. Yet, with the Korean experience and the recent Communist victory in China in mind, it was feared that, once the Korean War was over, China would redeploy its forces against the French in Indochina. The US let the logic of cold-war containment prevail. Moreover, France had committed itself militarily to the extent that the US would have found it difficult to deny assistance to such an important NATO ally, and one which it did not want to alienate in the crucial European theatre at a time when the US was pushing for the rearmament of West Germany.

The 1950s also saw diminishing American expectations of Allied out-of-area solidarity. Psychologically at least, the reshaping of US foreign policy after 1953 under the direction of John Foster Dulles was stimulated by the realization that only *American* power had been able to turn the tide of Communist aggression in Korea. This suggested that the US alone possessed the global capabilities to intervene effectively on behalf of Western interests. From a US perspective, moreover, British and French out-of-area policies remained too self-serving to address the global risks and opportunities presented by the steady emancipation of colonial territories. Last but not least, Soviet initiatives in the Third World worried American policy-makers. After Stalin's death in March 1953, the new Soviet leadership began to emphasize the importance of the Third World in Soviet foreign policy, by courting India as a key non-aligned country.[33] The significance of this development, as well as the acquisition by the Soviet Union of an indisputable and growing nuclear capability, was not lost in Washington. American global policies became shaped increasingly by the imperatives of the super-power relationship.

From an Alliance point of view, American global intervention during the late 1950s and 1960s seemed to tend towards unilateralism. Initially the NATO Allies of the US acquiesced rather passively, with the notable exception of Gaullist France. But global interventionism also drew an over-confident US into the Vietnamese quagmire to relive the earlier French experience on a larger scale. Ironically enough, it was now America's turn to appeal to NATO solidarity. When the Johnson Administration pointed out to the European NATO Allies in 1965 the strategic importance of South-east Asia and the Pacific as 'NATO's Western Flank',[34] it was using the same kind of geopolitical arguments that the European colonial powers had used 15 years before. Not only did Vietnam drain US energies, military resources and prestige, but it also came to be perceived in Washington as a wasteful product of dated cold-war containment policies, policies which did not reflect such changes as the Sino-Soviet split, the declining appeal of anti-Communism and the climate of super-power detente. The 1969 Nixon Doctrine was an attempt to adapt American global security policies to a rapidly changing international situation and, as a corollary, to pre-empt the effects on the Administration's foreign policy powers of growing domestic insurgency against the ability of the President unilaterally to commit American forces to combat abroad – an insurgency which would culminate in the 1973 War

Powers Act. Taking into account the strategic relief offered by the Sino-Soviet split, the Doctrine called on the Asian allies of the US, as well as on Iran, to do more for their own defence against local aggression. At the same time, it maintained existing treaty obligations, especially against aggression from nuclear powers. A concomitant of the Doctrine was the strengthening of regional powers allied with the US, such as Iran, through increased arms deliveries. In reaction to the Vietnam experience, the Nixon, Ford and Carter Administrations also refocused their security policies on traditional areas of American interest, such as Western Europe and the Middle East.

While this limited retrenchment enabled the US to plan its force posture for one-and-a-half wars only, instead of the previous two-and-a-half, global events in the 1970s raised new challenges which a non-interventionist domestic mood made it hard to confront. In 1975, Congress refused to authorize action to prevent the fall of Saigon and voted to cut off all American military and financial assistance to the pro-Western liberation movements in Angola[35] as part of a drive for greater Congressional control over US covert operations abroad. In a more general sense, the reluctant responses of the US to Soviet-Cuban actions in Angola, Zaire and the Horn of Africa revealed a new scepticism about automatic involvement in distant areas where American vital interests did not seem to be directly at stake. Whether this reflected a well-founded rejection of the vision that every event in the Third World had to be forced into an East–West matrix (the 'zero-sum game') or rather an American inability to cope effectively with growing turmoil in the Third World remains to be seen. It took deteriorating security conditions in the Persian Gulf, a traditional area of direct Western interest, for the US to shake off the double trauma of Vietnam and Watergate. Following the British withdrawal from the region, the demise of CENTO in 1979, the Iranian Revolution and the Soviet invasion of Afghanistan, the Carter Doctrine enunciated a new policy of containment in South-west Asia.[36] However, despite the build-up by the Carter and Reagan Administrations of rapid intervention forces for third-world contingencies (in the guise of the Rapid Deployment Joint Task Force (RDJTF)), the various political and military constraints which would govern their use continue to underline the narrowing margins of American global security policies since the 1970s.

Out-of-area solidarity as a transatlantic issue
The problem of Allied solidarity in out-of-area issues has often been discussed in terms of the US–European relationship. Indeed, while temporary coincidences of national interests and perceptions have allowed occasionally for limited Anglo-American and Franco-American out-of-area co-operation, broader transatlantic policy co-ordination outside the NATO area has not developed out of the regular out-of-area paragraphs in NATO communiqués. Rather, out-of-area issues appear to have been the source of strain from time to time between the US on the

one hand, and Britain and France, as well as smaller European NATO members – Belgium, Portugal and the Netherlands – on the other.[37] Support for this view is best found in the evolving pattern of Allied attitudes to crises in the Middle East, an area where Europe and America share traditional as well as vital interests.

Western attempts during the first half of the 1950s to align Egypt, Iraq, Iran, Pakistan and Turkey against a perceived Communist threat saw Britain and the US working at cross-purposes,[38] at a time when the dynamics of the Arab-Israeli antagonism and the sirens of third-world non-alignment should have called for close policy co-ordination on the part of the Western powers. This set the stage for the Suez crisis in 1956, in which, as noted earlier, Britain and France yielded to their last imperial temptation without informing (let alone consulting) their principal ally. Their attempt to regain physical control of the Suez Canal and to overthrow Nasser in the process not only led to an open clash with the United States, but also precipitated the loss of residual Anglo-French influence in the region. Politically, the action further aggravated the French position in Algeria. While the Suez Canal remained firmly in Egyptian hands, the Anglo-French intervention discredited the West in the Arab world and beyond, bolstered the cause of non-alignment and enabled the Soviet Union to recoup whatever loss of moral prestige it might have suffered as a result of its suppression of the Hungarian revolt.

Seventeen years later, immediate concerns about their dependence on Arab oil, and old frustrations at having been edged out of the Middle East by the US, led the European NATO Allies to dissociate themselves from American diplomatic and military efforts to end the 1973 Arab-Israeli War.[39] Except for Portugal, the Netherlands and – for a time – West Germany, the Western Europeans objected to the American use of NATO airfields on their territory to resupply Israel. European fears of horizontal escalation directly involving the Soviet Union increased when the US, in response to the perceived Soviet intention to send troops to Egypt allegedly to restore the cease-fire, called a military alert (Defense Condition (DEFCON) III) involving US forces worldwide. Diplomatically, the EEC members disavowed the American 'step-by-step' approach to the resolution of the conflict by endorsing the Arab interpretation of the UN Security Council Resolution 242 to the effect that Israel should immediately withdraw to its pre-June 1967 borders.[40] In turn, the US interpreted the Western European initiative as an implicit legitimation of the Arab attack on Israel.

Transatlantic confrontations over the Suez crisis and the 1973 Arab-Israeli War showed Western Europe and America in effect trading their interventionist and non-interventionist roles in the Middle East. The extent to which this suggests an evolution in the pattern of transatlantic reactions to out-of-area events is both real and relative. Quite apart from the substance of transatlantic out-of-area disputes, the differing geostrategic perspectives of the members of the Western Alliance constitute one inherent reason why Western Europe and America have tended to operate on different wavelengths in out-of-area matters. From a Western European perspective, 'out-of-area' covers a range of partly national, partly shared concerns. Seen from Washington, Western Europe is only one (albeit crucial) of the stakes in a global East–West contest from which, ultimately, there is no retreat. A second reason is the fact that the European NATO Allies themselves have shown repeatedly their differing reactions to out-of-area situations. While Britain and France have retained the vocation and a limited capability to play an extra-European role, the other Western European members of NATO have become extremely sensitive to any hint that they might be dragged into any kind of military involvement out-of-area through NATO. Portugal's appeals to Allied solidarity with respect to its engagement in Africa foundered on the unwillingness of, mainly, the Scandinavian and Benelux members of NATO to be associated with what their domestic constituencies perceived as support for colonialism of a particularly repressive kind. Even the immediate humanitarian motives underlying the 1978 Belgian-French intervention in Zaire did not dispel the basic scepticism of the other European NATO Allies towards the wider implications of the operation. In a more general sense, 'guilt by association', or the fear of being identified with what domestic constituencies perceive as colonial or neo-colonial interventions by another NATO member,[41] which had been a largely American out-of-area preoccupation during the earlier years of the Alliance, had now become a powerful sentiment in some Western European quarters of NATO. Spanish (and, to a lesser extent, Italian) criticisms of the British Falklands campaign is a recent illustration of this trend.[42]

Of course, the transatlantic aspect of Allied out-of-area differences has substantive dimensions as well. First, the uneasy coexistence since the early 1960s of change and continuity in the transatlantic relationship has helped to inhibit the emergence of any sustained Allied consensus on the management of Western global interests. Thus out-of-area issues have demonstrated Europe's contradictory pressures in favour and against US out-of-area involvement. During the 1973 Arab-Israeli War, Western Europe in effect criticized the US for unthinkingly leading the Alliance into a potential confrontation with the Soviet Union and for drawing down stocks. At the same time, many European policy-makers worried that the increasingly controversial Vietnam War would undermine US leadership and prestige in the Alliance. The tendency in Western Europe to oppose and yet expect American leadership simultaneously, as interests in specific circumstances required, was also demonstrated by the interpretation of the Nixon Doctrine as a sign of diminished US willingness to intervene globally on behalf of Western interests. France, which was discovering the limits of its own military and economic capabilities in Africa, deplored American non-intervention in Angola and the Horn of Africa, as well as the US refusal to participate in a multilateral scheme for sustained Western economic and military stabilization of Zaire and other pro-Western African states.[43] The renewal of American resolve in the world since 1980 can be seen, in part, as an attempt to stem the relative decline of US leadership during the previous decade.

Meanwhile, underlying changes affecting the Western European-US balance, such as European economic recovery and hesitant foreign policy co-ordination, did not result in greater transatlantic harmony towards out-of-area issues. The rapid liquidation of European colonial entanglements had coincided with the successful, but politically absorbing beginnings of the EEC. Thus, it was non-military co-operation, especially economic development co-operation, which tended to shape new relationships between the former colonial powers and the Third World. Indeed, the importance attached by policy-makers and electorates alike to the new 'North–South dialogue' seemed to result in a Western European tendency to 'purify' relations between the developing and the developed worlds and to divorce such relations from East–West security considerations. When Britain and France did intervene militarily in some of their former dependencies, they generally did so at the request of an endangered local government for purposes of political stabilization, in conjunction, at times, with humanitarian motives. Rather than providing for the protection of NATO's out-of-area interests, such British and French interventions responded to the wish to retain a 'unique', albeit reduced, national role in areas which Britain and France used to control. As the US discovered the necessary selectivity of European post-colonial out-of-area interventions meant that there was now hardly any prospect of the Western European NATO allies committing even token forces to South Vietnam. Thus SEATO, which had been established at American initiative to prevent a repetition of Dien Bien Phu, failed to provide a vehicle for British and French involvement in Vietnam.[44] France had not maintained a military presence in the area after 1957. By 1967 the French government announced that, to all intents and purposes, it no longer felt bound by SEATO.[45] Britain, although a more likely partner, was withdrawing most of its forces from East of Suez at about the time that the US Administration would have welcomed some of these forces in Vietnam.

Second, the evolution of the super-power relationship as such contributed to the growing scepticism in Western Europe about a global partnership with the United States. The Suez crisis had already shown how both super-powers, acting independently or in concert, might assume control of a dangerous out-of-area crisis provoked by manifestly lesser powers. The fact that the one major extra-European contingency of the early 1960s, the Cuban Missile Crisis, had been almost exclusively an affair of the super-powers confirmed the perception of the Western European countries that they no longer played any real part in the global management of the East–West contest. Improved Soviet-American relations after 1962 were interpreted by Western Europe as a signal for it to develop its own detente with the Eastern Bloc. As European NATO capitals acquired a major and vested interest in the maintenance of the detente process, they also further narrowed their perception of their vital security interests to the dimensions of their own continent, thereby exorcising their earlier preoccupations with schemes for a global Alliance.

Third, changes in NATO's global environment made it all the more difficult to identify, beyond the North Atlantic zone, new areas of common as well as vital transatlantic interests. As the extraordinary circumstances which had conditioned NATO's formative years came to an end, the Alliance grew more exposed to the new and often contradictory forces which shaped the further evolution of international relations. Its original as well as inherent ambiguity made the transatlantic relationship particularly sensitive to the centrifugal impact of the worldwide diffusion of power during the 1960s and the increasing turmoil in the Third World during the 1970s (which seemed to affect the USSR just as much as the West).[46]

The resulting temptation on both sides of the Atlantic to seek national answers to an increasingly complex security environment, at times apparent even in the area of NATO's formal treaty commitments, most clearly manifested itself in the almost wholly uncodified field of Western out-of-area interests. As the bipolarity of the international system became less pronounced, cold-war considerations lost their earlier grip on Western European foreign policies, as illustrated by Western European aloofness from the US engagement in Vietnam. A decade later, the European NATO members, by their ambiguous opposition to the Soviet invasion of Afghanistan, attested to their wish to insulate the limited but tangible benefits of East–West detente in Europe from untimely and unwelcome out-of-area challenges. While governments in Bonn, Paris and other European NATO capitals did call for a Soviet withdrawal from Afghanistan,[47] some of them also effectively resisted American efforts to impose Western sanctions on the Soviet Union. Moreover, the visits of President Giscard d'Estaing and Chancellor Schmidt to Moscow in May and July 1980 respectively, a few months after the invasion, hardly corresponded to basic US conceptions of the state of East–West relations at the time. Conversely, the new assertiveness of the Reagan Administration on the international scene tended to respond to US perceptions of American security interests and concerns in a more dangerous world. Thus, by yielding to their respective and often divergent perceptions of world events, the US and the European members of NATO at times have been creating the impression that the quest for Allied out-of-area solidarity had become, at best, a discretionary instrument to be tried in support of specific national actions, and, at worst, a nuisance when a NATO member, considering intervention out-of-area, sees no prospect of co-operation or support coming from other NATO Allies. These ambiguities attending the notion of Western solidarity out-of-area can acquire very real, as well as divisive dimensions under pressing circumstances. Thus the recurrent inability on the part of the Allies to find both unified and effective responses to state-sponsored terrorism has tended to generate at times irresistible pressures for unilateral national action, as was recently demonstrated by the controversial US air strike against Libya in April 1986.

To consult or not to consult?

A recurrent theme of NATO out-of-area disputes has been intra-Alliance recriminations that no – or no adequate – consultations were held before an individual Ally, or a small group of Allies, acted beyond the NATO area in ways which affected the interests of the other Allies. National expectations of prior consultations in these out-of-area disputes have been voiced mainly in the context of immediate crises, but they also have arisen with respect to non-military initiatives of certain NATO members in response to political developments in other parts of the world. This raises the question of the actual influence of NATO's consultative process on the formulation and execution of national out-of-area policies.

NO OBLIGATORY NORM

The North Atlantic Treaty contains no explicit provision on the subject of consultations about out-of-area issues. Nevertheless, there was an expectation of such consultations in the minds of those who attended the formation of the Alliance. These expectations were fostered by subsequent recommendations of the North Atlantic Council in the light of national practice and national declarations of intent.[48] Three different forms of consultations must be distinguished here.

First, in their most basic form Allied consultations may concern the notification of national decisions and the exchange of relevant information on a bilateral or multilateral basis. Thus, in April 1954 the Allies adopted a resolution urging NATO members to submit to the Council all political information likely to be of interest to other members.[49] During NATO's formative years, the intimacy of the Anglo-American special relationship manifested itself in the exchange of out-of-area intelligence, from which other NATO Allies also benefited,[50] but it was not until February 1983 that the Allies instituted regular meetings of experts on various regions of the world.[51] As regards notification of *national* out-of-area decisions, a 1955 Council Resolution *inter alia* subjected out-of-area diversions of forces to a partial notification regime. It called on NATO governments to inform the Council and the NATO Military Authorities (NMA) promptly of a final national decision to withdraw units from the NATO area of command to which they were assigned or earmarked in order to meet an emergency elsewhere.[52] It can be inferred from the Resolution that temporary withdrawals were exempted from this notification procedure. This step reflected Allied concerns that future out-of-area crises might endanger the military health of NATO. Many recalled that NATO had been solidified as a direct result of a major out-of-area emergency, namely Communist aggression in Korea. Indeed, extra-regional diversions of NATO forces have been a regular source of intra-Alliance frictions. A Pentagon report of 1950 complained that French casualties in Indochina since 1945 'had exceeded fifty thousand and officers are being lost . . . at a faster rate than they are being graduated from officer schools in France'.[53] In 1958 France had only two divisions committed to NATO's Central Front,[54] as a result of the Algerian War where 400,000 troops had been engaged since August 1956.[55] The United States, for its part, redeployed 30,000 troops from Europe to South Vietnam in 1966.[56] Just before granting independence to its colonial territories in 1974–5, Portugal had 134,000 troops stationed in Africa.[57]

Although the Council Resolution mentioned above has generally been observed by NATO governments, it should be recalled that it merely requires *notification* of out-of-area deployments (not *agreement*), and then only to the extent that such deployments are of a more or less permanent character, designed to cope with a serious and enduring emergency. Years of financial duress as experienced by Britain in fact have been far more effective in dealing with the problem of out-of-area diversions of NATO forces. Britain, it is worth remembering, subjected its 1954 Brussels Treaty pledge to continue to maintain four divisions and a tactical air force on the European mainland until 1998 to the double qualification of an acute overseas emergency or a financial crisis at home.[58] Over the years notification or non-notification to NATO of national out-of-area decisions, whether of a political or military nature, have elicited various reactions on the part of the other Allies, ranging from disinterest through acquiescence to sharp objections. The 1973 Arab-Israeli War provides a vivid example, when the US sent a cable in the middle of the night to Brussels to *inform* its NATO Allies that it had called a worldwide military alert involving American NATO forces in Europe.[59] While honest to a fault, Henry Kissinger's subsequent exegesis of this episode is hardly comforting to Western Europe:

> The Allies were really objecting not so much to timing as to absence of opportunity to affect our decision. But imminent danger did not brook an exchange of views and, to be frank, we could not have accepted a judgment different from our own. . . . Allies should be consulted whenever possible. But emergencies are sure to arise again; and it will not be in anyone's interest if the chief protector of free world security is hamstrung by bureaucratic procedure.[60]

From a European point of view, the intra-Alliance disputes caused by the 1973 Arab–Israeli War thus focus on the second form of Allied consultations. When can a NATO government be expected to seek Allied reactions to its stated policy intentions? This naturally provides an opportunity for the other Allies to influence the outcome of a national decision. With respect to out-of-area questions, the Alliance as a whole did evolve some guiding principles on prior consultations between 1956 and 1980. Taken together, the 1956 Report of the Committee of Three on Non-Military Co-operation, the 1967 Harmel Report and the 1974 Declaration on Atlantic Relations state that 'the members of the Alliance are firmly resolved to strengthen their practice of frank and timely consultations, bearing in mind that their common interests can be affected by events in other regions of the world'.[61] While the words 'frank and timely' imply that consultations should precede decision-making,[62] many uncertainties remain which government practice has only partially resolved. Judging from the record, there does not seem to be a binding obligation of prior consultations on the part of an Ally contemplating an out-of-area action. In the case of national decisions taken in the context of decolonization, the other Allies generally did not object to the lack of prior consultations by the European powers.[63] While Allied reactions to the Suez Crisis and the 1973 Arab–Israeli War strongly suggest that prior consultations are essential when national out-of-area actions present the risk of an armed confrontation with the Soviet Union, the need to act quickly – as in the Cuban Missile Crisis or in 1973 – is likely to pre-empt the norm.[64]

Third, consultations may be instrumental in bringing about concerted or parallel national actions as well as collective action out-of-area. Thus the possibility of American and British intervention in Lebanon and Jordan respectively was discussed in NATO shortly before it actually materialized in 1958.[65] By contrast, the 1978 intervention of Belgium, France and the US in Zaire was only discussed in NATO *after* the event.[66] Following the intervention, Belgium, Britain, France, West Germany and the US did not consult the other NATO Allies on their decision to meet in Paris in order to consider a multilateral approach to regime stabilization in Zaire and elsewhere in Africa.[67] This did not prevent the NATO Summit of May 1978 being in large part devoted to the problems affecting Western interests in Africa.[68] Instead of achieving consensus, Allied consultations following the Soviet invasion of Afghanistan exposed the differences of perceptions and policies when action was called for. It did not prove possible to go beyond calls in NATO communiqués for the withdrawal of Soviet forces.

CLASHING FOREIGN POLICIES
The fact that the need for a NATO norm for out-of-area consultations is disputed reflects the permanence of national interests and constraints on Allied attempts to foster political co-ordination through the consultative process. Intra-Alliance recriminations over the alleged lack of consultations have often failed to go to the heart of the matter, namely the uneasy coexistence within NATO of the original 12 national foreign policies, now expanded to 16.

While NATO is undoubtedly more than a short-term military alliance of the traditional kind, it has by no means reached the stage of a truly political alliance supported by shared decision-making.[69] This is particularly apparent with respect to out-of-area questions which, in lieu of binding treaty provisions, are merely covered by fluctuating expectations and reversible commitments on the part of NATO's pluralistic membership. Given also the fact that decisions by the North Atlantic Council are expected to be unanimous, it is no wonder that the Alliance as such has never had anything like a substantive out-of-area policy. Nevertheless, when successive outside pressures began to disprove the early notion that the codified recognition of common and vital interests within the NATO area would breed political conformity with respect to the wider world, two distinct remedies were tried.

First, there was de Gaulle's 1958 memorandum proposals that Britain, France and the US should form a tripartite 'directorate' for closer political co-ordination on global policy and strategy.[70] As well as addressing French concerns specifically, de Gaulle's move was prompted also by the realization at the time that changes in the international system no longer justified US dominance of the Alliance in out-of-area matters. What probably represented the most radical attempt to co-ordinate Allied foreign policies at large was rejected by Britain and the US, on the official ground that the creation of a directorate would institutionalize a hitherto informal intra-Alliance hierarchy. But Britain and the US also realized that the existing system of Alliance-wide consultations, by virtue of its very shortcomings in bringing about genuine policy co-ordination, in effect guaranteed the autonomy of their respective foreign policies. And to the extent that out-of-area events might require *ad hoc* Allied co-operation, both still regarded their special and exclusive relationship as the best instrument for this purpose. Whatever the intrinsic merits of tripartism might have been, nevertheless its rejection implied that national out-of-area unilateralism and the erosion of the cold-war consensus on the global threat to Western interests would continue to feed on each other. Having failed to lock up Allied out-of-area decision-making in tripartism, de Gaulle unilaterally recognized Communist China and criticized US policies in South-east Asia.[71] He also proceeded to develop his own kind of detente with the USSR. In the same period the US sought support from its NATO Allies for its war in Vietnam but to little avail.[72]

Second, initiatives to strengthen the mechanisms of political consultations in NATO have found it difficult to avoid two pitfalls. On the one hand, such initiatives have tended to mistake procedure for substance. Thus European procedural objections against the lack of Allied consultations preceding the American decision to call a worldwide military alert during the 1973 Arab–Israeli War at least partly masked substantive European-American disagreements on the nature and the resolution of the Arab-Israeli conflict,[73] which the repeated European Community (EC) declarations on the Middle East have confirmed.[74] On the other hand, strengthened bilateral and multilateral consultations might be used by a dominant NATO member to legitimate decisions which it has already firmly taken. The extent to which this can be the case remains, of course, a largely subjective question shaped by the specifics of each issue. As varying distributions of perceptions and interests will result in as many degrees of acquiescence or opposition to national policies, consultations might or might not assume a token character. By virtue of that diversity, out-of-area issues offer a fertile breeding ground for discontent in either case.

Implications
This outline of the basic dilemmas which have shaped the reactions of NATO members to out-of-area issues leads to the following general observations.[75]

First, the ways in which out-of-area issues historically have tended to mean different things to different NATO members confirms the 'open' nature as well as the uneven distribution of Western security interests and power beyond the North Atlantic Treaty zone. The reactions of NATO members to distant events have revealed, if anything, the uneasy nature of the distinction between out-of-area cases affecting the interests of only one Ally and cases affecting all the Allies or a group of them.

Second, both the limited premise of the Western Alliance and its manifest sensitivity to internal and external change constitute a constant warning against pitching expectations of Allied out-of-area solidarity too high. Indeed, undiscriminating attempts to develop common perceptions of, and united reactions to, out-of-area challenges manifestly run counter to the pluralism of the Alliance and might result therefore in undermining what solidarity exists in NATO's central concerns. Thus, the transatlantic dimensions of past Allied out-of-area disputes suggest in particular that such attempts are qualified by the fluctuating patterns of the overall European-American relationship. While US global policies continue to imply the pursuit of NATO (i.e. European) interests, they have also become more contestable as a result of the real and perceptual uncertainties surrounding America's ability to sustain its global power and the wisdom of US policies.

Third, the variety of national reactions to out-of-area events need not necessarily be a source of Western global weakness if it is seen as the most realistic basis for a conscious Allied policy of differentiated responses to challenges which, by their very nature, call for varying approaches. While regular, Alliance-wide consultations can help NATO members to clarify the out-of-area aspects of Western security, they cannot be expected to generate agreed out-of-area policies of NATO as an organization. National action is likely to remain the primary component of Allied reactions to concrete emergencies. In specific cases, national actions have proved to be amenable to *ad hoc* co-ordination, as opposed to integration, usually on a bilateral basis involving Britain, France and the US. Such instances of co-ordination also demonstrate the advantages, at least in a crisis, of bilateral or trilateral consultations as opposed to the more cumbersome process of Alliance-wide consultations. Moreover, while the question of actual or prospective Soviet involvement has been generally recognized as a crucial factor, its unifying impact on Alliance behaviour towards out-of-area crises has been more visible in NATO communiqués than on the level of policy planning. In turn this underlines the extent to which political considerations at the national level continue to determine the scope for concerted reactions to out-of-area events.

Fourth, reactions to British, French and American out-of-area military interventions have reflected Allied sensitivities to the possible diversion of resources away from the pursuit of NATO's central objectives. Historically, the Allied wish to maximize national force contributions to NATO has applied particularly to American forces, given both the actual and psychological importance of the US commitment to the security of Western Europe. But, while the Allied problem of American diversion to competing strategic theatres – such as the Pacific – has been long-standing, it assumes increased significance today as the interdependencies of global instability are putting additional demands on available US forces. Intra-Alliance management of the specific issues raised by current American strategic planning for South-west Asia will constitute therefore a large part of NATO's out-of-area agenda for the 1980s.

Fifth, both American and European out-of-area interventions have demonstrated in their respective ways the important – if not decisive – role of domestic factors in determining the limits and the modalities of extra-European military roles on the part of NATO members. On the whole, socio-economic, political and ethical considerations seem to have militated in favour of shorter, efficient and time-limited out-of-area interventions based on defensible motives. Conversely, critical domestic constituencies have contributed significantly to restrict, end or inhibit protracted, costly and debatable interventions undertaken or considered by their respective governments, especially in the case of the US during the 1970s. By manifesting themselves at the Alliance level as well, domestic criticisms have exerted pressure on controversial interventions by other NATO governments, as French Cabinets found in the late 1950s and as the Portuguese Salazar and Caetano regimes experienced in the 1960s and early 1970s.

II. GLOBAL DIMENSIONS OF WESTERN SECURITY: INTERESTS AND VULNERABILITIES

Discussions of NATO's out-of-area problem generally refer to the global vulnerabilities of Western security interests. The most often cited of these stem from threats to Western trade and resource security. Continued access to raw materials, such as oil and strategic minerals, constitutes a traditional source of concern on which, for the most part, the Allies appear to agree. These threats to trade and resource security are being connected, often in rather loose terms, with socio-economic and political instability in the Third World, resulting in domestic, interstate and regional conflict. The inability of many developing countries to service their foreign debt obligations, the rise of neo-protectionism and deteriorating terms of trade for low-income countries have led to concerns that resulting disruptions of the world economy and the precariousness of third-world structures, by feeding upon one another, may create a fertile breeding ground for future out-of-area crises.

Second, Soviet activity in the Third World, which acquired more menacing forms in the 1970s, has fed speculation about a systematic drive by the USSR to subvert Western economic and political interests in Africa, Central America, East Asia and elsewhere. Indications to that effect are seen in the expansion of Soviet power projection capabilities, particularly in the impressive naval build-up and the acquisition of overseas bases and facilities. This perceived threat seemed very real in December 1979, when the Soviet Union invaded Afghanistan. This massive intervention of Soviet forces outside the Soviet sphere of direct influence, the first since World War II and its aftermath, was interpreted by some as the start of a Soviet march to the oilfields of the Persian Gulf, thereby triggering fears of an impending 'resource war' between East and West.

Third, the recent recrudescence of terrorism against US and Western European citizens, property and interests in the Middle East and elsewhere, is again perceived by some as a dramatic manifestation of Western vulnerability to endemic violence in many areas of the Third World. In addition, terrorist attacks – such as the October 1982 bombing of the Western Multinational Force (MNF) in Beirut – have appeared to challenge the ability of Western powers, amongst them the United States, to influence decisively the out-of-area events in which they purport to intervene. When international terrorism against the West is manifestly sponsored by some governments, it tends also to infect interstate relations. And, as the US experienced in Lebanon, in the hijacking of the *Achille Lauro*, and with respect to Libya, Western attempts to strike back at terrorism abroad can either be frustrated, or have damaging domestic and international repercussions or both. Finally, Argentina's attempt to annex the Falkland Islands in 1982 served as a reminder of the way in which violent challenges to universally accepted principles of international order can result from the tendency of many governments to deflect mounting domestic problems by resorting to foreign aggression.

These developments have induced a renewed awareness within NATO of the wider threats to Allied security. It is therefore necessary to review briefly the main forms in which these threats manifest themselves and to assess, however tentatively, their gravity in terms of those vulnerabilities which the Allies tend to share.

Economic vulnerabilities

If there is any such thing as Western economic security[1] its main vulnerability stems from reliance on the supply of strategic raw materials (fuels – such as oil, uranium and coal – and non-fuel minerals), which are critical to the viability of Western economies – including those of Australia, Japan and New Zealand – and NATO's industrial base. The economic security risks involved are generally qualified in terms of import dependence and import vulnerability.[2] Dependence refers to the extent to which domestic consumption requirements are met by specific, potentially unstable foreign supply sources. Vulnerability refers to the probability that national minimum requirements will not be fulfilled as a result of interruptions, either at source or in transit, of the supplies themselves. Because dependence affects both importers and exporters, its security implications are less clear-cut than in the case of vulnerability.

OIL AND MINERALS

It is estimated that oil will continue to account for at least one-third of the energy demand in OECD countries between 1985 and 2000.[3] With respect to dependence, NATO members imported some 60% of their total oil consumption in 1983, of which two-thirds came from non-NATO sources, among which the Persian Gulf figured prominently.[4] Several, partly contradictory, trends affect NATO's present and near-term import dependence on oil. On the one hand, NATO members have quite dramatically reduced their oil imports since 1973, thereby reducing their overall dependence on Persian Gulf oil from 31% to 13% in 1983.[5] On the other hand, dependence on Gulf oil remains substantially higher for the European NATO members than for the US and Canada.[6] While national energy policies (supply diversification, substitution and conservation measures) since the 1973–4 oil crisis have lessened dependence, the effectiveness of these policies in the future tends to be qualified by the fact that some 55% of proven world oil resources are located in the Gulf area, in contrast to the more limited reserves of alternative and newer supply sources in Africa, Indonesia, the North Sea and South America.[7] International market forces in the wake of the 1980–3 recession have undermined the cartel policies of the Organization of Petroleum Exporting Countries (OPEC); thus by April 1986 crude oil prices had fallen to about $US 15 a barrel, and have dropped even further since then.[8] But OPEC still controls more than one-third of world production and, more importantly, about two-thirds of world oil trade. The future patterns of

Western import dependence therefore will be determined to a large extent by OPEC's internal cohesion in the light of the evolution of the world demand for oil.[9] The most important factors bearing upon the future credibility of the oil weapon (manipulation of oil production, prices and distribution or targeted oil embargoes) remain the ability and the willingness of conservative Arab oil producers to insulate the long-term economic interests which they have come to share with the West from the dynamics of the Arab-Israeli conflict.[10] With respect to import vulnerability, attacks on oil pumping and refinery installations in the course of the Gulf War between Iraq and Iran have underlined the potential for dangerous supply disruptions at source. While Western countries do have proven instruments to cope with disruptions, the future effectiveness of such economic crisis management might be reduced in several ways.

First, Western oil companies now enjoy less flexibility to redirect oil flows, while OPEC's basic control over oil production since the late 1960s, combined with its current policy of downstream diversification, renders the activation of surge capacity more dependent on discretionary producer decisions.[11] Second, the build-up of commercial and government stockpiles within the framework of the emergency oil-sharing scheme of the International Energy Agency (IEA) and parallel arrangements within the EEC at present are not supported adequately by clear and agreed intergovernmental policies on the acquisition, management and activation of these stockpiles.[12] Third, the establishment of the IEA in 1974 – in which, significantly, France does not participate – is no guarantee that its members are now immune from unilateralist temptations in the face of a renewed oil crisis. In a crisis with far-reaching political ramifications, national self-interest might well undermine the declared political will of IEA members to implement the oil-sharing scheme.[13]

The various concerns raised by mainly Western European dependence and vulnerability with respect to Gulf oil imports acquire an East-West dimension, albeit a theoretical one, when the economic and strategic implications of the Soviet energy problem are taken into account. So far a surplus of oil and gas has enabled the USSR to finance vital imports of grain and high-technology with hard-currency energy sales to the West, and to buy a measure of economic and political stability in Eastern European client states by meeting their rising energy needs.[14] The extent to which the USSR can continue to do both will depend largely on the uncertain evolution of Soviet domestic energy production, especially of oil. If Soviet oil production continues to tail off, the USSR might seek a way out of the resulting dilemma by trying to gain greater access to Gulf oil at concessionary rates for itself and Eastern Europe.[15] The implications for Western oil security would depend on the actual course of Soviet policy, as well as on the willingness of Gulf producers to step up preferential oil supplies to the Soviet Bloc.[16] Apart from the unlikely worst-case scenario involving a Soviet grab for some or all of the oilfields of the Gulf, a more plausible strategy would consist of pressuring Gulf states to supply oil to Eastern Europe on soft terms, in exchange for Soviet political and military restraint in the area.[17] While such an outcome would seem to be in the Western interest from a political and strategic point of view, it might still present certain economic dangers. Substantial Soviet Bloc imports of Gulf oil could increase Western European oil dependency by squeezing available quantities and raising prices,[18] and aggravate Western oil vulnerability if the USSR chose to back up its oil demands by exerting various forms of political and military pressure on producers.

Non-fuel minerals provide essential raw materials for defence and other high-technology industries. Hence they are particularly relevant to the military dimension of economic security. NATO members are heavily dependent on outside sources for the supply of critical materials such as chromium, cobalt, manganese, platinum, tantalum and titanium.[19] Yet, for a number of reasons, it is hard to assess the extent to which this translates into concrete economic security risks.[20] International market conditions, importance and substitution possibilities tend to vary for each mineral. Further uncertainties are the amount of ultimately recoverable world reserves, their geographical distribution (and hence the scope for supply diversification), as well as future producer attitudes and pricing structures. This helps to explain why Western import dependence on minerals as such does not present clear-cut security risks. Some suppliers are Western states themselves, while others – mainly Asian states – have close economic ties to the West.[21] Key African suppliers, such as Gabon (manganese), Guinea (bauxite), Morocco (phosphates), Zaire (cobalt) and Zimbabwe (ferrochromes), have been either unable or unwilling to emulate the Arab use of the oil weapon by subjecting Western consumer countries to any kind of 'mineral blackmail' for political purposes. In the face of deteriorating terms of trade they have generally assigned priority to continued exports in order to secure badly-needed hard currency earnings.[22] This also applies to the USSR which, so far, has been a reliable supplier of minerals. Despite vast Siberian reserves, the USSR does not appear to be in the position to derive political leverage from its fluctuating mineral exports to the West. Moreover, Soviet Bloc import dependence for a number of minerals appears to be increasing.[23]

South Africa constitutes a specific and, today, more worrying case. Since the 1960s, Western import dependence on South Africa for a wide range of minerals has grown significantly.[24] Thus, South Africa has become a crucial mineral producer, whose supply policies could affect Western economic security directly. Should a desperate white leadership in Pretoria resort to a mineral embargo in retaliation against stepped up Western economic and political sanctions against apartheid, the mineral import dependence of NATO members could suddenly acquire more threatening dimensions.[25] The availability of sizeable commercial and government-controlled stockpiles, however, could make a crucial difference in the hypothetical event of a South African mineral embargo. The US has maintained a strategic stockpile since 1939, while Britain, France and West Germany instituted modest (and hesitant) public stockpiling programmes in the 1970s. But acquisition, management and activation of mineral stockpiles are subject to various uncertainties, while no multilateral emergency sharing arrangements have been worked out so far.[26]

There appear to be three main concerns in the area of mineral import vulnerability. The first and lesser concern stems from almost endemic supply disruptions as a result of economic mismanagement (especially regarding transportation) by producer states. A second and more serious source of disruption is political and socio-economic instability within producer states. This has been the case particularly for African mineral exporters. The 1977 and 1978 invasions of Zaire were directed at Shaba province, which is rich in cobalt and copper. As a result of the Polisario insurgency in the Western Sahara, Morocco's phosphate exports had to be interrupted between 1976 and 1982. Repeated South African incursions deep into Angola since 1975 have halted Angola's iron ore production. In the French dependency of New Caledonia, sabotage closed down two important nickel mines in January 1985. The third area of concern is again South Africa. If racial tensions and civil and industrial unrest develop within South African mining areas, the risk of future supply disruptions in this key producer state can by no means be excluded.

TRADE AND TRADE ROUTES
Traditionally foreign trade has been a crucial ingredient of economic growth and prosperity for the European NATO members, and its importance to the US economy is rapidly increasing.[27] Both the US and its European Allies carry on a significant 'out-of-area' trade. In 1982 they exported to developing countries 39% and 21% of their total merchandise respectively. The figures for manufactured products were 40% and 25% in 1981.[28] By far the largest proportion of NATO members' imports of vital raw materials originates from overseas. Taken together, these two facts point to the critical importance to the US and Western European economies of unimpeded seaborne commercial traffic. There are three concerns, however, which affect the perceived vulnerability of this traffic.

First, there are numerous maritime 'choke points' at which littoral states, which now often possess relatively sophisticated weapons (precision-guided and cannon-launched guided projectiles), could interdict shipping. Well-known choke points in this context are the Straits of Hormuz and the Caribbean sea-lanes. Between 30% and 35% of Western European oil imports pass through the Persian Gulf,[29] and almost 50% of all US trade (including substantial amounts of crude oil) traverse the Caribbean basin.[30]

Yet, while the vulnerability of these specific choke points should not be underestimated, they are subject to several qualifications. Excess production capacity outside the Gulf and projects to increase pipeline capacity to by-pass the Straits of Hormuz tend to improve the Western ability to cope with maritime disruptions in the supply of oil.[31] Moreover, military threats are still more psychological than real. In the Gulf area many ships have been attacked by both Iraq and Iran,[32] but navigation in the Gulf has not been seriously interrupted. Iraq's use of the French-built *Exocet* surface-to-surface missiles against shipping also appears to be less devastating than was originally feared, while Iran's counter-threat to close the Straits of Hormuz to navigation has ceased to carry much military credibility. Similarly, the mysterious mining of the Red Sea in 1984, while damaging 19 commercial vessels, did not lead to the interruption of maritime traffic. Physical, military and over-riding political constraints thus appear to have prevented Iraq and Iran from interfering decisively with shipping in the Gulf, a move which would invite a determined and – one might assume – effective military response from the US and possibly Britain and France. Similar constraints seem to apply to both the ability and the willingness of Cuba – and certainly of Nicaragua – to interfere with shipping in the Caribbean.

Second, concerns about the perceived threat of the Soviet Navy operating in war astride Western sea lines of communication (SLOC) have become more pronounced since 1967 when, following the closure of the Suez Canal, the main oil flow to the West had to be re-routed around the Cape of Good Hope. This is still the case today, despite the reopening of the Canal to commercial traffic in June 1975 and the dredging programmes which were undertaken to increase its capacity, primarily because of the switch to VLCC (Very Large Crude Carriers). Further along the Cape Route, the South Atlantic constitutes the main transit area for Persian Gulf oil and vital African minerals bound for both the US and Western Europe. The threat posed by the Soviet Navy, especially submarines, to Western SLOC is linked, however, to the overall ability of the Soviet Union to project power on a global scale. While there is no doubt that Soviet capabilities in this regard have grown impressively over the past 15 years, they also remain constrained in several important ways which will be reviewed further on in this Chapter. At this point it suffices to say that Soviet attacks on Western shipping seem improbable, short of general war.

The third concern is the widespread tendency among littoral states to extend their sovereignty beyond the usual three-mile territorial sea zones. By 1984 at least 90 states had declared territorial sea zones in excess of 12 nautical miles, while several Latin American and African states claim zones of 200 nautical miles.[33] Apart from involving traditional economic interests such as fishing rights, these claims have acquired greater importance with the discovery of deep water sea-beds of minerals, especially major manganese nodule deposits in the Central Pacific basin. The North-South contest for the economic benefits of the sea and the West's vital interest in freedom of navigation for commercial and strategic purposes (right of innocent passage of warships, legal regime of international straits) are becoming increasingly hard to separate, as attested by the laborious conclusion of the Third United Nations Conference on The Law of the Sea (UNCLOS) in December 1982.[34] Yet, as has already been noted in the context of 'choke points', it remains doubtful whether littoral states will be able and willing to challenge effectively the existing maritime order.[35] The greater danger is perhaps that extensive neutral territorial seas could be used as a sanctuary by Soviet submarines.[36] Meanwhile, the Soviet Union, given its important merchant fleet, is coming to share the Western interest in freedom of navigation. Cases of open or tacit super-power co-operation in ensuring the free flow of maritime traffic are not inconceivable therefore, and such co-operation would certainly be effective in restraining littoral states.[37] Thus, it is worth mentioning that the USSR also contributed to the 1984 Red Sea mine-clearing operation. The US, for its part, has been underlining the Western commitment to maritime order by carrying out freedom-of-navigation exercises since 1979, notably in the Gulf of Sirte which is claimed by Libya.[38] Libya has reacted violently to such an assertion of maritime right.

Political vulnerabilities
In contrast to the economic aspects of NATO's out-of-area problem, it is much harder to identify the wider political threats to Allied security in terms of a calculus of interests and vulnerabilities. Political out-of-area interests tend to mean different things to different Allies, according to the extent and nature of their respective stakes in the world arena. As a result, national perceptions of political vulnerabilities will often diverge, both functionally and geographically. Moreover, the political aspects of out-of-area security are difficult to quantify. Attempts to do so, for instance, using geostrategic criteria related to the East-West contest, lead all too easily into 'zero-sum game' simplifications which do not reflect international realities. Thus there are various and at times recurrent sources of political vulnerability out-of-area, some of which may be partly shared by some NATO members while others may not.

DEPENDENT TERRITORIES
For Britain and France (and, to a much lesser extent, for Portugal, Spain and the Netherlands) residual vulnerabilities can stem from the few, and generally small, overseas dependencies which they still retain today. This was demonstrated vividly by the Falklands War between Argentina and Britain in 1982, the serious insurgency France faced in New Caledonia in 1984–5 and the persistent agitation for independence in some of the other French 'departements et territoires d'outre-mer' (DOM/TOM). These post-imperial vulnerabilities confront Britain and France with a number of difficult policy choices. On the one hand, both countries have incentives to liquidate the remainder of their imperial pasts which, apart from provoking anti-colonial sentiments at home and abroad, may entail significant diversions of national economic and military resources. Thus the costs of fortifying the Falklands against renewed Argentine aggression are being incurred at a time when Britain's contribution to the common defence of Europe is already felt to impose a considerable economic burden, and as Britain appears to be entering a period of flat real defence

funding.³⁹ On the other hand, self-determination by the local populations, a right acknowledged both in Britain and in France, may prolong British and French overseas presences. The retention of at least some dependencies may also serve wider national interests. This is certainly the case of the French DOM/TOMs which, apart from providing France with vital nuclear testing-grounds in Polynesia (Mururoa), help to preserve a distinctively French political and military presence beyond Europe. An important factor bearing upon the future policies of Britain, and perhaps also of France, towards remaining overseas dependencies might well be their possible strategic utility for the protection of or, conversely, the subversion of wider Western out-of-area interests.

EXTERNAL SECURITY OBLIGATIONS

Defence agreements maintained by individual NATO members with independent states outside the North Atlantic Treaty zone also constitute a potential source of political liability.⁴⁰ The US has bilateral and multilateral defence agreements, as well as military aid and co-operation agreements, with more than 50 states in Asia, Latin America and the Middle East. Britain has its (dormant) Five-Power Defence Arrangements with Australia, Malaysia, New Zealand and Singapore, Treaties of Friendship with a number of Persian Gulf states, and military co-operation agreements with seven African and Asian states. France maintains defence and military co-operation agreements with 15 African states and arms supply agreements with seven Arab states. In April 1985, Italy and the People's Republic of China (PRC) signed a framework agreement for defence technology co-operation, the first of its kind between the PRC and a Western nation.⁴¹ A substantial number of these international agreements entail no formal security obligations for the NATO members which are parties to them. Others tend to be ineffective or have fallen into abeyance because they no longer reflect current political realities.⁴²

Some agreements, however, when invoked by their local signatories, can expose these NATO members to possibly unwelcome out-of-area involvements. This could be the case with the 1954 Manila Pact, to which Britain and the US are parties, and with the 1971 Five-Power Defence Arrangements. Although both these multilateral agreements only call for consultations in the event of a threat to any party, nevertheless they represent residual out-of-area commitments which could become the source of political embarrassment for their NATO signatories. This is not simply a theoretical possibility, Vietnam's aggressive policies in Indochina have tended to revive the significance of the Five-Power Defence Arrangements, at least in the eyes of their local signatories.⁴³ Ambivalence towards the possible implications of external security obligations was reflected also at the time in the assurances of the Carter Administration to South Korea that the planned withdrawal of US ground forces would not impair the US security guarantee to that country. More recently, the withdrawal of French troops from Chad in November 1984 raised some doubts in Africa and the West about France's resolve to maintain its active security role in Africa. Although the fourth French military intervention in Chad in August 1983 took place in the absence of a formal fully-fledged bilateral defence agreement,[44] President Mitterrand felt obliged nevertheless to emphasize that France would honour integrally and immediately its defence agreements with African states;[45] thus in 1986 France sent troops back into Chad.

THIRD-WORLD RADICALISM

In many areas of the Third World, domestic conditions are afflicted with political and social fragmentation and exacerbated by economic stress, while growing disparities in national power tend to undermine the stability of interstate relations at the regional level.[46] Resulting domestic conflict, often supported by covert or overt foreign intervention, is thought by some to create conditions likely to cause the collapse of weak, pro-Western governments and their replacement by radical regimes hostile to the West and willing to associate themselves to varying degrees with the Soviet Union. However, the extent to which third-world radicalism contributes to Western global political vulnerability appears to be subject to important qualifications.

First, as a notion in itself, third-world radicalism does not differentiate between rhetoric and reality, nor does it reflect the fact that radicalism, depending on the issues and their specific circumstances, tends to mean different things to different states or combinations of states. Second, to the extent that domestic instability is a phenomenon common to many third-world countries, it will affect both radical and pro-Western regimes. Especially in Africa, the plight of such 'radical' states as Angola, Ethiopia or Mozambique appears to be at least as serious as that of Sudan or Zaire. Hence the advent of radical regimes by itself does not seem to constitute sufficient proof of a serious and lasting threat to Western interests. As already noted, third-world regimes – whatever their political complexion – often appear anxious to preserve or attract Western foreign investment and aid, as the rather moderate policies of Angola's Marxist MPLA government or Mozambique have attested. The recent economic recession and its aftermath have only confirmed the basic dependence of the Third World on the capitalist economies. Some radical states (Ghana and Tanzania being recent examples) have thus been led to accept or consider the strict economic tutelage of the Western-dominated International Monetary Fund (IMF), in exchange for crucial balance-of-payments assistance. Moreover, following the example of Mozambique, Angola joined the second 1979 Lomé Convention between the EEC and 58 African, Caribbean and Pacific Ocean countries in April 1985.[47] And the radicalism of third-world regimes may betray hidden factional power struggles and thereby their own vulnerability to domestic challenges. The crucial role of Cuban troops and Soviet Bloc advisers in keeping particular factions in power in Afghanistan, Angola, Ethiopia, Mozambique or South Yemen against domestic opposition cast doubts over the long-term prospects of radical regimes, some of which (such as Algeria, Guinea and Guinea Bissau) are now trying to move away from the Soviet Union.[48] Militarily, these same regimes appear to be too embattled domestically to pose a significant external threat, while their overall military capabilities should not be over-rated.

Third, the complex dynamics of third-world turmoil and the limitations of its foreign policy instruments – notably the signature of Treaties of Friendship and Co-operation – have often prevented the USSR from taking full advantage of the advent of radical regimes. Soviet policies towards the Third World appear to be hindered by the nationalist or irredentist ambitions of radical states close to the Soviet Union. The radicalism of Libya, Syria and Vietnam may also serve to realize old and new regional ambitions on their part which do not always coincide with the complex foreign policy considerations of the Soviet Union.[49] Thus its close connections with the USSR did not prevent Iraq from attacking Iran in 1980, thereby provoking a potentially highly destabilizing conflict which so far has forced the Soviet Union – in circumstantial accord with the US – to maintain an uneasy neutrality towards the two belligerents. The limits to any natural identity of interests between the USSR and radical states in the Third World have also found implicit recognition on the ideological level, where the USSR has displayed great caution in acknowledging the 'socialist' nature of particular regimes. Early Soviet endorsement of the Afghan Taraki regime in 1978 constituted a costly exception to this rule.

In terms of trade, aid and investment the Soviet Union has relatively little to offer to developing countries. This was highlighted by the recent famine crisis in pro-Soviet Ethiopia, where the tardy and limited food aid provided by the Soviet Union contrasted painfully with the large-scale relief operations undertaken by Western governments and private organizations. Diplomatically, the USSR tends to remain on the periphery of the various multilateral attempts to find negotiated solutions to the Middle Eastern conflict, the independence of Namibia and regional turmoil in Central America. And Soviet diplomacy has been notably unsuccessful in Pacific Asia. The USSR was also unable to interfere with the move to Rhodesian independence in 1979–80 or to supplant the US in Khomeini's Iran and it has been manifestly unwilling – at least so far – to provoke the US by attempting to subvert the Persian Gulf states. The invasion and continued occupation of Afghanistan by Soviet troops has dealt a severe blow to Soviet political prestige in the Third World and has caused major embarrassment to Soviet friends and allies within the Non-Aligned Movement, notably India and Cuba.[50] The destruction in September 1983 of a South Korean civilian aircraft by the Soviet Air Force did little to restore the image of the USSR in the Third World and in Asia in particular.[51]

This leaves only military initiatives, namely massive arms transfers, as well as the despatch of Cuban troops and Soviet Bloc advisers in support of preferred local client factions, as the main instruments on which the

USSR must rely to make its impact felt in the Third World. The distinctly one-dimensional nature of the Soviet Union's relationship with its few third-world allies has tended to constrain Soviet global influence in two other ways. It has prevented these allies from assisting in the development of Soviet diplomatic and political options on the international scene, and it has not been conducive to the Marxist penetration of third-world societies – as the remarkable slowness of the Ethiopian revolutionary regime in introducing a Soviet-style constitution suggests.[52]

Military vulnerabilities

Third-world conflicts, whether Soviet-inspired or not, recurrently have brought into sharp relief Western economic or political vulnerabilities which otherwise might have tended to remain unclear. This suggests that NATO members, notwithstanding the established geographical limits to the Alliance, do share a general objective beyond those limits, namely to prevent, by military force if necessary, conflict in the Third World from threatening those critical interests upon which they agree most. But while this clearly suggests the need for national military capabilities in support of national or shared out-of-area interests, various problems affect the use and the effectiveness of such capabilities. Some of these problems are related to the political and military Alliance dimensions of the out-of-area issue and will be discussed further in Chapter III. Others, however, stem from the two main contingencies which NATO members face or could be facing in out-of-area crises: limited but trying third-world conflicts (so-called 'small wars'); and conflicts involving direct and full-scale Soviet aggression. A brief assessment of the extent of the threats posed by both these contingencies will clarify the ways in which NATO members are and are not militarily vulnerable out-of-area.

SMALL WARS

Small wars refer to conflicts ranging from domestic insurgency to large-scale interstate wars which, if necessary, both super-powers can contain in order to avoid a direct armed confrontation between them.[53] Small wars tend to originate in the inter-related volatilities which characterize domestic, interstate and regional conditions in the Third World. Whatever their complex origins and overlapping labels (anti-colonialism, anti-imperialism, separatism, irredentism, religious or ideological messianism, etc.) small wars can still be exploited by Soviet global opportunism. To the extent that they are involved at all, NATO members (essentially Britain, France and the US, but occasionally also smaller Allies, such as Belgium in the case of the 1977 and 1978 Shaba crises) will have shifting, at times contradictory but generally limited, stakes in such conflicts. Thus, apart from cases where specific and vital national interests appear to be immediately at stake (as in British sovereignty over the Falkland Islands), the many grey areas of small wars offer those NATO members few reliable criteria on which to base a calculus of interests, threats and appropriate responses. Because of their complexity, local circumstances are easily misinterpreted, and may be contradicted by the possible regional or even global dimensions of the conflict. The resulting policy dilemmas experienced by those NATO members involved can be particularly intractable, as in the case of America which, as a super-power, sees its foreign policy permanently exposed to the many and often conflicting pressures from a turbulent international environment.

The general question of involvement in small wars is fraught with perplexities and the military dimensions of involvement can be hazardous and complex. First, small wars tend to pose shifting and exacting requirements in terms of doctrine, manpower, training and equipment. Due to the increased conventional power of many third-world states, as well as covert or overt interventions by external powers through the provision of arms, military advisers or even combat troops, small wars can turn into protracted and mixed conflicts in which high-intensity conventional phases and low-intensity insurgency operations alternate.[54] A relatively minor operation, such as the American-led intervention in Grenada in October 1983 (which had to be executed swiftly for domestic political reasons in the US), involved about 6,000 paratroops, marines and rangers, a naval task force of 12 ships and some dozens of transport aircraft and helicopters. The operational complexities of small wars can be compounded by the growing terrorist component of international violence. This was underlined by the October 1983 bombing of the US and French headquarters of the Western MNF in Beirut, in which 239 American marines and 58 French soldiers were killed. This dramatic event, which contributed to the US military withdrawal from Lebanon in February 1983, suggests more generally that the present-day exigencies of small wars do not allow NATO the luxury of intellectual confusion as to the goals of small war interventions. Such confusion seemed to be present in the Western intervention in Beirut which, in the case of the US contingent, saw a force, deployed to keep the peace, later taking sides and engaging Druze militias backed by Syria for more than local reasons.

Second, operational complexities tend to be compounded by the fact that small wars, despite their exacting military requirements, still deal with limited objectives, at least from the point of view of outside powers which happen to intervene in them. But the deep-rooted experiences of the First and Second World Wars have oriented Western, and especially American, military doctrine and force structure towards a type of conflict which, by virtue of its clear-cut and total nature, is least likely to occur today.[55] While US strategists did attempt to develop a theory of limited war in the late 1950s, the US engagement in Vietnam also demonstrated the shortcomings of that theory when applied to a shifting (and messy) combat environment.[56] Moreover, the Vietnam War, as well as the present crisis in Central America, underline America's predicament which stems from the necessity of maintaining its global interests and super-power credibility *vis-à-vis* the USSR, and the equally compelling necessity to avoid being pressed into assuming a global policing role. Because the question of whether or not to intervene abroad is likely to be controversial in the US, the limitations which the US Administration would seek to impose in small wars will themselves tend to be unclear.

Third, success in small wars often depends ultimately on patient, protracted and low-key local in-fighting. As NATO members intervening in support of pro-Western but corrupt and disorganized regimes have come to experience, the potential dynamics of that process may extend to far-reaching political and administrative interference in the affairs of such regimes.[57] Not only are highly visible Western interventionary forces ill-suited to such a task but, for understandable reasons, NATO governments and their military forces generally will be reluctant, if not unwilling, to deepen their involvements in such conflicts beyond strictly military forms of intervention.

The political and military problems raised by involvement in small wars have been contributing to the notion, widespread among Western civilian and military decision-makers alike, that military interventions in small, out-of-area wars can be risky ventures. As a result, those NATO members concerned have sought, with varying degrees of success, to insulate themselves from small-war risks. Britain, France and the US have engaged in bilateral or multilateral diplomacy, encouraged regional security co-operation and adjusted their arms supply policies. They have sought to strengthen key regional partners and, with greater or lesser consistency, to generate doctrines and capabilities tailored to small-war conditions, more recently in the form of rapid deployment forces. Ultimately these policies reflect a shared desire to avoid, when possible, direct military involvement in small wars. The Carter and Reagan Administrations have thus stressed repeatedly deterrence of Soviet aggression in South-west Asia as the primary purpose of the US Rapid Deployment Force, now subsumed in the US Central Command (USCENTCOM).[58] In doing so, they have been acknowledging what has become a fact of US security policies, namely reluctance to fight wars which might present more risks than a Grenada-type operation and which are already clearly less crucial than a Soviet drive for Western Europe, the Persian Gulf or North-east Asia.

Efforts by the Reagan Administration to improve US small-war capabilities[59] so far have not been complemented by a clear consensus in Washington as to the role and method of military power in securing US foreign policy objectives,[60] for instance in the small wars in El Salvador and Nicaragua and with respect to state-sponsored terrorism.[61] Thus, limited covert operations by Special Forces would seem to constitute an effective retaliation against state-sponsored terrorism. Yet, in its air raid on Libya in April 1986, the US chose to employ large and highly visible military forces, including two carrier task forces and 155 fighter aircraft, against a limited number of Libyan ground targets. This decision is likely to fuel the internal policy debate in Washington on the appropriate use of military force.

Given these constraints, NATO governments have generally come to consider the prospective length of involvement as the decisive criterion for the way in which they might intervene militarily in small, out-of-area wars. Rather than expose themselves to a protracted and costly process of creeping escalation, with no decisive results on the ground and no tangible political benefits for the intervening power, they have instead opted for interventions which could be expected to be short and effective enough not to undermine the relation between ends and means of involvement (as in Zaire 1977–8, Chad 1983 and Grenada 1983). The future ability and willingness of Britain, France and the US to heed this criterion may well affect the importance of that other constraint on military interventions out-of-area by NATO members – public and political opinion at home.

THE SOVIET MILITARY THREAT

The ability of a state to use military force far beyond its borders is determined generally by the availability of in-place forces abroad and by adequate power projection capabilities, namely a capable blue-water navy, supported by strategically located bases, sufficient long-range air transport and significant amphibious forces. The success or failure of distant military interventions is seen to hinge on the judicious co-ordination of these three components. In assessing the ability of the Soviet Union to mount successful military operations outside the NATO area, a basic distinction should be made between areas which are contiguous or close to Soviet borders and those which are more distant.

Its relative proximity to the USSR and Soviet-occupied Afghanistan, as well as its vital economic importance to the West, designate the Persian Gulf as the one region on which Allied concerns over the Soviet military threat out-of-area continue to focus most. Here, in theory at least, the Soviet Union could take full advantage of its very large airborne force (seven divisions of about 7,300 men each), and beat the main Western powers in a race to occupy the oilfields. By contrast, the US seems to face a daunting task in projecting and sustaining sufficient military power at such a great distance from home, in an area where it would hardly have bases readily available. But apart from the political improbability of such a scenario, various factors raise doubts about the feasibility of a Soviet military *fait accompli* in the Persian Gulf.[62] Thus, the forbidding terrain and primitive transportation infrastructure of Iran could delay considerably a Soviet overland advance into Iran and onwards to the Gulf. Any such advance would entail a major military operation, requiring elaborate measures to upgrade the usually low combat readiness of troops in the southern Military Districts of the Soviet Union. In turn, this could give the US the warning time needed to deploy sufficient rapid intervention units and airpower to be able to meet the Soviet overland threat in central Iran and to interdict Soviet airborne assault and aerial resupply operations.

A more likely threat might be a limited Soviet move into northern Iran in the context of a long-term, step-by-step military penetration of the area. Such a move would present the USSR with three basic advantages: it would be more feasible from a military standpoint; it would fit into an overall strategy of gradually pressuring local regimes into compliance with

Soviet objectives; and, by virtue of its seemingly limited nature, it would tend to encourage a hesitant, rather than a determined, military response on the part of the US and its NATO Allies.

The steady build-up of its conventional rapid deployment forces since 1980 has put the US in a better position to deter Soviet military moves towards the Persian Gulf than was the case in December 1979, when the Soviet Union invaded Afghanistan. And while simultaneous contingencies in South-west Asia, Europe and possibly elsewhere would dangerously stretch American military resources, it is a problem which would presumably affect the USSR as well – albeit to a lesser extent. Meanwhile, the unpredictable origins of potential threats to Gulf security – an external Soviet threat, internal destabilization of the Gulf states, or both – as well as the reluctance of states like Saudi Arabia to accept US forces on their soil, generate continuing uncertainties as to the basic purpose and the means of US military planning in the area. Ultimately, it could well be the quality of US relations with key Arab states (which might or might not provide it with critical bases in the area before and during a conflict) which, to a large extent, would determine the military margin of manoeuvre of the West in South-west Asia.[63]

More distant areas, such as Africa, Latin America and the Pacific, have also come within reach of Soviet military power. The Soviet Union has been steadily acquiring a global military capability during the past 15 years. Yet the main components of that capability continue to be subject to various constraints, the effect of which may well be compelling in situations which would trigger a military response on the part of the United States, possibly assisted by one or more of its NATO allies.

With respect to in-place forces abroad, the Soviet and Eastern Bloc military presence in Africa is of impressive, if not of colonial proportions, reaching about 35,200 troops and advisers stationed in more than 11 countries.[64] But the bulk of these forces are engaged, as already noted, in securing endangered client regimes against numerous internal and external threats. Moreover, only the Cuban contingent forms a large regular combat force, the others consisting mainly of advisers who are involved in training and familiarizing indigenous forces with Soviet equipment. In Africa, Eastern Bloc troops are unlikely to engage opponents other than weak local forces under favourable political and military circumstances except, as in the past, South African incursions into Angola. In Cuba the continued presence since 1962 of a Soviet brigade, as a unit separate from the acknowledged Soviet training mission to the Cuban Armed Forces,[65] mainly serves to underline Soviet support for the Castro regime, but the alleged threat posed by Soviet ground forces in Cuba, which led to what seemed to many to be a rather artifical Soviet-American crisis in 1979,[66] remains hard to define in the absence so far of a forthright Soviet guarantee to defend Cuba militarily if necessary. In Nicaragua, the Eastern Bloc military presence has succeeded in tying down some US military resources, although not yet to the detriment of other US strategic commitments in Europe, North-east Asia and the

Pacific.[67] But certainly this has led to a substantial intensification of the American military presence in Central America, an area where Soviet policies will not play a critical role and where the USSR will almost certainly not allow an escalation into a direct confrontation with the US. More generally, the Soviet Union has experienced the third-world allergy to foreign military presences which extends both to East and West. This was demonstrated in 1972 when Egypt abruptly dismissed 6,000 Soviet military advisers.

The perceived growth of Soviet power projection capabilities as such is mainly related to the emergence of the Soviet Navy as a modern and powerful force. In 1986 it deployed a very large and still expanding submarine force (448 strategic delivery, cruise-missile and attack units) and 289 major surface combatants.[68] Apart from the strategic targeting of NATO territory with nuclear weapons, the Soviet Navy poses two other main threats to the Allies, both inside and outside the NATO area: interdiction of Western use of the sea; and the projection of military force against targets ashore.

With permanent deployments (augmented periodically by large task force exercises) in the Pacific, the Indian Ocean and the Caribbean, as well as a regular patrol off the West African coast, the Soviet naval presence has acquired worldwide dimensions.[69] Impressive as these deployments may be, nevertheless they call for several qualifying remarks. Judging from fleet composition and deployment patterns, the main peacetime function of the Soviet Navy is to underline the global nature of Soviet interests. Under crisis or war conditions, however, the credibility of the Soviet Navy would be put to more severe tests. The Soviet ability to interdict shipping effectively, for instance, would suppose a clear ability to deny Western command of the seas, to be acquired through sustained operations in distant waters against possibly several, on the whole more capable, Western navies.[70] In fulfilling this requirement the Soviet Navy would have to face important operational constraints, stemming from geographical handicaps and, barring the availability of a warm-water port on the Indian Ocean, over-extended lines of communication between the Atlantic and Asian-Pacific theatres and rather poor maritime surveillance capabilities in distant areas. Moreover, Soviet naval logistics still suffer from limited replenishment and rearming capabilities at sea. Finally, while the Soviet Navy has gained access to ports in many regions of the world, only a few of these naval facilities provide both secure and extensive forward maintenance and logistic support.

A better measurement of the actual threat posed by the Soviet Navy outside the NATO area is perhaps to be found in the disposition and ability of the Soviet leadership to exploit fully the range of political and military options offered by the inherent flexibility of sea-power.[71] The effective use of sea-power, which for the major NATO members is a matter of both tradition and necessity, may not carry the same familiarity and appeal to a state geared primarily and traditionally to land warfare.[72]

With respect to the air component of Soviet power projection capabilities, Soviet land-based Naval Aviation does pose a significant threat to Western surface navies when within range.[73] The USSR gave ample evidence of its ability to airlift considerable amounts of troops and equipment in the 1973 Arab-Israeli war (massive resupply of Egypt and Syria), Angola and Ethiopia (transport of Cuban troops and their equipment in 1975–6 and 1977–8 respectively, together with one major deployment exercise of Soviet airborne forces), and Afghanistan (since 1979). But US long-distance airlift capabilities, which have been significantly enhanced since 1980, also reveal the comparative weaknesses of Soviet Military Transport Aviation, namely a limited number of heavy-lift aircraft and a lack of in-flight refuelling capacity.[74] Finally, the amphibious component of Soviet power projection capabilities remains clearly inferior to Western forces, even when discounting the probability that a substantial proportion of the almost 236,000 marines from six NATO members (as opposed to only 16,000 Soviet Naval Infantry troops) would have to be retained for operations within the NATO area.[75] This is accentuated by the fact that US marine forces form an autonomous corps with much larger independent staying power than Soviet amphibious forces.

Implications
From what has been said, actual and potential threats to wider Western security interests are manifold and, in many respects, inevitable. Some threats present, or could present, security risks, the gravity of which is difficult to measure. A calculus of shared Western out-of-area interests and external threats to these interests therefore cannot be established in any comprehensive and conclusive way. This suggests the following implications.

First, any wider interests which NATO members may have in common still need a shared perception of an impending threat – a renewed Arab oil embargo, another 'Afghanistan', escalating anti-Western terrorism – to be brought into sharp relief. Yet the NATO Allies will find it hard to satisfy this prerequisite, if only because the US – as a super-power engaged in a worldwide contest with the USSR – will tend to make more of such threats than Western Europe, while subsequent European endorsement of US early threat perceptions will by no means be automatic.

Second, most existing out-of-area vulnerabilities, whether shared by NATO members or not, are there to be managed rather than solved. And where they can be anticipated and identified in time, future out-of-area challenges – such as changing economic and strategic factors in the Arctic region[76] – can become the subject of appropriate national and co-ordinated policy responses on the part of NATO members. While intra-Alliance management may be desirable if not indispensable in some cases, appropriate national initiatives remain an essential precondition to intergovernmental co-operation. For both constitutional and political reasons, the NATO Alliance may often not be the appropriate forum for such co-operation, especially in the economic field, where other Western organizations such as the IEA, the OECD and the EEC have well-established competences. Moreover, for geographical or other reasons, Western or Western-oriented nations which are not NATO members, such as Australia, Israel or Japan, may be in a better position to manage certain wider Western interests in direct and indirect ways (See Chapter III).

Third, management often begins at home, as illustrated by domestic policies designed to reduce oil import dependency or by the development of national power-projection capabilities.

Fourth, the management of crises arising from third-world turmoil and radicalism should reflect the fact that such crises are not dominantly regional, poverty-related or Soviet-induced, but generally are a mixture of these elements. Admittedly, there are limits here to the fine tuning of national policy to the various dimensions of these crises, but then some comfort may be taken from the fact that the shifting interaction between these dimensions generates complexities which tend, in the process, to hedge against clear-cut and lasting 'losses' for the West as a whole. This suggests that there often will be scope for Western reactions which, politically and militarily, can show restraint or even aloofness towards many endemic crises in the Third World.

Fifth, the East–West dimension of NATO's out-of-area problem is both real and relative. The 'presence' of the USSR in many parts of the globe is a logical and, in time, inevitable corollary to its super-power status and rivalry with the West. Meanwhile, the force of third-world nationalism, as well as the rising economic costs of global involvement, have been forcing the Soviet Union to shelve any systematic plan for worldwide domination which it might have harboured and instead to pursue essentially opportunistic policies. Soviet activism in the Third World has confirmed what was already known about the Soviet Union: a one dimensional dependence on military strength and a basic lack of economic, ideological and cultural appeal. NATO members draw – and should continue to draw – upon their contrasting and comparative advantages over the USSR. By addressing the structural causes of global disorder, co-ordinated Western action to stabilize the international economic and monetary system, to sustain development co-operation with third-world countries and to pursue active bilateral and multilateral diplomacy constitute tangible and intangible assets which, in the longer term, may be more effective in influencing any global correlation of forces than military power only.

Sixth, the availability of viable military options nevertheless forms an essential prerequisite for a credible management by NATO members of some of their more pressing out-of-area vulnerabilities. Such options help to deter Soviet global adventurism, to contain or defuse dangerous small wars and to encourage local states to maintain or develop ties with the West. Expressed in terms of their combined conventional power projection capabilities, the major NATO members do have military options which remain credible enough to restrain the Soviet Union and, *a fortiori*, unfriendly local states, as Libya's reaction to the US retaliatory air raid of

April 1986 seems to indicate. Even in the crucial South-west Asian theatre, where the USSR enjoys the important advantage of geographical proximity, other factors may well add up to a regional military balance of sorts between East and West.

Rather than military capabilities as such, it is the way in which they are used which appears to be most controversial. Small-war challenges, when taken up, tend to undermine the timely and cost-effective use of precious military resources diverted from the NATO area as an instrument of a broader and more coherent policy. The operational uncertainties which exist can be compounded when internal subversion combines with an external threat, as for instance in any possible Soviet-led destabilization of the Persian Gulf states (the case of British – and Iranian – assistance to Oman in the Dhofari Rebellion might be cited here). Sharp but limited, open or covert, military interventions by NATO members may diminish or make manageable some of the hazards implied by such dangerously ambiguous contingencies. Beyond that, the way in which military action is used out-of-area by NATO members is necessarily influenced by wider factors, such as the basic readiness of the US and its major NATO allies to accept irreducible risks entailed by the use of force, the overall military balance between both super-powers and the state of East–West relations.

III. MANAGING OUT-OF-AREA CHALLENGES INSIDE AND OUTSIDE NATO

This final Chapter will examine the current prospects for out-of-area security management. To what extent are out-of-area issues an Alliance concern? If they are, how much unity of policy is possible and how much is desirable? What are the implications for the defence of Western Europe in light of the transatlantic debate on 'burden-sharing' and 'division of labour'?

The answers to these questions may vary greatly, depending on the type and the gravity of particular contingencies. In terms of their effect on the Alliance, out-of-area issues divide themselves into at least two quite separate types of contingencies. First, there are the many, often distant and diffuse contingencies, which are hard to define as challenges to the Alliance as a whole, because they affect only one Ally or a small group of Allies. At the same time, such contingencies can affect relations between NATO members and therefore tend to be construed as Alliance problems. Second, there are those extra-European threats which directly involve the USSR, and therefore engage the expectations underlying NATO's *raison d'être*, namely the deterrence of Soviet aggression.

Drawing on present cases of policy frictions as well as co-operation out-of-area, this Chapter will first review the main ways in which NATO members appear to respond to, and actually to manage, the first type of contingency. Later it will consider the Alliance management of the Soviet threat beyond Europe.

Exploiting convergence and divergence

Apart from clear-cut cases of direct Soviet intervention, as in Afghanistan, there is no convincing reason why the members of an Alliance which exists for the overriding purpose of providing security in Europe, should necessarily agree on issues in other regions of the world. To expect the contrary would be to subject allied solidarity to unnatural tests which risk jeopardizing agreement on NATO's more central security concerns. Conversely, out-of-area issues need not constitute a preordained source of dispute between allies. As their more recent experiences in two such important regions as the Middle East and Central America seem to suggest, convergence as well as divergence determine the extent to which intra-Alliance relations beyond Europe need special management.

DIVERGENCES ARE BOTH REAL AND RELATIVE

In the Middle East, Western Europe and the US continue to hold different views of the Soviet threat to the region, of the relative weight of indigenous issues and of the amount of pressure to be applied to Israel with respect to Palestinian self-determination, as well as the more controversial aspects of Israel's security policy as a whole.[1] Yet since the early 1980s there has also been a *de facto* narrowing of the gap between European and

US approaches to the region. The Middle East has become less prominent in US foreign policy, partly because of greatly reduced US dependence on Gulf oil and the diminished Arab threat to Israel since the 1978 Camp David Accords and the Israeli-Egyptian Peace Treaty. Moreover, their manifest inability to exert a decisive influence on the imbroglio of the Middle Eastern peace process, as well as the terrorist factor, have been forcing Western Europe and America into a diplomatic and physical retreat from the area until the regional actors themselves come forward with constructive initiatives and have restored a minimum of local stability.[2] Given the relative impotence of external powers, Western Europe has more or less come to realize the futility of developing new political initiatives of its own, at least for the moment. The Euro-Arab dialogue, set up in the aftermath of the 1974 Arab oil embargo, has been stagnating since 1980. Western Europe was glad to be able to support the 1982 Reagan Plan, which marked a movement towards greater US recognition of Palestinian aspirations. Following the failure in February 1986 of the joint Jordanian/Palestinian Accord on joint action for peace, the EEC Foreign Ministers made it known in June 1986 that, for the time being, they would not launch a new European initiative for the Middle East. In the Persian Gulf, once an area of major out-of-area Alliance disputes, the Allies are by now in unequivocal agreement that the Iraq-Iran War should be ended so as to prevent a direct Iranian victory or a spread of Islamic fundamentalism, either of which could trigger a highly dangerous destabilization of the entire region to the possible benefit of the Soviet Union. Apart from an implicit Western security guarantee to the six member states of the Gulf Co-operation Council (GCC), France and the US, in particular, have found themselves taking Iraq's side in the war.

At a more fundamental level, Western Europe and the US continue to share a broad strategic interest in preventing the intractable conflicts in the area from exacerbating two main threats: an interruption of oil supplies; and the extension of Soviet influence in the Arab world which could lead to a regional East–West confrontation which then might spill over into the European theatre. In addition, NATO members are committed to the security of Israel within internationally-recognized borders. Yet there remain enough factors here to fuel intra-Alliance divergences, affecting both perceptions and policies. Local or external actors may make unexpected moves which, by aggravating regional and domestic instabilities, could provoke different reactions in the NATO members involved. US attempts to align the NATO nations in a campaign to stamp out terrorism in Lebanon, Libya and elsewhere have tended to backfire. Many European NATO governments, with the exception of Britain, worried that the US air strike against Libya in April 1986 was a counter-productive response to state-sponsored terrorism.[3] The reinforcement of the strategic link between the US and Israel since the advent of the Reagan Administration can be expected to be discomforting to at least some European NATO governments. France, for its part, will probably maintain an autonomous policy towards the region, where its growing commercial interests may well outweigh any conflicting Alliance considerations.

Central America is a relative newcomer to the agenda of Allied out-of-area disputes but, with the Grenada issue as well as continuing turmoil in Central America, this region has become a fertile breeding-ground for both transatlantic and intra-European tensions in recent years. Britain decided not to allow the 1983 US intervention in Grenada to lead to a major Anglo-American crisis, in which it would have received ample support from the other European NATO members.[4] Whatever the legal questions posed by this action, its successful outcome helped confer *de facto* legitimacy to an operation which, in the end, seems to have had no lasting effect on transatlantic relations. This may not be the case with respect to American bellicosity in Central America, where the US is concerned about countering domestic and regional subversion which it sees as potentially damaging to its security. Although in wartime, Western control of the area would be vital to the reinforcement and resupply of NATO forces, European peacetime interests in Central America and the Caribbean remain very modest. This helps to explain why transatlantic tensions over this issue tend to assume the character of a philosophical debate on the conduct of North-South relations. Yet there is a real concern in European NATO capitals that the current US policy of applying military and economic pressure on Nicaragua may eventually drag the US into direct and protracted involvement, and thereby serve Soviet regional goals. Not only would this divert US energies and resources from the Alliance, but it would also tend – as during the Vietnam War – to undermine European domestic support for NATO.[5]

This seems to have been realized on both sides of the Atlantic, judging from recent attempts to soothe irritations. During its latter period of power, the French Socialist Government moderated its anti-American stance with respect to Central America, most notably by discontinuing its military aid to Nicaragua.[6] With the gradual improvement of El Salvador's international image and corresponding doubts about the Sandinistas' commitment to democratic pluralism in Nicaragua, European policy-makers now tend to show more appreciation of the dilemmas confronting the US and of the risks to their residual dependencies and commitments in the area.[7] The US Administration, for its part, no longer makes serious attempts to turn the Central American crises into an Alliance problem, but, given the facts of geography, their differing stakes in the region and their unequal roles in the world, Europe and the US must learn to live with irreducible divergences over this issue. Thus the US is still inclined to see Western European political support for the 1984 Contadora Peace Plan and economic aid to Nicaragua as rather gratuitous attempts on the part of its NATO partners to carve out a political niche in the Central American conflict.[8] Conversely, Western Europe will consider US ambivalence towards regional negotiations and, more generally, the Marxist regime in Nicaragua as indicative of a basic unwillingness on the part of the US to come to terms with some revision of its traditional preponderance in the Western hemisphere.[9] Such transatlantic differences are fed in no small measure by varying estimates of the Soviet threat and, correspondingly, of the prospects for moderate (non-radical) reformist political regimes following a course of genuine non-alignment in Central America.

Transatlantic differences over third-world policy are often mitigated by parallel, albeit more subtle, divergences among the European NATO members themselves. First, Britain, France – and to a certain extent Italy – do acknowledge the military dimensions of third-world contingencies and, within limits, the possible need for Western military action. The smaller European NATO members, however, tend to be sceptical of, or clearly opposed to, military interventions outside the context of the UN collective security system. Second, the various privileged ties between European NATO members and third-world countries are a breeding-ground for occasional intra-European conflicts of national interest, as the Falklands issue has shown. With no negotiated solution yet in sight, this issue remains a latent source of tension between Britain and some of its NATO partners with close ties to Argentina and Latin America in general (Italy, Spain, but also the US). As the issue of the Argentine aggression of 1982 tends to recede into the background, and as Argentina holds to a democratic path, Britain may find the measure of Allied support which it was able to muster at the time, will erode in the longer term.[10] This may be all the more the case since there are hardly any East–West or strategic considerations at the moment which would build up a compelling case for Allied solidarity over the political future of the Falklands Islands. In Africa, the two Western interventions in Zaire in 1977 and 1978 have been indicative of Belgium's resentment at French inroads into its former colony.[11] And Spain's position with respect to its North African enclaves of Ceuta and Melilla may well not receive support from other European NATO members, depending on strategic developments in North Africa and on the evolution of the related Gibraltar issue.[12]

EUROPEAN ROLES IN SUPPORT OF WIDER WESTERN
SECURITY INTERESTS

European NATO members, acting on a national, bilateral or multilateral basis, have always played out-of-area roles which address some third-world security challenges. Economically, most European NATO members actively combat underdevelopment, that crucial source of third-world instability, by sustaining the largest amounts of aid in the West to low-income countries, as well as by organizing large-scale humanitarian and disaster relief operations.[13] Where the US finds itself handicapped by its anti-Soviet, pro-Israeli super-power profile, European NATO members are in a position to generate goodwill and influence for the West. Thus the US has come to recognize the wider strategic utility in the Middle East of French, British and Italian privileged connections in some Arab capitals, resulting, for example, in politically important arms sales to Iraq and other Gulf states. At times Western Europe can also help to mitigate the consequences of Washington's foreign policy biases and errors. Thus, it can at least be argued that the European-Arab entente on the Palestinian question and its long-term regional repercussions has been limiting the damage done to the West's standing in the region by US deference to Israeli intransigence on this issue.

Also, Europe's extensive historical experience of the limited utility of military force in third-world conflicts can help to save the US from rash interventions, which risk antagonizing both local actors and key NATO partners. British and French pleas with the US for moderation towards a perceived Soviet activism in the Third World are not necessarily rationalizations of an alleged Western European impotence out-of-area. The US is sometimes reluctant to recognize that Britain and France, working through broadly-based groupings, such as the Commonwealth and the community of Francophone states in Africa, can quietly promote policies congenial to Western interests. In Africa, Britain was the principal architect, albeit in close co-operation with America, of the 1979 Rhodesian peace settlement, which left both South Africa and the Soviet Union on the sidelines. Following the US intervention in Grenada in 1983, the Commonwealth has been active in addressing ways to reduce the various vulnerabilities faced by small states and to supplement the mechanisms of the UN collective security system.[14] With 17 Central American member states, the Commonwealth could play a stabilizing role in an area which now figures so prominently among US security concerns. Without necessarily involving Britain directly, Commonwealth peace-keeping forces and intra-Commonwealth assistance may help to defuse third-world turmoil (as Tanzania did in the Seychelles in 1977 or Papua New Guinea in Vanuatu in 1980). In 1985-6 the Commonwealth was also involved in the search for a negotiated solution to the mounting domestic crisis in South Africa.

France, for its part, remains the leading Western actor in large areas of sub-Saharan Africa. In 1984 the eleventh Franco-African Summit, attended by delegations from 37 African states, confirmed the considerable influence retained by France on the continent.[15] Similarly, with respect to Central America, as well as Angola and Mozambique, there may be scope for some political roles on the part of Spain and Portugal respectively.

The image of a 'civilian' Europe which leaves the defence of wider Western interests to the US is hardly supported by the record of security involvements out-of-area on the part of Western European NATO members. Britain and France maintain a fairly comprehensive range of military activities out-of-area which, on the whole, have been effective in meeting widespread third-world security challenges in the lower and middle regions of the conflict spectrum. First, there is the strengthening of friendly governments against the threats of external aggression and internal subversion through arms transfers, advisers, security assistance and, where needed, direct military intervention. In this, Britain and France each display a certain degree of role specialization by virtue of geography. In early 1986, in the strategically important Gulf area, Britain had nearly 400 servicemen on loan to every littoral state except Iraq and Iran, a very successful practice which the US is prevented by law from emulating.[16] The British military presence in Belize, a Commonwealth member, guarantees the security of one of the few Central American democracies, thereby also relieving America from an additional burden in the area.[17] France concentrates on Africa, where it had more than 7,000 troops and 1,000 advisers permanently deployed in 1985, and in the Pacific.[18] Most importantly, Britain and France have shown repeatedly that they are not unwilling to stage direct military interventions out-of-area. Significantly enough, these interventions represented either the US assisting in a wider, European military effort, or actions carried out independently of the US.[19]

Second, Britain and France contribute substantially to various international peacekeeping operations in the Middle East, along with Denmark, Italy, the Netherlands, Norway and Canada.[20] European participation in the Multinational Force and Observers to the Sinai (MFO) and, earlier, in Beirut (MNF) in particular represent an important measure of support for US policies for the Middle East. Some other European NATO members also play certain security roles in the wider world. While prohibited by constitutional and historical reasons from assuming overt political and military roles out-of-area, West Germany has become a very important indirect exporter of arms to the Third World.[21] The closest West Germany came to an out-of-area intervention was its successful anti-terrorist operation at Mogadishu, Somalia in 1977. This is a field in which West German specialists have built up an international reputation comparable to that of their British and French counterparts.[22] The Netherlands and Spain retain small garrisons in their remaining Caribbean and North African dependencies, while Portugal has forces on loan to Angola and Mozambique. Both Iberian NATO members possess forces which they could decide to employ out-of-area under certain circumstances and conditions. Finally, it is worth noting that Belgium, among the smaller European NATO members, has appeared willing to participate militarily in the two Western interventions in Zaire.

POLICY CO-ORDINATION ON A 'VARIABLE GEOMETRY' BASIS

The foregoing suggests a *de facto* decentralization and, by implication, that national out-of-area activities complement those of other nations, in accordance with the comparative advantages enjoyed by individual Allies beyond Europe. Rather than constituting an unspecified goal in itself, policy co-ordination should functionally promote complementarity between national activities out-of-area. In practice, this is already taking place in several ways. First, at the level of practical policy aimed at safeguarding concrete interests, Britain, France and the US tend to show greater recognition of each other's postures out-of-area than national rhetoric sometimes suggests. Thus, judging from less known bilateral *quid pro quo*, it can be safely assumed that the US does appreciate certain

British and French activities and capabilities.[23] Conversely, by deferring in practice to the US where their specific interests tend to be marginal or the political costs of opposition seem prohibitive, most European NATO members do recognize that the US cannot run its foreign policy on the basis of a permanent opinion poll among its various allies.[24]

Second, the Allies have been investigating how intergovernmental co-operation may enhance the effectiveness of national action. This is reflected in the number of Allies involved, as well as in the nature of such co-operation. Thus Western concerted action out-of-area comprising Britain, France and the US as core actors has been enlarged occasionally to include other NATO members, if their participation appeared to be related to the goals of the operation as well as to their national self-interest (Belgium in Zaire, Italy in the MNF, and West Germany in Namibia are examples of this trend). Co-operation may be of an economic, political or military nature or a combination of these, but co-operation clearly produces the best results when it takes place on a temporary basis for a specific and identifiable purpose.

Third, such co-operation based on 'variable geometry' is reflected in the flexible and informal approach to consultations: choice of forum, timing and intentions remain discretionary. There are enough fora where governments can meet to discuss the wider aspects of Western security. Regular bilateral political-military talks provide a basic, but essential means of consultations. The 'principal nations' have two main fora outside NATO where they can discuss out-of-area questions *en marge* of official agendas: the 'Berlin Group', comprising Britain, France and the US – with their special responsibilities for Berlin – and West Germany; and the annual economic summits of the leaders of the seven major industrial democracies (Britain, Canada, France, Italy, Japan, US, West Germany). Some European members of NATO have the European Political Co-operation (EPC) mechanism as well as the Western European Union (WEU) at their disposal. And there is NATO itself, where Alliance-wide exchanges of views on out-of-area developments take place on a regular basis within the North Atlantic Council, the Defence Planning Committee (DPC) and other bodies of the Organization. Allied views on a wide range of past and present trouble-spots in the world have thus been reflected in the biannual communiqués of the Council and the DPC.[25] And in a crisis not directly implicating the USSR, such as the second Western intervention in Zaire in 1978, NATO was already seen to function as one of the possible channels of communication between those Allies involved, as well as a political sounding board in the aftermath of the crisis.

Current consultative practices within and outside NATO appear adequate to deal functionally with the many out-of-area questions not directly involving the Soviet Union, even though the present arrangements will not always satisfy bureaucratic preoccupations with procedures. No amount of institutional reform can conceal the fact that the political will to co-operate, especially at crucial moments, remains the key factor in reaching substantive agreement. In view of this, proposals for streamlining Allied decision-making in out-of-area matters are subject to the following qualification.[26] Many out-of-area events, it should be recalled, are primarily dealt with on the basis of national action. To the extent that intergovernmental co-operation may prove necessary, it appears that the approach of the 'principal nations' already tends to function in practice, with a core group of nations able and willing to intervene out-of-area diplomatically, militarily or both, on the basis of restricted consultations held on the margin of, or wholly outside, NATO. On the other hand, a direct Soviet challenge out-of-area should clearly remain a matter for the Alliance as a whole, even though this may actually complicate the elaboration of co-ordinated responses. Therefore, there seems to be no direct need for formalizing the 'principal nations' practice. Irrespective of whether a 'principal nations' group would leave NATO's present consultative structure untouched, nevertheless it may antagonize at least some of the smaller Allies and undermine their commitment to NATO's central concerns.

FUNCTIONAL AND GEOGRAPHICAL INTERDEPENDENCE

The interdependence of functional and geographical issues is seen most clearly in the Middle East, where Western oil and geopolitical interests have been intersecting in various and often divisive ways. The most recent and vivid example of this remains the 1973 Arab-Israeli War, when the US considered Europe's 'stooping for oil' to be one of the primary causes of the perceived unreliability of NATO Allies during and after the conflict.[27] The interaction between economic and out-of-area controversies among the Allies is also apparent when Western Europe objects to the use of economic sanctions by the US against pro-Soviet states which also happen to be strategically important. A recent example of this was the imposition of a trade embargo by the US against Nicaragua in May 1985. Another issue which is often connected with out-of-area debates is the question of conventional arms transfers by NATO members to sensitive areas in the Third World. Not only have arms exports become critical to the economic viability of independent European weapons industries, but for European governments they also constitute a preferred way – and often the only way – to play a security role in certain areas.[28] As a result, competition rather than co-operation characterizes US, British and French arms transfer policies to third-world states. Where Britain and France seek to remain reliable and accessible suppliers, the US is traditionally concerned about the impact of unrestrained arms transfers on military balances in volatile regions of the Third World. Yet urgent political and strategic considerations have forced the US repeatedly to reverse its declaratory policies, thereby undermining its predictability as an arms supplier, at times to the benefit of the Soviet Union.[29]

Western summit meetings still represent the best instrument for developing a more comprehensive approach towards a wide range of interrelated, functional and geographical issues. Thus NATO summits have been devoting increasing attention to such problems as Western oil security, non-alignment, underdevelopment, East-West economic relations and international terrorism.[30] The annual seven-nation economic summits can deal with functional issues which may exceed NATO's competence. But 'summitry' by no means constitutes a panacea, as it remains subject to most of the constraints affecting Western out-of-area policy co-ordination in general. Although summits are supposed to engage the political will of Heads of State and Government, they have a mixed record of effectiveness. In order to reach substantive decisions which are effectively followed up, summits must seek to avoid both superficial preparation and bureaucratic ritualization. Here as elsewhere, much depends on the abilities and personal relationships of Western political leaders.[31]

MANAGING DOMESTIC OPINION

Earlier in this Paper domestic opinion was seen at times to play a major role in determining the scope and direction of national out-of-area policies. Acting under pressure of special interests and public opinion at large, legislatures no longer limit themselves to setting the basic objectives of foreign and defence policies. They also tend to intervene actively in the day-to-day implementation of these objectives. This exposes government action more directly to the vagaries of the domestic political process at a time when global turmoil and rapidly shifting geostrategic pressures make greater demands on the coherence, flexibility and predictability of national policy responses. The constraints of domestic opinion also tend to reproduce themselves at the Alliance level, where democratic governments find it all the more difficult to reduce out-of-area policy divisions between them, divisions which are fed by the activities of politically influential interest groups at home. This is clearly the case with transatlantic frictions over both Israel and Central America, and, indeed, as it was over Vietnam. Conversely, increasing domestic pressures for concerted Western action may, for better or for worse, submerge existing policy differences between Allied governments, for example, with respect to the desirability of economic sanctions against South Africa.[32]

In handling their respective domestic opinions, Allied governments face difficulties. In Britain and France, short of a major government crisis, the ruling party can usually count on the support of its majority in parliament for its wider security policies.[33] In the US, by contrast, the constitutional doctrine of separated powers – as well as the breakdown of the so-called bipartisan approach to foreign policy since Vietnam – tends to pit Congress and the President against one another.[34] They can also result in differences between the House and Senate, thus forcing American Administrations to resort to unsatisfactory stop-gap measures.[35] Whether over defence budgeting, the deployment of US forces in hostilities abroad, foreign economic and military assistance programmes or foreign intelligence operations, Congress has clearly reduced the scope for presidential discretion to the point of weakening the effectiveness of American security policies and, thereby, the structures of Western security. By manipulating – and sometimes effectively blocking – US arms transfers and economic assistance programmes, Congress risks antagonizing recipient countries whose friendships might have served wider US security interests.[36] While the constraints of the 1973 War Powers Act may have been exaggerated,[37] nevertheless these constraints complicate and politicize US use of military force abroad.[38] This is especially the case in ambiguous, undeclared 'small wars' of the kind continuing in Lebanon; the deployment there of US Marines in the context of the Western MNF thus led to protracted disputes between the US Department of Defense and Congress.[39]

Political and human factors, rather than institutional or even constitutional reform, are likely to be decisive in handling domestic opinion at the national level. But this should not prevent all Allied governments, and the US in particular, from following a number of prudent rules.[40] They should avoid public rhetoric which they cannot subsequently back up with concrete policies. Governments, which have both the will and the capability to use force abroad if necessary, should restrict themselves to morally defensible interventions which involve minimal numbers of conscripts, can be concluded successfully and quickly. In turn, this implies a good appreciation of the various circumstances in an out-of-area crisis which warrant reliance on, respectively, internal crisis-management, regional policing, external intervention or some combination of these.[41] Governments contemplating out-of-area action should also make full use of NATO as a sounding board for the range of domestic opinions existing within the Alliance. Finally, governments should refrain from participating in multinational military or peacekeeping interventions if it is likely that they will be unable to sustain their participation. Forced withdrawal of one participant not only strains relations with the others, but can also endanger and discredit the entire operation.[42]

The Alliance and the global containment of the Soviet Union
Out-of-area events which directly implicate the Soviet Union are challenges, direct or indirect, to the Alliance as a whole. The main issues at stake here revolve around the central question: should the European NATO members contribute politically and militarily to US-determined strategies aimed at the global containment of the Soviet Union? There is a wide range of answers to this question and it cannot be answered on the basis of principle. Proposals for managing the Alliance dimensions of the global East–West contest will have to address the potential for harmful internal divisions which exists, taking into account Western European insistence that out-of-area policies remain a matter for national decision.

THREAT ASSESSMENTS AND OBJECTIVES
The most logical approach to this issue would be to institute closer political contacts between Allies than those implied in the 'frank and timely consultations' recommended by NATO texts in the past. This was

considered by the Allies in the aftermath of the 1982 Bonn Summit which, judging from subsequent NATO ministerial communiqués, represents the most current and authoritative call for reinforced political consultations on out-of-area issues.[43] Such consultations would build upon existing consultative principles and procedures for the purpose of sharing threat assessments and identifying common objectives. The Allies, if they wish, can derive some guidance here from the various inter-related policy statements found in successive NATO communiqués since 1981. Taken together, these statements could be said to demonstrate a certain evolution of Alliance thinking on out-of-area matters since the earlier, and rather vague, admission by NATO members that 'their common interests can be affected by events in other regions of the world' (see Chapter I). Judging from the global range of economic, political and military issues (for example Western oil security, underdevelopment, non-alignment and terrorism) which have found their way into NATO communiqués, the Alliance appears to have gradually adopted a wider security concept than the literal text of the North Atlantic Treaty would suggest.[44] Thus, with respect to threat assessment, the Allies have now come to recognize that their collective interests may be involved if there is economic and political instability in third-world areas. With respect to the identification of common objectives, the Allies have reached agreement on the principle that NATO members, who are in a position to do so, will endeavour to support foreign nations, if their security, independence or territorial integrity are threatened and they have requested one or more NATO members to give assistance.[45]

These policy statements would seem to establish objective criteria by which to ascertain whether Soviet and Soviet-inspired actions do indeed qualify as a challenge to the Alliance as a whole under the terms and in the spirit of Article V of the North Atlantic Treaty. Yet the danger remains that these attempts at sharing assessments and predictions of Soviet behaviour will founder on the inevitable subjectivity of the assumptions underlying US, British, French and other national out-of-area policies. Thus, transatlantic and, to a lesser extent, intra-European divergences over the divisibility of East–West detente and the nature of third-world conflict will continue to interact with differing assessments of the nature of the Soviet state, with divergent estimates of Soviet aggressiveness and argument about the constraints on Soviet global policies. Thus recently, many Western Europeans have perceived the USSR as less willing to allow itself to be used by third-world states in local conflicts, and more reluctant to take on more responsibilities in the Third World. This is clearly not the American view. Whether or not the highwater mark of Soviet expansionism has passed becomes – almost inevitably – a matter of transatlantic conjecture, debate and even acrimony.

Furthermore, there are difficulties with the idea of closer consultation, at least in crisis. First, attempts to reconcile differing perceptions and responses may be hard, not least because perceptions and risks change under the pressures engendered by crisis. Second, Britain, France and the

US, while paying lip service to the notion of more and better consultations, appear to be satisfied on the whole with the existing habits of multilateral political consultations in the North Atlantic Council and its subordinate bodies, supplemented where needed by *ad hoc* bilateral contacts.[46] This should come as no surprise, since it has been precisely the limitations of present consultative mechanisms which have helped to preserve the foreign policy autonomy of NATO's three main out-of-area actors. Third, at the transatlantic level, Western Europe and the US tend to expect different things from consultations, whether reinforced or not. While Western Europe seeks to keep abreast of US policy towards the USSR without necessarily wanting to share responsibility for any moves, the US seems to believe that the observance of the mere appearance of consultation will gain it Western European endorsement of its policies. Hence George Ball's scratchy description of the Europeans as 'merely voyeurs of the world's troubles'.[47] Fourth, the *nature* of such reinforced consultations remains unclear: would they be limited to the exchange of national views on political issues only? Or would they also be aimed at harmonizing these views, possibly including military matters as well? While the latter proposition is certain to raise objections from various quarters within the Alliance, the former adds little to existing practice. Fifth, depending on the circumstances of specific out-of-area contingencies, it may not always be either feasible or desirable to adhere strictly to the pre-eminent competence of the North Atlantic Council for the political aspects of consultations. While there is agreement on the general principle that the Council is the best organ for providing overall political guidance to other NATO consultative or executive bodies, the Allies tend to disagree on the extent to which protracted deliberations in the Council should be allowed to delay military decision-making in the Defence Planning Committee (DPC) in the event of Soviet armed action out-of-area. The choice of forum would be of particular importance for the purpose of hearing France's reactions to or securing French participation in any action that NATO might contemplate, as France can be expected to stay outside NATO's integrated defence activities as supervised by the DPC.

This suggests, then, that the prospects for reinforced NATO consultations, as a means of managing the political repercussions of Soviet actions out-of-area, should not be overestimated. However, this should not prevent the Allies from maintaining or introducing new forms of co-operation at the working level which, especially in crisis, could help members to reach agreement – at least as to the facts – at the political level. Thus, more systematic attention could be devoted to out-of-area developments in the regular reports in which the Allies pool their national intelligence. Similarly, out-of-area incidents could play a larger role in the political and military crisis-management exercises which the Allies conduct every year. Together these measures might enhance Allied capability for emergency consultations in an out-of-area crisis with direct East-West implications.[48]

Beyond such incremental improvements at the NATO level, it is the quality of super-power relations themselves which may broaden or narrow the scope for Allied agreement on the political aspects of the global East-West contest. Transatlantic tensions over a range of issues, including out-of-area questions, are likely to increase if Western Europe were to feel that what it would regard as unwarranted US antagonism towards the USSR was reducing its freedom of manoeuvre in Europe or elsewhere. Britain and France especially share an interest in insulating their 'unique' roles in the Third World from the super-power contest. Conversely, the Western Europeans tend to support any American initiatives which show that out-of-area events need not always pit East and West against one another. Thus, following a call by President Reagan in 1984 for periodical consultations at a political level with the USSR in order to prevent regional crises from degenerating into global confrontations, both super-powers have held informal exchanges of views on Afghanistan, the Middle East, the Far East, Central America and southern Africa since the first half of 1985, and President Reagan laid considerable stress on the resolution of five regional disputes in his speech to the UN on 24 October 1985.[49]

All this implies additional responsibilities for both the US and the European members of NATO. Policy-makers in Washington should realize that their calls for Western unity against the Soviet global threat will have to be supported by a willingness to move beyond the mere form of consultation. They should take the substance of Allied views more into account. This should also be seen as the logical corollary of the erosion of US post-war economic and political predominance. Where once the US could act alone (and could afford to), this will not often be the case in the future. Western Europe, for its part, should realize that parochial approaches to Western security co-operation out-of-area will deprive it of any real influence on US global policies and thus unduly expose its interests to the risks of the super-power contest. A transatlantic understanding along those lines would imply that East–West detente is divisible, but only up to a certain point and only for some purposes.[50] Ultimately, it also implies a Western European willingness to give political endorsement to some US military efforts in support of wider Western interests, even if the US can never assume that support in advance.

MILITARY ASPECTS: MANAGING THE IMPLICATIONS OF US PLANS FOR SOUTH-WEST ASIA

The military dimension, which this Paper can only discuss in general terms, brings some of the political issues mentioned above into sharper focus. From the outset an important distinction should be made between peacetime and wartime conditions. In the event of an armed confrontation between East and West leading to a general war, NATO's out-of-area problem would tend to lose much of its present meaning. Given the experience of the two world wars and what one must assume to be no less (and probably greater) interdependence of various strategic theatres since then, the operational imperatives of such an East–West war would cause the peacetime controversies surrounding Article VI of the North Atlantic Treaty to pass into oblivion.[51] This leaves the *peacetime* containment of the Soviet global military threat, and the additional demands which this puts on American strategy worldwide, as the main out-of-area source of difficulties for the organization of Allied defence co-operation. There are two aspects to these difficulties. First, NATO's old problem of national force diversions out-of-area now manifests itself in the designation, for contingency use by the US Central Command (USCENTCOM), of US forces which are already declared to NATO. Second, such dual-tasking of US forces tends to restate the wider, interlocking problems of transatlantic burden-sharing and division of labour in much more urgent terms.

This complex of issues goes back to around 1977, when US military planners started recognizing that the US would need greater freedom of manoeuvre in the employment of its armed forces in order to be able to deal with two, mutually reinforcing problems: the relative decline of American military power since Vietnam; and the new threats posed by the Soviet Navy and force projection capabilities, particularly in the Indian Ocean, South-west Asia and the Pacific. Given finite resources for defence, the achievement of greater strategic flexibility could only take place at the expense of the unquestioned priority which NATO traditionally held in US strategy overseas and force planning. By revealing the paucity of US military options in South-west Asia, events in Iran and Afghanistan in 1979–80 accelerated the movement towards greater strategic flexibility. In the first half of 1980 the US informed the other Allies that, for planning purposes, American naval, marine and air forces would no longer be swung automatically from the Pacific to the NATO area in the event of Soviet aggression against Western Europe. Since 1980 NATO planners have also had to face up to the fact that, in the event of a prior conflict in South-west Asia, many units declared to NATO could not be redirected to a subsequent conflict in Europe. On paper at least, the magnitude of the repercussions on NATO's deterrent and defensive posture has been increasing with the steady expansion of the manpower available to USCENTCOM since 1980 (290,600 at full strength in 1986, expected to reach a total of 440,000 in 1989).[52]

Judging from successive ministerial communiqués since May 1980, as well as from the Document on Integrated NATO Defence in the Annex to the 1982 Bonn Summit Declaration, America's Allies have come, albeit reluctantly, to acknowledge that they have no alternative but to allow the US greater force mobility in support of vital Western strategic interests out-of-area.[53] They also have developed a number of procedures and criteria for national force deployments out-of-area which amplify the limited notification regime established by the 1955 Council Resolution on Important Changes in National Defence Efforts (see Chapter I). Thus the Allies agree to subject national deployments to multilateral consultations within the appropriate NATO bodies, and to consider appropriate remedial measures which need not necessarily be confined to the deploying Ally.[54] The implementation of these measures, namely the facilitation and the compensation of mainly US out-of-area deployments in support of collective vital interests, calls for the following remarks. Consultations prior to national deployments apply only to situations in which there is a challenge to the Alliance as a whole. Thus Britain did not consult with NATO before deciding to send a task force to retake the Falklands. With respect to the remedial measures themselves, facilitation is the least problematic, because transit rights and authorization to refuel ships and airplanes can be granted on a bilateral basis and need not await any multilateral political consultation in a crisis. Facilitation represents an out-of-area contribution which almost all the Allies can make, and one might expect most progress to take place in this field.[55]

Compensation measures are more problematic because they bring up, inevitably, NATO's wider defence burden-sharing issues. There are several points to be made here. First, confusion may arise as to precisely what should be compensated for and in what circumstances. Under the present terms of NATO's defence planning system the need for compensation arises, strictly speaking, only for out-of-area diversion of national forces which are assigned or earmarked to NATO or designated as 'other forces for NATO'. Out-of-area deployment of forces which are not thus committed to NATO therefore do not qualify for compensation, at least technically. To complicate the matter further, whether out-of-area diversions of national forces which are committed to NATO actually do call for compensation depends on the exact and detailed status of those forces, which, in turn, is subject to variations. These variations are recorded in the annual national replies to NATO's Defence Planning Questionnaire (DPQ), in which NATO members (except France, Iceland and Spain) indicate the existing as well as planned level and commitment of their forces as a measure of their respective progress in implementing NATO's Force Goals. NATO members which are in a position to do so will state their military plans out-of-area by implication, generally by qualifying NATO-programmed commitments of specific national forces in their national DPQ replies. National plans for out-of-area deployments therefore need not terminate the commitment of forces to NATO. This is the case with USCENTCOM forces. Most of these forces are dual-tasked, in that they have a primary European reinforcement role which they retain. Their diversion out-of-area is envisaged for contingency purposes only, although periodic peacetime deployments of selected naval units to the Persian Gulf and the Indian Ocean do take place. But, given the magnitude of a USCENTCOM deployment at full strength, the military eventuality of simultaneous contingencies in Europe and South-west Asia, and the overall political sensitivity of the issue, the US felt obliged to initiate NATO consultations on what, in European eyes at least, constituted – in the terminology of the 1955 Council Resolution – 'an important quantitative or qualitative change' in the force contribution of NATO's most powerful member. Second, the prospects for the adoption of military significant compensation measures in the area of Allied Command Europe (ACE) look rather uncertain at present.[56] Due to various delays, the Allies were unable to incorporate the provisional measures of compensation recommended by the South-west Asia Impact Study into NATO's Force Goals for 1985–90 agreed in May 1984.[57] Moreover, as a result of tight defence budgets and increasing military manpower problems in Western Europe, additional out-of-area Force Goals for 1985–90 adopted by the Allies in November 1984 consist mainly of follow-on studies focusing on the feasibility of compensation.[58] It was also agreed that any concrete recommendations following from these studies would have to be evaluated financially and militarily against competing priorities within the framework of NATO's normal defence planning process. More tangible compensatory measures are now included, or are expected to be included, in the Force Goals for 1987–92 and 1989–94.

Given perennial US criticisms of European defence efforts, this implies a real danger that the question of compensation in Europe for wider US defence efforts will become bogged down in the defence burden-sharing controversy. A recent episode in that controversy was the proposal made by Senators Nunn and Roth in 1984 to reduce progressively US force levels in Europe, should the European NATO members fail to improve their performance in meeting previously agreed Alliance defence goals.[59] Against the background of America's growing absorption with Soviet challenges in the Third World,[60] the Nunn-Roth Amendment, although defeated, seemed to confirm European experiences going back to Korea and Vietnam, that the threat of US troop reductions in Europe tends to be greatest when the US becomes militarily overcommitted out-of-area.[61] On the American side, there is an understandable temptation to use the compensation and burden-sharing issues as interchangeable arguments for greater overall defence efforts on the part of the European NATO members.

However, in keeping with the psychology of intra-Alliance relations, lumping both issues together risks exacerbating transatlantic problems without solving global ones.[62] It may feed European suspicions that, by agreeing to greater defence efforts at home, they would be assisting a US shift away from NATO towards global unilateralism. This is bound to undermine American efforts to secure the degree of European co-operation on which the implementation of American global military strategy manifestly depends. There are, in other words, powerful political arguments for maintaining a distinction between burden-sharing issues within the NATO area and out-of-area compensation measures which involve wider division-of-labour concepts between the Allies. The extent to which such a distinction can be maintained in practice will depend essentially on two factors: the evolution of the Soviet military threat within and outside the NATO area in relation to available Western forces; and a greater willingness on the part of the Allies to address each other's preoccupations – Western Europe by becoming more aware of US frustrations, the US by giving at least its main NATO partners a greater say in its global strategies. This was recognized by the EEC Foreign Ministers at their informal meeting in the Netherlands on 7–8 June 1986, when they decided to intensify political consultations with the US on regional crises outside Europe.

In addition to facilitation and compensation of US global defence efforts, America has also been calling for greater European security involvement, particularly in South-west Asia, for instance through bilateral economic and military assistance to local states, co-operation in the development of contingency plans and participation (actively or as observers) in regional military exercises in the Middle East and elsewhere.[63] These calls have been reflected indirectly in NATO communiqués stating that member nations have a wide and diverse range of possibilities from which to choose in making useful contributions to the promotion of stability and deterrence out-of-area.[64] The scope for such an expansion of European security roles out-of-area appears to be determined by at least three interacting factors. First, European NATO members can be expected to point out that – as noted here – there is in fact no lack of security activities on their part. Their political willingness to tie these and any additional activities more closely to American strategy towards South-west Asia would depend very much on the extent to which Britain and France are able to influence US perceptions of the regional threat posed by the Soviet Union. Given the fact that American planners feel obliged to work almost exclusively on the basis of worst-case scenarios (for instance a Soviet invasion of Iran, Soviet local use of theatre nuclear forces and chemical weapons), it seems important that Western Europe is able to exert a moderating influence here by reminding its US counterparts that most of the out-of-area events which would seem to call for Western military intervention, in fact are unlikely to stem from Soviet actions.

Second, continuing limitations on British and French capabilities for mounting larger-scale military operations overseas underscore the inevitability of an allied division of labour in which the US must continue to bear the brunt of generating decisive military power out-of-area. It is true that during the Falklands Campaign Britain demonstrated how forces could be employed selectively beyond the NATO area.[65] Since 1983 improvements in Britain's out-of-area capabilities, as well as the 1983 reorganization of existing French interventionary forces into the 47,000-strong *Force d'Action Rapide* (FAR), may signal a greater readiness in Europe to help, under certain circumstances, to share the defence burden of USCENTCOM.[66] But at least some of Britain's specialist out-of-area forces are now declared to NATO, while the French FAR should certainly not be identified with USCENTCOM forces. Although the FAR also has an out-of-area role, it responds primarily to French strategic needs in Europe where it could rapidly reinforce NATO's Central Sector. The primacy of NATO commitments would also apply to a putative Italian Rapid Intervention Force with a Mediterranean vocation.[67] Long-range naval deployments by NATO's 'second echelon powers' (Canada, Italy and the Netherlands) also imply some out-of-area capabilities, but they are likely to remain intermittent at best. European out-of-area capabilities thus amount to the ability to redeploy, for specific purposes, forces which could be missed in NATO. European military assets, limited as they already are by budgetary and increasing manpower constraints, are likely to be best employed at home. Efforts to improve these assets should primarily be directed to ensuring their combat sustainability, thus providing more deterrent and defensive capability within the NATO area.[68]

In terms of strategic flexibility and political manageability, co-ordinated (if variable) naval deployments (especially British and French) to the Indian Ocean would seem to be the most cost-effective contribution that Europe could make to US military efforts in South-west Asia.[69] On the other hand, putting what would necessarily be limited numbers of British or French troops ashore alongside USCENTCOM forces may appear to be less manageable, not only politically but also militarily.[70] Britain, France and the US have had relatively little experience, and even less success, in staging joint interventions. This would require a measure of shared decision-making which NATO's main out-of-area actors have not yet been able to evolve, as the experience of the Western MNF in Beirut showed.[71] Furthermore, joint military planning by Britain, France and the US may well founder as they try to answer difficult questions. How unambiguous is the Soviet threat to South-west Asia? What does the answer to this question imply for the composition of national forces, as well as for the strategy and doctrine underlying any joint operations? Are forces to provide a trip-wire or a credible conventional defence? Should geographic or nuclear escalation be contemplated? To what extent should nations report back to the North Atlantic Council and the DPC for political-military clearance?

Third, European NATO members already assist American military efforts out-of-area – directly and indirectly – in important ways. In South-west Asia, there is the indispensable function performed by Diego Garcia, which the US has been leasing from Britain since 1966, as well as possible *en route* support provided by the French bases of La Réunion and Mayotte in the southern Indian Ocean. France is also the only NATO member to maintain permanent forces in the area, namely 3,800 troops in Djibouti and a naval force. Outside South-west Asia, the remaining British and French dependencies in the Caribbean, the South Atlantic and the Pacific tend to acquire increasing strategic value for the projection of air and naval power, as demonstrated by the vital logistic role of Ascension Island during the Falklands Campaign. Significantly, France is considering modernizing and expanding its air and naval facilities in New Caledonia.[72]

Finally, France continues to deploy significant numbers of pre-positioned forces (*forces de présence*) beyond Europe, while Britain, in addition to its garrison forces, conducts temporary out-of-area deployments to demonstrate commitment, to exercise capability and to practice strategic mobility in the event of a crisis.[73]

These security roles are more than symbolic on the part of Western Europe in helping to secure South-west Asia, parts of Africa and other regions of the world in the Western interest. Nevertheless, the ultimate significance of such Western European roles tends to be more political than military, as it would appear essential to the transatlantic management of NATO's out-of-area problem that the US should not be seen as bearing sole responsibility for the global containment of the Soviet military threat, or acting as the only Western agent in attempting to manage the wide range of security threats which could arise in the Third World.

CONCLUSIONS

The discussion in this Paper does not leave one with a simple view of NATO's out-of-area problem. It should be clear that out-of-area security challenges remain difficult to define objectively. It is inevitable that beyond NATO's formal area of commitment, shifting and ambiguous pressures will provoke different estimates of national self-interest in different situations. Yet, given the growth of global interdependence, it is also inevitable that the requirements of alliance make themselves felt beyond the geographical limits which were drawn rather arbitrarily in 1949. Analysis made it necessary to subject out-of-area issues to a host of distinctions and qualifications which, in the end, may seem to bring into question the very notion of out-of-area security. Thus, the difficulty of assessing which out-of-area events will find which of the Allies consulting together, let alone acting jointly, extends even to what would seem to be the most unifying of possible out-of-area threats, namely Soviet military challenges beyond Europe.

This also means that there are no easy answers to NATO's out-of-area problem. The recommendations outlined in Chapter III represent nothing particularly novel or striking, but at least they may facilitate the management of a problem which is built into the very nature of the Atlantic Alliance. To sum up, the Allies appear *less* willing to confront each other openly over out-of-area issues, at least for the time being. Such restraint in national rhetoric is, of course, partly circumstantial. Between 1980 and 1983 there was an overriding need to close ranks in the face of strong Soviet pressures to prevent NATO from deploying intermediate-range nuclear missiles in Europe. Another factor is the compatibility in outlook of the present, moderately conservative governments in three NATO countries, Britain, the US and West Germany. France, when under a Socialist government, was very traditional (and rather conservative) in terms of its foreign policy in this period. At the same time, there may now be a deeper realization in NATO capitals that, even where domestic pressures accentuate differences over national policies out-of-area, sterile and ultimately counterproductive public arguments should be resisted as much as possible. This is not to say that exchanges of national views should remain confined to low-profile, bilateral consultations only. Much continues to depend here on the overall evolution of super-power and, by implication, transatlantic relations.

Second, divisive as some past out-of-area issues may have been, nevertheless it appears that many other extra-European events have had little or no political impact on relations among the Allies. Either their relevance to Allied security was considered to be negligible or NATO members chose to remain indifferent towards these events. Sweeping demands for Allied unity out-of-area as a reflection of the recurrent temptation to escape from the vicissitudes of alliance therefore should be treated with scepticism. Instead the Allies require some objective criteria by which to determine what measures need to be taken in response to out-of-area events. For the time being, these criteria are still best found in NATO's original objectives amplified in the 1967 Harmel Report, namely the management of the Soviet threat to Western Europe through a combination of defence and detente. This means that it is those out-of-area situations which are likely to divide the Allies to the benefit of the USSR which require the greatest degree of unanimity. Judging from the historical record so far, such cases have tended to generate strong intra-Alliance pressures to bring the attending dispute under control to defuse the issue. From a military viewpoint, it means that national policy responses, whether co-ordinated or not, should be calibrated in such a way to prevent local disputes from escalating, so far as possible, into direct East–West confrontations within the NATO area. Observance of these two principles need not undermine the political credibility and the military effectiveness of national and joint reactions to out-of-area threats. On the contrary, the US and its European NATO partners can deploy a comprehensive range of complementary assets – economic, diplomatic and military – in support of the wider dimensions of Western security.

Britain, France and the US are not alone in sustaining security roles out-of-area. By pursuing gradual increases of their defensive capabilities, various regional actors contribute informally to a global balance of power congenial to vital Western interests. In South-west Asia the six members of the Gulf Co-operation Council (GCC) have been developing – albeit slowly – their practical defence co-operation since 1980, considerably assisted by the Western powers. In East Asia, the military component of the Japanese-US alliance is being strengthened with a growing number of joint air, ground and naval exercises, some joint contingency planning and a Japanese commitment to achieve a Pacific sea-lane defence up to 1,000 nautical miles from the Japanese coast. In the South Pacific, Australia and New Zealand are both stepping up their national defence efforts in response to increased Soviet maritime activities in the area.

The American need for greater strategic mobility and flexibility should not be seen in the context of South-west Asia only, but rather as a trend which could manifest itself elsewhere, for instance in Central America. In this respect NATO's South-west Asia Impact Study and its follow-up constitute the first instructive multilateral exercise in adjusting Allied defence planning to new and wider strategic realities. In order to yield positive results, such an exercise should not be allowed to get bogged down in estimates – especially at the transatlantic level – of the relevance of worst-case scenarios beyond Europe. While these scenarios cannot be disregarded, they are also least likely to materialize. Both these aspects should be reflected realistically in Allied defence planning.

European security co-operation out-of-area?
As a result of increased attention to out-of-area issues since the late 1970s, consideration has been given to the prospects for European concerted action beyond the NATO area.[1] Like European defence co-operation as a whole, a distinctly European security role out-of-area might serve to

counter Congressional pressures for a withdrawal of US troops from Europe. It would also be an attempt to improve the transatlantic management of out-of-area issues by adjusting NATO's existing consultative arrangements to changes in the overall European-US balance. The main difficulty is to develop forms of co-operation which are significant and compatible with the security framework provided by the Atlantic Alliance.

On the other hand, various constraints limit both the scope and the effectiveness of European co-operation out-of-area. Only Britain and France maintain a comprehensive, although modest, capability for interventions out-of-area, the use of which, moreover, would be contingent on the absence of a major East–West crisis in Europe. A credible European capacity for autonomous action would have to rest on Anglo-French military co-operation out-of-area, yet for geographical, historical and political reasons there have been remarkably few instances of such co-operation since the ill-fated 1956 Suez expedition.[2] Politically, the fact that the notion of European defence co-operation tends to mean different things to different NATO members inhibits the development of a coherent perspective on a European security identity. Institutionally, each of the possible frameworks for European political consultation and co-ordination on out-of-area questions appears to suffer from drawbacks. The Eurogroup may be deemed too close to NATO's integrated military structure, especially by a key out-of-area actor such as France, which so far has refused to join this informal organization for European collaboration in the military-technical and public relations fields. Largely at the French initiative, the Western European Union (WEU) has been enjoying a well-publicized political revival. At their October 1984 meeting in Rome, the Defence and Foreign Ministers of the seven WEU members (Belgium, Britain, France, Italy, Luxembourg, the Netherlands and West Germany) agreed, among other things, to study and consult on the consequences of out-of-area crises for European security. But, due to its limited membership, the WEU by no means represents Europe. Broader-based consultations are provided by European Political Co-operation (EPC) in which the 12 EEC members can discuss the economic and political aspects of security, without any geographical limitations. While their largely overlapping memberships have resulted in a growing interaction of the EPC and NATO, European Defence Ministers have not been allowed so far to meet within the EPC framework, as recommended by the 1981 Genscher-Colombo Plan. Also, two strategically important flank countries – Norway and Turkey – remain outside both the EEC and the EPC. Finally, decision-making in the EPC can be blocked effectively by those smaller members – like Ireland, Denmark and Greece – who are reluctant or clearly unwilling to align themselves with the majority. Short of an unexpected turn in events, these military, political and institutional constraints could limit the prospects for European security co-operation out-of-area, even though 'variable geometry' and 'dual velocity' approaches may occasionally achieve results. Apart from concerting policy on specific issues leading to joint political interventions – as in South Africa – the EPC has also been instrumental in bringing about, albeit laboriously, European participation in the multinational peacekeeping force (MFO) in the Sinai. However, British, Dutch, French and Italian participation in the 1984 mine-clearing operation in the Red Sea (together with the US) was not prepared within the EPC framework. This illustrates how, at even slightly higher levels of conflict and instability where swift action may be required, European NATO members prefer to revert to national action supplemented where needed by bilateral or multilateral *ad hoc* co-operation.

In the vital relationship with the US, on the other hand, European security co-operation out-of-area eventually could create more political problems than it would solve. As a response to US global unilateralism and periodic concentration on other regions of the world, such as the Pacific and Central America, European co-operation may be basing itself on perceptions which correspond imperfectly and only temporarily to the reality of the future directions of US security policy. For its part, the US will at least question whether European co-operation can result in an overall improvement of the West's security posture out-of-area. Influential quarters in Washington are inclined to think that European co-operation defines itself in its opposition to American policies, rather than in terms of any substantial contribution to order outside the NATO area, a view superficially confirmed by the largely 'civilian' input of the EEC and EPC so far. The EEC reaction to the recent Libyan affair has not improved Congressional and US popular sensitivity to the notion of a positive European security role beyond the NATO area. Given the vital importance of its transatlantic connection, Western Europe has only a limited margin of manoeuvre in articulating separate perspectives on the substance of major out-of-area issues, which the US could not easily dismiss as objectionable manifestations of 'moral equidistance' and 'political-military neutralism'. The British initiative leading to an EEC call for Afghan neutrality in February 1980 may be considered as an instructive precedent in this respect.

This suggests that a European security identity is perhaps fraught with even greater difficulties outside the NATO area than within it. European security co-operation out-of-area, however well-intentioned, may not necessarily be the only or even the best way to ensure that European views are presented persuasively to the US. Such an objective could be pursued more directly by strengthening the European voice in NATO's existing consultative arrangements; updating the 1967 Harmel exercise could provide the impulse for this. On the other hand, if the primary objective is to demonstrate European commitment to the defence of wider Western interests, Britain, France and some other European Allies have more direct and concrete means at their disposal unilaterally to promote Western security interests in the world beyond the narrow confines of NATO's geographical area.

Notes

Chapter I

[1] Raymond Aron, *Paix et Guerre entre les Nations* (Paris: Calmann-Levy, 1962), p. 440, quoted by Guy de Carmoy, *Les Politiques Etrangères de la France 1944-1966* (Paris: La Table Ronde, 1967), p. 74.
[2] See Theodore Draper, 'The Western Misalliance', *The Washington Quarterly*, vol. 4, no. 1 (Winter 1981), pp. 16–7.
[3] See Douglas Stuart, 'NATO Out-of-Area Disputes: From the Washington Talks to the RDF', *Atlantic Quarterly*, vol. 2, no. 1 (Spring 1984), pp. 50–3.
[4] See Anthony Verrier, *Through The Looking Glass. British Foreign Policy in an Age of Illusions* (London: Jonathan Cape, 1983), pp. 58–60.
[5] On 12 March 1986, 52.5% of the Spanish voters were in favour of continued Spanish membership in NATO. In May 1986 Spain presented a nine-point plan to the other Allies outlining the principles which would govern its military participation in NATO. Intra-Alliance talks on this Spanish plan and its related military aspects are expected to begin in the second half of 1986. On 10 July 1986 Spain and the US started negotiations on the adjustment of their bilateral military relations.
[6] See Christopher Coker, (1) 'The Western Alliance and Africa 1949-1981', *African Affairs*, vol. 81, no. 324 (1982), pp. 324–31; and (2) *NATO, the Warsaw Pact and Africa* (RUSI Defence Studies Series: Macmillan, 1985), pp. 82–6.
[7] Coker, *ibid*, (1) p. 326.
[8] Coker, *ibid*, (1) pp. 328–9; see also Ch. III, note 51.
[9] See *Statement on Defence Estimates 1975*, Cmnd 5976 (London: HMSO, 1975). The principal reductions in out-of-area commitments proposed by the 1975 Defence Review included the withdrawal of the British contribution to the ANZUK force in Singapore which had been created pursuant to the 1971 Five-Power Defence Arrangements for Malaysia and Singapore (see also n. 18), the withdrawal from Gan and Mauritius and the cancellation of the Simonstown base agreement with South Africa. These measures completed the steady retreat from East-of-Suez responsibilities, the major milestones of which had been British withdrawals from India (1947), Egypt (1956), Iraq (1958), Aden (1967) and the Persian Gulf (1971). An overseas military presence was only retained in Cyprus, Gibraltar and in the dependent territories of British Honduras (which became independent as the State of Belize in 1981), Diego Garcia, the Falkland Islands and Hong Kong, while the withdrawal of a Gurkha battalion from Brunei was to be subject to consultations with the Sultan of Brunei. The permanent deployment of two frigates in the Caribbean was terminated in 1976. Reductions in capabilities affected British specialized reinforcement forces for NATO's flanks, which also were best designed for out-of-area missions, see *ibid.*, Ch.I, p. 12. After 1976 British maritime forces were no longer committed to the defence of NATO's Mediterranean flank.
[10] *Statement on Defence Estimates 1980*, Cmnd 7826, (London: HMSO, 1980) vol. I, para. 408.
[11] See John Baylis, *Anglo-American Defence Relations 1939-1980. The Special Relationship* (London: The Macmillan Press, 1981), in particular Ch.II.
[12] *Ibid.*, pp. 40–42. See also Ra Jong-yil, 'Special Relationship at War: The Anglo-American Relationship during the Korean War', *The Journal of Strategic Studies*, vol. 7, no. 3 (September 1984), pp. 301–17.
[13] See F.S. Northedge, *Descent From Power. British Foreign Policy 1945-1973* (London: George Allen & Unwin, 1974), pp. 199–202. The Commonwealth occasionally acted as a brake on Anglo-American unity in out-of-area matters, as demonstrated by the important Commonwealth summit meetings of 1951 and 1952 at which Britain felt obliged to take Nehru's views on the Korean War into account.
[14] See Verrier (*op. cit.* in note 4), *passim*.
[15] However, the US did become a member of the Military Committee of the Baghdad Pact in 1957; see Northedge, (*op. cit.*, in note 13), pp. 124–5 and pp. 188–9. Following the withdrawal of Iraq in 1959, the Pact was renamed the Central Treaty Organization (CENTO) in which the US participated as an associate.

[16] See James H. Wyllie, *The Influence of British Arms. An Analysis of British Military Interventions since 1956* (London: George Allen & Unwin, 1984), pp. 60–61.
[17] See Baylis (*op. cit.* in note 11), Ch. 5.
[18] By 31 March 1976, Britain had withdrawn all its forces from Singapore, except for a small contribution to the integrated air defence system.
[19] See Coker (*op. cit.* (1) in note 6), p. 321; Pierre Lellouche and Dominique Moisi, 'French Policy in Africa: a Lonely Battle Against Destabilization', *International Security*, vol. 3, no. 4 (Spring 1979), pp. 110–11; and Alfred Grosser, *The Western Alliance: European-American Relations since 1945* (London: Macmillan, 1980), Ch. 5, *passim*.
[20] In December 1952 the North Atlantic Council issued a public statement expressing 'its wholehearted admiration' and 'continuing support' for the French struggle 'against Communist aggression' (the statement is reproduced in the North Atlantic Assembly, Political Committee, *Interim Report of the Sub-Committee on Out-of-Area Security Challenges to the Alliance* AB207 PC/OA(84)2 (Brussels: International Secretariat, November 1984), p. 27. US bilateral financial assistance to France in Indochina already had been considered by the Truman Administration in late 1949; in July 1950 it went into effect, see Stanley Karnow, *Vietnam – A History* (New York: The Viking Press, 1983), p. 177. Subsequently, the amount of US aid was stepped up several times, reaching a total of $2.6 bn between 1950 and 1954, according to Stuart (*op. cit.* in note 3), p. 54.
[21] France deeply resented US abstention and dissension in UN debates on the Algerian question, as well as US criticisms of French policies (notably on the part of Senator John F. Kennedy) towards Algeria, see Coker (*op. cit.* (2) in note 6), pp. 32–4, and Grosser (*op. cit.* in note 19), Ch. 5.
[22] From the French point of view, de Gaulle's memorandum proposals were not unprecedented. Under pressure of the Gaullist faction in the French Parliament one of the last governments of the Fourth Republic, headed by Prime Minister Felix Gaillard, had publicly announced early in 1958 that, as far as French territory was concerned, the emplacement of US IRBM would be made conditional, among other things, on the degree of Allied co-operation beyond the NATO area; see de Carmoy (*op. cit.* in note 1), p. 62 and p. 70. De Gaulle attempted at least twice to broaden the premise of the Alliance, on 17 and 25 September 1958, see Draper, (*op. cit.* in note 2), pp. 29–30.
[23] For a list of the major bilateral co-operation agreements signed between France and the new African states in the early 1960s, see John Chipman, 'French Military Policy and African Security', Adelphi Paper no. 201 (London: IISS, Summer 1985), p. 25. For Franco-African agreements in force at present, see Ch. III, note 18.
[24] *Ibid.*, pp. 6–8.
[25] On 29 August 1963 de Gaulle called for the unification of North and South Vietnam into a single, neutral state. On 27 January 1964, France accorded diplomatic recognition to Communist China. Both French moves were made without prior Allied consultations. Subsequent French calls for an end to US intervention in South Vietnam were made on 12 June 1964 and 1 September 1966.
[26] See Lellouche and Moisi (*op. cit.* in note 19), pp. 119–20.
[27] Three phases can be distinguished in the evolution of French military interventions in Africa. Between 1960 and 1964 French forces intervened eight times, in Cameroon, Congo-Brazzaville (twice), Chad, Gabon (twice), Mauritania and Niger in order to stabilize local regimes threatened by military uprisings, tribal agitation and civil disorder. After a sharp decline between 1964 and 1974, with interventions taking place only in the Central African Republic and Chad, both the frequency and the level of French military actions in Africa increased markedly after 1975. The largest deployments took place in Chad, against Libyan-backed Muslim rebels: some 2,000 ground troops supported by units of *Jaguar* strike aircraft by 1978 and even larger deployments during the 1983 *Opération Manta*. In December 1977 French bombing missions over the Western Sahara were staged from Senegal, in support of the Mauritanian government against Algerian-backed Polisario forces. In response to the 1977 and 1978 invasions of Zaire's Shaba province, France airlifted

1,500 Moroccan troops to the area and sent 600 of its own troops the following year. See Lellouche and Moisi (*op. cit.*, in note 19), pp. 117–18; *Strategic Survey 1978* (London: IISS, 1979), pp. 15–16, 100-101 and Chipman (*op. cit.* in note 23), pp. 5–15.

[28] Since the mid-1970s the number of French troops stationed in Africa has varied between 6,000 and 10,000; repeated interventions in Chad and related deployments to the Central African Republic since 1980–81 account for the main variations; for the precise figures over the period 1975–86, see *The Military Balance*, (London: IISS, annual). France also has more than 1,000 military advisers in more than 20 African states, see Chipman (*op. cit.* in note 23), p. 24. During the second half of the 1970s France also maintained its permanent naval presence in the Indian Ocean (bases in Djibouti, La Réunion), even deploying one of its aircraft carriers to the area during much of 1977 and 1978, see *Strategic Survey 1978* (*op. cit.* in note 27), p. 15.

[29] See Coker (*op. cit.* (1) in note 6), p. 332.

[30] Lellouche and Moisi (*op. cit.* in note 19), p. 131.

[31] See Scott L. Bills, 'The United States, NATO and the Colonial World', in Lawrence S. Kaplan and Robert W. Clawson (eds.), *NATO After Thirty Years* (Wilmington, DE: Scholarly Resources, 1981), pp. 149–64.

[32] See Karnow (*op. cit.* in note 20), pp. 171–2, 175–6.

[33] See Adam B. Ulam, *Expansion and Coexistence. Soviet Foreign Policy 1917-1973* (New York: Praeger Publishers, 1974, 2nd ed.), pp. 560–62.

[34] See 'The Western Flank', *New York Times*, 4, 6 and 9 January 1967. For European reactions to the US engagement in Vietnam, see Grosser (*op. cit.* in note 19), pp. 237–43.

[35] *Strategic Survey 1975*, pp. 2, 32. The subsequent so-called Clark Amendment (1979) banning military assistance to anti-Communist insurgents in Angola was lifted by the US Congress in 1985, see also Ch. III, note 36.

[36] In his State of the Union message to Congress on 23 January 1980, President Carter declared the Persian Gulf to be an area of vital US interest which would be defended 'by use of any means necessary, including military force'.

[37] The Netherlands and Belgium had to bow to US interference with their decolonization policies in Indonesia/West Irian (1949, 1962) and Congo (1962) respectively.

[38] Fears of Egyptian nationalism siding with the Soviet camp had led the US to apply pressures on Britain to extricate itself from Egypt and the Sudan, as part of a more general US wish to replace Britain in the Middle East. Contradictory schemes to align Arab states, as well as Turkey, into a pro-Western multilateral alliance revealed Anglo-American policy differences towards the area. Britain sought to link the evacuation of its Suez base with the formation of a regional defence arrangement including Egypt, which would have enabled Britain to retain a military role in the area in the event of an aggression against a member of the Arab League or Turkey. After having initially supported such a scheme, the US turned to the idea of an openly anti-Communist pact comprising Iran, Iraq, Pakistan and Turkey. Once the US started sponsoring the 'Northern Tier' concept as a means to close the circle of containment between NATO and SEATO, Nasser drew the conclusion that the West was subordinating the Arab cause against Israel to its cold-war preoccupations. The creation of the Baghdad Pact also gave Egypt reason to question the West's commitment to its 1950 Tripartite Declaration, in which Britain, France and the US sought to harmonize their divergent policies on arms supplies to Israel and the Arab states. In deciding to join the Pact, Britain considered that the short-term benefit of securing a multilateral safeguard for its military presence in Iraq outweighed the risk of hostile reactions on the part of Arab nationalism.

[39] For a first-hand account, see Henry Kissinger, *Years of Upheaval* (London: Weidenfeld & Nicolson and Michael Joseph, 1982), pp. 707–22.

[40] The European declaration on the Middle East was released following a meeting of the EEC Foreign Ministers in Brussels on 6–7 November 1973. Subsequently the EEC members, in addition to pursuing a separate Euro-Arab

dialogue, issued joint declarations on the resolution of the Arab-Israeli conflict in 1977 and on 13 June 1980 (The Declaration of Venice by the EEC Heads-of-Government Summit).
[41] See Stuart (*op. cit.* in note 3), pp. 55–6.
[42] *Ibid.*, p. 56.
[43] See Lellouche and Moisi (*op. cit.* in note 19), pp. 131–3.
[44] In a separate Protocol to the Manila Treaty of 8 September 1954, on which SEATO was based, the designated area of the Treaty (Article 8) was extended to include the territories of Cambodia, Laos and Vietnam. Thus these states, although not members of SEATO, were put under the protection of the Organization. Apart from the US, of the eight members of SEATO only Australia, New Zealand and Thailand committed forces to operations in South Vietnam; their involvement was not pursuant to any policy of SEATO as such.
[45] In view of de Gaulle's 1963 policy statement on Vietnam (see note 25), France retreated to an observer status in SEATO in April 1965 and withdrew its military mission to SEATO in May 1965; it ceased financial contributions to the Organization after June 1974.
[46] See *Strategic Survey 1975*, p. 3.
[47] On 19 February 1980, the EEC Foreign Ministers meeting in Rome gave their support to a British proposal for a Soviet withdrawal from Afghanistan against an international guarantee of Afghan neutrality.
[48] See Frederic L. Kirgis, Jr., 'NATO Consultations as a Component of National Decisionmaking', *American Journal of International Law*, vol. 73 (1979), pp. 372–406.
[49] *NATO – Facts and Figures* (Brussels: NATO Information Service, 1981), p. 120.
[50] Various bilateral defence links which had existed between Britain and the US previous to the formation of NATO were extended further between 1948 and 1950. In particular, several agreements were signed on the bilateral exchange of classified military information and intelligence, see Baylis (*op. cit.* in note 11), pp. 40–3.
[51] See *NATO – Facts and Figures* (*op. cit.* in note 49), p. 122, and *Atlantic News*, no. 1497 (24 February 1983). Working groups of regional experts now meet twice a year in Brussels in five working groups (Middle East, Latin America, Africa, South-east Asia, Eastern Europe).
[52] North Atlantic Council Resolution on Important Changes in National Defence Efforts, 5 October 1955, NATO Doc. CM(55)82 (Final) (unclassified).
[53] Quoted by Karnow (*op. cit.* in note 20), p. 178.
[54] De Carmoy (*op. cit.* in note 1), pp. 70–71, 73–4.
[55] *Ibid.*, p. 205.
[56] See Kirgis (*op. cit.* in note 48), p. 38. In 1968, at the height of the Vietnam War, the US had some 10 of its 19 Army divisions deployed in South-east Asia, as well as 9 of the 28 USAF tactical fighter wings.
[57] *The Military Balance 1974–1975*, p. 25.
[58] Documents Relating to the Accession to the North Atlantic Treaty of the Federal Republic of Germany ('Paris Agreements' of 23 October 1954), Protocol No. II on Forces of the Western European Union, Article 6.
[59] Kirgis (*op. cit.* in note 48), p. 400.
[60] Kissinger (*op. cit.* in note 39), p. 713.
[61] These documents are reproduced in *NATO – Facts and Figures*, (*op. cit.* in note 49), pp. 269–93.
[62] Kirgis (*op. cit.* in note 48), pp. 376–7.
[63] *Ibid.*, pp. 398–9.
[64] *Ibid.*, p. 405. From a reconstruction of Allied reactions to the procedure followed by the US in the case of the 1973 worldwide alert, it appears that the Western Europeans actually appreciated the fact that the urgency of the situation did not allow for prior consultation. What they did object to was mainly the fact that NATO's political and military authorities were not provided simultaneously with prompt and adequate information on the circumstances which had prompted the US alert.
[65] *Ibid.*, p. 398.
[66] Coker (*op. cit.* (1) in note 6), p. 333. Coker mentions that, despite the lack of prior consultations, NATO's channels of communication were used throughout the crisis.
[67] Kirgis (*op. cit.* in note 48), p. 401.
[68] Coker (*op. cit.* (1) in note 6), p. 334.
[69] The issue of a common, Atlantic foreign policy had been raised already in 1956 by the West German Chancellor Adenauer in talks with Secretary of State Dulles, see Draper (*op. cit.* in note 2), pp. 28–9.

70 See note 22.
71 See note 25.
72 In 1964, for instance, Secretary of State Rusk asked NATO members to give greater support to South Vietnam, see US Senate, Committee on Foreign Relations, 91st Congress, 2nd Session, *Background Information relating to South-East Asia and Vietnam* (Washington DC: USGPO, 6th rev. ed., June 1970).
73 Kissinger (*op. cit.* in note 39), mentions on p. 723 that he proposed regular out-of-area consultations at the Deputy Foreign Minister level during the ministerial meeting of the North Atlantic Council of December 1973, shortly after the Arab-Israeli war.
74 See note 40.
75 For four instructive overviews of NATO's out-of-area problem, see William P. Bundy, 'Alliance Crisis and Consensus: Western Experience'; Kenneth Hunt, 'Crisis and Consensus in the West – The Boundaries of Shared Interests'; A.W. De Porte, 'The North Atlantic Alliance: External Threats and Internal Stress', in *Naval War College Review*, November-December 1984, pp. 37–9; and Gregory F. Treverton, 'Making the Alliance Work – The Alliance and Western Europe' (London: Macmillan, 1985), Chs 4, 6. See also the more detailed and very interesting papers presented at an international conference on *The Atlantic Alliance and its Borders exposed to Crisis*, organized by The Trans-European Policy Studies Associations (TEPSA, Brussels), The University Center for International Studies (UCIS, Pittsburgh) and the Istituto Affari Internazionali (IAI, Rome) in Brussels on 2 and 3 July 1986.

Chapter II

1 See Hanns W. Maull, *Raw Materials, Energy and Western Security* (London: IISS, 1984), pp. 7–25; David Deese and Joseph Nye (eds), *Energy and Security* (Cambridge, MA: Ballinger Publ. Co., 1980), *passim*.
2 *Ibid.*
3 See Fereidun Fesharaki and David T. Isaak, *OPEC, The Gulf and the World Petroleum Market. A Study in Government Policy and Downstream Diversification* (Boulder, CO/London: Westview Press/Croom Helm, 1983), pp. 28–31.
4 See Tom Cutler (Chairman of NATO's Petroleum Planning Committee), 'NATO and Oil Supply Vulnerability. The Role of the Petroleum Planning Committee', *NATO Review*, vol. 32, no. 5 (October 1984), p. 31.
5 *Ibid.*
6 *Ibid.*
7 See Maull (*op. cit.* in note 1), pp. 114–7.
8 OPEC did succeed in imposing higher price levels on consumer countries in 1973–4 (an average increase from $US 1.50 to $US 9.50 a barrel between 1973 and June 1974, and imposition by the Arab OPEC members of oil embargoes targeted against the US and the Netherlands) and again in 1979–80 (an average increase from $20 to $35 a barrel between September 1979 and January 1981). In 1981–2 and subsequent years falling prices due to demand decline (economic recession, domestic conservation and substitution measures) as well as to increased competition from alternative, non-OPEC sources, have put OPEC under increasing pressure to cut its official prices in response to the prevailing oil glut.
9 OPEC's effectiveness as a cartel has suffered from internal tensions, with some members (Iran, Nigeria) breaking agreements on oil production and price in response to their own economic difficulties.
10 Past oil crises affecting NATO members took place in 1951 (nationalization of the Anglo-Iranian Oil Company), 1956 (Suez Crisis), 1967 and 1973 (Arab-Israeli wars accompanied by Arab oil embargoes), and 1979–80 (following the Iranian Revolution and the outbreak of the Gulf War between Iraq and Iran).
11 See Maull (*op. cit.* in note 1), pp. 121–30.
12 At US initiative the IEA was established in November 1974 in response to Western disarray during the 1973–4 oil crisis. Its current emergency oil-sharing scheme can be triggered if the IEA Secretariat, in consultation with governments, finds that a member country, or the members as a whole, experience or can be expected to experience a 7% or greater shortfall in oil supplies compared to historical base period consumption levels. Although IEA members agree on the necessity for stockpiles (90 days of imports or consumption), current national stockpile

levels and policies differ widely, see Maull (*op. cit.* in note 1), pp. 339–49. As of 31 May 1986 the US Strategic Petroleum Reserve (SPR) held about 500 million barrels (source: US Department of Energy, quoted in *International Energy Statistical Review* (Washington DC: Central Intelligence Agency, 29 July 1986, p. 15.

[13] In 1969 and 1972 Washington warned the OECD that, in the event of a future oil crisis, the US would not divert domestic oil resources to Western Europe as it had done during the 1956 and 1967 crises. The 1973–4 crisis saw Britain and France effectively blocking the implementation of the OECD European oil-sharing scheme which would have allocated oil to the embargoed Netherlands. This demonstrated how national attempts to seek unilaterally national or bilateral solutions to shared oil vulnerability can damage Western internal solidarity and external credibility. During the 1979–80 oil crisis the IEA oil-sharing arrangements were not triggered.

[14] Soviet energy sales to NATO members have been discussed mainly in the context of Siberian gas deliveries to France, Italy and West Germany, made possible by the construction of a special pipeline connecting the Urengoi gas-fields and Western Europe. The 1982 unilateral US sanctions against Western European equipment deliveries to the USSR for the construction of the pipeline reopened the 'functional' out-of-area debate within the Alliance on Allied solidarity towards the management of East-West economic relations. After much transatlantic controversy, agreement was reached within the IEA on the principle that Western European import dependency on Soviet gas should be kept at a level sufficiently low to prevent the USSR from using its gas supplies as a lever to exert political pressure on European NATO. According to EEC estimates, the Soviet gas share of total energy consumption in France, Italy and West Germany would rise from 3.4% in 1982 to only 5.4% in 1990, see John Van Oudenaren, *The Urengoi Pipeline. Prospects for Soviet Leverage* (Santa Monica, CA: The Rand Corporation, 1984), p. 21. West Germany has limited its import of Soviet gas to 6% of its total energy consumption (see *Strategic Survey 1983–1984*, p. 55). In the 1990s Western European (as well as Japanese) gas import dependence and vulnerability might well focus on the Persian Gulf and Africa (Algeria, Libya, Nigeria), as OPEC countries will expand their international gas trade.

[15] See Dennis Ross, 'Considering Soviet Threats to the Persian Gulf', *International Security*, vol. 6, no. 2 (Fall 1981), pp. 159–80, and Thane Gustafson 'Energy and the Soviet Bloc', *International Security*, vol. 6, no. 3 (Winter 1981/1982), pp. 65-89; see also Maull (*op. cit.* in note 1), pp. 130-8. During the 1970s the USSR imported small amounts of crude oil from OPEC countries, primarily from Iraq until the outbreak of the Gulf War in 1980.

[16] It may be recalled in this context that Iraq, one of the Arab states closest to the USSR, did not participate in the 1973 oil embargo.

[17] See Maull (*op. cit.* in note 1), pp. 135–6.

[18] See Ross (*op. cit.* in note 15), p. 170.

[19] In 1979–80 US and EEC mineral import dependence amounted to 90% and 97% for chromium ore, 100% for cobalt, 100% and 99% for manganese ore, 100% for platinum and tantalum, and 87% and 100% for titanium ore, see Maull (*op. cit.* in note 1), pp. 284–5.

[20] For a detailed risk assessment for each non-fuel mineral critical to the steel industry, see Maull (*op. cit.* in note 1), pp. 190–282.

[21] For example, molybdenum is exported by Canada, Chile and the US, niobium by Brazil and Canada, titanium ore by Australia and Norway, potash by Canada, France, Spain and West Germany, bauxite by Australia, vanadium by Finland; important Asian mineral exporters are China and South Korea (tungsten, vanadium) as well as Malaysia (tantalum, titanium); see Maull (*op. cit.* in note 1), pp. 284–5.

[22] See Maull (*op. cit.* in note 1), pp. 286-287. In relative contrast to OPEC's use of the oil weapon, the great diversity of mineral markets so far has contributed to limit the effects of concerted action by suppliers. While formal and informal cartels operate among bauxite, cobalt and platinum producers, their policies have not threatened Western mineral security, see Maull, pp. 37–8, 283, 286.

[23] *Ibid.*, pp. 291–3.

[24] South Africa is a crucial exporter of

chromium, manganese, platinum, vanadium and other minerals, see Maull (*op. cit.* in note 1), pp. 284–5.

[25] For limited economic sanctions imposed by NATO members on South Africa since mid-1985, see Ch. III, note 32.

[26] See Maull (*op. cit.* in note 1), pp. 343–53, and *Strategic Survey 1981–1982* (London: IISS, 1982), pp. 43–4.

[27] Between 1960 and 1982 European NATO members increased their exports of goods and non-factor services as a percentage of their GNP from 21% to 32%, while US exports increased from 5% to 9% of GNP during the same period. These figures (which exclude Iceland and Luxembourg) are compiled from the *World Development Report 1984* (New York: Oxford University Press, 1984, published for the World Bank), pp. 226–7.

[28] *Ibid.*, pp. 240–43.

[29] See the North Atlantic Assembly (*op. cit.* in Ch. I, note 20), p. 13.

[30] See *The Report of the President's National Bipartisan Commission on Central America* (New York: Macmillan Publ. Co. 1984), p. 110.

[31] Iraq especially sees increased oil exports through the creation of new outlets as vital to its economic survival in the protracted war against Iran. With its Gulf outlet blocked as a result of the war and its pipeline through Syria closed down since 1982, Iraq has been attempting to complement its single existing outlet through Turkey with pipeline projects in Jordan (shelved in November 1984) and Saudi Arabia (two new pipelines, the first of which was completed in September 1985), see *Strategic Survey 1984–1985*, p. 70 and *1985–1986* (London: IISS), p. 129.

[32] *Journal of Defense & Diplomacy*. vol. 2, no. 10 (October 1984), p. 15.

[33] Brazil, El Salvador, Nicaragua, Ghana and Somalia among other states.

[34] The Convention on the Law of the Sea of 30 April 1982, provides for the universal establishment by littoral states of territorial sea zones up to 12 nautical miles, 200 nautical miles exclusive economic zones and the creation of an International Seabed Authority to manage the economic resources of the sea. The US announced on 9 July 1982 that it would not sign the Convention and, instead, it concluded an interim agreement with Britain, France and West Germany on deep seabed mining. Nevertheless, the European signatories of the interim agreement reserved the right to ratify the Convention at a later date. By March 1985 only 11 states (among them France, Japan and the USSR) had ratified the Convention, which needs 60 ratifications to enter into force.

[35] See Michael Vlahos, 'Designing a Third World Navy', *Journal of Defense & Diplomacy*. vol. 3, no. 3 (March 1985), p. 62.

[36] Michael Akehurst, *A Modern Introduction to International Law*. (London: George Allen and Unwin, 1977), p. 166.

[37] See Johan Jørgen Holst, 'The Navies of the Superpowers: Motives, Forces, Prospects', and Michael Howard 'Order and Conflict at Sea in the 1980s', in Jonathan Alford (ed.), *Sea Power Influence – Old Issues and New Challenges* (London: IISS, 1980), pp. 53, 75.

[38] Such exercises were challenged by the Libyan Air Force in August 1981, which led to the shooting down of two Libyan Su-22 fighters by two US F-14s from the aircraft carrier *Nimitz*. On 24 March 1986, US planes attacked Libyan missile sites and sank two Libyan patrol boats in the Gulf of Sirte, after being fired upon by Libyan forces in international waters.

[39] The direct economic burden arising from the Falkland Islands Campaign consisted of the costs of the 1982 Task Force operation (£780 million), the replacement costs of equipment lost in that operation (estimated at £900 million) as well as garrisoning and operational costs (£624 and £684 million in 1983–4 and 1984–5 respectively). Due to the completion of a strategic airfield in May 1985 and force stabilization measures, projected garrisoning and operational expenditures are expected to decline from 1985 onwards (£525,450 and £300 million in 1985–6, 1986–7 and 1987–8 respectively). (Figures provided by the Ministry of Defence Press Service, London).

[40] For a general account per region of known defence and military co-operation agreements which are in force at present, see *The Military Balance 1985–1986* (London: IISS, 1985).

[41] Reported in *Defense & Foreign Affairs Weekly*, 22–28 April 1985, p. 2. Italy is reported to have signed another major military co-operation agreement with

India, see *Defense & Foreign Affairs Weekly*, 13–19 May 1985, p. 2.

[42] For example, agreements in abeyance are US mutual security agreements with Iran (1959), Ethiopia (1975) and some other African states. Other agreements have repeatedly shown their limited relevance, such as the 1947 Rio Treaty which did not prevent the US from eventually siding with Britain during the Falklands War.

[43] See *Strategic Survey 1980-1981* (London: IISS, 1981), p. 99.

[44] The 1960 bilateral defence agreement between Chad and France was terminated in 1976 and replaced by an agreement on technical military co-operation only.

[45] As stated by President Mitterrand in Bujumbura, Burundi, on 11 December 1984; see also Ch. III, note 15.

[46] This has been seen to be the case in Africa in particular, see Neil Macfarlane, 'Africa's Decaying Security System and the Rise of Intervention', *International Security*, vol. 8, no. 4 (Spring 1984), pp. 127–51, and *Intervention and Regional Security*, Adelphi Paper no. 196 (London: IISS, 1985).

[47] See *Le Monde*, 18 April 1985, p. 7.

[48] Thus in April 1985 President Chadli was the first Algerian president to pay an official visit to the US since Algeria's independence in 1962.

[49] For Soviet reservations about Libyan intervention in Chad, see Oye Ogunbadejo, 'Qaddafi's North African Design', *International Security*, vol. 8, no. 1 (Summer 1983), pp. 166–9; for Vietnam's attempts to preserve its Indochinese policies from Soviet interference, see *Strategic Survey 1982-1983* (London: IISS, 1983), pp. 97–8; for Cuban-Soviet policy divergencies towards Angola and the Eritrean secession, see Mark N. Katz, 'The Soviet-Cuban Connection', *International Security* vol. 8, no. 1, (Summer 1983), pp. 94–7.

[50] The Soviet invasion of Afghanistan was condemned overwhelmingly by the UN (General Assembly resolution ES-6/2 of 14 January 1980, approved by 104 votes to 18, 18 abstentions) and by the Islamic Conference of Foreign Ministers at its extraordinary meeting in Islamabad of 27–29 January 1980.

[51] See *Strategic Survey 1983-1984* (London: IISS, 1984), pp. 91–4.

[52] Ethiopia's adoption of a new constitution has been postponed several times. A draft constitution is now scheduled for final approval in September 1986. See also R. Craig Nation and Mark V. Kauppi, *The Soviet Impact in Africa*, (Lexington, MA: Lexington Books, D.C. Heath & Company, 1984).

[53] See Eliot A. Cohen, 'Constraints on America's Conduct of Small Wars', *International Security*, vol. 9, no. 2 (Fall 1984), pp. 151–3.

[54] *Ibid.*, pp. 153, 162, 174, 179.

[55] *Ibid.*, pp. 165–6, 170–71.

[56] According to this theory, limited wars are political wars fought with the primary intention of communicating strategic interests and objectives to the adversary through the discretionary manipulation of military power, see Stephen Peter Rosen, 'Vietnam and the American Theory of Limited War', *International Security*, vol. 7, no. 2, (Fall 1982), pp. 83–113.

[57] See Cohen (*op. cit.* in note 53), pp. 168–70.

[58] *Ibid.*, pp. 171–2.

[59] After a period of underfinancing and undermanning during the 1970s, new units have been added to US Special Operations Forces (SOF), equipment is being upgraded and command-and-control problems addressed in the creation of a Joint Special Operations Command and a Joint Special Operations Agency. See Caspar W. Weinberger, *Annual Report to the Congress: Fiscal Year 1986*, (Washington DC: USGPO, 4 February 1985), pp. 41–2, and Angelo Codevilla, 'The Challenge of Special Operations', *Journal of Defense & Diplomacy*, vol. 3, no. 6 (June 1985), pp. 19–27. With 500 Mobile Training Teams (MTT), US special forces have been involved in security assistance to almost 60 countries in the last 10 years.

[60] Such is the impression produced by diverging statements made by Secretary of State Shultz and Secretary of Defense Weinberger in late 1984 on the role of military power in US foreign policy. While Shultz, referring primarily to terrorist threats, advocated *inter alia* US use of military power abroad if necessary (25 October and 9 December 1984), Weinberger stressed the limitations affecting the utility of military power by spelling out 6 basic conditions for its use (28 November 1984), see *Strategic Survey*

1983–1984 and *1984–1985*, (London: IISS, 1984 and 1985), pp. 45 and 34. Excerpts from their statements are reproduced in *Survival*, vol. 27, no. 1 (Jan/Feb. 1985), pp. 30–35.

[61] For the problems of guerrilla war in Central America (El Salvador, Guatemala) see *The Report of the President's National Bipartisan Commission* (*op. cit.* in note 30), pp. 111–20. See also Col. John D. Waghelstein, 'Post-Vietnam Counterinsurgency Doctrine', *Military Review*, vol. 65, no. 5 (May 1985), pp. 42–9; and Victor H. Krulak, 'Strategic Implications of "The Little War"', *Strategic Review*, vol. 13, no. 2 (Spring 1985), pp. 31–6. For the shortcomings of Soviet counter-insurgency doctrine and operations, see Ross S. Kelly, 'Soviet Low-Intensity Operations: Moving to Center Stage', *Defense & Foreign Affairs*, January 1985, pp. 28–9, 37. For a controversial assessment of the problems which affected the conduct of the third French intervention in Chad in 1983–4, see 'Colonel Spartacus', *Les documents secrets: Opération Manta, Tchad, 1983-1984* (Paris: Plon, 1985).

[62] See *Strategic Survey 1980–1981* and *1982–1983* (London: IISS, 1981 and 1983), pp. 19 and 133–8; Joshua M. Epstein, 'Soviet Vulnerabilities in Iran and the RDF Deterrent', as well as Dennis Ross, 'Considering Soviet Threats to the Persian Gulf', *International Security*, vol. 6, no. 2 (Fall 1981), pp. 126–58 and 175–78 respectively. Barry R. Posen and Stephen Van Evera, 'Defense Policy and the Reagan Administration: Departure from Containment', *International Security*, vol. 8, no. 1 (Summer 1983), pp. 19–23; Geoffrey Kemp, 'Military Force and Middle East Oil', in Deese and Nye (eds.), (*op. cit.* in note 1), pp. 376–80.

[63] See *Strategic Survey 1982–1983*, pp. 82–3, and Epstein, *op. cit.* in note 62, p. 157. Apart from Diego Garcia (the sole US-only base in South-west Asia), Oman (which allows a limited but full-time US presence at 5 airbases) and Bahrain (unofficial base of the 5 naval units of the US Middle East Force), USCENTCOM does not have permanent bases in the area due to the unwillingness of local states to identify themselves too closely with American security interests. While the US has negotiated since 1979 access arrangements with Djibouti, Egypt, Kenya and Somalia as well as overflight and refuelling rights with Portugal, Liberia and Morocco, these agreements would give USCENTCOM staging areas on a contingency basis only, to be determined by the various host-nations. Similarly, US use of 3 important, forward NATO bases in eastern Turkey would depend on Turkish approval; on 10 October 1985, the Turkish Prime Minister Ozal publicly ruled out letting the US use bases in Turkey for its RDF under the bilateral defence arrangements existing between both countries. See also Raphael Iungerich, 'US Rapid Deployment Forces – USCENTCOM – What Is It? Can It Do The Job?', *Armed Forces Journal International*, October 1984, pp. 88–106.

[64] According to *The Military Balance 1985–1986* (London: IISS, 1985), the Eastern Bloc military presence in Africa is distributed as follows: Soviet, East German and Cuban forces in Angola (21,000), Ethiopia (7,000), Mozambique (1,150); Soviet and East German forces in Algeria (1,250), Libya (1,800); Soviet and Cuban forces in Congo (600); Soviet forces in Mali (200); Soviet forces in rest of Africa (900); East German forces in Guinea (125); North Korean forces in Madagascar (100), the Seychelles (40), Uganda (40), Angola (1,000).

[65] *Ibid.*, p. 30, which puts the total Soviet military presence in Cuba at some 8,700 troops, advisers and technicians. The USSR also mans a large intelligence collection facility in Cuba which is targeted at monitoring electronic communications in the US.

[66] See Gloria Duffy, 'Crisis Mangling and the Cuban Brigade', *International Security*, vol. 8, no. 1 (Summer 1983), pp. 67–87.

[67] The Nicaraguan Armed Forces total 62,850 troops, which makes them the largest in Central America after those of Mexico; they are being equipped with Soviet tanks, armoured vehicles, attack helicopters and air defences. About 10,000 Cuban troops are in Nicaragua, of which 3,000 are military advisers; military advisers from the Soviet Union (50) are also present, see *The Military Balance 1985–86*, p. 30.

[68] *Ibid.*, pp. 21, 24–5.

[69] In the Indian Ocean the Soviet naval presence (since 1968) consists on average

of 25 ships, all of which are detached from the Soviet Pacific Fleet. The Soviet Navy also maintains a regular West Africa patrol of about 6 ships, an average of 3 to 4 ships in the Caribbean and regularly deploys larger task forces to the area for limited periods of time. There has also been a marked increase of Soviet 'trawlers' in South American waters and Soviet fishing vessels in the Pacific.

[70] With a combined active force of about 310 principal surface combatants and 145 attack submarines, the US, British and French navies alone represent a formidable long-distance power projection force, which could be further augmented locally by other Western navies (Australia, New Zealand). It is worth noting that the South African Navy, which officially no longer aims to protect and convoy international shipping around the Cape, nevertheless could pose an interdiction threat to the Soviet Navy in wartime; on the changing mission of the South African Navy, see Coker (*op.cit* (2) in Ch. I, note 6), pp. 142–3. Thanks to the availability of forward maintenance and logistic support in areas where they do not have bases (such as the western Indian Ocean, the south Atlantic and the south-eastern Pacific), the US, British and French navies can carry out protracted operations in distant theatres.

[71] In wartime a primary task of the Soviet Navy would be to maintain a defence perimeter around the homeland, which would significantly limit its flexibility to intervene effectively in distant areas. This points to the basic and unresolved question as to whether Soviet naval expansion stems from geopolitical aggressiveness or, rather, from strategic defensiveness – or both at once.

[72] Between 1946 and 1975 the US engaged its navy in 177 cases (out of a total of 215 cases involving some employment of US armed forces), 100 of which involved the navy alone. By comparison, the USSR engaged its navy in only 43 cases between 1944 and 1979 (out of a total of 190 cases involving some employment of Soviet forces), see Barry M. Blechman and Stephen S. Kaplan, *Force Without War: US Armed Forces as a Political Instrument* (Washington: Brookings Institution, 1978), cited in Laurence Martin, 'The Use of Naval Forces in Peacetime', *Naval War College Review*, Jan-Feb. 1985, p. 9.

[73] See *Strategic Survey 1980–1981*, pp. 31–6, and *Strategic Survey 1982–1983*, pp. 128–33. At present, Soviet long-range naval reconnaissance aircraft operate from Cam Ranh (Vietnam), Al-Anad (South Yemen, a forced redeployment from Asmara, Ethiopia, in mid-1984) and Cuba. Guinea and Somalia terminated Soviet access for naval reconnaissance in 1977.

[74] However, the USSR is expected to deploy a new *Antonov-400* transport aircraft in 1987 or 1988, which will enhance its heavy airlift capabilities significantly over long distances.

[75] See *The Military Balance 1985–1986*, pp. 11, 25, 42, 46, 53, 55, 57, 58, 60. However, the USSR does possess a sizeable fleet of amphibious ships (79) and craft (99), among which 2 *Ivan Rogov*-class amphibious assault ships since the late 1970s.

[76] See Simon Ollivant, *Arctic Challenge to NATO*, Conflict Studies, no. 172 (London: The Institute for the Study of Conflict, 1984).

Chapter III

[1] For example, the Israeli annexation of the Golan Heights in December 1981, the Jewish settlements in the Arab-occupied territories and the Israeli invasion of Lebanon in June 1982. The issues of the Jewish settlements and Israeli brutalities in Lebanon have led repeatedly to divergent European and US votes on UN Security Council and General Assembly resolutions.

[2] For recent US attitudes towards the Middle East peace process, see *Strategic Survey 1984–1985* and *1985–1986*, pp. 34–5, 64–5; and pp. 75–6, 110-11. Western concerns about the terrorist factor in the Middle East have been fuelled *inter alia* by the following events: the bombings of the US Embassy in Beirut in April 1983; the bombing of the Western MNF in Beirut in October 1983; the bombing of the US and French Embassies in Kuwait in December 1983; numerous abductions and murders of US, British and French citizens since December 1983, often with Libyan or Syrian involvement; the hijacking of a US TWA civilian airliner in June 1985; and the hijacking of the Italian liner *Achille Lauro* in October 1985. See Robert C. McFarlane (Assistant to President Reagan

for National Security Affairs), 'Deterring Terrorism', *Journal of Defense & Diplomacy*, vol. 3, no. 6 (June 1985), pp. 7-8, 63.

³ For US attitudes to state-sponsored terrorism, see e.g. remarks made by Secretary of State Shultz in Honolulu on 17 July 1985, and by Vice-President Bush to the IISS on 3 July 1985. On 14 and 21 April 1986, the EEC Foreign Ministers agreed to restrict the activities of Libyan missions in Western Europe. They also pledged more diplomatic efforts to defuse the US–Libyan crisis in the Mediterranean region in order to avert further US military action against Libya, see *International Herald Tribune*, 23 April 1986, p. 1.

⁴ Although Washington did consult London before the intervention in Grenada, such consultations appear to have been held *pro forma* only. The intervention went ahead as planned, despite the fact that Britain had expressed 'very considerable doubts' on the ground that an intervention clearly would violate international law. See *The Economist*, 10-16 March 1984, pp. 31-40, and Philip Windsor, 'Some Reflections on Grenada', *Atlantic Quarterly*, vol. 2, no. 1 (Spring 1984), pp. 1-11.

⁵ See Joseph Cirincione (ed.), *Central America and the Western Alliance* (New York/London: Holmes & Meyer, printed for the Carnegie Endowment for International Peace and the IISS, 1985); see also *International Herald Tribune*, 18 March 1985, and *The Guardian*, 19 August 1985.

⁶ In August 1981, French Foreign Minister Claude Cheysson recognized the Salvadorean rebels as a 'representative political force'. In January 1982 France announced military assistance of $US 16 million to Nicaragua (supply of helicopters and naval reconnaissance craft). By comparison French economic assistance to Nicaragua for 1985 amounted to $US 15 million. The newly-elected Gaullist government announced in March 1986 that, as of 1986, France would no longer provide *new* financial aid to either Cuba or Nicaragua.

⁷ Some well-known European personalities published an open letter in *Le Monde* of 21 March 1985, urging the US Congress to approve proposals by the Reagan Administration for US aid to the Nicaraguan rebels (the 'contras').

⁸ Various NATO members give bilateral development aid to Nicaragua. In 1985 Canada, the Netherlands and Norway reaffirmed and increased their respective aid levels, see *Defense & Foreign Affairs Weekly*, 17-23 June 1985, p. 1. Following the meeting in Costa Rica on 28-29 September 1984 of the 21 Foreign Ministers of the EEC, Spain, Portugal, the 4 Contadora and the 5 Central American states, the EEC announced a five-year, $US 268 million aid package to the region (rebuffing a last-minute US appeal to exclude Nicaragua from the programme). On 16 May 1985, the EEC Commission proposed to double the aid level to Central America, including Nicaragua, over the next five years. At their Costa Rica meeting the EEC Foreign Ministers also endorsed the so-called Contadora Peace Plan for Central America.

⁹ In its report of January 1984, the President's National Bipartisan Commission on Central America (the 'Kissinger Commission') made more than 50 recommendations for regional reform and economic reactivation, aimed at four interrelated goals: further democratization; economic growth; human development and security. As a result, the US provided Central American and Caribbean nations in Fiscal Year (FY) 1983 with $US 625.2 m. and $US 265.5 m. in the context of the so-called Caribbean Basin Initiative (CBI) of 1983. Total US aid to Central America and the Caribbean increased to $US 1,234.2 m in FY 1984 and 1,374.5 m in 1985. For FY 1986 the Reagan Administration has requested $US 1,457.2 m for Central America and the Caribbean. With respect to Nicaragua, the US vetoed a $US 60 m loan to that country from the Inter-American Development Bank in March 1985. On 1 May 1985, the Reagan Administration issued an Executive Order (no Congressional approval needed) instituting economic sanctions (total trade embargo, suspension of landing rights in the US for Nicaraguan airplanes and ships, cancellation of bilateral Treaty of Friendship) against Nicaragua, which became effective on 6 May 1985. Additional sanctions considered by the Administration include a declaration of default on Nicaragua's official debt, a

freeze on Nicaraguan assets in the United States, tight restrictions on travel by American citizens to Nicaragua and a break in diplomatic relations. Militarily, the US has intensified its activities in the region while keeping its permanent presence at a relatively low level (15,700 troops in 1985, according to *The Military Balance 1985-6*, p. 13). US military activities include continuing series of large-scale regional exercises, the build-up of military infrastructure in Honduras, unmanned reconnaissance flights over Nicaragua from Palmerola, Honduras, and increased levels of security assistance to 14 Central American and Caribbean nations (from $US 137.7 to 334.5 m in FY 1983–4, and from $81.3 to 196.5 m for El Salvador in particular over the same period). And after much wrangling both Houses of the US Congress finally approved on 31 July 1985, $US 27 million in direct, but 'non-lethal' aid to anti-Sandinista rebels in Nicaragua ($US 13 m in 1985 with the total aid package running only until 31 March 1986), as part of a $US 25.4 bn Foreign Aid Authorization Bill for FY 1986 and 1987 (see also notes 35, 36, 48, *infra*). President Reagan signed the Bill on 19 August 1985. Similar Congressional wrangling over further US assistance to the Nicaraguan rebels took place in the first half of 1986, finally leading to the approval by the House of Representatives of a $100 m package of mainly military aid ($70m) on 26 June 1986. On 27 June 1986 the International Court of Justice ruled that US aid to the Nicaraguan rebels breached customary international law forbidding the use of force and intervention in the affairs of another state.

[10] On 9 April 1982, all EEC members embargoed arms sales to Argentina. On 30 April 1982 the US, after a failed mediation attempt, announced publicly its support for Britain in the conflict. Subsequently, Allied political support for Britain was expressed in ministerial communiqués issued by NATO's Eurogroup, Defence Planning Committee and North Atlantic Council on 6, 7 and 18 May 1982 respectively. But already on 2 November 1982 the US voted in favour of a UN resolution calling for negotiations on the principle of British sovereignty over the Falkland Islands.

[11] See Coker (*op. cit.* (1) in Ch. I, note 6), pp. 127–8.

[12] See Bernard Labatut, 'Ceuta et Melilla', *Studia Diplomatica*, vol. 38, no. 4, pp. 409–72.

[13] In 1983 the eight most prosperous European NATO members devoted $US 12.174 m or 0.64% of their GNP in ODA, as opposed to $US 7.950 m or 0.24% of GNP for the US. Figures are compiled from *The World Development Report 1984* (*op. cit.* in Ch. II, note 27), p. 252.

[14] See paragraph 11 of the communiqué issued by the Commonwealth Heads of State at their meeting in New Delhi in November 1983, as well as their Goa Declaration on International Security in annex to the New Delhi communiqué. On the security problems of small and very small states, see George H. Quester, 'Trouble in the Islands: Defending the Micro-States', *International Security*, vol. 8, no. 2 (Fall 1983), pp. 160–75, and Jonathan Alford, 'Security Dilemmas of Small States', *The World Today*, vol. 40, Nos. 8-9 (August-September 1984), pp. 363–9.

[15] Held in Bujumbura, Burundi, on 11–12 December 1984 and attended by President Mitterrand, 17 African Heads of State with 20 other African countries represented at Ministerial level. Only Burkina Faso (ex-Upper Volta) boycotted the Summit; see also Ch II, note 45.

[16] See *Statement on the Defence Estimates 1985* (London: HMSO, Cmnd. 9430-I, 1985), paragraph 452, and T.A. Boam, 'Defending Western Interests Outside NATO: The United Kingdom's Contribution' *Armed Forces Journal International*, October 1984, pp. 116–20.

[17] At the request of the local government Britain maintains a balanced force of some 1,500 troops in Belize to deter Guatemala from enforcing its claim on the former British colony. There is also a Canadian training team in Belize which, pursuant to an agreement of 3 June 1985, will step up its assistance to the Belize Defence Force, see *Defense & Foreign Affairs Weekly*, 17–23 June 1985, p. 5.

[18] In 1985 France had bilateral military technical assistance and defence agreements in force with 23 African states (defence agreements with Cameroon, the Central African Republic, Djibouti, Gabon, Ivory Coast, Senegal and Togo). See *The Military Balance 1985–1986*, p. 89.

[19] Between August 1983 and October 1984 France deployed a total of 3,300 troops to Chad to safeguard the Habré Government against rebel forces supported by Libyan forces (*Opération Manta*). Following a Franco-Libyan military withdrawal agreement in September 1984, France redeployed about 2,000 of its troops to the neighbouring Central African Republic and the rest to France, leaving about 130 military advisers in Chad. US involvement with Chad included the despatch of military supplies and advisers, the deployment of AWACS aircraft to Sudan in 1983, and the disclosure by the State Department in November 1984 that, according to US satellite information, the majority of Libyan forces and their equipment had stayed in Chad in violation of the withdrawal agreement with France. In February–March 1986 France sent aircraft and 750 troops back into Chad (*Opération Epervier*) in what has now become its fifth military intervention there since the early 1960s; see *Strategic Survey 1983–1984; 1984–1985* and *1985–1986*, pp. 104–7 and 104–6, and 177–9. On the Aden evacuation mounted by the Royal Navy in January 1986, see *Statement on the Defence Estimates 1986* (London: HMSO, Cmnd 9763–I, 1986), p. 38; see also Conclusion, note 2.

[20] In early 1986 participation by NATO members in the five peacekeeping operations in the Middle East was distributed as follows: UNIFIL (Lebanon): France (1,380), Italy (48), Norway (861); UNFICYP (Cyprus): Britain (750), Canada (515), Denmark (341); UNDOF (Syria/Israel): Canada (226); UNTSO (Middle East): Canada (20); MFO (Sinai): Britain (38), France (40), Italy (90, 3 minesweepers), the Netherlands (105), US (1,200); MNF (Lebanon, 1982–4): Britain (87), France (2,000), Italy (2,038), US (1,800); See *The Military Balance 1983–1984, 1984–1985* and *1985–1986*.

[21] See Articles 26 and 87(e) of the 1949 Basic Law of The Federal Republic of Germany; *White Paper 1985 – The Situation and the Development of the Federal Armed Forces* (Bonn: Federal Minister of Defence, on behalf of the Federal Government, 1985), pp. 25–6, as well as Joachim Krause and Gale A. Mattox, 'West German Arms Sales to the Third World Countries', *Atlantic Quarterly*, vol. 2, issue 2 (Summer 1984), pp. 171–82. On 7 October 1985, Bonn authorized important West German arms sales to Saudi Arabia.

[22] See Ross S. Kelly, 'How West Germany Tackles Its Special Operations Challenge', *Defense & Foreign Affairs*, April 1985, pp. 32–3; and 'France's Special Operations Forces', *ibid.*, June 1985, p. 33.

[23] Thus, as part of the Anglo-US deal of March 1982 on the acquisition by Britain of US *Trident* II SLBM, Britain reportedly agreed to maintain its naval deployments in the Indian Ocean and to keep its two amphibious assault ships in service, see *The Sunday Times*, 7 April 1985, p. 18.

[24] See *International Herald Tribune*, 9 May 1985, p. 3.

[25] See, for instance, the following ministerial communiqués of the North Atlantic Council: 31 May 1979, (paragraph 13) and 14 December 1979 (par. 15) on the Middle East peace process, (par. 16) on the Rhodesian peace settlement, 13 December 1980 (par. 5) on the Iraq-Iran War.

[26] See Karl Kaiser, Winston Lord, Thierry de Montbrial and David Watt, *Western Security: What Has Changed? What Should Be Done* (New York: Council on Foreign Relations, 1981), pp. 44–6. The authors recommend the formation of a core group of nations (Britain, France, Japan, West Germany) which are able and willing to accept concrete obligations out-of-area. This group could be expanded on an *ad hoc* and temporary basis to include other nations, as out-of-area events require. See also Phil Williams, 'Revitalizing The Western Alliance: Proposals for Change', *Atlantic Quarterly*, vol. 2, no. 2 (Summer 1984), pp. 120–5.

[27] Conversely, during the 1970s Western Europe condemned the deliberate failure on the part of the US to develop a national energy policy complementing European efforts at reducing import dependency on Gulf oil. Attempts by the Nixon and Ford Administrations to shield US consumers from high world oil prices by encouraging domestic consumption were reversed in 1978, when the US finally committed itself to a national energy policy at the seven-nation economic summit in Bonn.

[28] In 1984 France exported twice as many arms by value as in 1983, at a total value of about $US 4.8 bn. Of these, 76.6% went

to North Africa and the Middle East (especially Saudi Arabia and the UAE), 9% to the Far East, 2.2% to Latin America and the Caribbean and 1.6% to Africa.

[29] See *Strategic Survey 1984–1985*, pp. 65, 70, as well as note 36.

[30] See, for instance, the passages on Afghanistan, Korea, the Gulf War and terrorism in the *Declaration on Security* in annex to NATO's *Bonn Summit Declaration* of 10 June 1982. In 1984 and 1986 the leaders of the seven major industrial democracies, meeting in London and Tokyo respectively, pledged to fight terrorism. In their Tokyo statement on terrorism issued on 5 May 1986 they specifically identified Libya as a source of state-sponsored terrorism; see also note 3.

[31] See Gregory F. Treverton, 'Defence Beyond Europe', *Survival*, vol. 24, no. 5 (September-October 1983), pp. 223–6.

[32] On 8 July 1985 Canada announced limited trade and investment sanctions against South Africa, while France cut off all new investment in South Africa on 24 July 1985. Following the imposition by Pretoria of the state of emergency in 36 South African districts on 20 July 1985 (extended to the Cape Town area on 25 October 1985), the EEC Foreign Ministers (meeting in Helsinki on 31 July and 1 August 1985) threatened South Africa with co-ordinated coercive measures; at their Luxembourg meeting of 10 September 1985 they adopted a list of limited measures to be implemented by EEC members individually. (Britain joined with its EEC partners in endorsing these measures on 25 September 1985.) In the US, after separate votes in the House of Representatives and the Senate in June and July 1985, the House voted overwhelmingly on 1 August 1985 in favour of a compromise Bill imposing limited measures on South Africa. President Reagan, anticipating Congressional pressure, introduced limited economic sanctions against South Africa on 9 September 1985. In 1985 and the first half of 1986 Britain, the US and West Germany, later joined by France, remained opposed to full-scale, 'punitive' measures against South Africa. On 26 July 1985, Britain and the US abstained on a French-inspired UN Security Council Resolution calling for voluntary sanctions against South Africa. On 23 May 1986, they vetoed a UNSC Resolution calling for selective sanctions. On 4 March 1986 Pretoria had lifted the 1985 state of emergency in all 36 districts concerned, only to reimpose it on 12 June 1986, this time in the whole of South Africa. At their summit meeting in The Hague on 26–7 June 1986, the EEC leaders appeared to be deadlocked over whether to impose further joint sanctions. In view of growing domestic pressures for action against South Africa, they finally adopted a compromise and agreed to consider selected economic sanctions (ban on new investment and on the import of coal, iron, steel and gold coins) in three months' time, should Pretoria fail to respond to a peace mission by the British Foreign Secretary, Sir Geoffrey Howe.

[33] See Loic Bouvard, 'The Legislative Role of the French Parliament in Crisis Management', *Naval War College Review*, November–December 1984, pp. 80–85.

[34] See Richard Haass, *Congressional Power: Implications for American Security Policy*, Adelphi Paper no. 153 (London: IISS, Summer 1979); Eliot A. Cohen, 'Constraints on America's Conduct of Small Wars', (*op. cit.* in Ch. II, note 53), pp. 155–60 and 163–5.

[35] This is particularly the case with respect to foreign aid spending authority. Thus the July 1985 agreement reached by both Houses of Congress on a Foreign Aid Authorization Bill ended a legislative impasse which had lasted four years.

[36] For Congressional opposition to US arms sales to moderate Arab states such as Jordan, Kuwait and Saudi Arabia, see *Strategic Survey 1984–1985*, pp. 65–70, and *The Sunday Times*, 28 July 1985, p. 19. In June–July 1985 the US Congress repealed the 1975 Clark Amendment banning US military aid to anti-Communist insurgents in Angola. US covert military aid to the UNITA guerrillas was resumed in 1986. This has led Angola – a country whose co-operation remains crucial to the success of the Reagan Administration's policy of Constructive Engagement in southern Africa – to cease talks with the US on a Namibian settlement; see *Strategic Survey 1985–1986*, p. 189. Similarly, Congressional imposition of sweeping political conditions on the provision of development and military aid may discourage further attempts on the part of

various third-world states (such as Mozambique) to move away from the Soviet Bloc; see various provisions in the *International Security and Development Cooperation Act of 1985*, S. 960, 99th Congress, 1st Session, 1985.

[37] See Haass (*op. cit.* in note 34), pp. 19–22. For a pessimistic view, see John R. Silber, 'Central America and the War Powers Act. An Emerging Constitutional Crisis', *NATO's Sixteen Nations*, November-December 1984, pp. 26–30.

[38] The 1973 War Powers Act subjects Presidential discretion to deploy unilaterally US armed forces abroad in situations not involving a national emergency to a maximum period of 92 days. Congress can end such deployments at any given moment during that period. Deployments longer than 92 days require explicit Congressional authorization in the form of a declaration of war. In its attitude towards the War Powers Act, the Reagan Administration has generally refrained from taking advantage of a June 1983 ruling by the US Supreme Court striking down so-called legislative vetoes in Acts passed by Congress (Article 5(c) of the War Powers Act being particularly affected by the Supreme Court ruling).

[39] See *Strategic Survey 1983–1984*, p. 45.

[40] *Ibid.*

[41] See Jonathan Alford (*op. cit.* in note 14), pp. 366–69.

[42] Thus US withdrawal from Lebanon in February 1984 seems to have taken place without much consultation with the three other Western participants in the MNF. Although the US, British and Italian contingents stayed in Beirut until February 1984, and the French contingent until March 1984, the MNF had ceased to operate as such after the September 1983 Chouf Battle between the Lebanese Army and Druze militias supported by Syria, see also note 71.

[43] See paragraph 5(e) of the Bonn Declaration of 10 June 1982. On the significance of the Bonn Declaration for out-of-area questions, see Fredo Dannenbring (NATO's Assistant Secretary-General for Political Affairs), 'East-West Relations: Are There Common NATO Positions?', *NATO Review*, vol. 32, no. 5 (October 1984), pp. 3–5.

[44] See the North Atlantic Assembly (*op. cit.* in Ch. I, note 20), p. 10.

[45] As stated by every ministerial communiqué of the North Atlantic Council between May 1981 and May 1984.

[46] See the North Atlantic Assembly (*op. cit.* in Ch. I, note 20), p. 11.

[47] *International Herald Tribune*, 2 May 1979.

[48] See Amos A. Jordan, 'NATO and the Out-of-Area Challenge', in Joseph Godson (ed.), *Challenges to the Western Alliance* (London: Times Books, 1984), pp. 135–6.

[49] The call was made by President Reagan in Autumn 1984 in the UN General Assembly. The talks on the Middle East (after an interruption of seven years) were held in Vienna on 19, 20 February 1985 and in Stockholm on 26, 27 June 1986, those on Afghanistan in Washington on 18, 19 June 1985, and those on southern Africa in Paris. Further talks were held on the Far East in Moscow on 12, 13 September 1985, and on Central America in Washington on 31 October, 1 November 1985 and Moscow on 21 May 1986. The US was represented at the level of Assistant-Secretary of State. See also USIS, 25 October 1985 for President Reagan's speech to UN General Assembly on 24 October 1985. In his 1985 UN speech President Reagan called for US-Soviet initiatives to support regional efforts at negotiated settlements of the conflicts in Afghanistan, Angola, Cambodia, Ethiopia and Nicaragua.

[50] Europe and the US have thus come to agree to disagree on the motives and the lessons of the Soviet invasion of Afghanistan. They concur in their support for the successive UN General Assembly resolutions on Afghanistan and a diplomatic solution to the conflict. Yet European NATO governments seem less disposed than ever to jeopardize the tangible benefits of East-West detente in Europe over the Afghan issue. Thus the practice of regular Franco-Soviet summit meetings, which the Socialist government in Paris had interrupted since 1981 in protest against the continued Soviet occupation of Afghanistan, was resumed in 1985. The US continues to see the presence of Soviet troops in Afghanistan as an obstacle to the improvement of bilateral relations with Moscow. On 9 May 1985 the State Department revealed that the US had been giving $US 4 m in humanitarian aid to the Afghan resistance

since August 1984. On 31 July 1985, Congress authorized $US 15 m in further humanitarian aid. In October 1985, it was reported that the Congress had secretly approved another $US 300 m in aid for the Afghan resistance, see *International Herald Tribune*, 11 October 1985, p. 4.

[51] There is a growing recognition at NATO Headquarters and elsewhere of the need for effective Allied responses to Soviet military challenges in key geographical zones at the periphery of the North Atlantic area. These include the Arctic and the Northern Cap zone, the northern approaches to the Greenland/Iceland/United Kingdom (GIUK) gap, the eastern Mediterranean beyond the territories of Greece and Turkey, South-west Asia and the south Atlantic/Cape route. See William T. Tow, 'NATO's Out-of-Region Challenges and Extended Deterrence', *Orbis*, vol. 28, no. 4 (Winter 1985), pp. 829–56. But, given existing inhibitions against any extension of the NATO area, these peripheral defence concerns cannot be adequately addressed by the Alliance as such under peacetime conditions. Thus NATO's contingency planning for the protection of Allied shipping in the South Atlantic, Cape and Indian Ocean areas exists mainly on paper. Maritime contingency plans cannot be implemented or exercised in any form without specific authority of NATO's political and military authorities, nor do they in any way imply the acceptance by NATO members of additional naval commitments. Moreover, the existing shortage of escort ships within the NATO area seriously questions the viability of protective operations south of the Tropic of Cancer and in the Indian Ocean in the event of a generalized conflict. The most which seems to have been achieved so far are occasional NATO naval exercises extending beyond the North Atlantic area, such as *Operation Venture* (August 1981, involving the South Atlantic).

[52] See Iungerich (*op. cit.* in Ch II, note 63), p. 95.

[53] See Worth H. Bagley, *Sea Power and Western Security*, Adelphi Paper no. 139 (London: IISS, Winter 1977); the author analyses, among other things, how a more flexible use of Western sea power can serve strategic interests beyond the NATO area and, thereby, enhance deterrence of the USSR on land.

[54] See ministerial communiqués of NATO's Defence Planning Committee since May 1981, and Geoffrey E. Pattie, 'Western Security Beyond the NATO Area', *Strategic Review*, vol. 12, no. 2 (Spring 1984), p. 43.

[55] At the Alliance level it was agreed in general terms in December 1982 that European NATO members would not again withhold landing rights for US planes *en route* to a Middle Eastern crisis (as had been the case in October 1973); see *Strategic Survey 1982–1983*, p. 56. In 1983 it was reported that eight NATO members provided overflight rights and *en route* support for annual USCENTCOM exercises in South-west Asia during 1980–82, see Tow (*op. cit.* in note 51), p. 853.

[56] More progress has been achieved in the area of Allied Command Atlantic, where out-of-area measures have been incorporated in the regular Force Goal package for 1985–90.

[57] At the end of 1981 Washington began exerting pressures at the level of the NAC and DPC in order to obtain Allied political and, where possible, military support for US out-of-area policies in South-west Asia. In response, the other Allies requested a thorough *Study on the Implications for NATO of the US Strategic Concept for South-west Asia* before committing themselves. This South-west Asia Impact Study, first mentioned in the ministerial DPC communiqué of 7 May 1982 (par. 8), progressed slowly in 1982–3 due to US reluctance to specify its highly confidential and repeatedly changing contingency plans for South-west Asia. Later in 1983, final approval of the Study by the NATO Military Authorities was blocked by a Greek-Turkish dispute about the wording of a passage describing procedures in the Aegean Sea. Thus the Study could be approved on an unofficial basis only by the DPC in June 1984. This means that the search within the Alliance for out-of-area compensation measures now must take place without agreed underlying concepts and analyses.

[58] See par. 10 of the Ministerial DPC communiqué of 5 December 1984. Meanwhile 10 NATO members have committed themselves to generate 600 commercial ships to supplement US capabilities to reinforce NATO, while nine NATO members have similarly committed

themselves to increase their contributions of civil long-range cargo and passenger aircraft. More generally, out-of-area compensation means that the transatlantic Allies will have to achieve greater co-ordination of their respective defence roles and national mobilization decisions.

[59] See Phil Williams, 'The Nunn Amendment, Burden-sharing and US Troops in Europe', *Survival*, vol. 27, no. 1, January–February 1985, pp. 2–10, and William V. Roth, 'After the Nunn-Roth Amendment', *NATO's Sixteen Nations*, vol. 30, no. 3 (June–July 1985), pp. 15–22.

[60] This trend is partly connected with the emergence of a current opinion in the US favourable to a 'maritime strategy', and a certain fatigue with the 'Atlanticist' tenets of a security policy inherited from an earlier generation of policy-makers; see Robert W. Komer, *Maritime Strategy or Coalition Defence?* (Cambridge, MA: Abt Books, 1984); Keith A. Dunn and William O. Staudenmaier, 'Strategy for Survival', *Foreign Policy*, no. 52 (Fall 1983), pp. 22–41; Jeffrey Record and Robert J. Hanks, *US Strategy at the Crossroads* (Washington DC: Institute for Foreign Policy Analysis, July 1982). A much discussed concept in this context is that of 'horizontal escalation' which, in conjunction with forward defence in Europe, opens the theoretical prospect of widespread simultaneous operations. Although horizontal escalation has been dropped as a declaratory strategy under the second Reagan Administration, nevertheless it continues to influence current US acquisition and force planning policies, see John M. Collins, *US–Soviet Military Balance 1980–1985* (Washington DC: Pergamon-Brassey's, 1985), p. 103.

[61] See *Strategic Survey 1983–1984*, p. 45.

[62] For US out-of-area burden-sharing assessments, see US Department of Defense, *Report on Allied Contributions to the Common Defense* (Washington DC: USGPO, March 1983), pp. 60–61.

[63] See the North Atlantic Assembly (*op. cit.* in Ch. I, note 20), p. 21. In 1980 the US briefly suggested the establishment of a multinational naval force in the Indian Ocean; this was rejected by the European NATO Allies. On 10 June 1986 US Secretary of Defense Weinberger, in a speech to the 'Sea Link' Symposium in Annapolis, pleaded for a NATO naval presence in the Persian Gulf as well as in the Indian and Pacific Oceans.

[64] See Ministerial DPC communiqués of 2 June 1983 (par. 7) and 7 December 1983 (par. 11).

[65] See *Strategic Survey 1982–1983*, pp. 121–3.

[66] See *Statement on the Defence Estimates 1985* (London: HMSO, Cmnd 9430-I, 1985), par. 455, and 1986 (London: HMSO, Cmnd 9763-I, 1986), pars 439-42; J. Farwell, 'The Joint Force Headquarters for Out-of-Area Operations', *Air Clues*, June 1985, pp. 210-212; Giovanni de Briganti, 'Forces d'Action Rapide: France's Rapid Deployment Forces', *Armed Forces Journal International*, October 1984, pp. 122. French out-of-area capabilities suffer especially from insufficient military airlift and sealift assets, as demonstrated during the 1983–4 intervention in Chad.

[67] See Yannis Valinakis, 'Italian Security Concerns and Policy', *The International Spectator*, vol. 19, no. 2 (April-June 1984), pp. 110–4; Luigi Caligaris and Maurizio Cremasco, *Italian Rapid Intervention Force*, Paper IAI/02/85 (Rome: Istituto Affari Internazionali, 1985), p. 18.

[68] See ministerial communiqués of the Council and the DPC since May 1980.

[69] See A.L. Roberts, *Peace Beyond NATO: The Challenge to Europe* (London: Seaford House Papers, 1983), p. 119; Dov S. Zakheim, 'Toward a Western Approach to the Indian Ocean', *Survival*, January-February 1980, pp. 7–14. Drawing on their respective naval presences in the Persian Gulf, Britain, France and the US have been discreetly escorting their own oil tankers and cargo ships in the Hormuz area since September 1985. These have been national initiatives, with no agreed division of labour between these three NATO members.

[70] See Roberts, (*op. cit.* in note 69). For a lucid analysis of the many constraints bearing upon the use of force by NATO members in the Middle East, see Anthony H. Cordesman, 'The Uses of Force in the Middle East', conference paper presented in Brussels on 2–3 July 1986 (see Ch I, note 74).

[71] See Luigi Caligaris, 'Western Peacekeeping in Lebanon: Lessons of the MNF', *Survival*, vol. 24, no. 6 (November–December 1984), pp. 262–8, and note 42. France especially can be expected to resist

truly multinational co-operation out-of-area. In the past France refused to allow the US navy access to the Comoros and La Réunion, see Coker (*op. cit.* (2) in Ch. I, note 6), p. 225. While at the French military level there now seems to be a movement towards open recognition of the need for joint contingency planning (see remarks to that effect by the French naval Chief of Staff Y. Leenhardt, 'Réflexions pour une stratégie navale d'avenir', *Défense Nationale*, août-septembre 1985, p. 26), strict bilateralism remains the norm at the political level. There are exceptions to the rule, as demonstrated by the participation of a French ship in NATO's 'United Effort/Teamwork 84' amphibious exercise north of the Arctic Circle .
[72] Implementation of the French defence plans in New Caledonia over the next three years would cost an estimated $US 40 m., see *Defense & Foreign Affairs Weekly*, 29 April – 5 May 1985, p. 4. In this context, the former French Defence Minister, Charles Hernu, has been quoted as saying: 'If France is the world's third naval power, it is largely due to the Pacific and everything represented by the Western Pacific', *ibid.*, 20–26 May 1985, p. 4.
[73] For British and French deployments as of early 1986, see *The Military Balance 1985–1986*, pp. 43, 48–9. For British out-of-area exercises, see *Statement on the Defence Estimates 1984* (London: HMSO, Cmnd.9227-I, 1984), paragraph 450 and Annex B. In 1986 Britain will conduct a major strategic mobility exercise to test its ability to respond rapidly to an out-of-area crisis, see *Statement on the Defence Estimates 1986* (London: HMSO, Cmnd 9763-I, 1986), Annex B.

Conclusions

[1] See Bernard Burrows and Geoffrey Edwards, *The Defence of Western Europe* (London: Butterworths European Studies, 1982), Ch 9, pp. 117–29; A.L. Roberts (*op. cit.* in Ch III, note 69); James Eberle, John Roper, William Wallace and Phil Williams, 'European Security Cooperation and British Interests', *International Affairs*, vol. 60, no. 4 (Autumn 1984), pp. 545–60; Trevor Taylor, *European Defence Cooperation*, Chatham House Paper No. 24 (London: RIIA/Routledge & Kegan Paul, November 1984), Ch 7, pp. 67–80. Maurizio Cremasco, 'The Do-It-Yourself Syndrome. The European Approach to the Out-of-Area Question', Conference Paper presented in Brussels on 2–3 July 1986 (see Ch I, note 74).
[2] See Jonathan Alford, 'The Prospects for Anglo-French Military Co-operation Out-of-Area: A British View', in a forthcoming IFRI book. Britain and France did co-operate (not always smoothly) in the 1986 evacuation of Aden (see Ch III, note 19). In this context it may be worth mentioning that Dutch and French forces stationed in the Antilles hold combined tactical exercises *Deux Tricolores* on a regular basis.

ADELPHI PAPERS

The following is a selection of those available. They are distributed by Jane's Publishing Co. Ltd and may be ordered at a current price of **£3.50 ($US 6.50)** from: Marketing Services Department, Jane's Publishing Co. Ltd, 238 City Road, London EC1V 2PU.

180 **A Regional Security Role for Africa's Front-Line States: Experience and Prospect**
    Robert S. Jaster. Spring 1983
181 **Nordic Security** Erling Bjøl. Spring 1983
182–4 **Defence and Consensus: The Domestic Aspects of Western Security: Parts I–**
    Papers from the IISS 24th Annual Conference. Summer 1983
185 **Targeting for Strategic Deterrence** Desmond Ball. Summer 1983
186 **The Soviet Economic Crisis: Prospects for the Military and the Consumer**
    David Fewtrell. Winter 1983
187 **Soviet Theatre Nuclear Forces: Part I: Development of Doctrine and Objectives**
    Stephen M. Meyer. Winter 1983/4
188 **Soviet Theatre Nuclear Forces: Part II: Capabilities and Implications**
    Stephen M. Meyer. Winter 1983/4
189 **The Conduct of East–West Relations in the 1980s: Part I**
    Papers from the IISS 25th Annual Conference. Summer 1984
190 **The Conduct of East–West Relations in the 1980s: Part II**
    Papers from the IISS 25th Annual Conference. Summer 1984
191 **The Conduct of East–West Relations in the 1980s: Part III**
    Papers from the IISS 25th Annual Conference. Summer 1984
192 **Western Security and Economic Strategy Towards the East**
    David Buchan. Autumn 1984
193 **Deterrence in the 1980s: Part III: The Role of Conventional Air Power**
    Lt-Col. D.J. Alberts, USAF. Winter 1984
194 **France's Deterrent Posture and Security in Europe: Part I: Capabilities and Doctri**
    David S. Yost. Winter 1984/5
195 **France's Deterrent Posture and Security in Europe: Part II: Strategic and Arms-Control Implications** David S. Yost. Winter 1984/5
196 **Intervention and Regional Security** Neil Macfarlane. Spring 1985
197 **New Technology and Western Security Policy: Part I**
    Papers from the IISS 26th Annual Conference. Summer 1985
198 **New Technology and Western Security Policy: Part II**
    Papers from the IISS 26th Annual Conference. Summer 1985
199 **New Technology and Western Security Policy: Part III**
    Papers from the IISS 26th Annual Conference. Summer 1985
200 **The Prospects and Implications of Non-nuclear Means for Strategic Conflict**
    Carl H. Builder. Summer 1985
201 **French Military Policy and African Security** John Chipman. Summer 1985
202 **Sino-Soviet Relations after Mao** Gerald Segal. Autumn 1985
203 **Soviet Policy Towards West Germany** Roland Smith. Winter 1985
204 **Spain: Domestic Politics and Security Policy** Gregory F. Treverton. Spring 1986
205 **Power and Policy: Doctrine, the Alliance and Arms Control: Part I**
    Papers from the IISS 27th Annual Conference. Spring 1986
206 **Power and Policy: Doctrine, the Alliance and Arms Control: Part II**
    Papers from the IISS 27th Annual Conference. Spring 1986
207 **Power and Policy: Doctrine, the Alliance and Arms Control: Part III**
    Papers from the IISS 27th Annual Conference. Spring 1986
208 **The Two Koreas: Catalyst for Conflict in East Asia?** Peter Polomka. Summer 1986
209 **South Africa and its Neighbours: the Dynamics of Regional Conflict**
    Robert S. Jaster. Summer 1986
210 **Deterrence, War-fighting and Soviet Military Doctrine**
    John Van Oudenaren. Summer 1986